The Three Stooges®

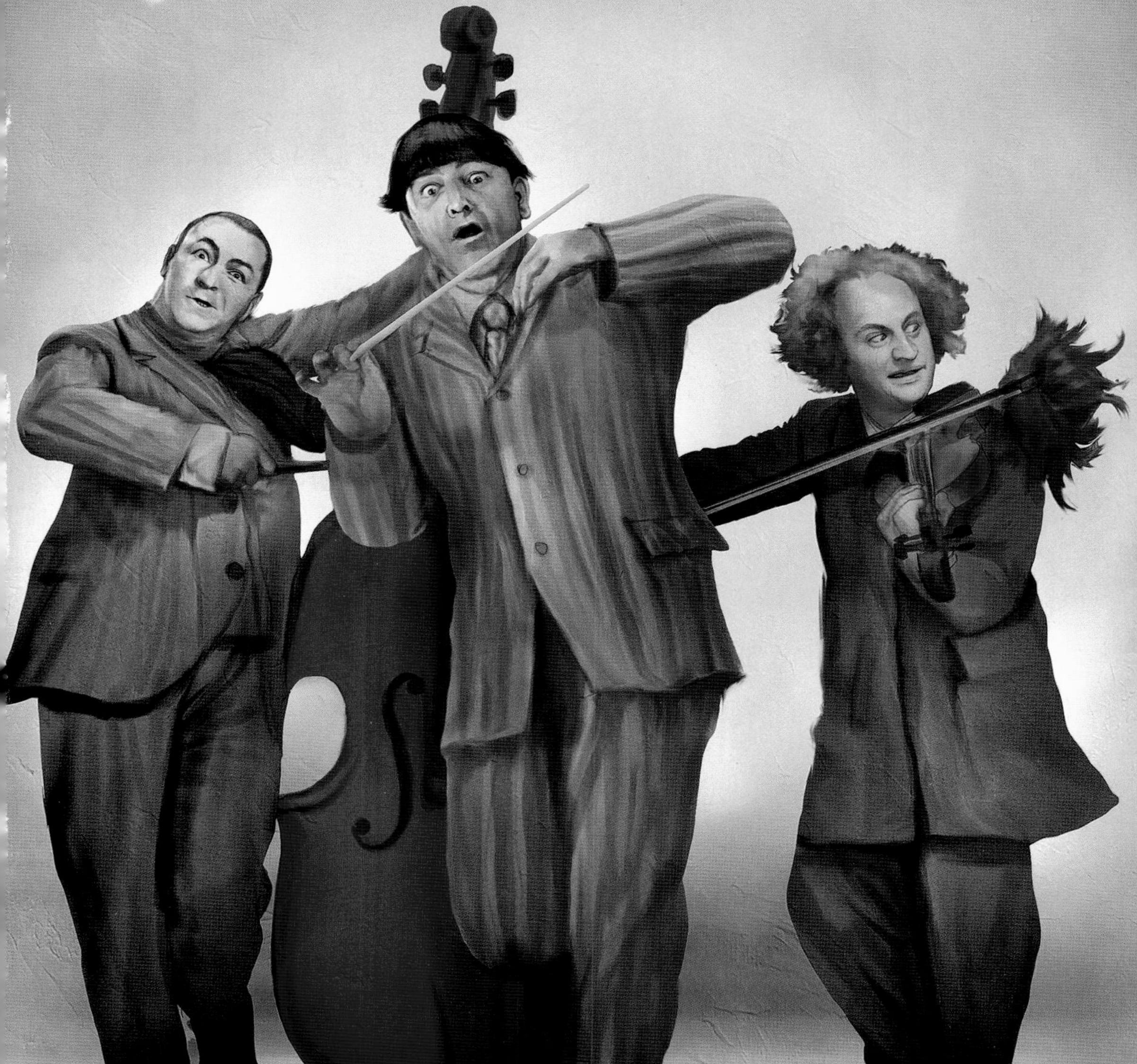

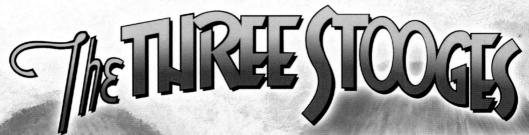

The Three Stooges

TRIPLE KNUCKLE HEADER
STORY- S.A. CHECK
PENCILS- BILL GALVAN, INKS- BOB SMITH
COLOR & LETTERS- ADRIAN ROPP

THE BIG NYUK, NYUK, NYUK
STORY- J.C. VAUGHN
PENCILS & INKS- BRENDON & BRIAN FRAIM
COLORS- TRAVIS WALTON, LETTERS- NATALIE JANE

BURGERSAURUS STOOGE
STORY- S.A. CHECK,
PENCILS & INKS- BRENDON & BRIAN FRAIM
COLORS & LETTERS- ADRIAN ROPP

NIGHT OF THE LIVING STOOGE
STORY- S.A. CHECK
PENCILS & INKS- BRENDON & BRIAN FRAIM
COLOR- TRAVIS WALTON, LETTERS- NATALIE JANE

RED, WHITE, & STOOGE
STORY- S.A. CHECK
PENCILS & INKS- BRENDON & BRIAN FRAIM
COLORS & LETTERS- DAN CONNER

SCAREDY STOOGE
STORY- S.A. CHECK
PENCILS- BILL GALVAN, INKS- BOB SMITH
COLORS & LETTERS- DAN CONNER

THE CURSE OF FRANKENSTOOGE
STORY- CHRISTOPHER HILL
PENCILS & INKS- BRENDON & BRIAN FRAIM
COLORS- MATT WEBB, LETTERS- DAN CONNER

TRICK OR EAT
STORY- JAMES KUHORIC
PENCILS & INKS- ADRIAN ROPP
COLORS & LETTERS- DAN CONNER

AMERICAN MYTHOLOGY PRODUCTIONS:

www.AMERICANMYTHOLOGY.net
Facebook: /AmericanMythologyComics
Twitter: @AmericanMytho

AMERICAN MYTHOLOGY PRODUCTIONS

THE THREE STOOGES VOLUME 1 TRADE PAPERBACK. First printing. Published by American Mythology Productions, LLC, P.O. Box #325, Bel Air, MD 21014 www.americanmythology.net.
ISBN 978-1-945205-06-4

THE THREE STOOGES
VOLUME ONE: THE BOYS ARE BACK

FEATURING STORIES FROM THE FOLLOWING COMICBOOKS:
THE BOYS ARE BACK, STOOGE-A-PALOOZA, RED, WHITE, & STOOGE
THE CURSE OF FRANKENSTOOGE, AND HALLOWEEN HULLABALOO

MIDWAY MADNESS
BOOBS IN THE WOODS
ORIGINALLY PUBLISHED IN
DELL FOUR COLOR #1170 (1961)
STORY- JERRY BELSON, ART- SPARKY MOORE

BEACH BOO-BOOBS
ORIGINALLY PRESENTED IN
THE THREE STOOGES #44 (1969)

HOUSE OF MANY MONSTERS
ORIGINALLY PRESENTED IN
THE THREE STOOGES #24 (1965)
BY SPARKY MOORE
COLOR REMASTERING- ADRIAN ROPP
SPECIAL ASSISTANCE- BRENT SEGUINE
RESTORATION- DAN CONNER

PIE HARD
MOE-STEST FRUIT PIES PARODY AD
STORY- JAMES KUHORIC
PENCILS & INKS- BILL GALVAN
COLORS & LETTERS- ADRIAN ROPP & MIKE WOLFER

STOOGE MONKEYS PARODY AD
STORY- JAMES KUHORIC, ART- S.L. GALLANT

SOUR NOTE
ART- CHRIS SCALF, LAYOUT- ADRIAN ROPP

COVER GALLERY PAGES
FEATURING ART BY
CHRIS SCALF
GREG LAROCQUE & MELISSA MEADOWS
MARK WHEATLEY
ADRIAN ROPP
JON PINTO
BILL GALVAN & BOB SMITH

COVER ART- JON PINTO
LAYOUT AND DESIGN- DAN CONNER
SPECIAL THANKS TO JAMES KUHORIC AND MIKE WOLFER
AMERICAN MYTHOLOGY PUBLISHER- MICHAEL BORNSTEIN
MARKETING MANAGER- BARLOW JONES

EXTRA SPECIAL THANKS TO
ANI KHOCHOIAN, ERIC LAMOND,
ANDREA DELESDERNIER,
AND ALL OF THE THREE
STOOGES FAMILY MEMBERS!

HEY KIDS - NEVER HIT, POKE, OR SMACK YOUR FRIENDS AND FAMILY. LEAVE ALL THAT
PRETEND SILLINESS TO US STOOGES AND LAUGH ALONG WITH OUR HIJINKS! NYUK, NYUK, NYUK!

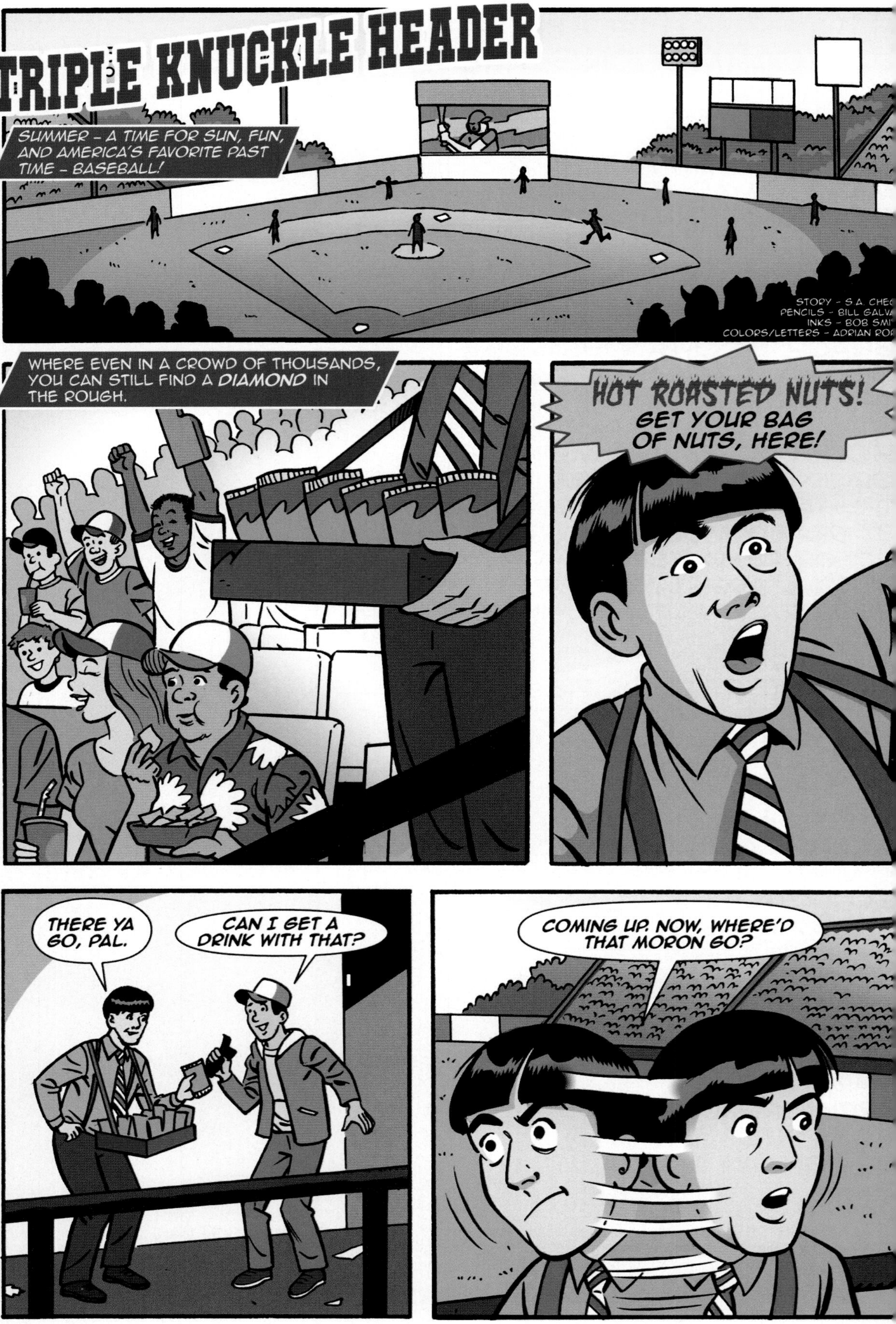
TRIPLE KNUCKLE HEADER
SUMMER – A TIME FOR SUN, FUN, AND AMERICA'S FAVORITE PAST TIME – BASEBALL!
STORY – S.A. CHEC
PENCILS – BILL GALVA
INKS – BOB SMI
COLORS/LETTERS – ADRIAN RO
WHERE EVEN IN A CROWD OF THOUSANDS, YOU CAN STILL FIND A DIAMOND IN THE ROUGH.
HOT ROASTED NUTS! GET YOUR BAG OF NUTS, HERE!
THERE YA GO, PAL.
CAN I GET A DRINK WITH THAT?
COMING UP. NOW, WHERE'D THAT MORON GO?

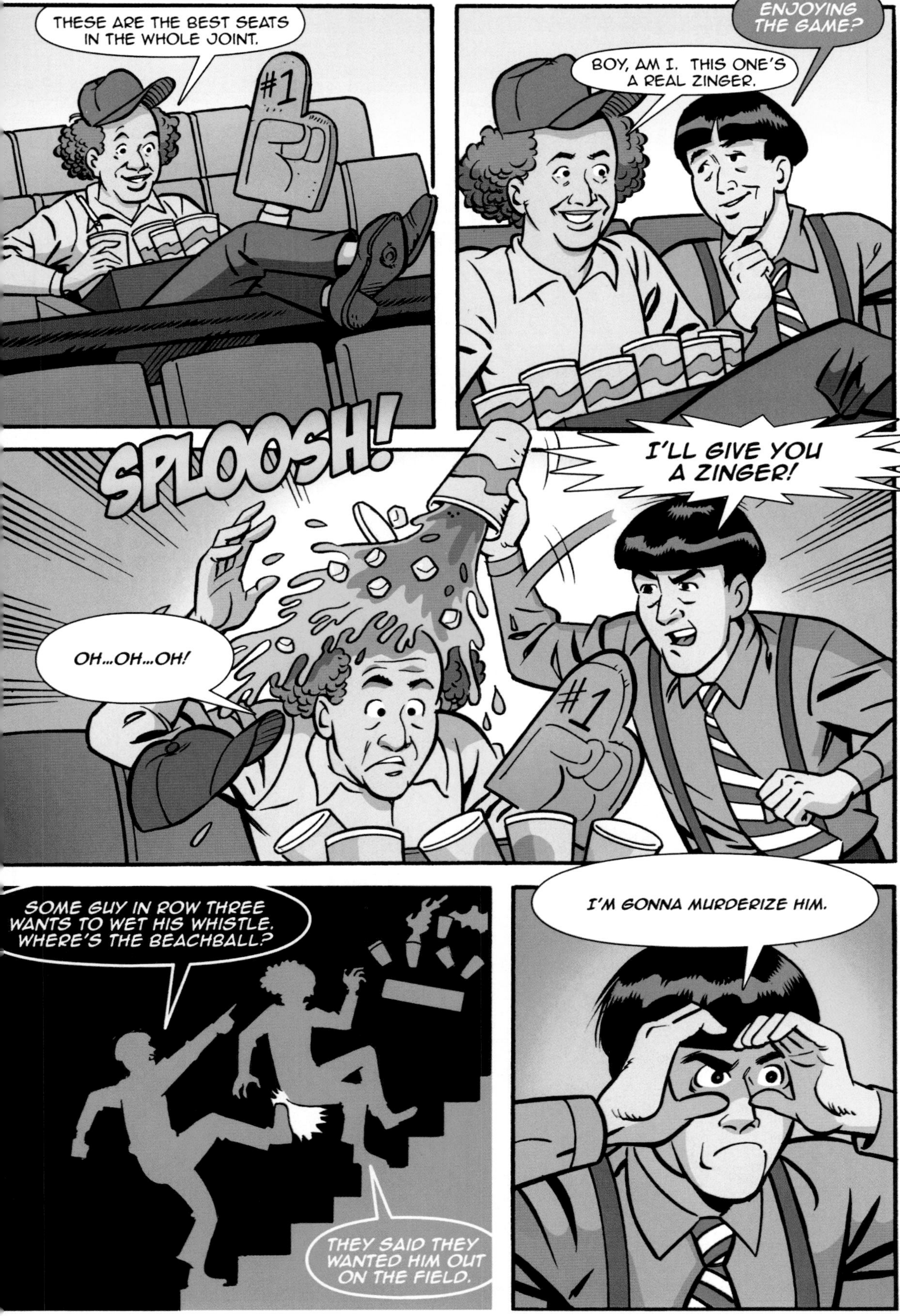
THESE ARE THE BEST SEATS IN THE WHOLE JOINT.
#1
ENJOYING THE GAME?
BOY, AM I. THIS ONE'S A REAL ZINGER.
SPLOOSH!
I'LL GIVE YOU A ZINGER!
OH...OH...OH!
#1
SOME GUY IN ROW THREE WANTS TO WET HIS WHISTLE. WHERE'S THE BEACHBALL?
THEY SAID THEY WANTED HIM OUT ON THE FIELD.
I'M GONNA MURDERIZE HIM.

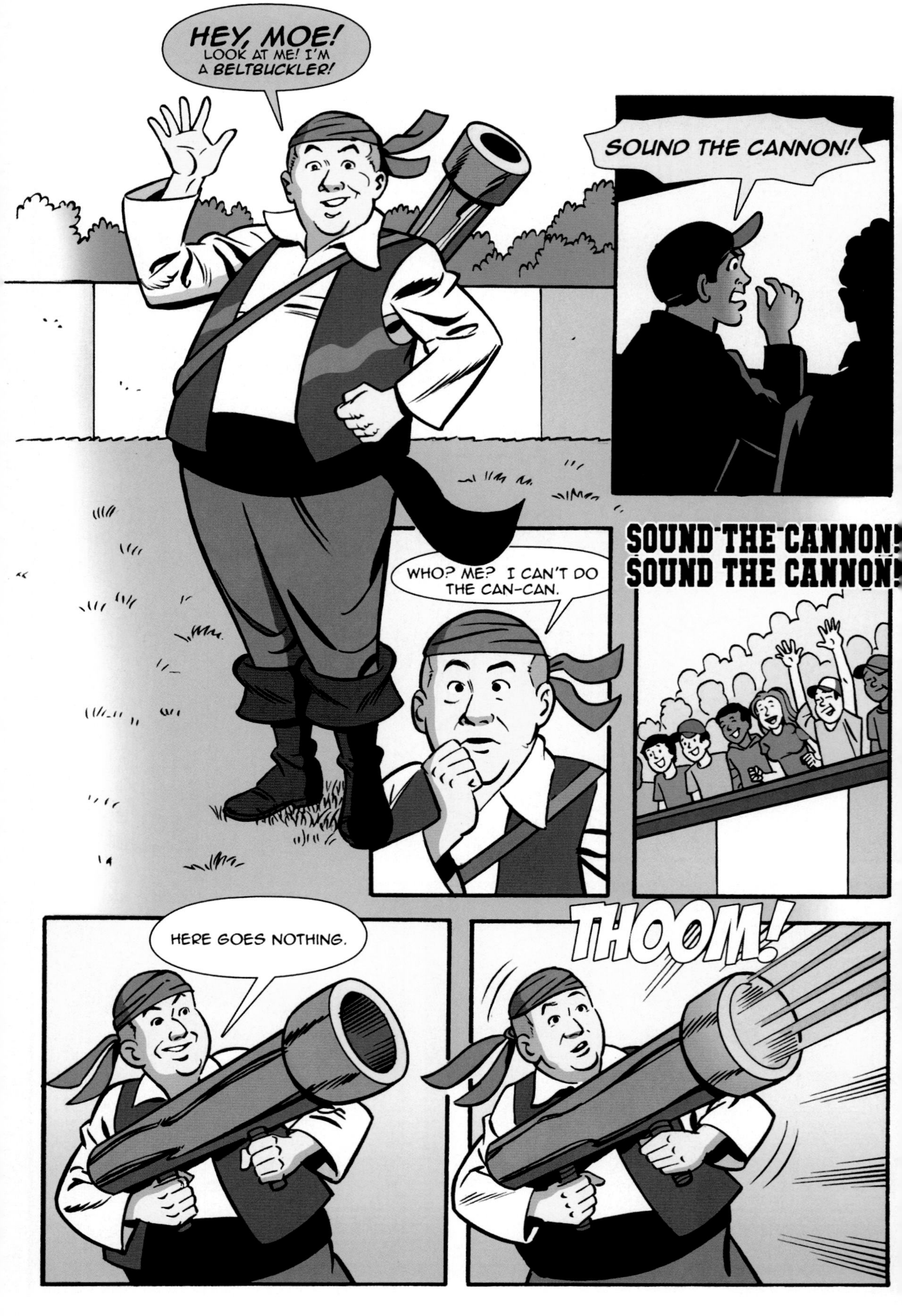
HEY, MOE! LOOK AT ME! I'M A BELTBUCKLER!
SOUND THE CANNON!
WHO? ME? I CAN'T DO THE CAN-CAN.
SOUND THE CANNON! SOUND THE CANNON!
HERE GOES NOTHING.
THOOM!

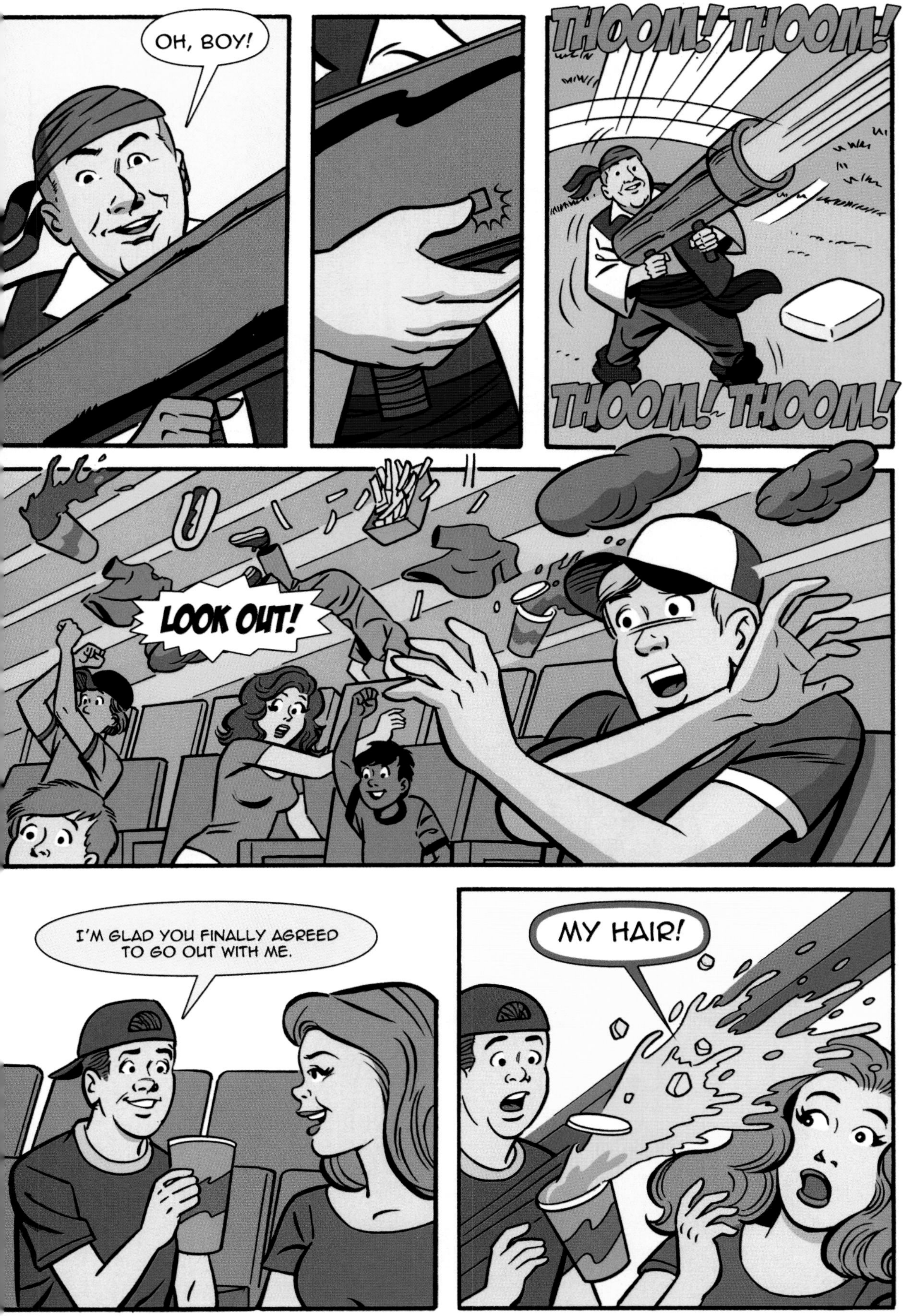
OH, BOY!
THOOM! THOOM!
THOOM! THOOM!
LOOK OUT!
I'M GLAD YOU FINALLY AGREED TO GO OUT WITH ME.
MY HAIR!

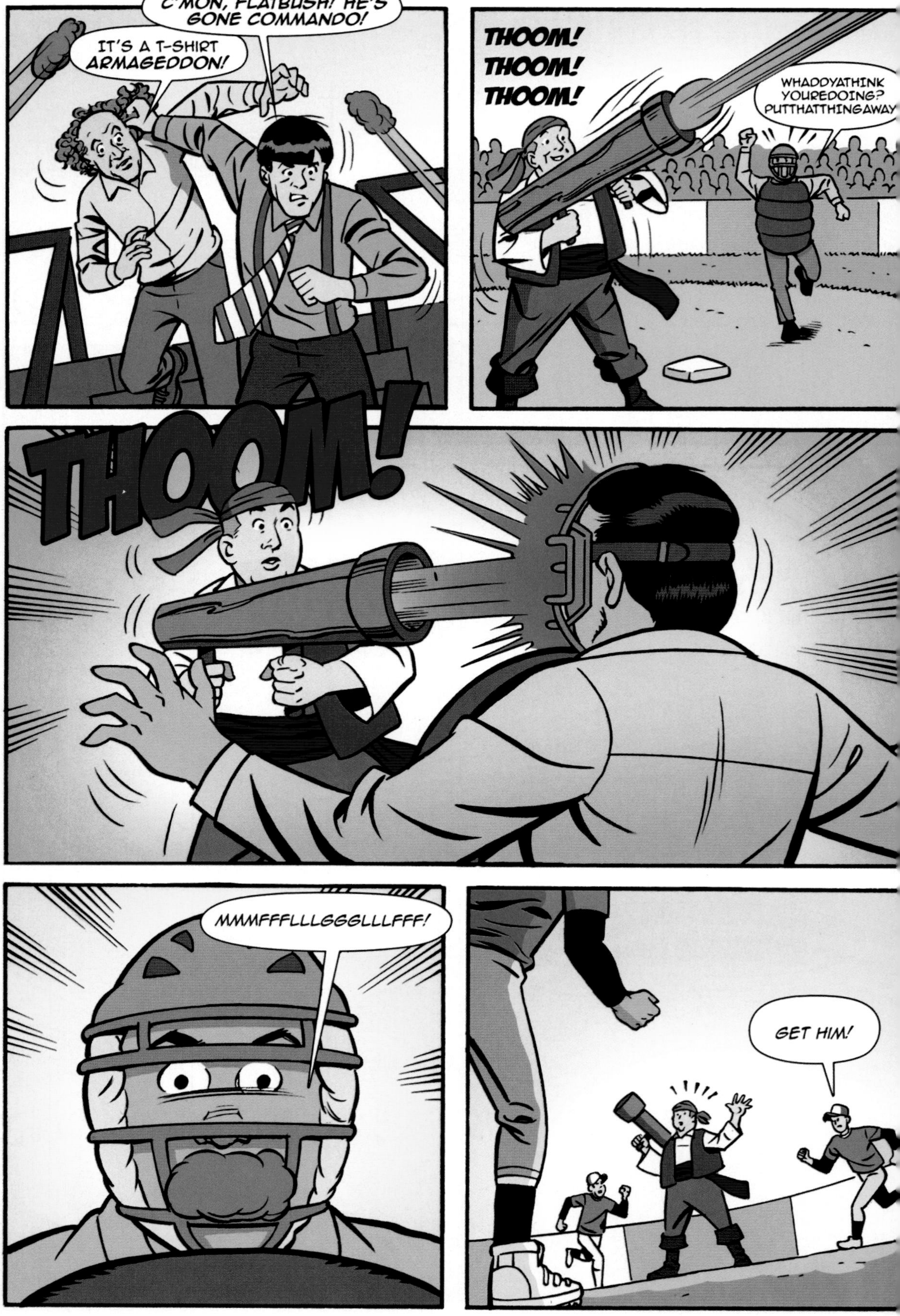
C'MON, FLATBUSH! HE'S GONE COMMANDO!
IT'S A T-SHIRT ARMAGEDDON!
THOOM! THOOM! THOOM!
WHADDYATHINK YOUREDOING? PUTTHATTHINGAWAY
THOOM!
MMMFFFLLLGGGLLLFFF!
GET HIM!

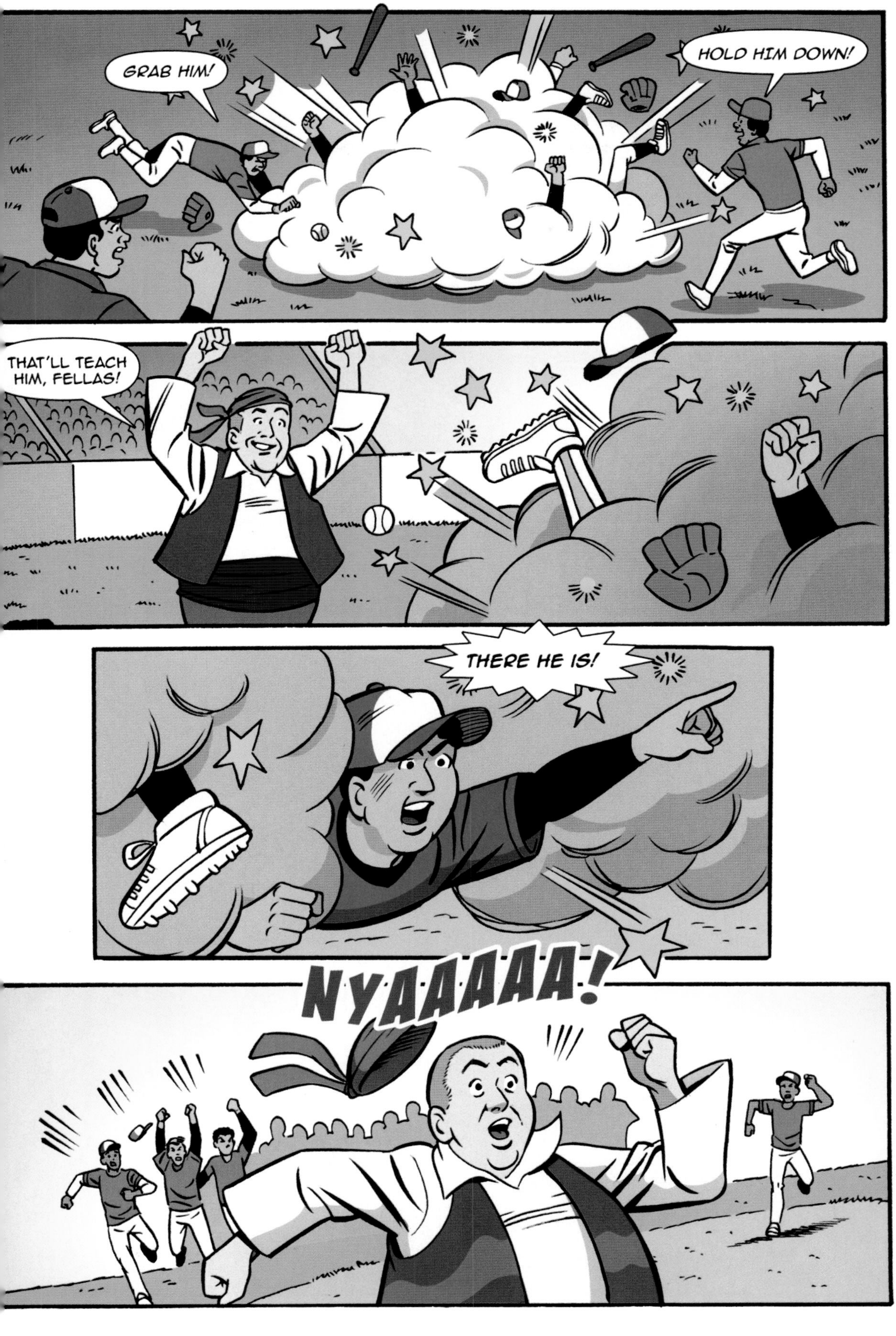
GRAB HIM!
HOLD HIM DOWN!
THAT'LL TEACH HIM, FELLAS!
THERE HE IS!
NYAAAAAA!

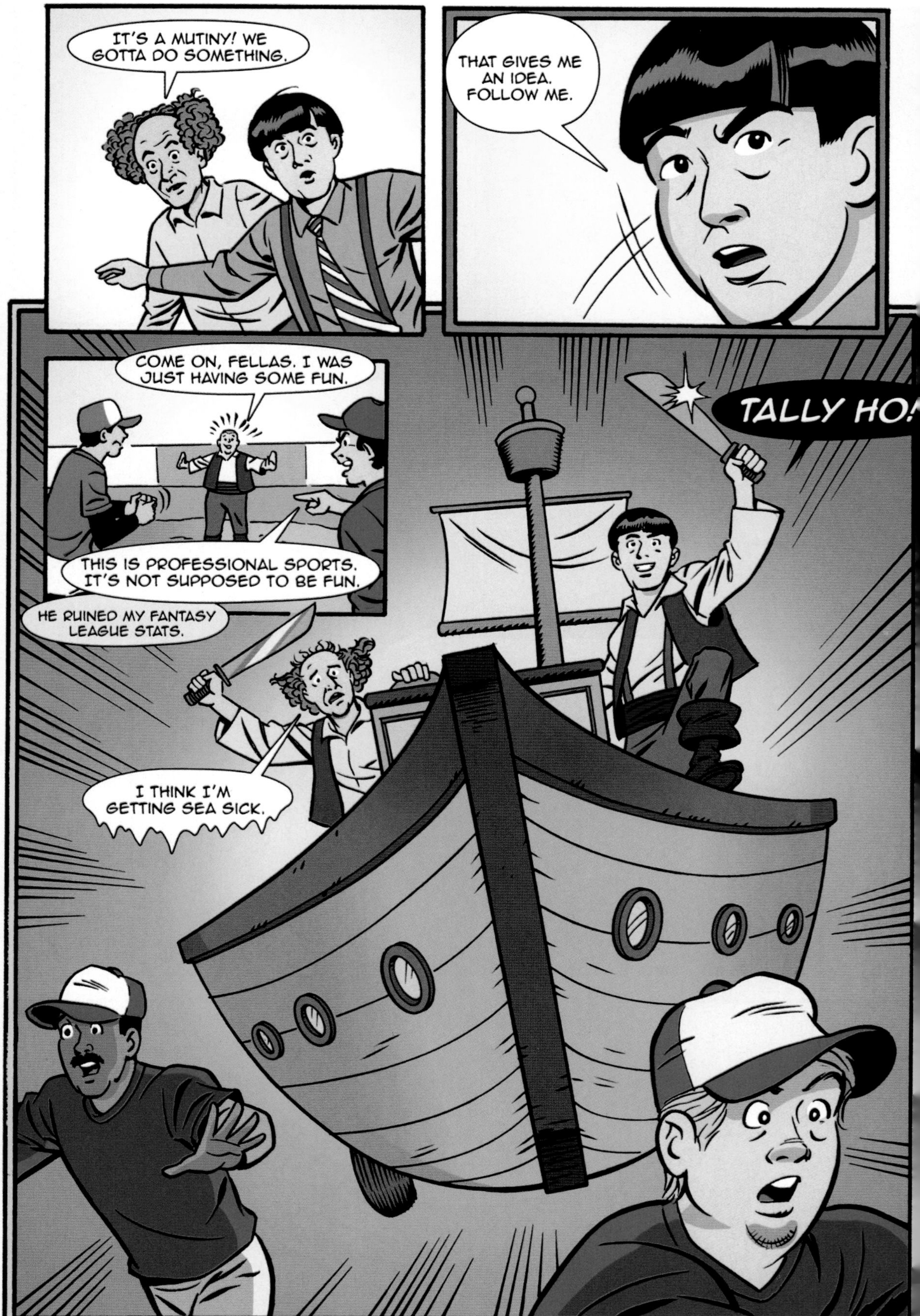
IT'S A MUTINY! WE GOTTA DO SOMETHING.
THAT GIVES ME AN IDEA. FOLLOW ME.
COME ON, FELLAS. I WAS JUST HAVING SOME FUN.
THIS IS PROFESSIONAL SPORTS. IT'S NOT SUPPOSED TO BE FUN.
HE RUINED MY FANTASY LEAGUE STATS.
TALLY HO!
I THINK I'M GETTING SEA SICK.

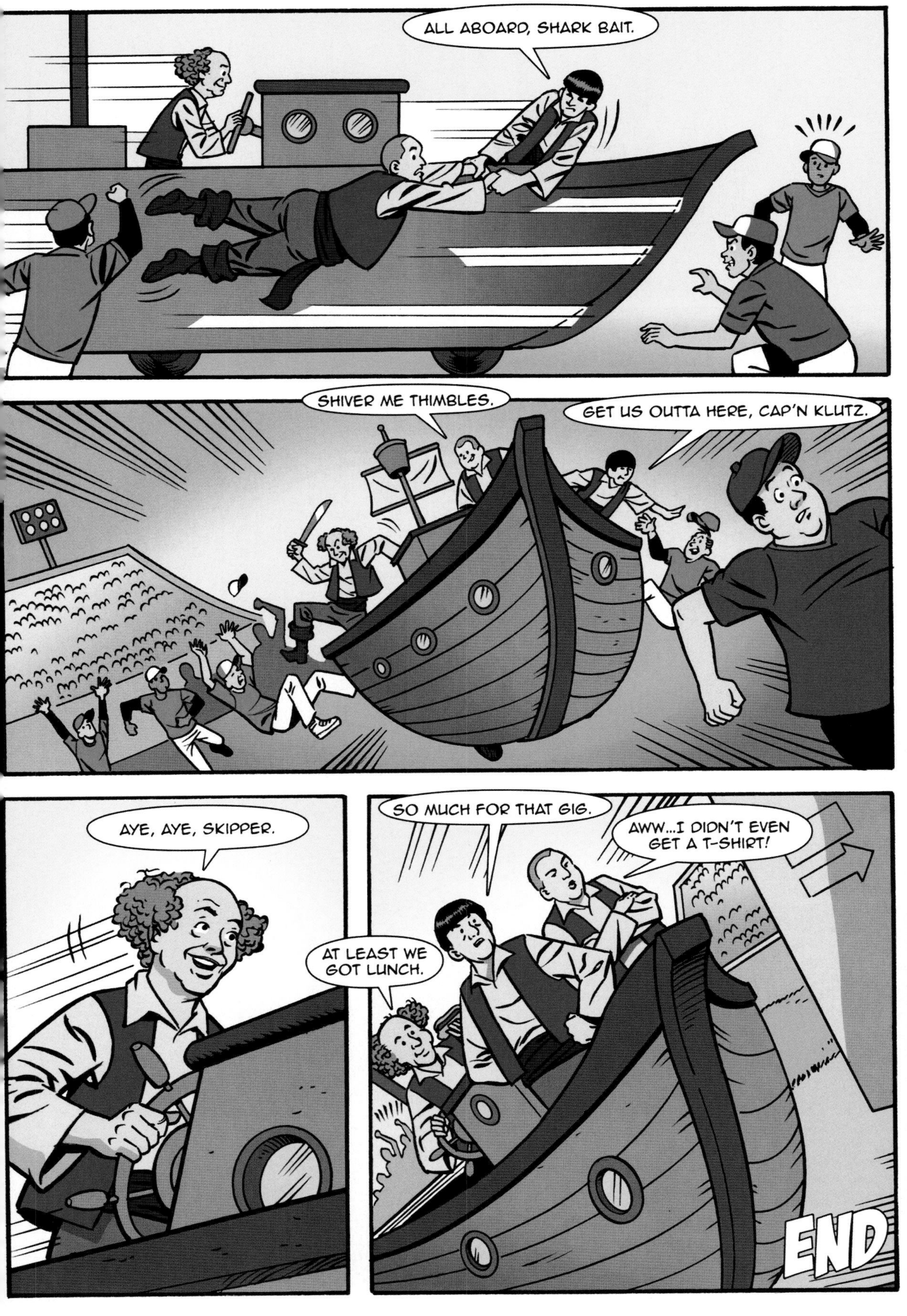
ALL ABOARD, SHARK BAIT.
SHIVER ME THIMBLES.
GET US OUTTA HERE, CAP'N KLUTZ.
AYE, AYE, SKIPPER.
SO MUCH FOR THAT GIG.
AWW...I DIDN'T EVEN GET A T-SHIRT!
AT LEAST WE GOT LUNCH.
END

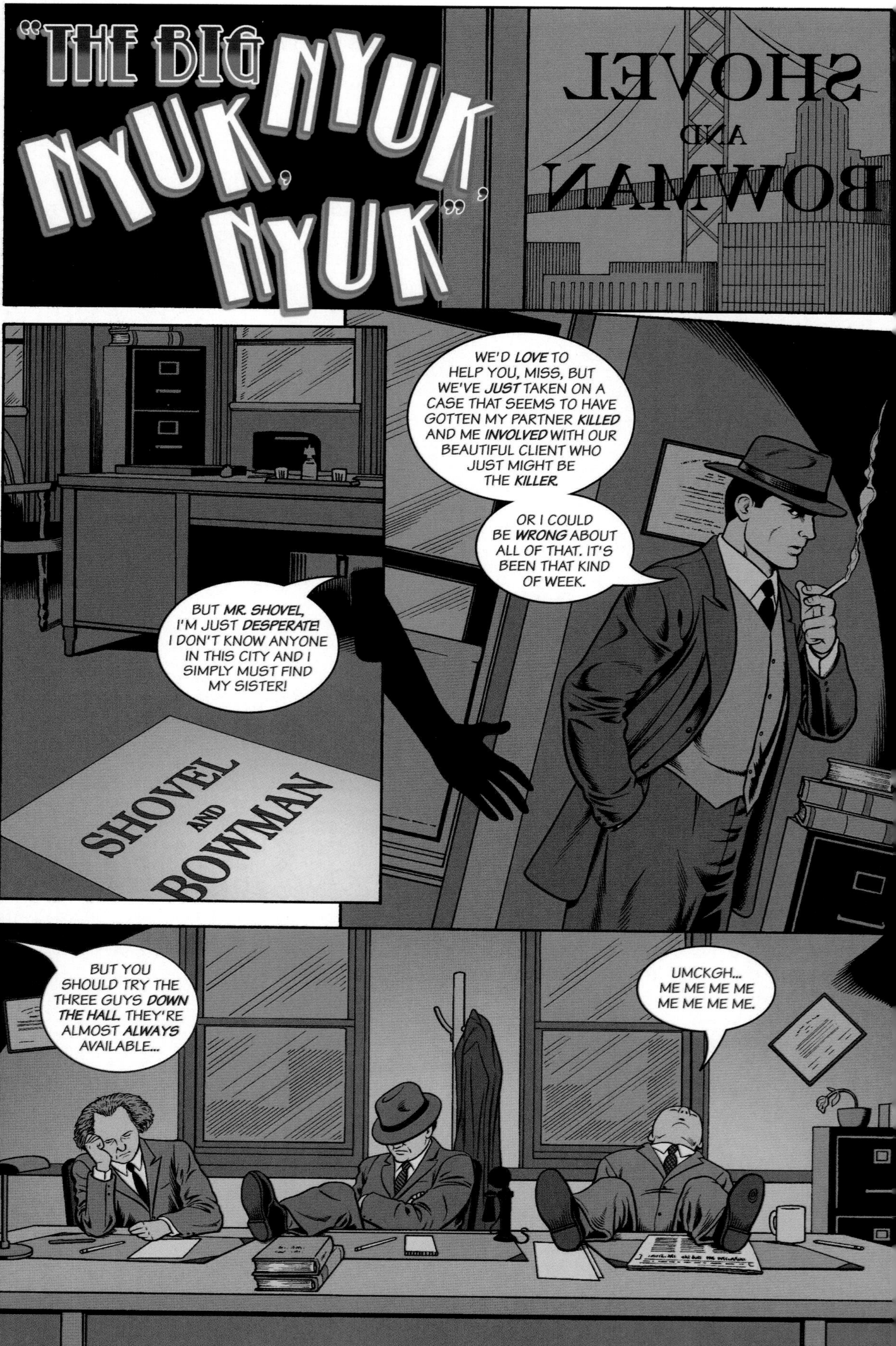
"THE BIG NYUK, NYUK, NYUK"
SHOVEL AND BOWMAN
WE'D LOVE TO HELP YOU, MISS, BUT WE'VE JUST TAKEN ON A CASE THAT SEEMS TO HAVE GOTTEN MY PARTNER KILLED AND ME INVOLVED WITH OUR BEAUTIFUL CLIENT WHO JUST MIGHT BE THE KILLER.
OR I COULD BE WRONG ABOUT ALL OF THAT. IT'S BEEN THAT KIND OF WEEK.
BUT MR. SHOVEL, I'M JUST DESPERATE! I DON'T KNOW ANYONE IN THIS CITY AND I SIMPLY MUST FIND MY SISTER!
SHOVEL AND BOWMAN
BUT YOU SHOULD TRY THE THREE GUYS DOWN THE HALL. THEY'RE ALMOST ALWAYS AVAILABLE...
UMCKGH... ME ME ME ME ME ME ME ME.

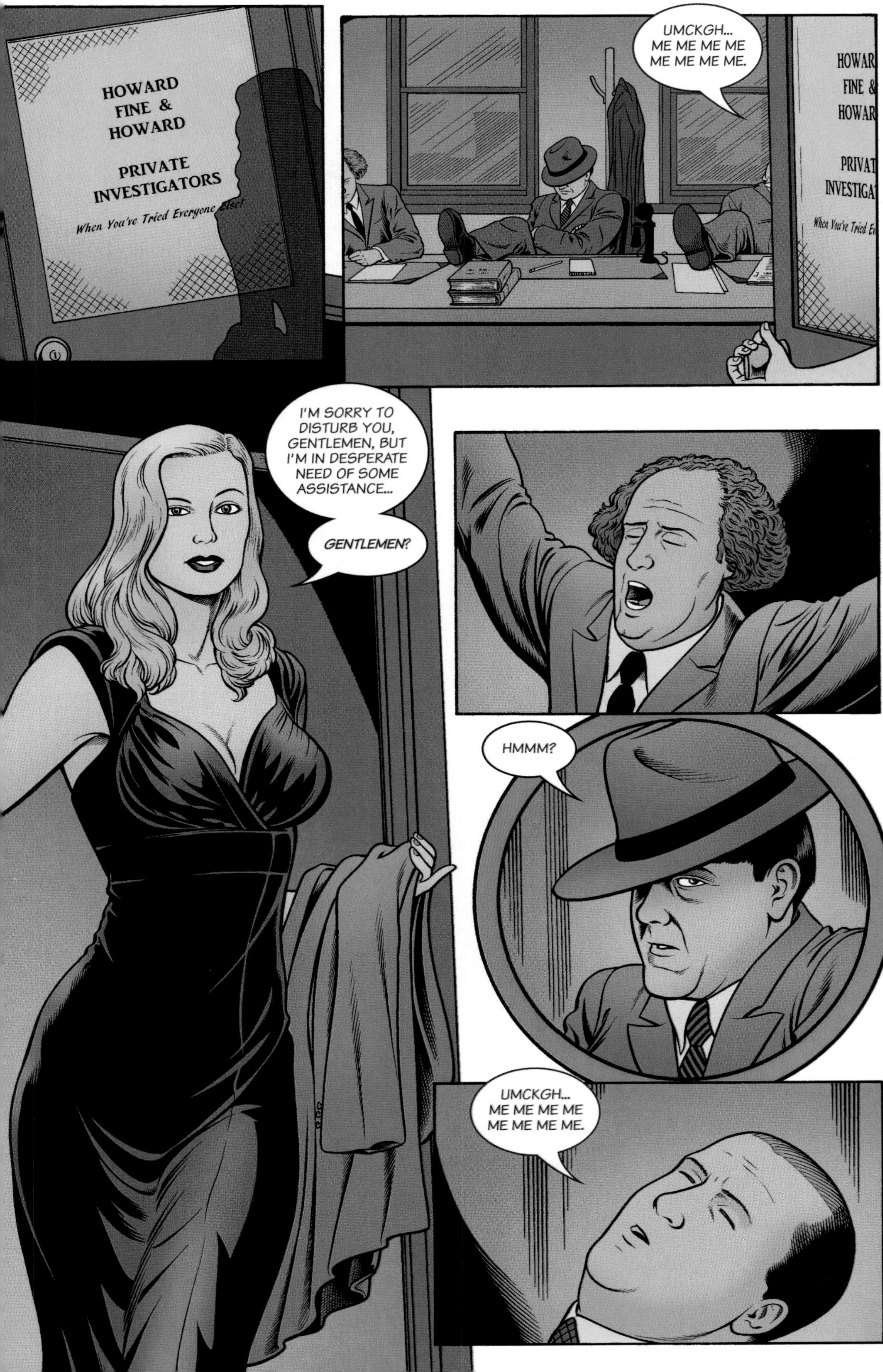
HOWARD
FINE &
HOWARD
PRIVATE
INVESTIGATORS
When You've Tried Everyone Else!
UMCKGH... ME ME ME ME ME ME ME ME.
HOWARD
FINE &
HOWARD
PRIVATE
INVESTIGAT
When You've Tried Ev
I'M SORRY TO DISTURB YOU, GENTLEMEN, BUT I'M IN DESPERATE NEED OF SOME ASSISTANCE...
GENTLEMEN?
HMMM?
UMCKGH... ME ME ME ME ME ME ME ME.

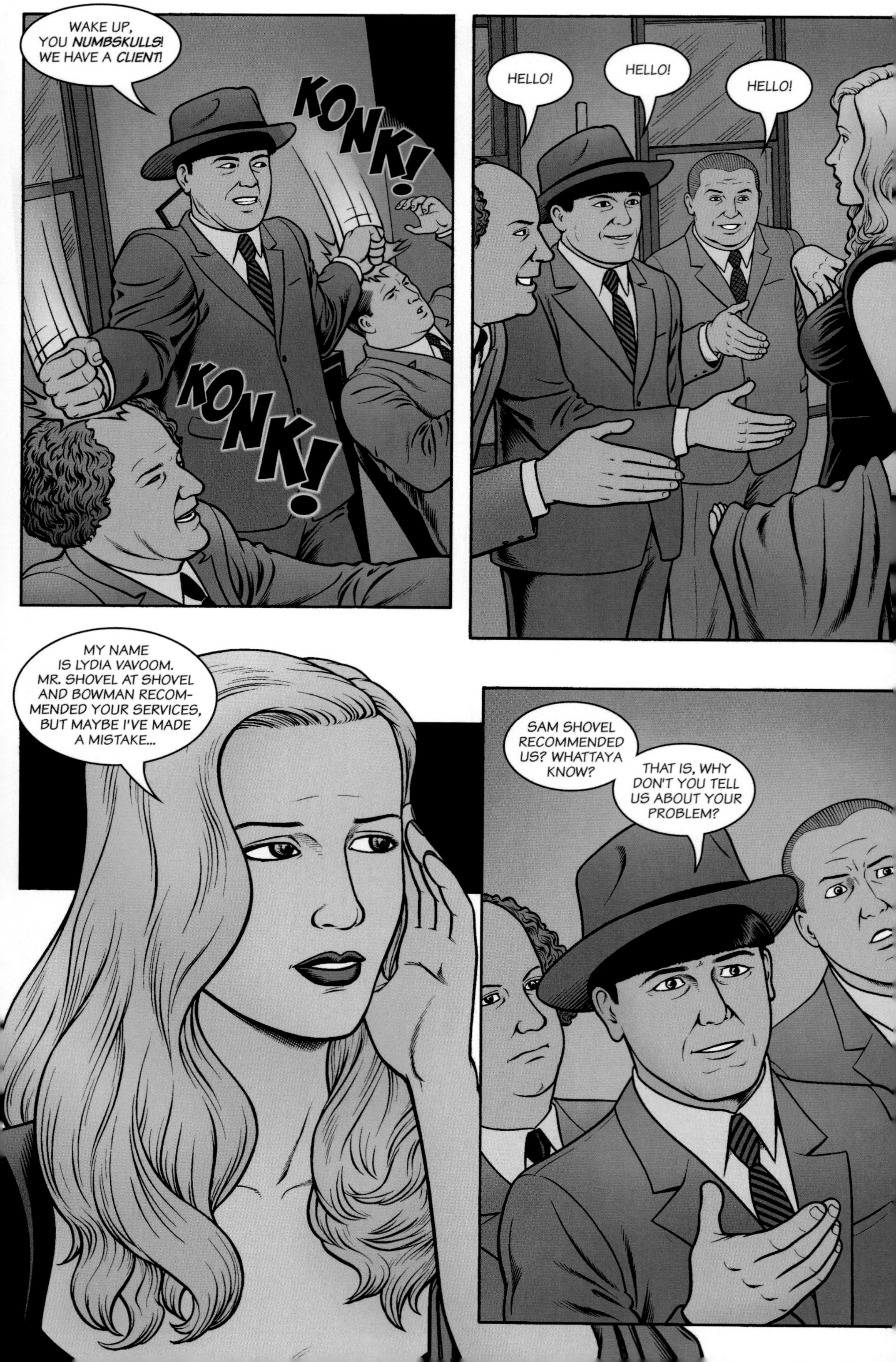
WAKE UP, YOU NUMBSKULLS! WE HAVE A CLIENT!
KONK!
KONK!
HELLO!
HELLO!
HELLO!
MY NAME IS LYDIA VAVOOM. MR. SHOVEL AT SHOVEL AND BOWMAN RECOMMENDED YOUR SERVICES, BUT MAYBE I'VE MADE A MISTAKE...
SAM SHOVEL RECOMMENDED US? WHATTAYA KNOW?
THAT IS, WHY DON'T YOU TELL US ABOUT YOUR PROBLEM?

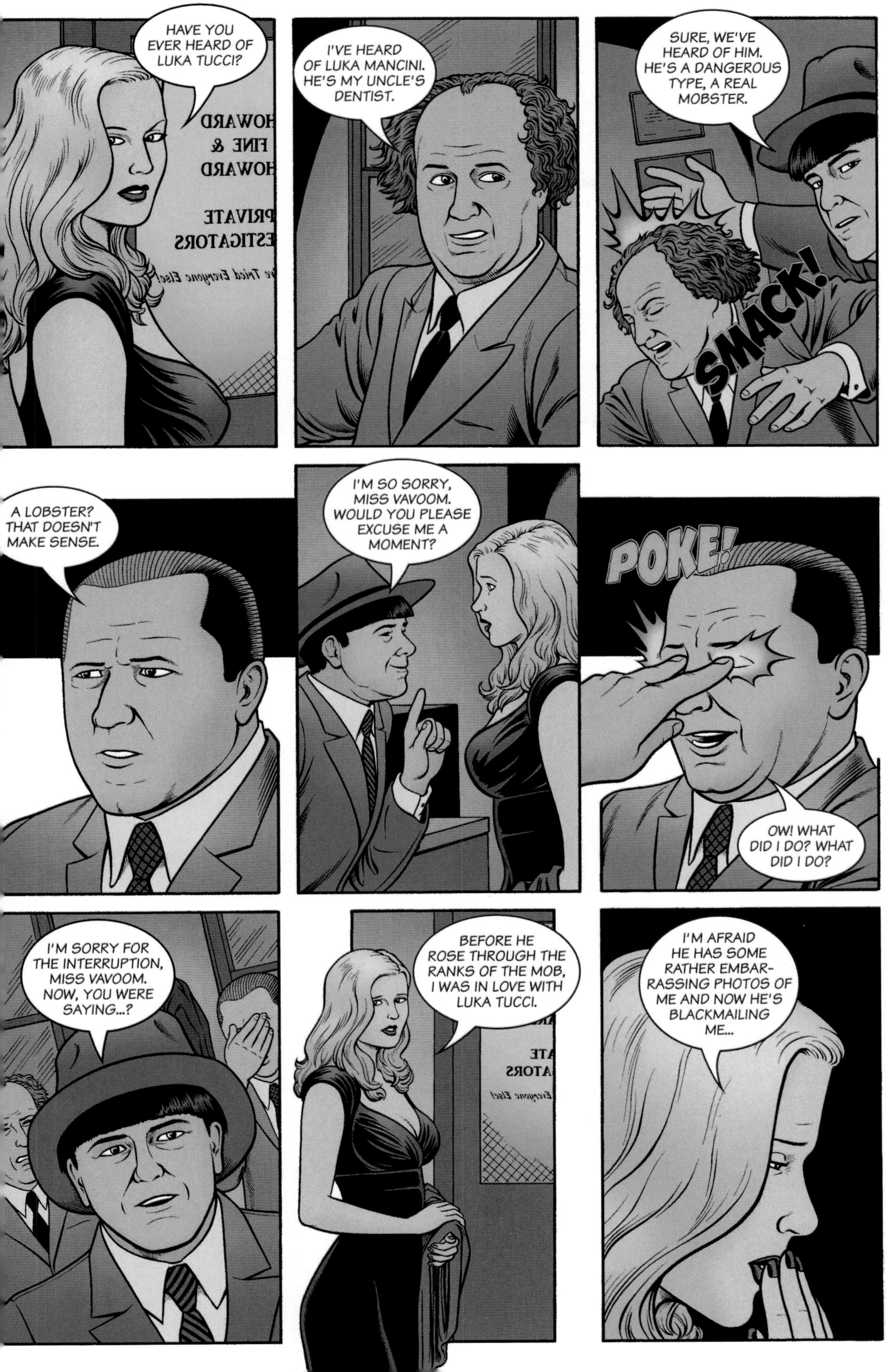
HAVE YOU EVER HEARD OF LUKA TUCCI?
I'VE HEARD OF LUKA MANCINI. HE'S MY UNCLE'S DENTIST.
SURE, WE'VE HEARD OF HIM. HE'S A DANGEROUS TYPE, A REAL MOBSTER.
SMACK!
A LOBSTER? THAT DOESN'T MAKE SENSE.
I'M SO SORRY, MISS VAVOOM. WOULD YOU PLEASE EXCUSE ME A MOMENT?
POKE!
OW! WHAT DID I DO? WHAT DID I DO?
I'M SORRY FOR THE INTERRUPTION, MISS VAVOOM. NOW, YOU WERE SAYING...?
BEFORE HE ROSE THROUGH THE RANKS OF THE MOB, I WAS IN LOVE WITH LUKA TUCCI.
I'M AFRAID HE HAS SOME RATHER EMBAR-RASSING PHOTOS OF ME AND NOW HE'S BLACKMAILING ME...

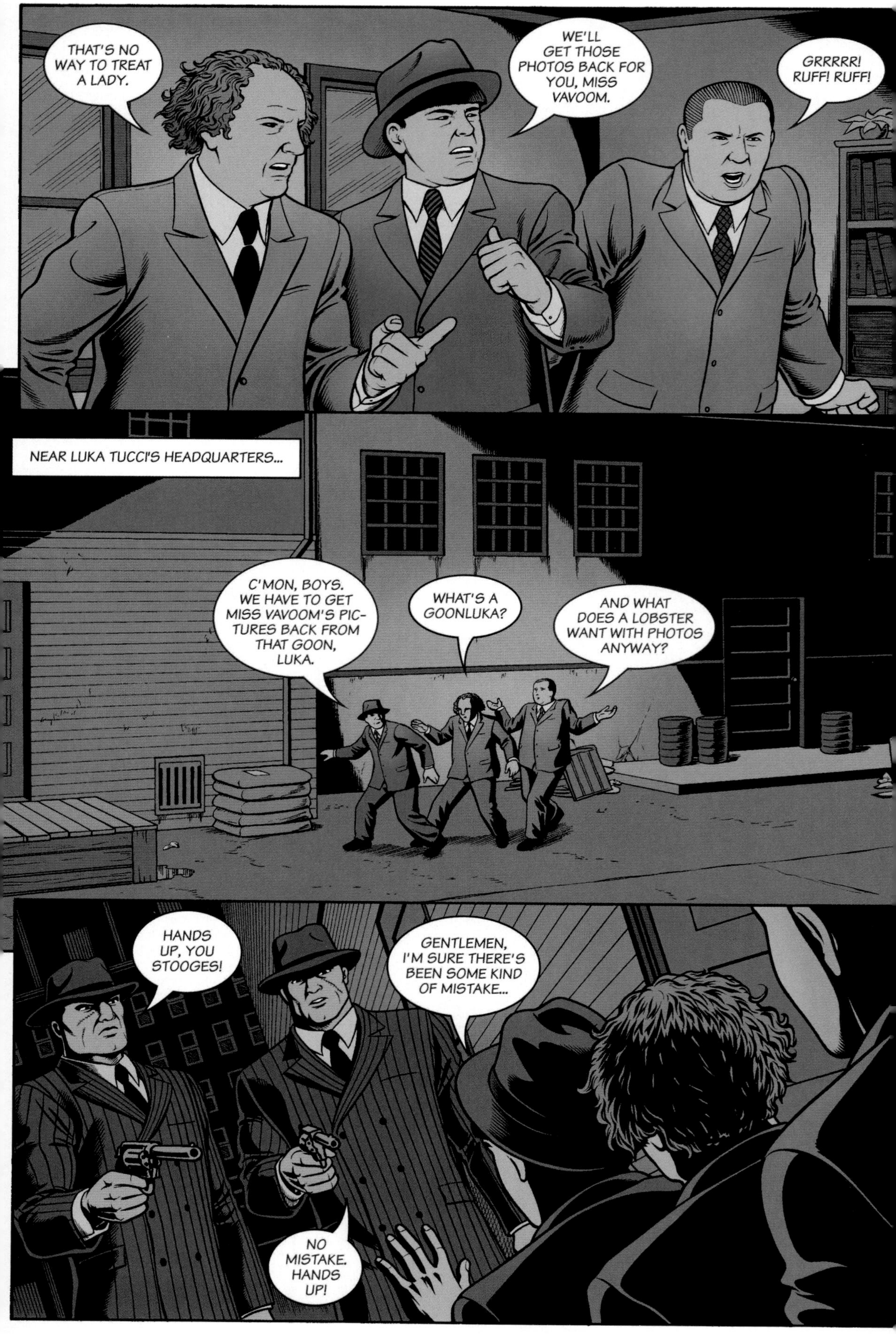
THAT'S NO WAY TO TREAT A LADY.
WE'LL GET THOSE PHOTOS BACK FOR YOU, MISS VAVOOM.
GRRRRR! RUFF! RUFF!
NEAR LUKA TUCCI'S HEADQUARTERS...
C'MON, BOYS. WE HAVE TO GET MISS VAVOOM'S PICTURES BACK FROM THAT GOON, LUKA.
WHAT'S A GOONLUKA?
AND WHAT DOES A LOBSTER WANT WITH PHOTOS ANYWAY?
HANDS UP, YOU STOOGES!
GENTLEMEN, I'M SURE THERE'S BEEN SOME KIND OF MISTAKE...
NO MISTAKE. HANDS UP!

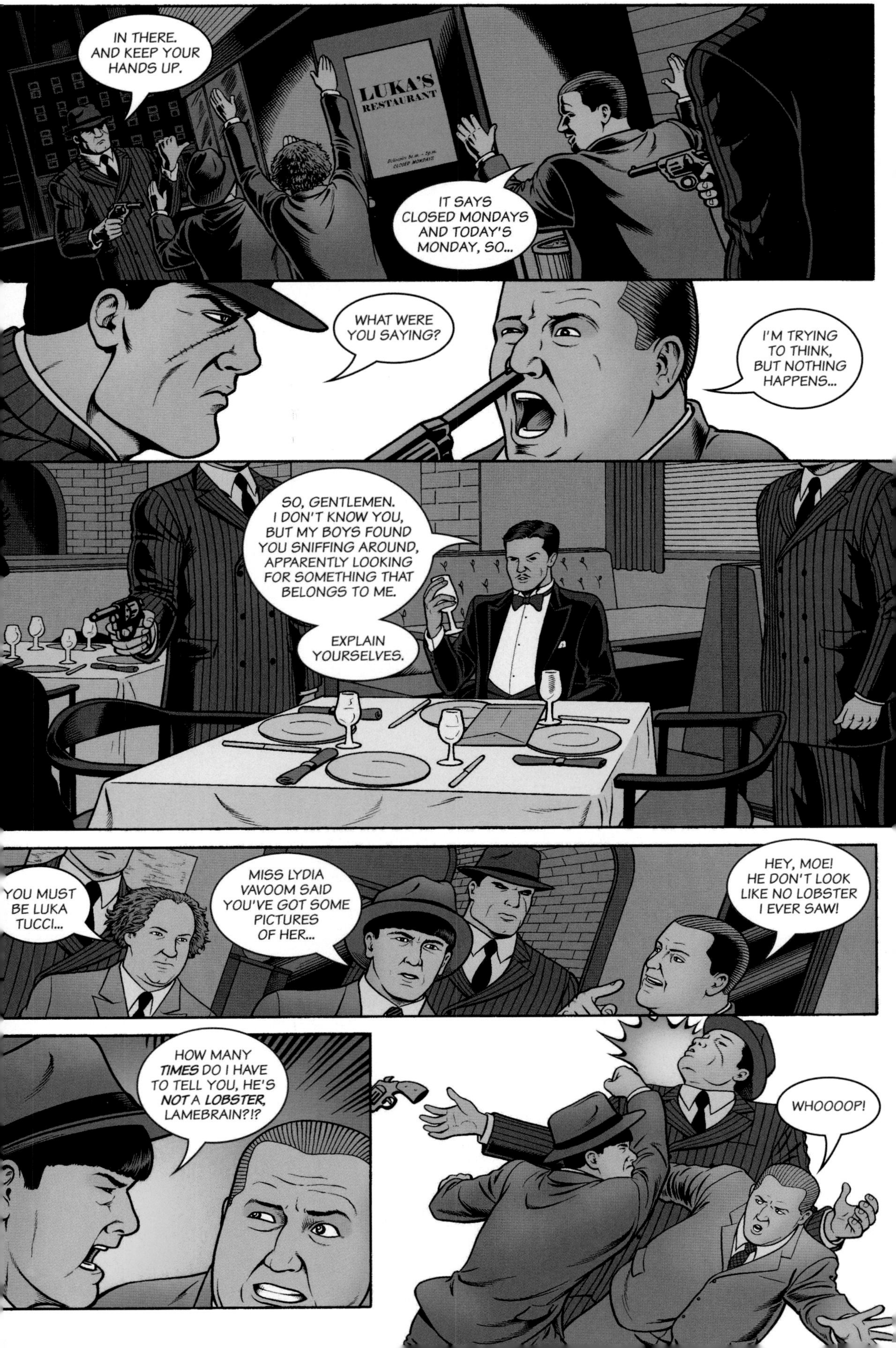
IN THERE. AND KEEP YOUR HANDS UP.
LUKA'S RESTAURANT
CLOSED MONDAYS
IT SAYS CLOSED MONDAYS AND TODAY'S MONDAY, SO...
WHAT WERE YOU SAYING?
I'M TRYING TO THINK, BUT NOTHING HAPPENS...
SO, GENTLEMEN. I DON'T KNOW YOU, BUT MY BOYS FOUND YOU SNIFFING AROUND, APPARENTLY LOOKING FOR SOMETHING THAT BELONGS TO ME.
EXPLAIN YOURSELVES.
YOU MUST BE LUKA TUCCI...
MISS LYDIA VAVOOM SAID YOU'VE GOT SOME PICTURES OF HER...
HEY, MOE! HE DON'T LOOK LIKE NO LOBSTER I EVER SAW!
HOW MANY *TIMES* DO I HAVE TO TELL YOU, HE'S *NOT* A *LOBSTER*, LAMEBRAIN?!?
WHOOOOP!

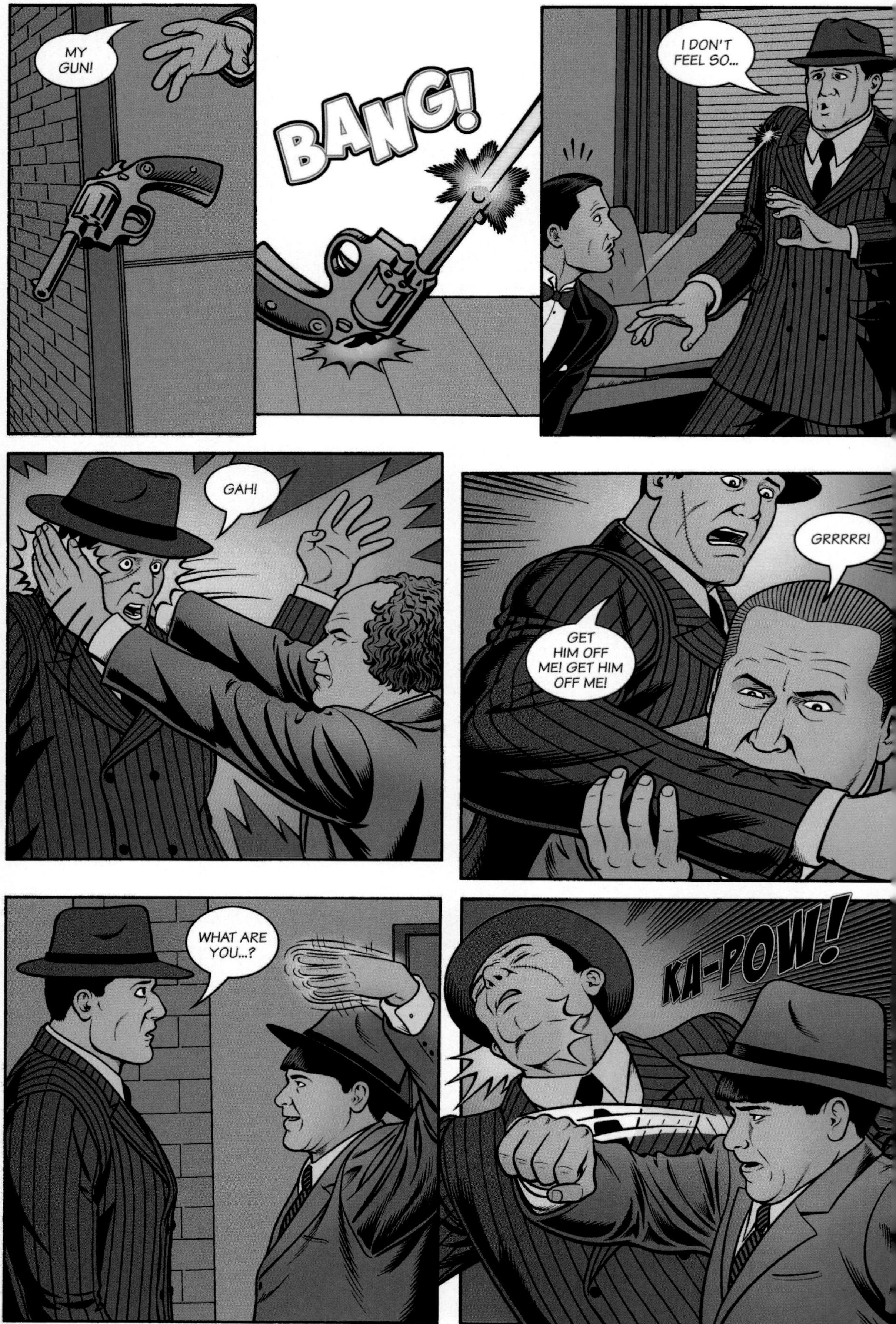
MY GUN!
BANG!
I DON'T FEEL SO...
GAH!
GRRRRR!
GET HIM OFF ME! GET HIM OFF ME!
WHAT ARE YOU...?
KA-POW!

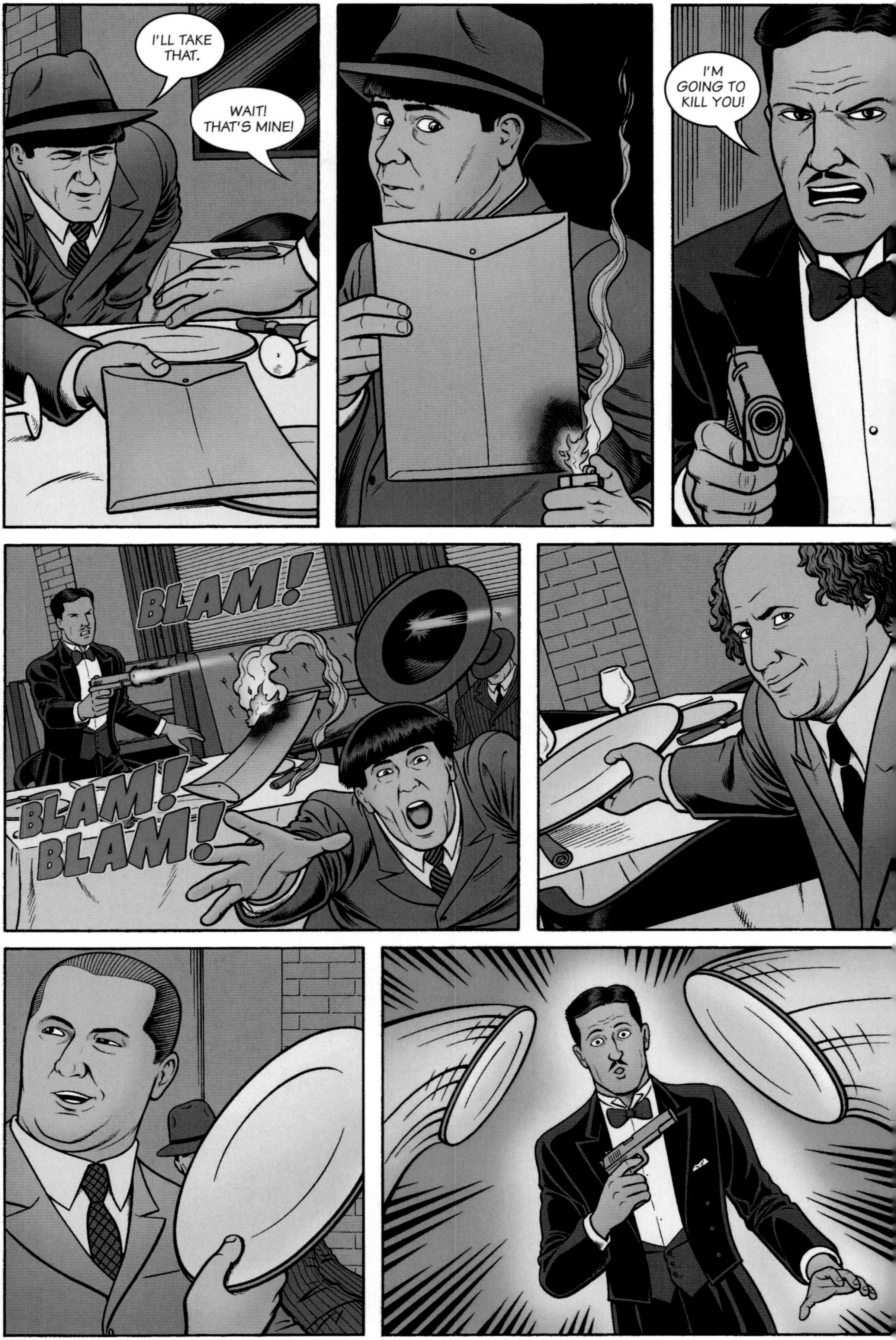
I'LL TAKE THAT.
WAIT! THAT'S MINE!
I'M GOING TO KILL YOU!
BLAM!
BLAM! BLAM!

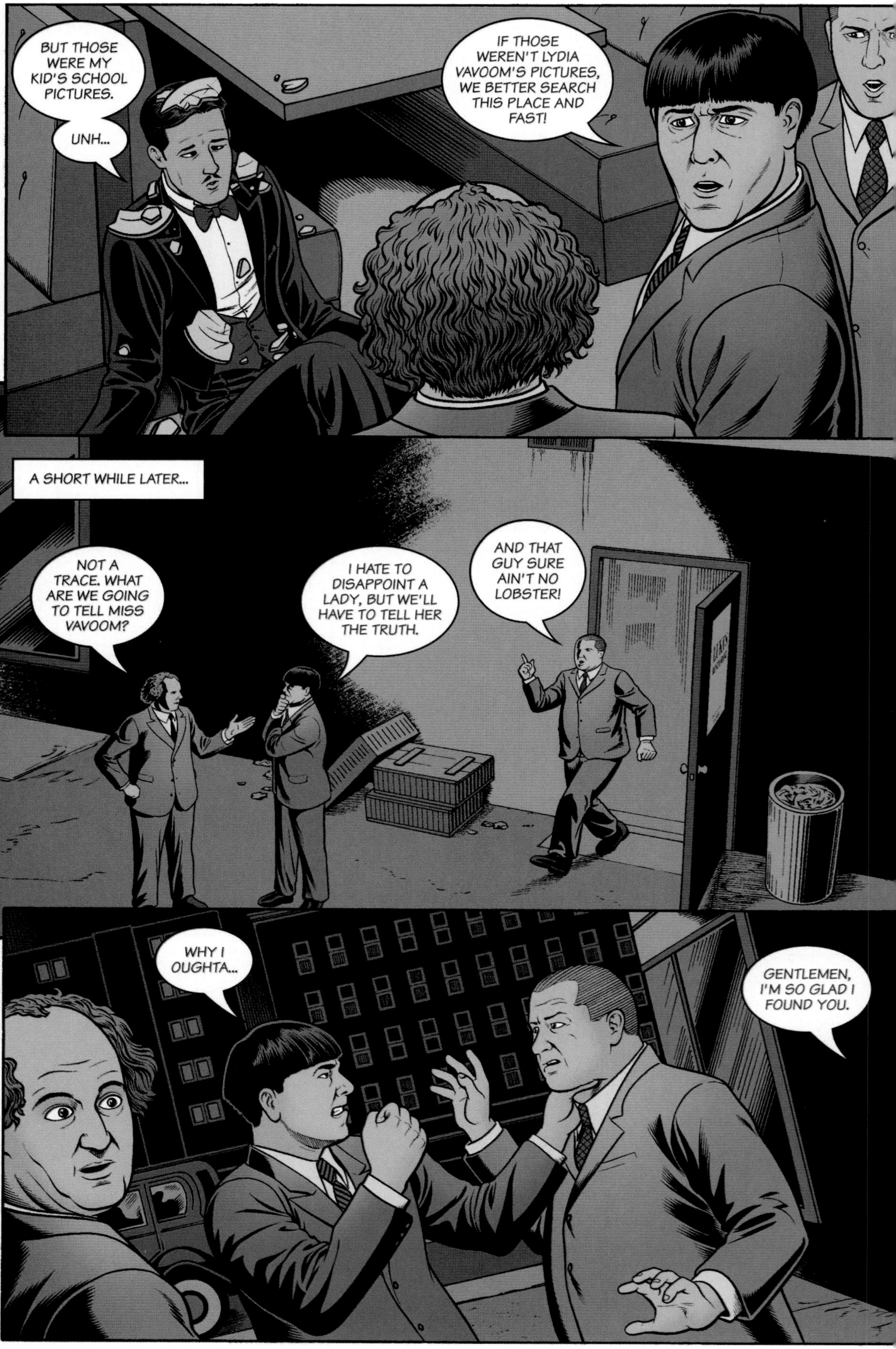
BUT THOSE WERE MY KID'S SCHOOL PICTURES.
UNH...
IF THOSE WEREN'T LYDIA VAVOOM'S PICTURES, WE BETTER SEARCH THIS PLACE AND FAST!
A SHORT WHILE LATER...
NOT A TRACE. WHAT ARE WE GOING TO TELL MISS VAVOOM?
I HATE TO DISAPPOINT A LADY, BUT WE'LL HAVE TO TELL HER THE TRUTH.
AND THAT GUY SURE AIN'T NO LOBSTER!
WHY I OUGHTA...
GENTLEMEN, I'M SO GLAD I FOUND YOU.

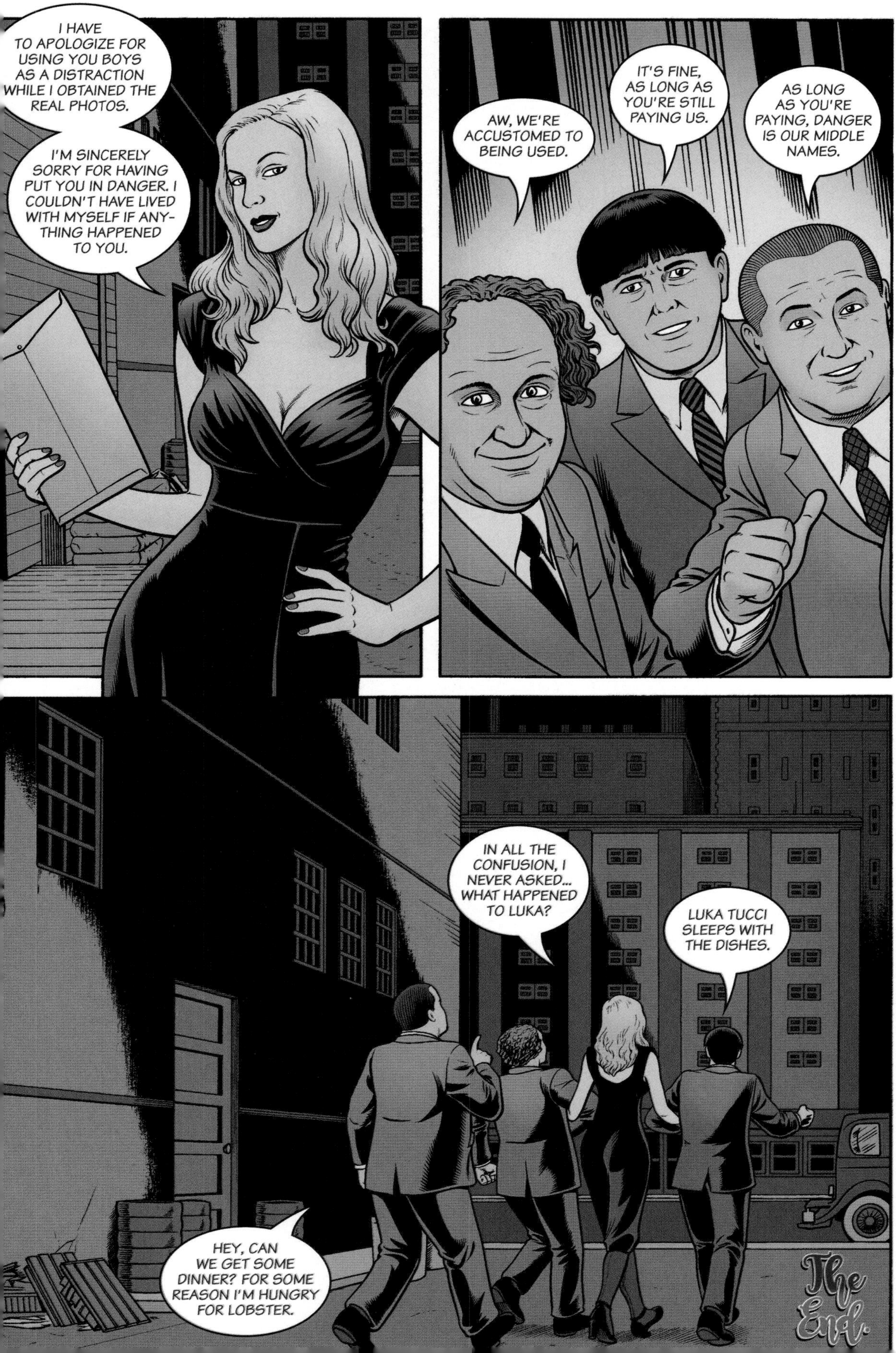
I HAVE TO APOLOGIZE FOR USING YOU BOYS AS A DISTRACTION WHILE I OBTAINED THE REAL PHOTOS.
I'M SINCERELY SORRY FOR HAVING PUT YOU IN DANGER. I COULDN'T HAVE LIVED WITH MYSELF IF ANYTHING HAPPENED TO YOU.
AW, WE'RE ACCUSTOMED TO BEING USED.
IT'S FINE, AS LONG AS YOU'RE STILL PAYING US.
AS LONG AS YOU'RE PAYING, DANGER IS OUR MIDDLE NAMES.
IN ALL THE CONFUSION, I NEVER ASKED... WHAT HAPPENED TO LUKA?
LUKA TUCCI SLEEPS WITH THE DISHES.
HEY, CAN WE GET SOME DINNER? FOR SOME REASON I'M HUNGRY FOR LOBSTER.
The End.

BURGERSAURUS STOOGE

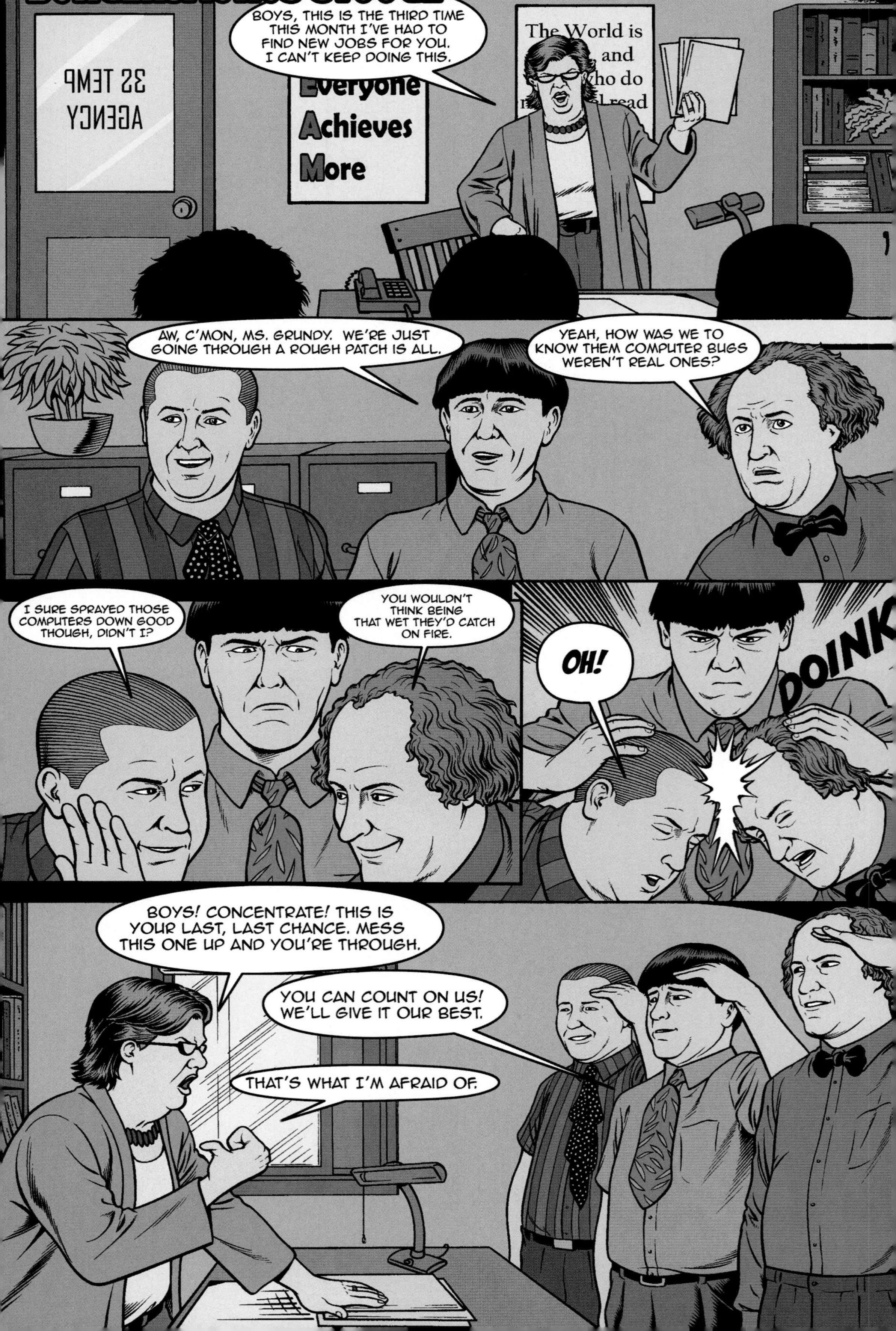
3S TEMP AGENCY
Everyone Achieves More
BOYS, THIS IS THE THIRD TIME THIS MONTH I'VE HAD TO FIND NEW JOBS FOR YOU. I CAN'T KEEP DOING THIS.
AW, C'MON, MS. GRUNDY. WE'RE JUST GOING THROUGH A ROUGH PATCH IS ALL.
YEAH, HOW WAS WE TO KNOW THEM COMPUTER BUGS WEREN'T REAL ONES?
I SURE SPRAYED THOSE COMPUTERS DOWN GOOD THOUGH, DIDN'T I?
YOU WOULDN'T THINK BEING THAT WET THEY'D CATCH ON FIRE.
OH!
DOINK
BOYS! CONCENTRATE! THIS IS YOUR LAST, LAST CHANCE. MESS THIS ONE UP AND YOU'RE THROUGH.
YOU CAN COUNT ON US! WE'LL GIVE IT OUR BEST.
THAT'S WHAT I'M AFRAID OF.

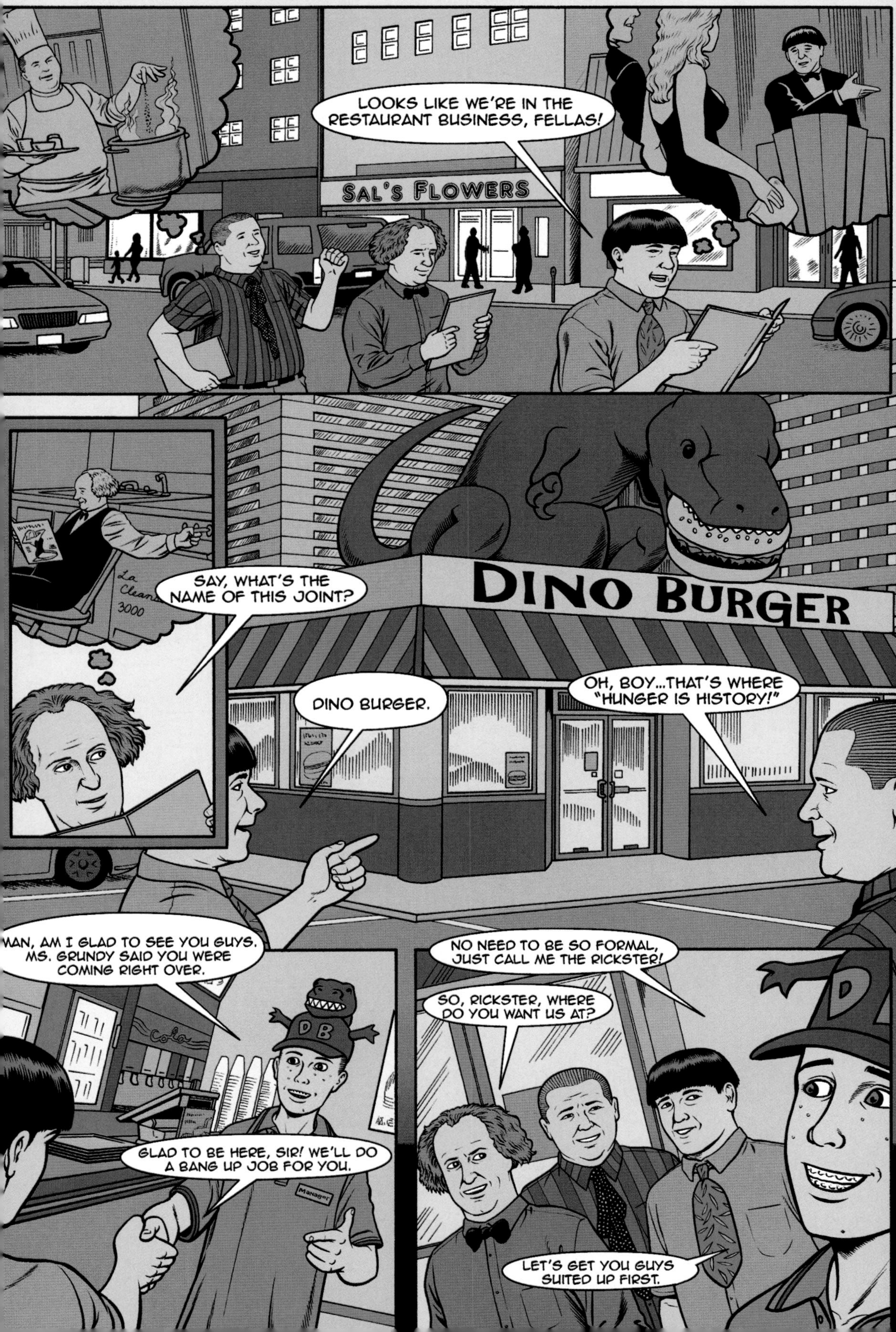
LOOKS LIKE WE'RE IN THE RESTAURANT BUSINESS, FELLAS!
SAL'S FLOWERS
DINO BURGER
SAY, WHAT'S THE NAME OF THIS JOINT?
La Cleaner 3000
DINO BURGER.
OH, BOY...THAT'S WHERE "HUNGER IS HISTORY!"
MAN, AM I GLAD TO SEE YOU GUYS. MS. GRUNDY SAID YOU WERE COMING RIGHT OVER.
DB
Cola
GLAD TO BE HERE, SIR! WE'LL DO A BANG UP JOB FOR YOU.
Manager
NO NEED TO BE SO FORMAL, JUST CALL ME THE RICKSTER!
SO, RICKSTER, WHERE DO YOU WANT US AT?
LET'S GET YOU GUYS SUITED UP FIRST.

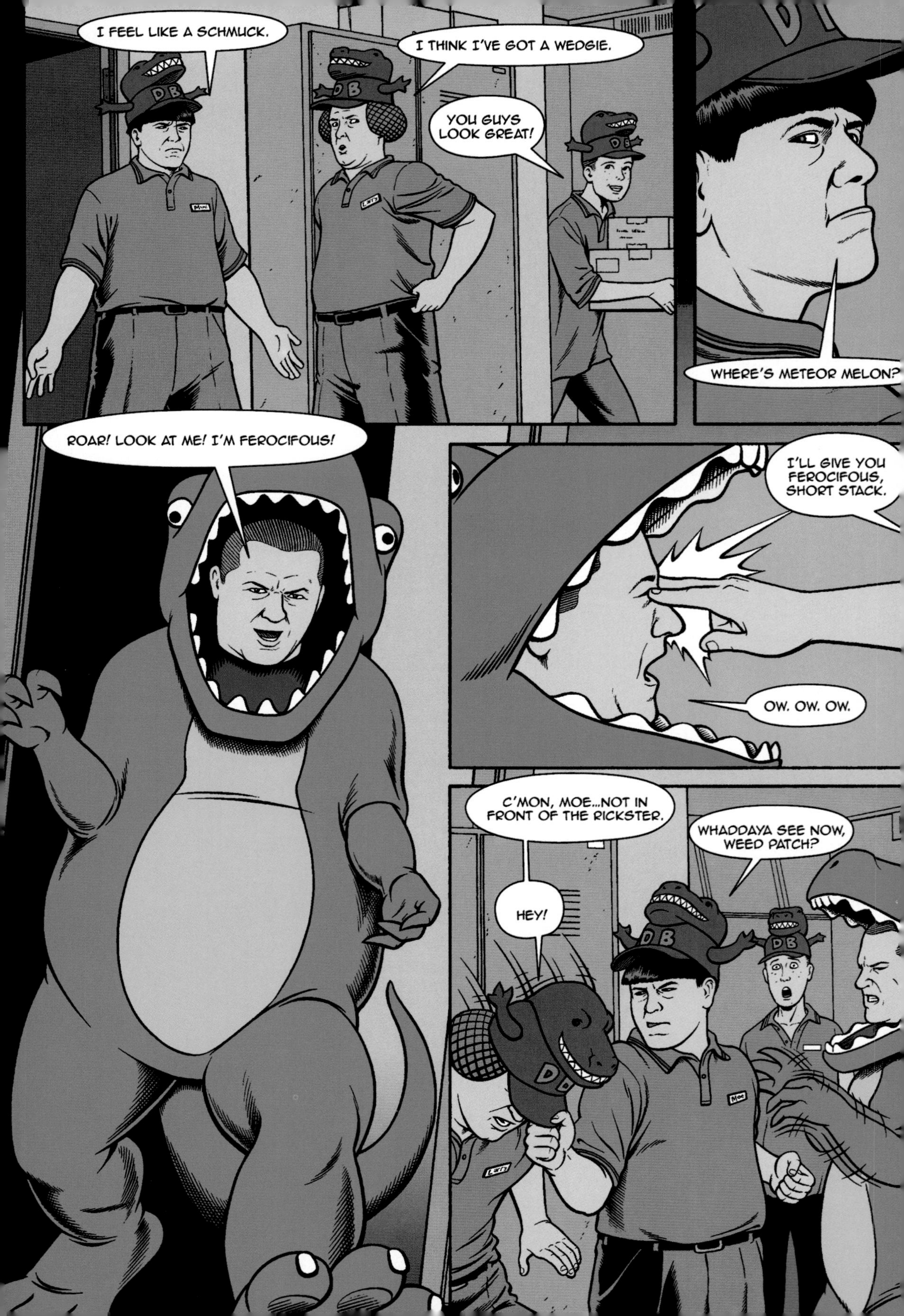
I FEEL LIKE A SCHMUCK.
I THINK I'VE GOT A WEDGIE.
YOU GUYS LOOK GREAT!
WHERE'S METEOR MELON?
ROAR! LOOK AT ME! I'M FEROCIFOUS!
I'LL GIVE YOU FEROCIFOUS, SHORT STACK.
OW. OW. OW.
C'MON, MOE...NOT IN FRONT OF THE RICKSTER.
HEY!
WHADDAYA SEE NOW, WEED PATCH?

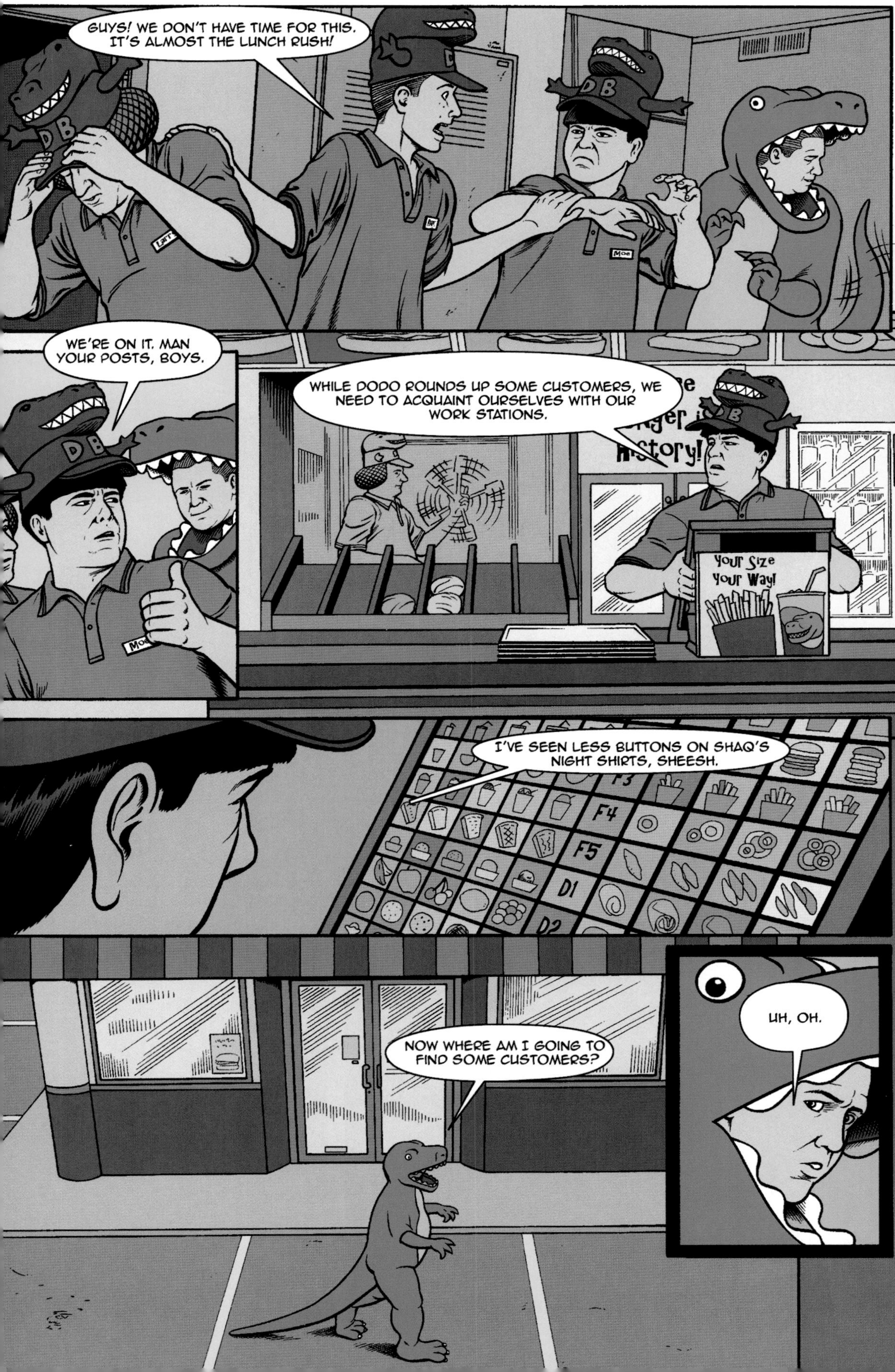
GUYS! WE DON'T HAVE TIME FOR THIS. IT'S ALMOST THE LUNCH RUSH!
WE'RE ON IT. MAN YOUR POSTS, BOYS.
WHILE DODO ROUNDS UP SOME CUSTOMERS, WE NEED TO ACQUAINT OURSELVES WITH OUR WORK STATIONS.
[redacted]
Your Size Your Way!
I'VE SEEN LESS BUTTONS ON SHAQ'S NIGHT SHIRTS, SHEESH.
F3
F4
F5
D1
D2
NOW WHERE AM I GOING TO FIND SOME CUSTOMERS?
UH, OH.

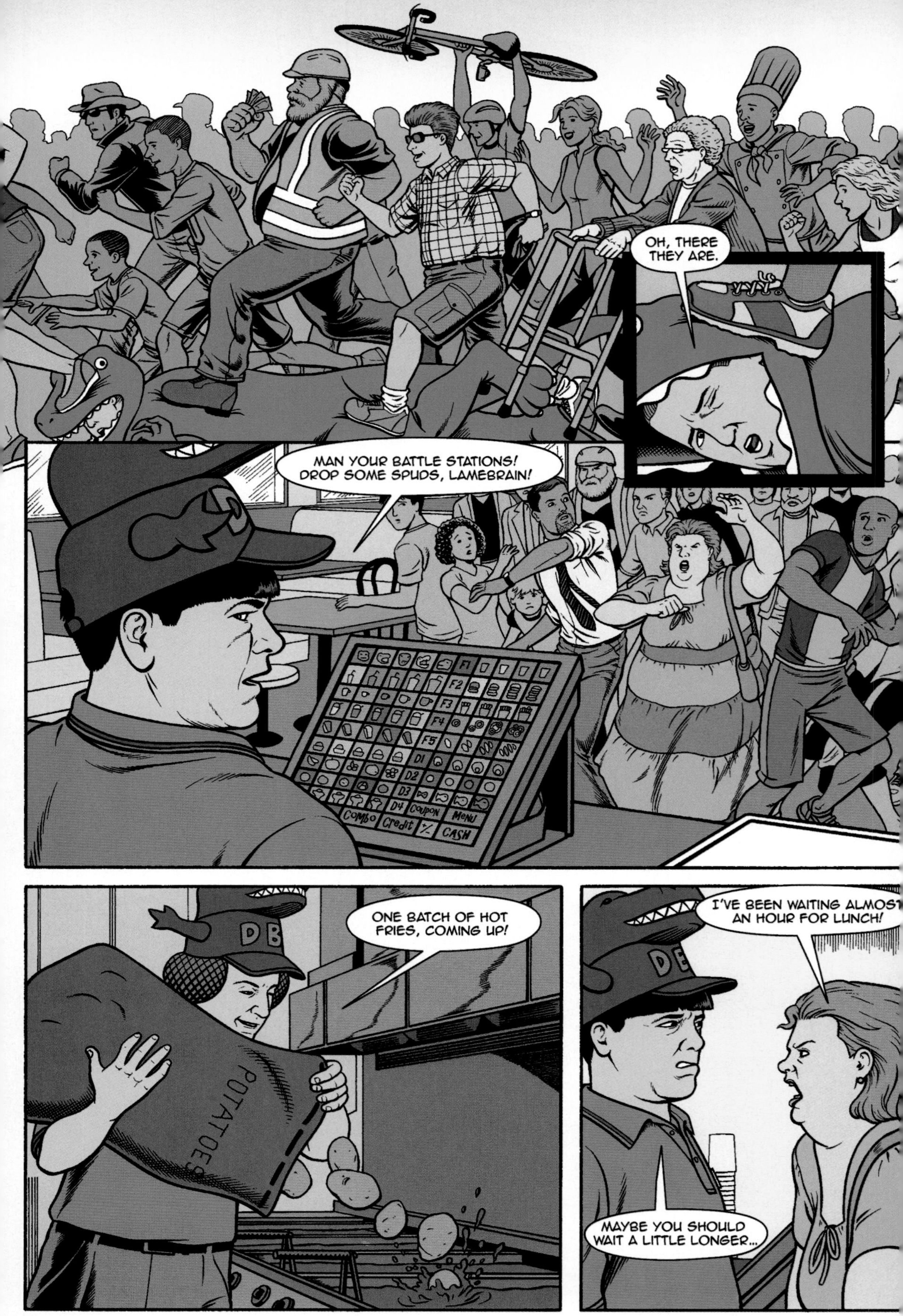

OH, THERE THEY ARE.
MAN YOUR BATTLE STATIONS! DROP SOME SPUDS, LAMEBRAIN!
F1
F2
F3
F4
F5
D1
D2
D3
D4
COUPON
MENU
COMBO
Credit
%
CASH
ONE BATCH OF HOT FRIES, COMING UP!
DB
POTATOES
I'VE BEEN WAITING ALMOST AN HOUR FOR LUNCH!
MAYBE YOU SHOULD WAIT A LITTLE LONGER...

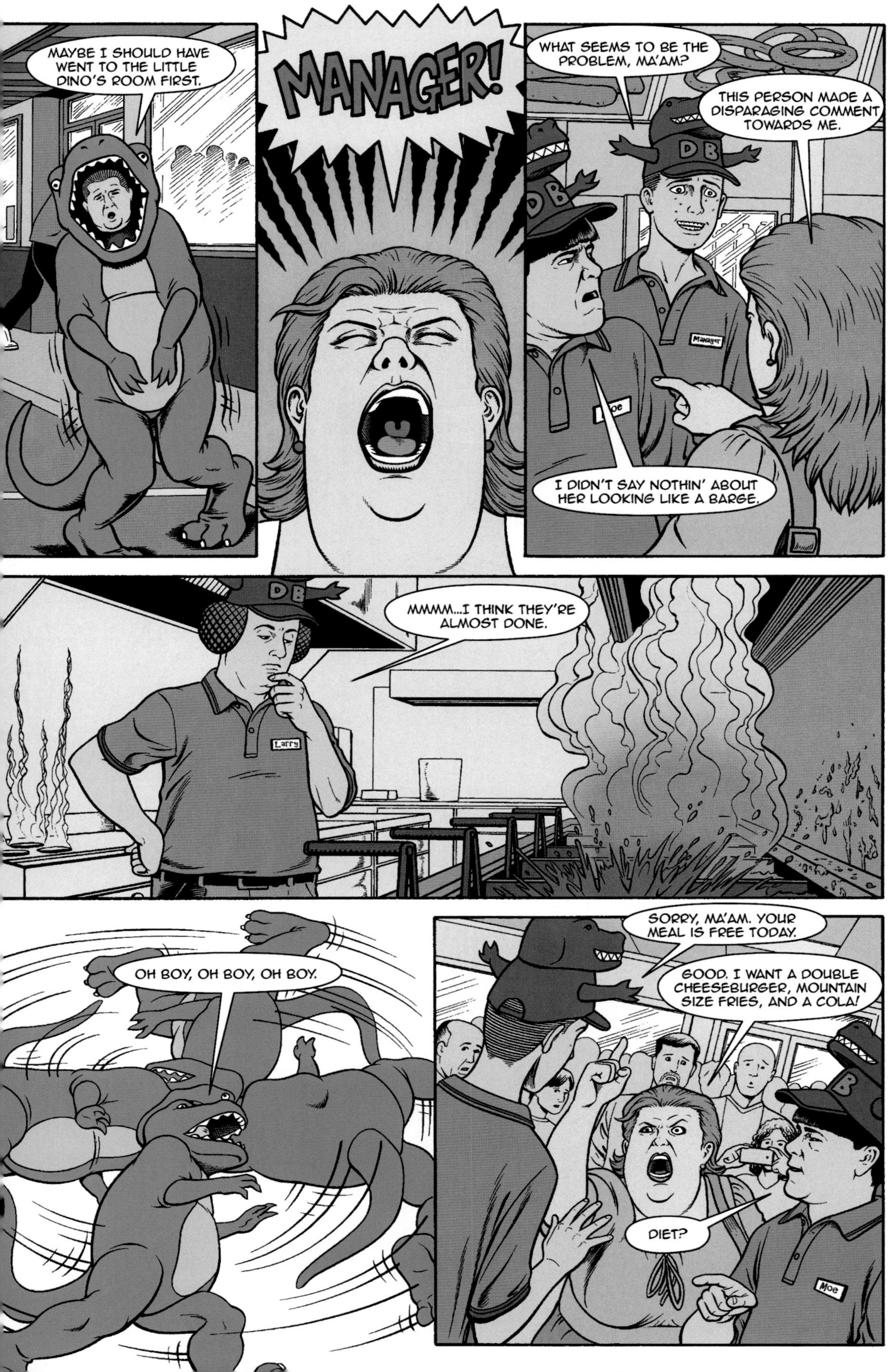
MAYBE I SHOULD HAVE WENT TO THE LITTLE DINO'S ROOM FIRST.
MANAGER!
WHAT SEEMS TO BE THE PROBLEM, MA'AM?
THIS PERSON MADE A DISPARAGING COMMENT TOWARDS ME.
DB
Manager
Moe
I DIDN'T SAY NOTHIN' ABOUT HER LOOKING LIKE A BARGE.
DB
MMMM...I THINK THEY'RE ALMOST DONE.
Larry
OH BOY, OH BOY, OH BOY.
SORRY, MA'AM. YOUR MEAL IS FREE TODAY.
GOOD. I WANT A DOUBLE CHEESEBURGER, MOUNTAIN SIZE FRIES, AND A COLA!
DIET?
Moe

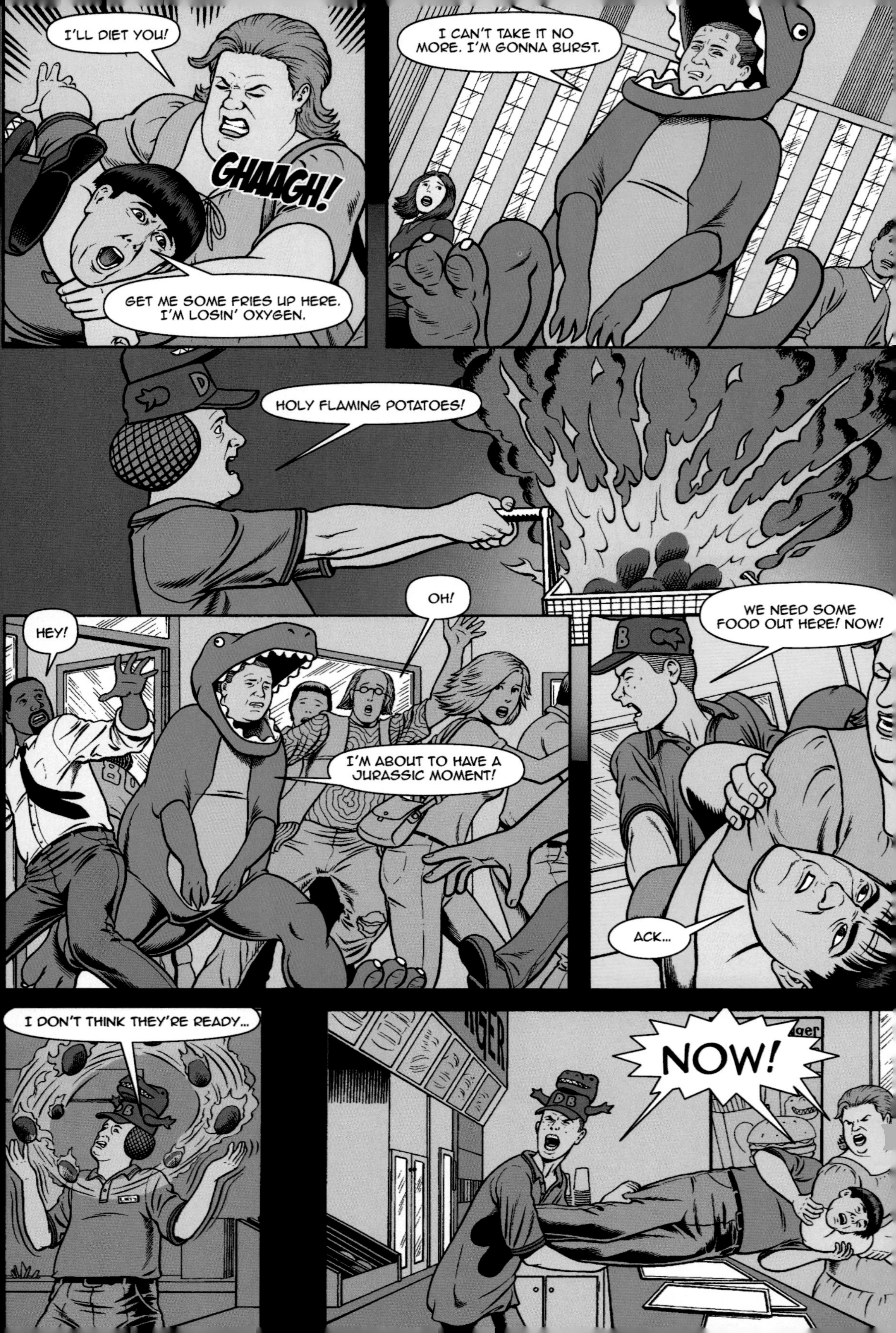
I'LL DIET YOU!
GHAAAGH!
GET ME SOME FRIES UP HERE. I'M LOSIN' OXYGEN.
I CAN'T TAKE IT NO MORE. I'M GONNA BURST.
HOLY FLAMING POTATOES!
HEY!
OH!
I'M ABOUT TO HAVE A JURASSIC MOMENT!
WE NEED SOME FOOD OUT HERE! NOW!
ACK...
I DON'T THINK THEY'RE READY...
NOW!

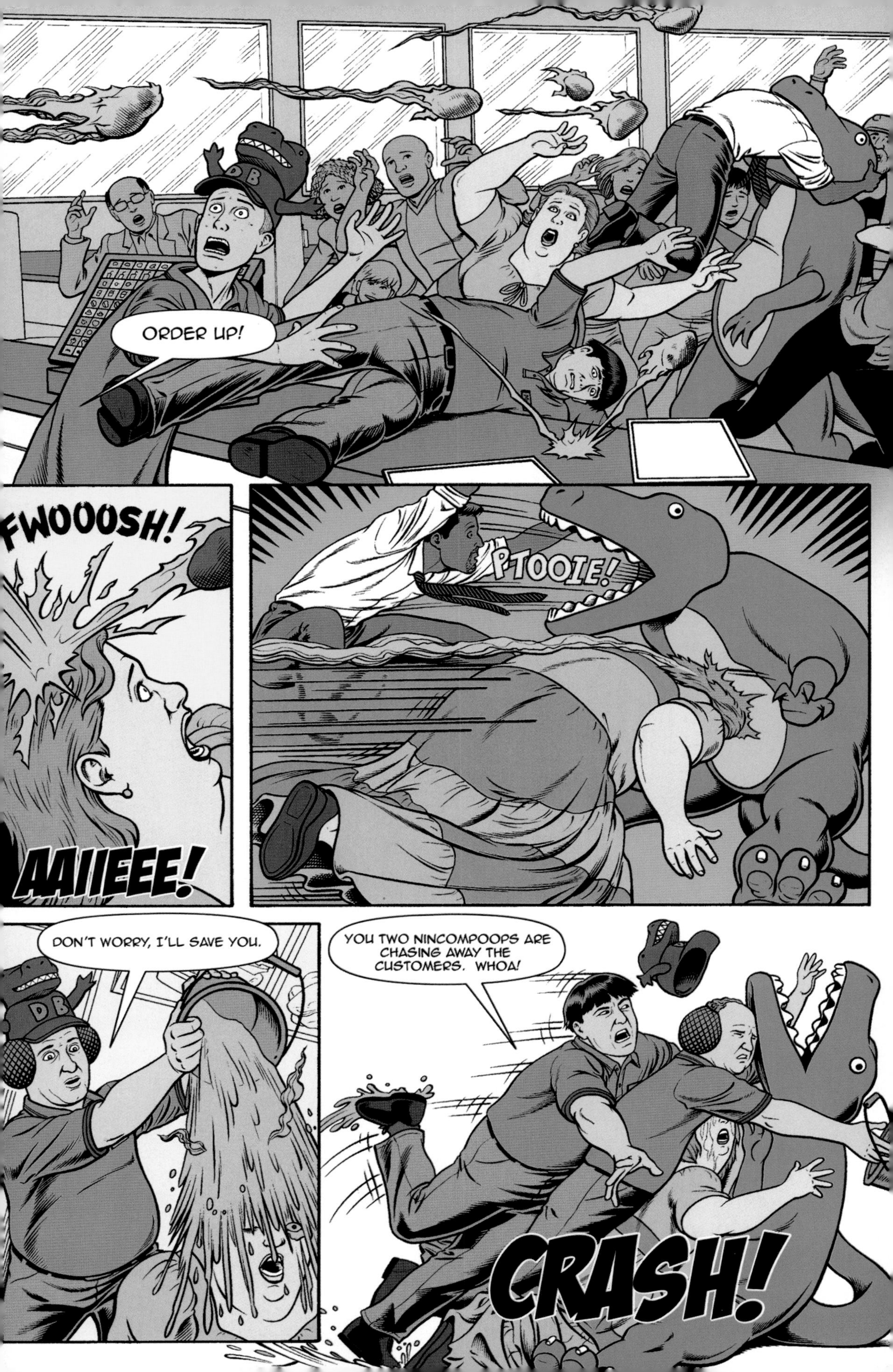
ORDER UP!
FWOOOSH!
AAIIEEE!
PTOOIE!
DON'T WORRY, I'LL SAVE YOU.
YOU TWO NINCOMPOOPS ARE CHASING AWAY THE CUSTOMERS. WHOA!
CRASH!

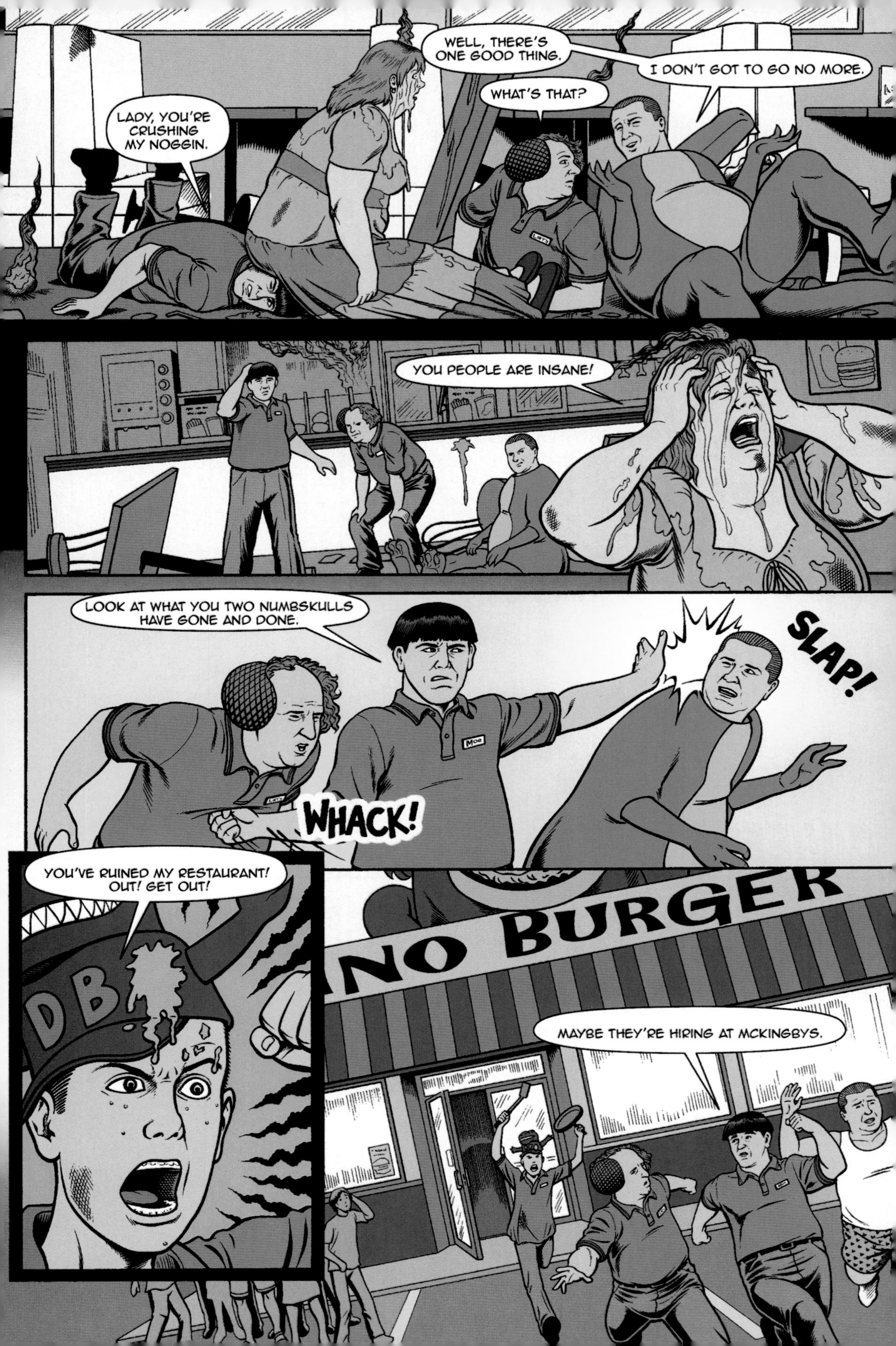
WELL, THERE'S ONE GOOD THING.
WHAT'S THAT?
I DON'T GOT TO GO NO MORE.
LADY, YOU'RE CRUSHING MY NOGGIN.
YOU PEOPLE ARE INSANE!
LOOK AT WHAT YOU TWO NUMBSKULLS HAVE GONE AND DONE.
SLAP!
WHACK!
YOU'VE RUINED MY RESTAURANT! OUT! GET OUT!
NO BURGER
MAYBE THEY'RE HIRING AT MCKINGBYS.

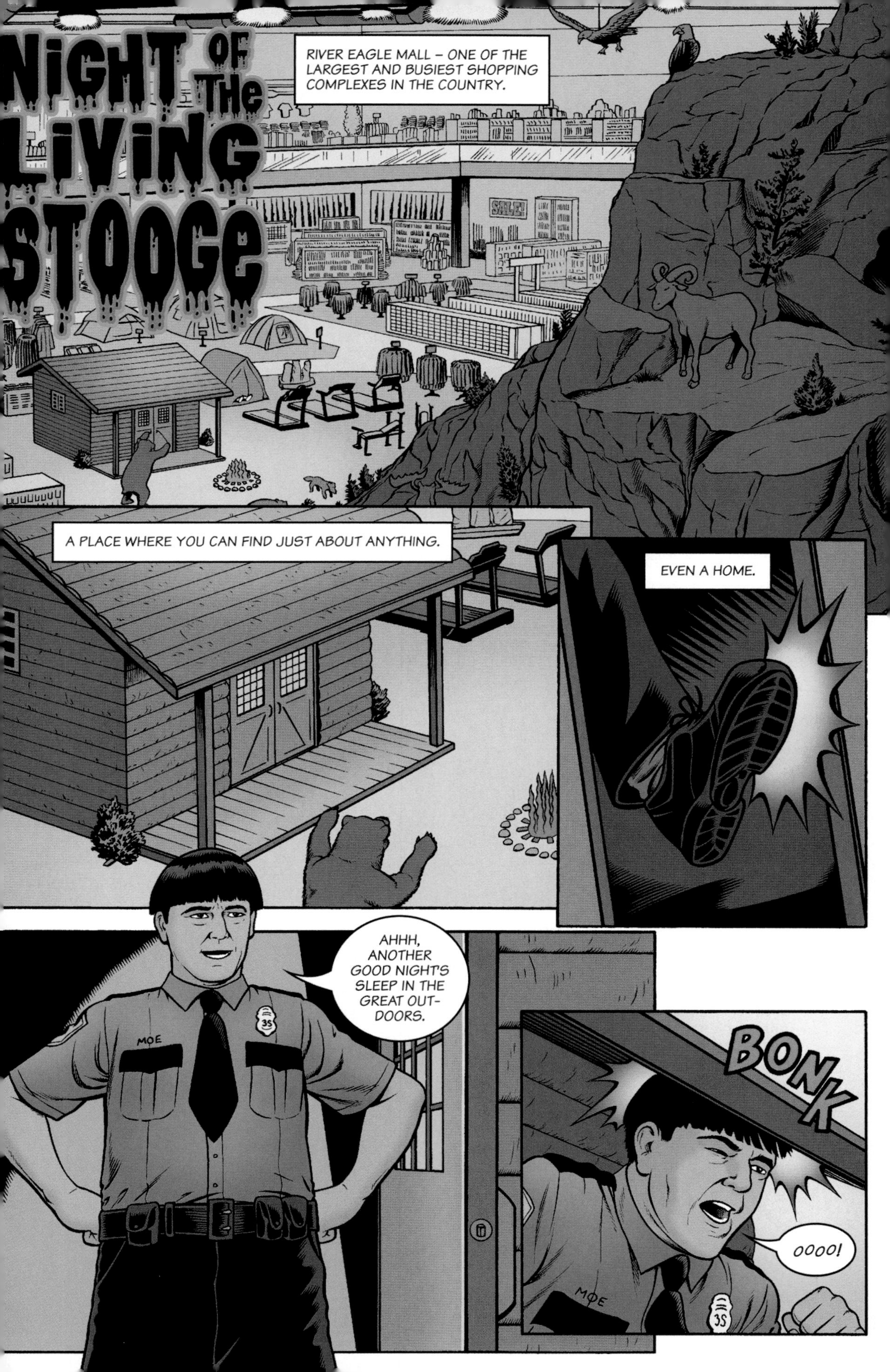
NIGHT OF THE LIVING STOOGE
RIVER EAGLE MALL – ONE OF THE LARGEST AND BUSIEST SHOPPING COMPLEXES IN THE COUNTRY.
SALE!
A PLACE WHERE YOU CAN FIND JUST ABOUT ANYTHING.
EVEN A HOME.
AHHH, ANOTHER GOOD NIGHT'S SLEEP IN THE GREAT OUT-DOORS.
MOE
BONK
OOOO!
MOE

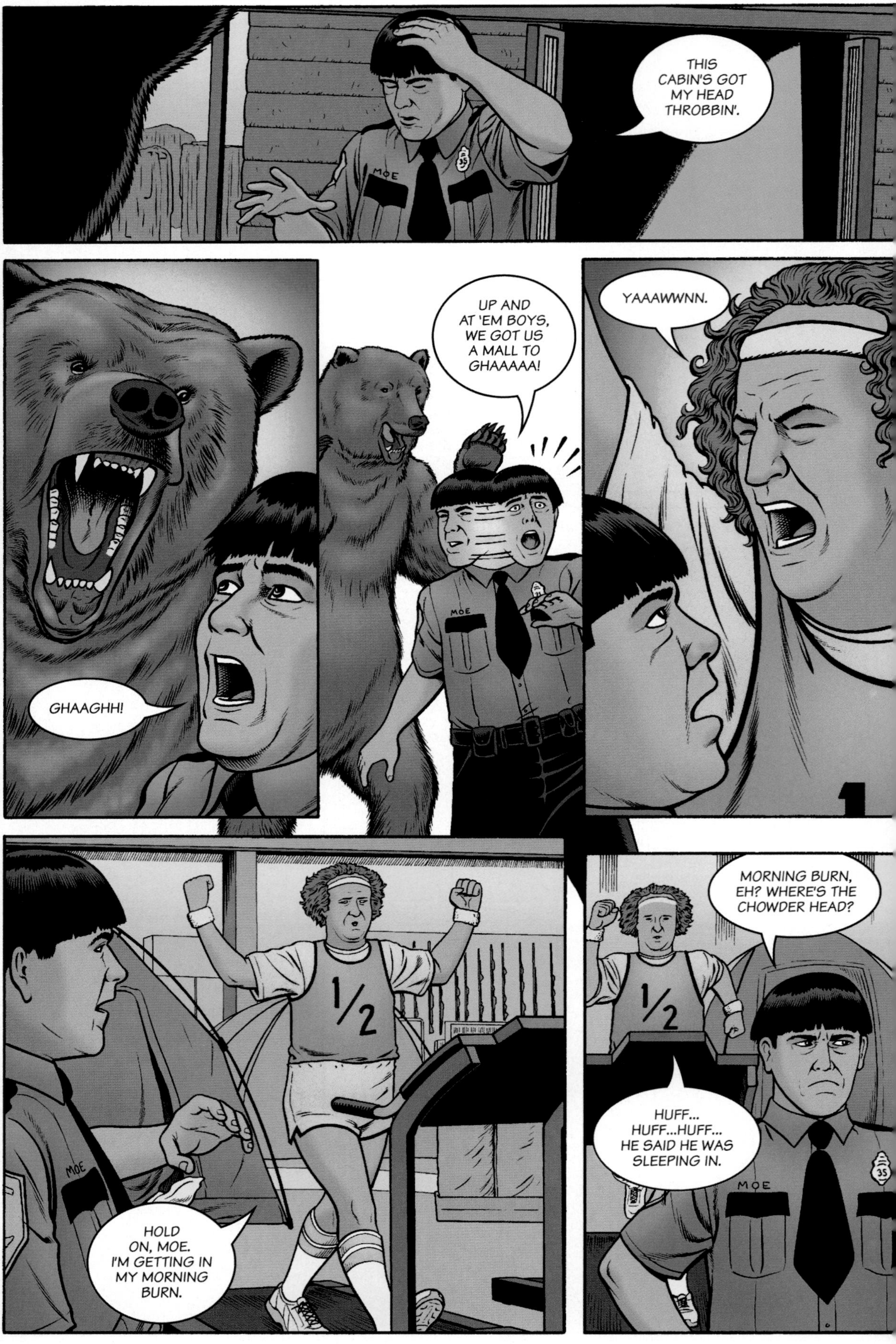
THIS CABIN'S GOT MY HEAD THROBBIN'.
GHAAGHH!
UP AND AT 'EM BOYS, WE GOT US A MALL TO GHAAAAA!
YAAAWWNN.
HOLD ON, MOE. I'M GETTING IN MY MORNING BURN.
MORNING BURN, EH? WHERE'S THE CHOWDER HEAD?
HUFF... HUFF...HUFF... HE SAID HE WAS SLEEPING IN.

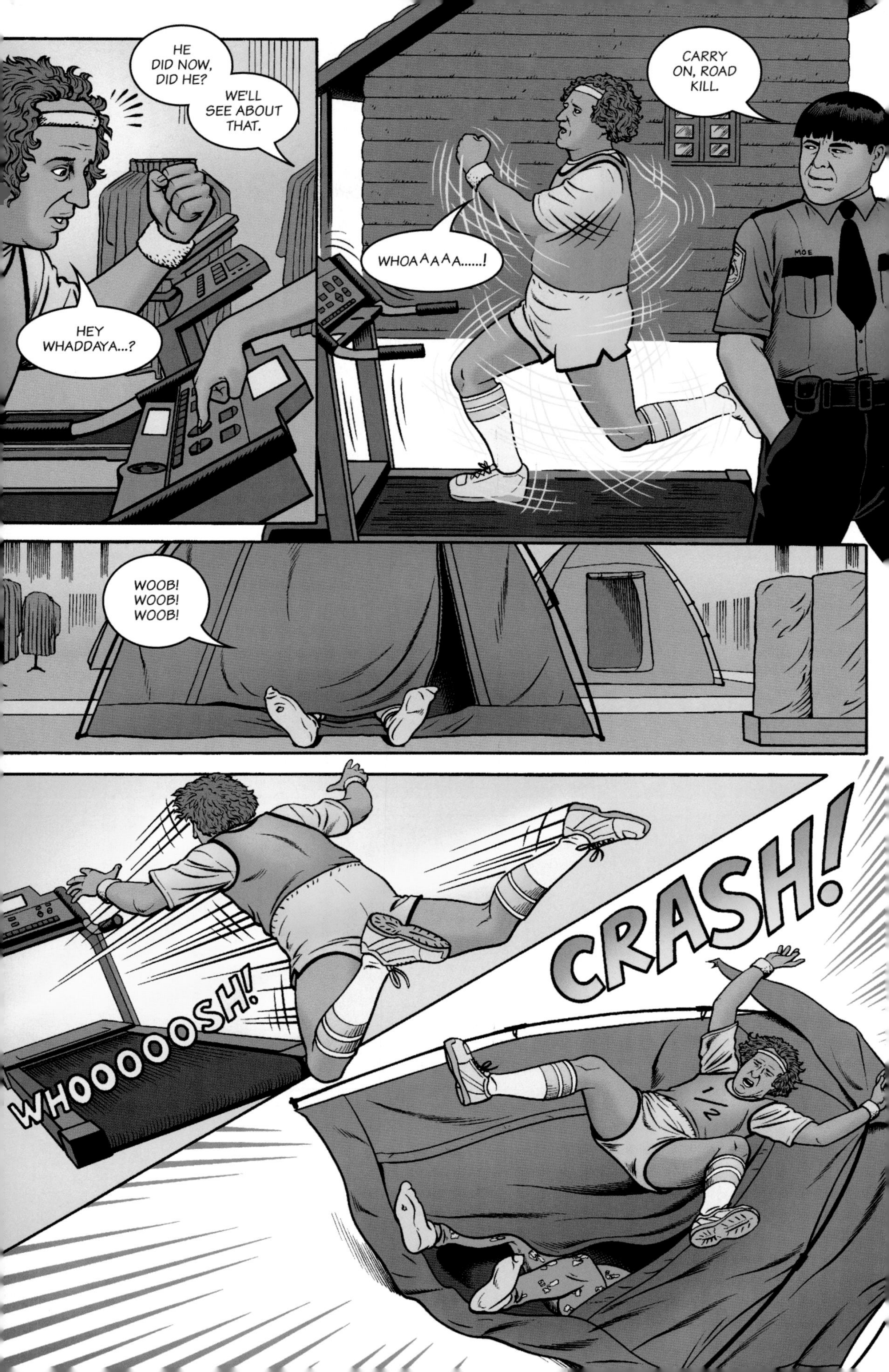
HE DID NOW, DID HE?
WE'LL SEE ABOUT THAT.
HEY WHADDAYA...?
CARRY ON, ROAD KILL.
MOE
WHOAAAAA......!
WOOB! WOOB! WOOB!
WHOOOOOOSH!
CRASH!

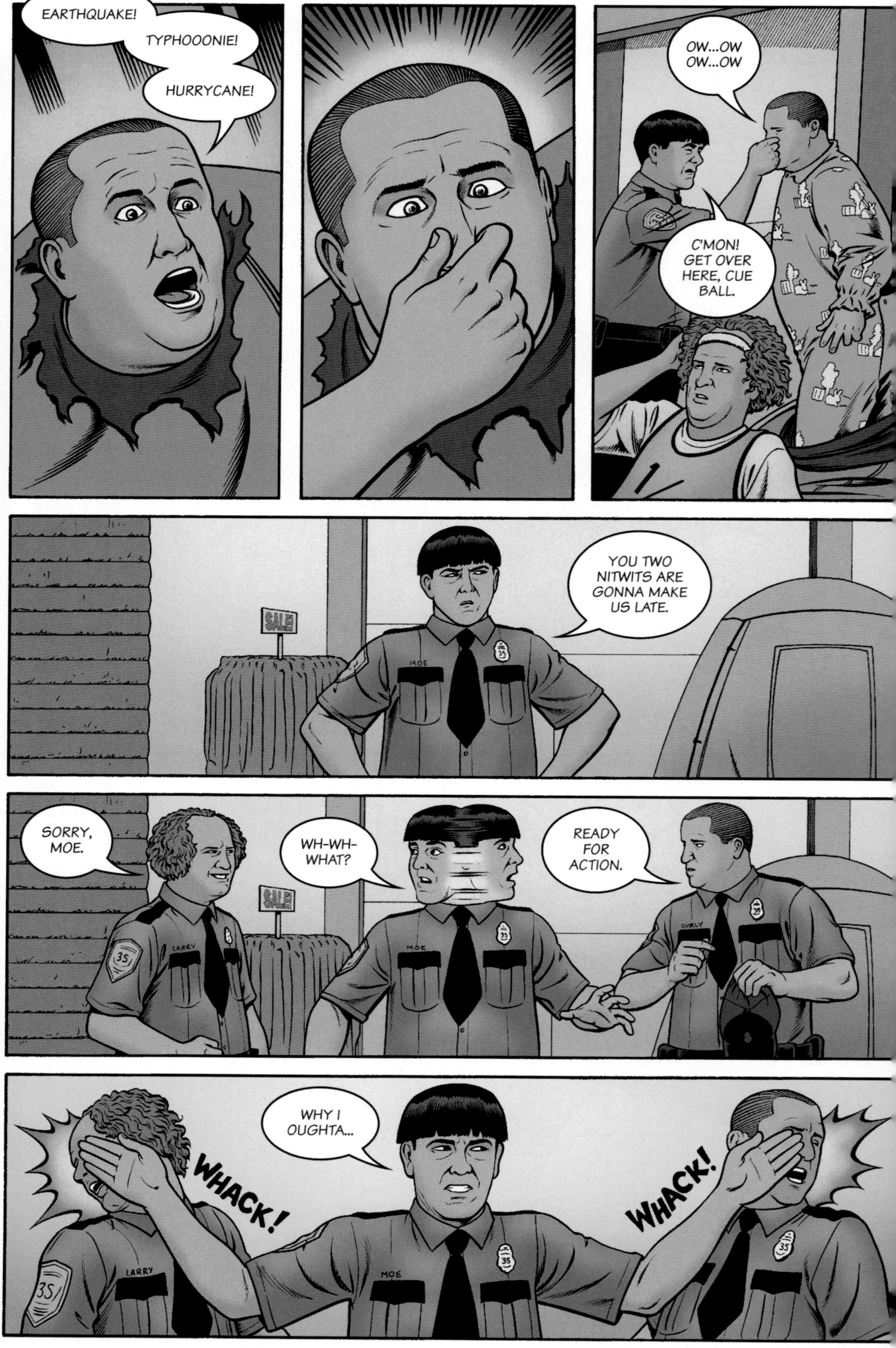
EARTHQUAKE!
TYPHOOONIE!
HURRYCANE!
OW...OW OW...OW
C'MON! GET OVER HERE, CUE BALL.
YOU TWO NITWITS ARE GONNA MAKE US LATE.
SALE!
SORRY, MOE.
WH-WH-WHAT?
READY FOR ACTION.
LARRY
MOE
CURLY
WHY I OUGHTA...
WHACK!
WHACK!

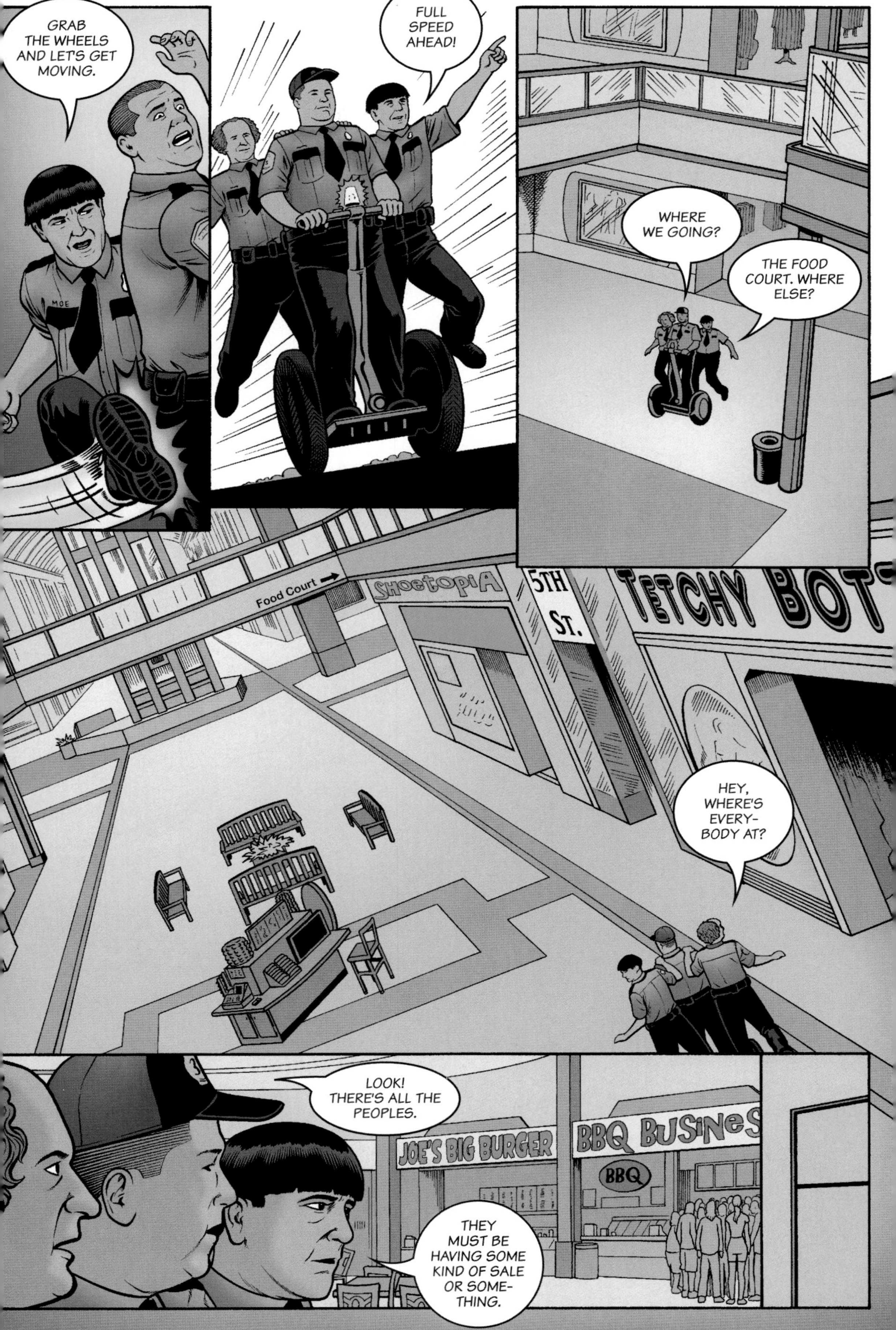
GRAB THE WHEELS AND LET'S GET MOVING.
MOE
FULL SPEED AHEAD!
WHERE WE GOING?
THE FOOD COURT. WHERE ELSE?
Food Court
SHOETOPIA
5TH ST.
TETCHY BOT
HEY, WHERE'S EVERY-BODY AT?
LOOK! THERE'S ALL THE PEOPLES.
JOE'S BIG BURGER
BBQ BUSINES
BBQ
THEY MUST BE HAVING SOME KIND OF SALE OR SOME-THING.

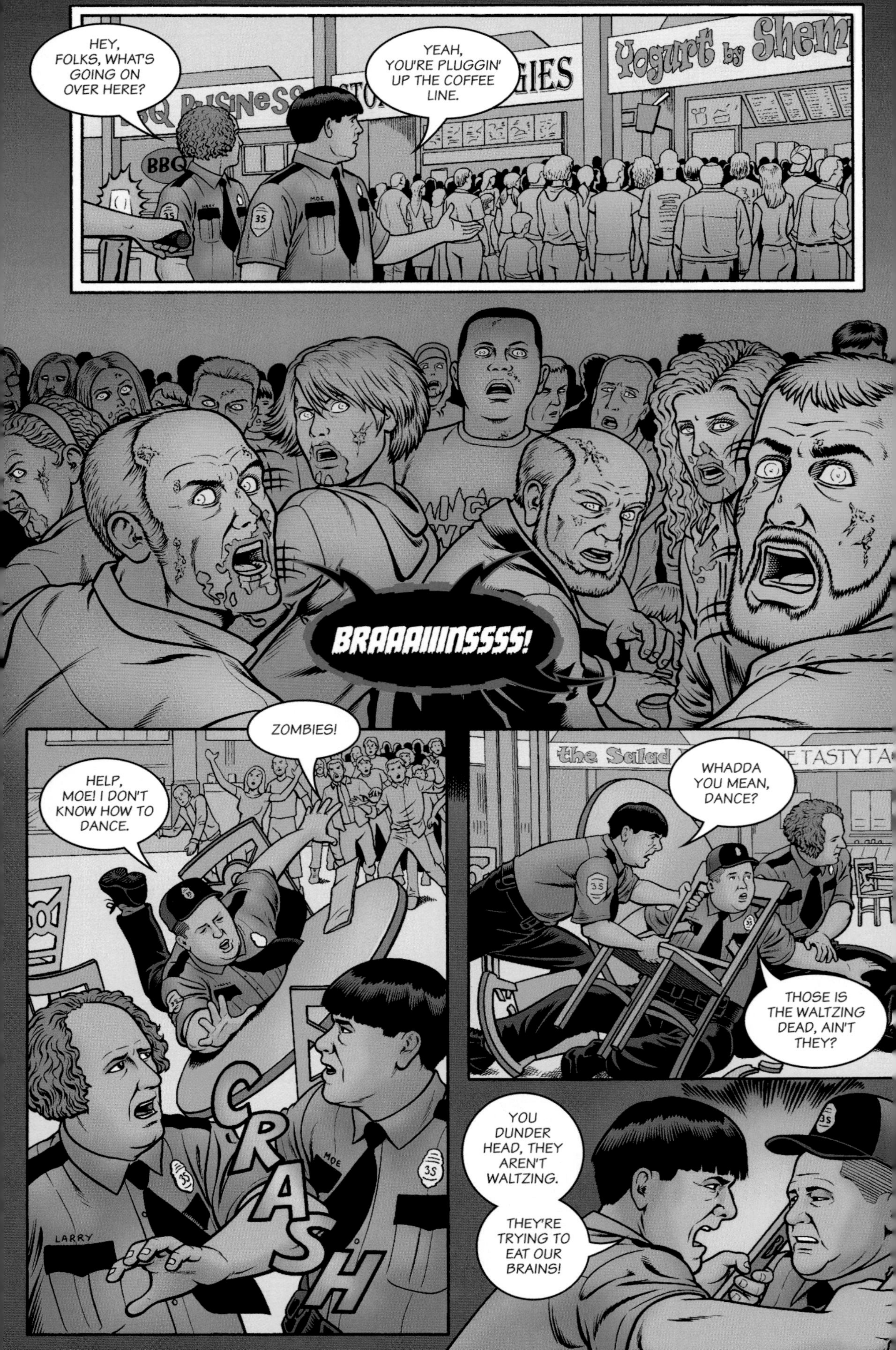
HEY, FOLKS, WHAT'S GOING ON OVER HERE?
YEAH, YOU'RE PLUGGIN' UP THE COFFEE LINE.
BBQ
Yogurt by Shem
BRAAAIIINSSSS!
ZOMBIES!
HELP, MOE! I DON'T KNOW HOW TO DANCE.
CRASH
WHADDA YOU MEAN, DANCE?
THOSE IS THE WALTZING DEAD, AIN'T THEY?
YOU DUNDER HEAD, THEY AREN'T WALTZING.
THEY'RE TRYING TO EAT OUR BRAINS!

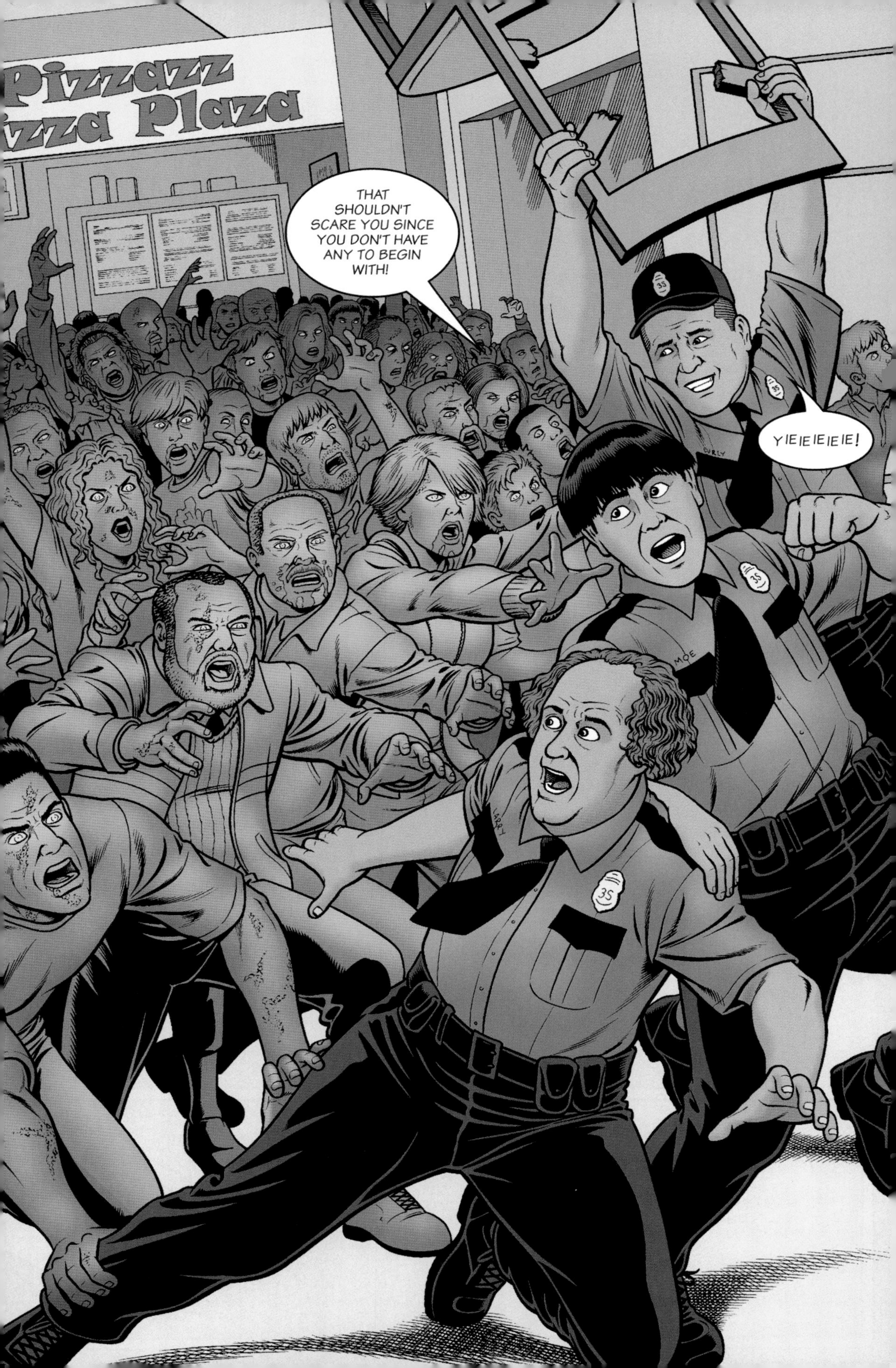
Pizzazz
Pizza Plaza
THAT SHOULDN'T SCARE YOU SINCE YOU DON'T HAVE ANY TO BEGIN WITH!
YIEIEIEIEIE!

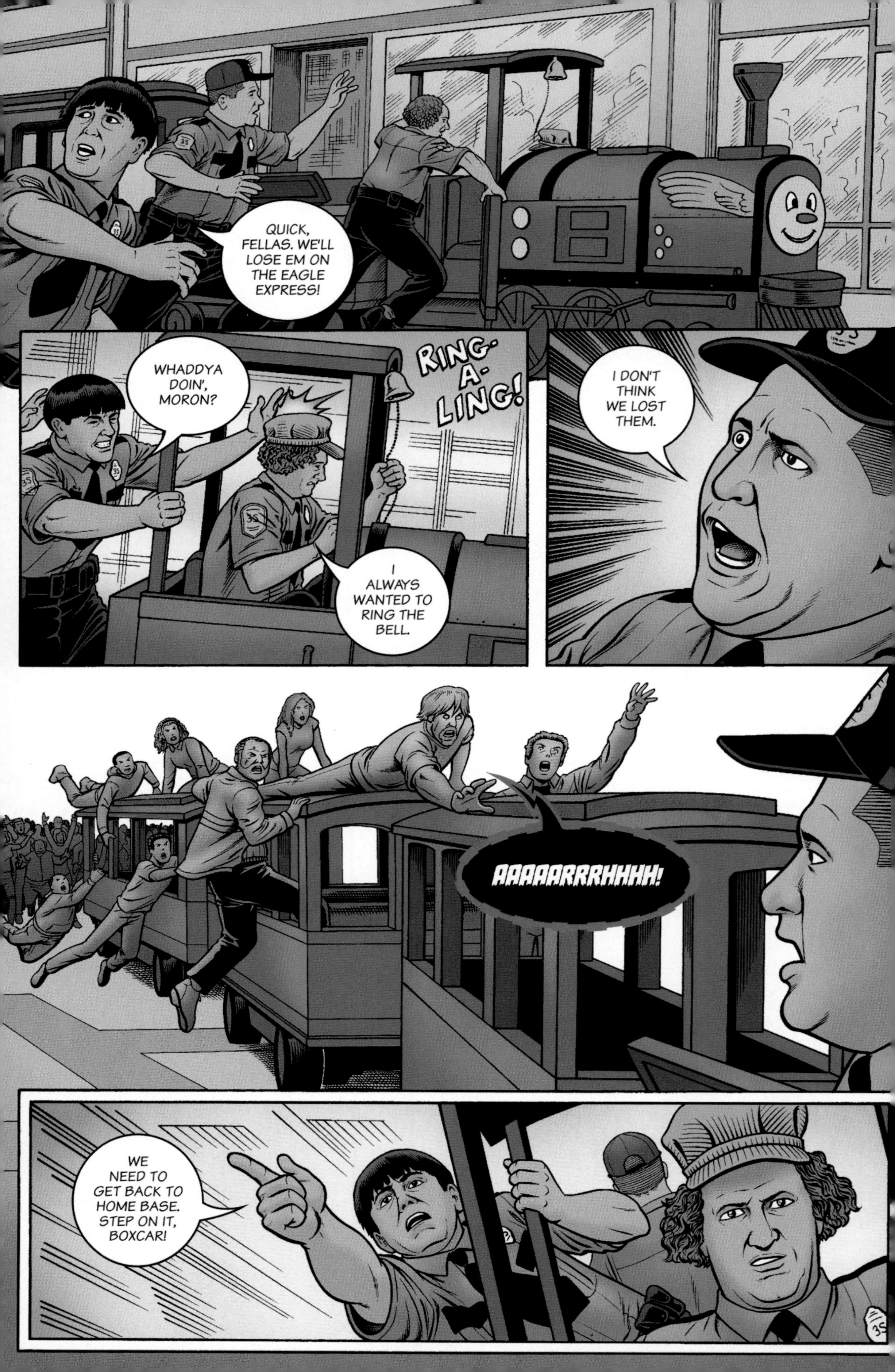
QUICK, FELLAS. WE'LL LOSE EM ON THE EAGLE EXPRESS!
WHADDYA DOIN', MORON?
RING-A-LING!
I ALWAYS WANTED TO RING THE BELL.
I DON'T THINK WE LOST THEM.
AAAAARRRHHHH!
WE NEED TO GET BACK TO HOME BASE. STEP ON IT, BOXCAR!

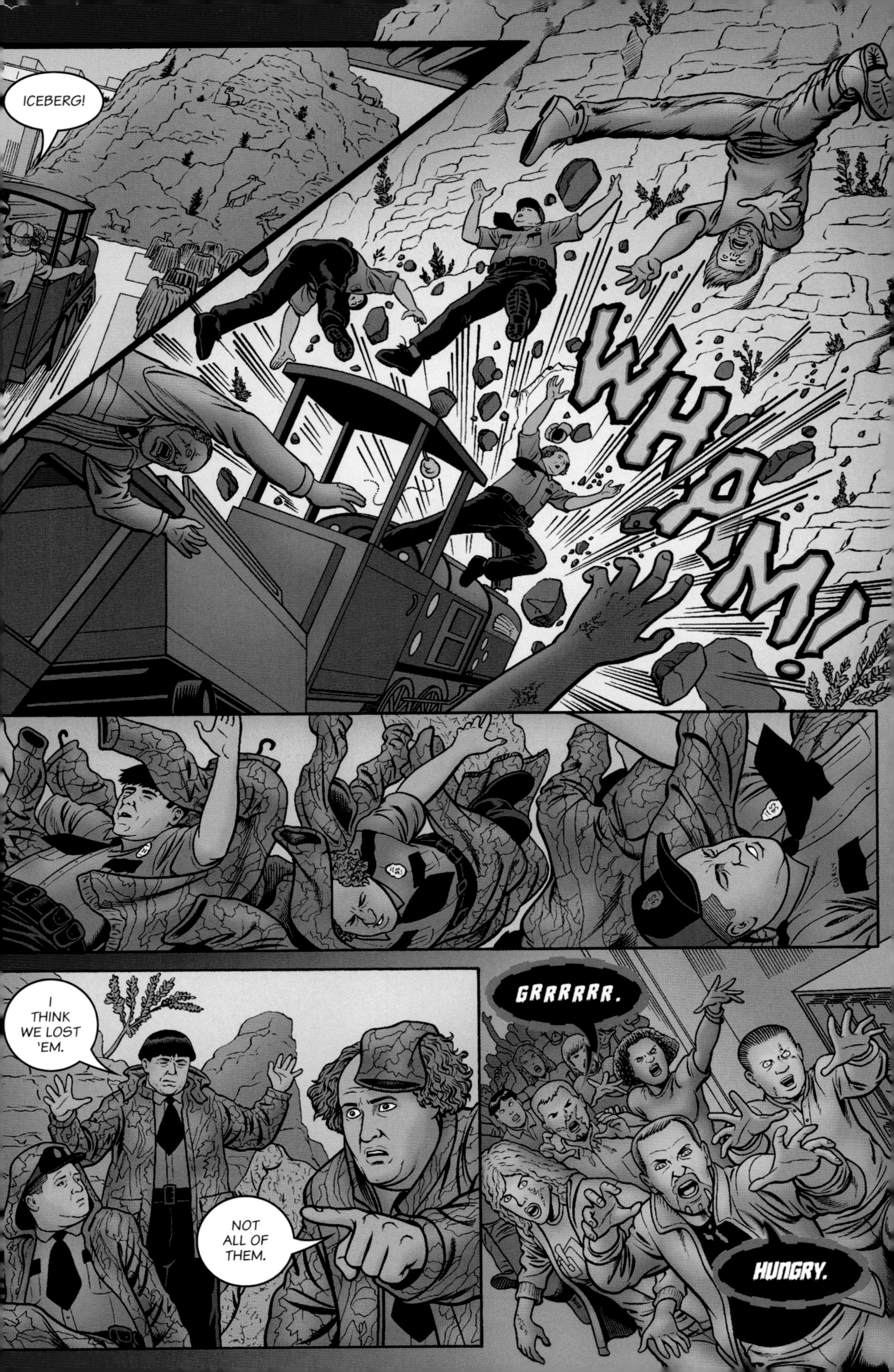
ICEBERG!
WHAM!
I THINK WE LOST 'EM.
NOT ALL OF THEM.
GRRRRRR.
HUNGRY.

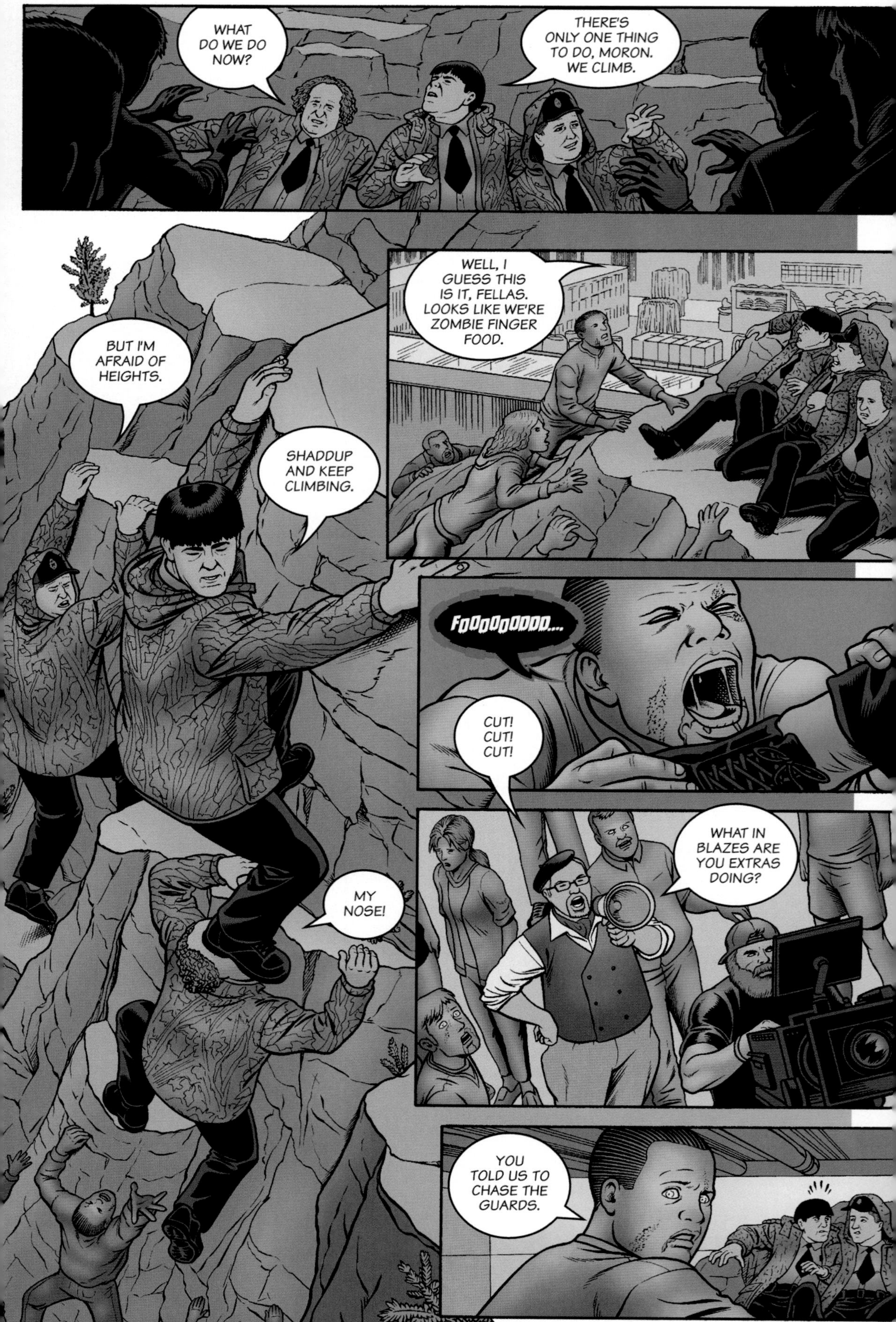
WHAT DO WE DO NOW?
THERE'S ONLY ONE THING TO DO, MORON. WE CLIMB.
BUT I'M AFRAID OF HEIGHTS.
SHADDUP AND KEEP CLIMBING.
MY NOSE!
WELL, I GUESS THIS IS IT, FELLAS. LOOKS LIKE WE'RE ZOMBIE FINGER FOOD.
FOOOOOOOOD....
CUT! CUT! CUT!
WHAT IN BLAZES ARE YOU EXTRAS DOING?
YOU TOLD US TO CHASE THE GUARDS.

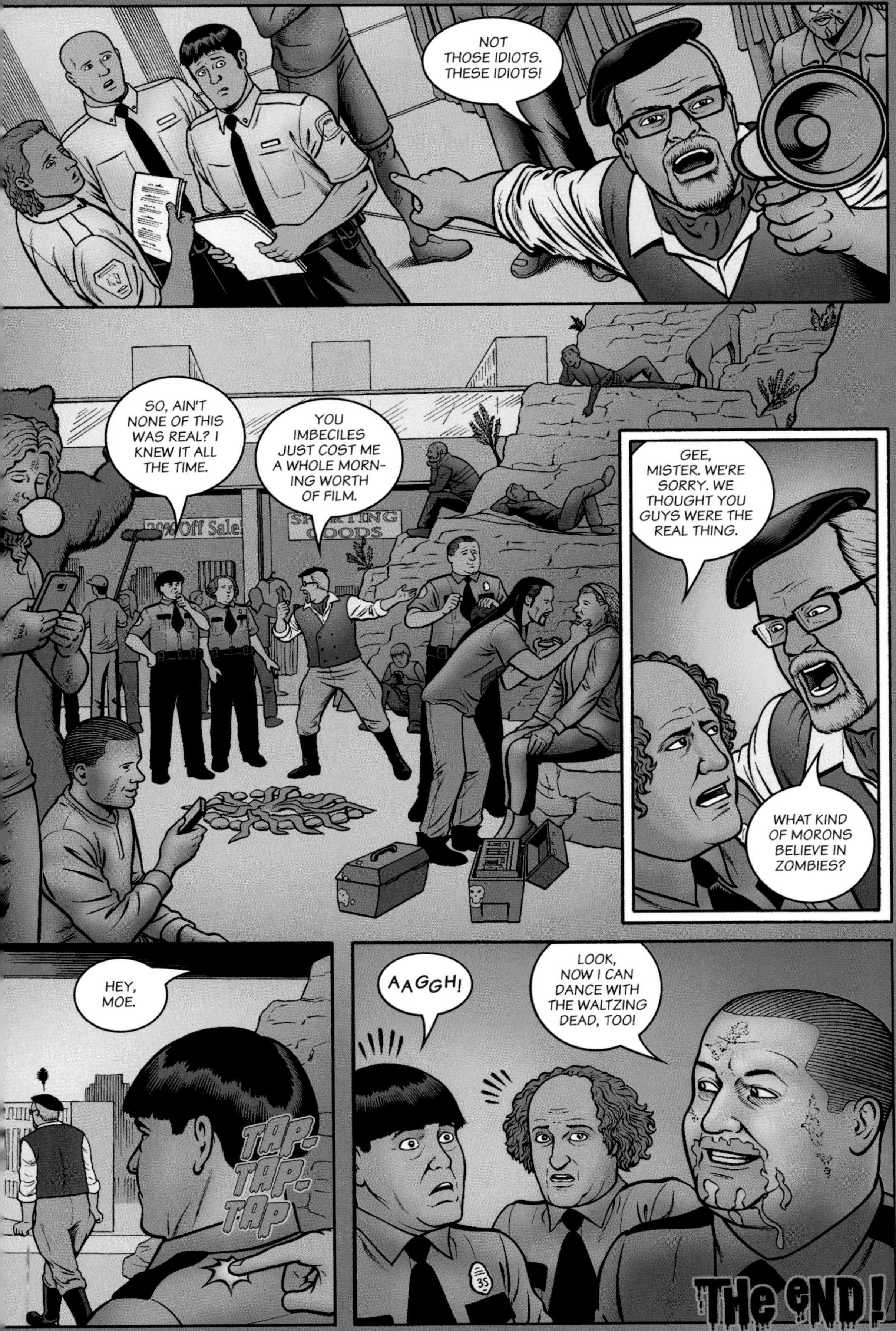
NOT THOSE IDIOTS. THESE IDIOTS!
SO, AIN'T NONE OF THIS WAS REAL? I KNEW IT ALL THE TIME.
YOU IMBECILES JUST COST ME A WHOLE MORNING WORTH OF FILM.
20% Off Sale!
SPORTING GOODS
GEE, MISTER. WE'RE SORRY. WE THOUGHT YOU GUYS WERE THE REAL THING.
WHAT KIND OF MORONS BELIEVE IN ZOMBIES?
HEY, MOE.
TAP-TAP-TAP
AAGGH!
LOOK, NOW I CAN DANCE WITH THE WALTZING DEAD, TOO!
THE END!

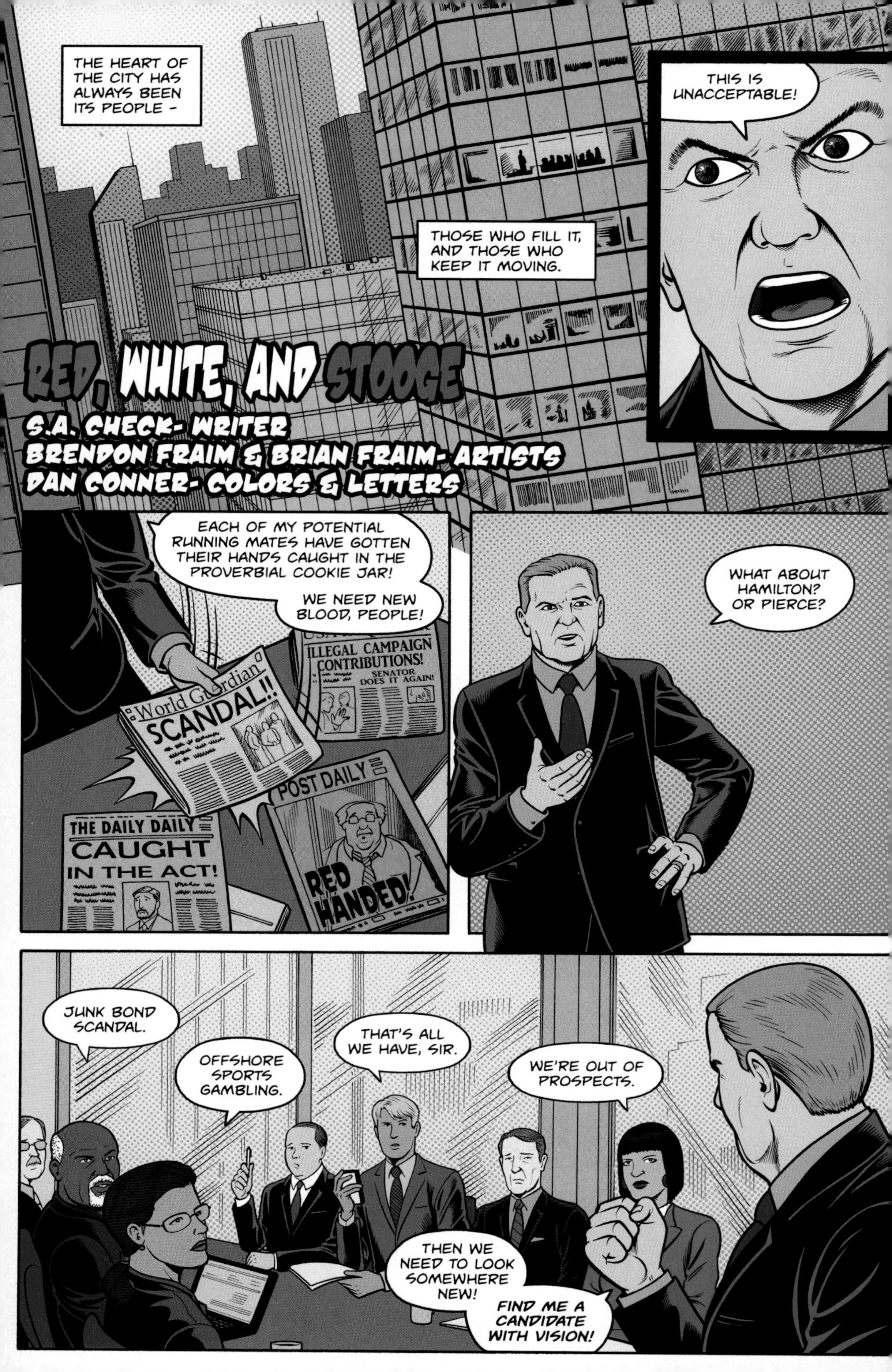
THE HEART OF THE CITY HAS ALWAYS BEEN ITS PEOPLE -
THIS IS UNACCEPTABLE!
THOSE WHO FILL IT, AND THOSE WHO KEEP IT MOVING.
RED, WHITE, AND STOOGE
S.A. CHECK- WRITER
BRENDON FRAIM & BRIAN FRAIM- ARTISTS
DAN CONNER- COLORS & LETTERS
EACH OF MY POTENTIAL RUNNING MATES HAVE GOTTEN THEIR HANDS CAUGHT IN THE PROVERBIAL COOKIE JAR!
WE NEED NEW BLOOD, PEOPLE!
ILLEGAL CAMPAIGN CONTRIBUTIONS!
SENATOR DOES IT AGAIN!
World Guardian
SCANDAL!!
POST DAILY
THE DAILY DAILY
CAUGHT IN THE ACT!
RED HANDED!
WHAT ABOUT HAMILTON? OR PIERCE?
JUNK BOND SCANDAL.
OFFSHORE SPORTS GAMBLING.
THAT'S ALL WE HAVE, SIR.
WE'RE OUT OF PROSPECTS.
THEN WE NEED TO LOOK SOMEWHERE NEW!
FIND ME A CANDIDATE WITH VISION!

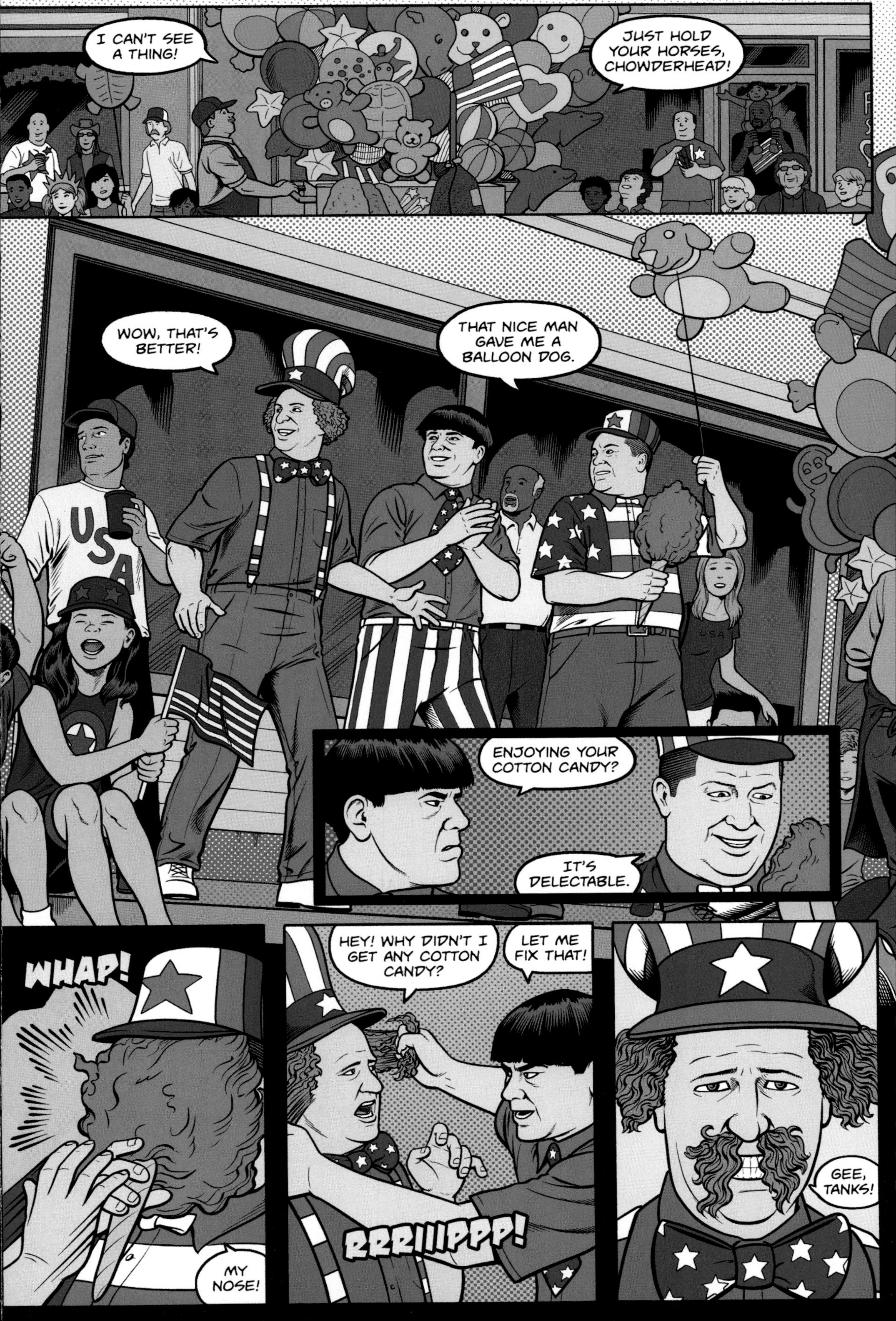
I CAN'T SEE A THING!
JUST HOLD YOUR HORSES, CHOWDERHEAD!
WOW, THAT'S BETTER!
THAT NICE MAN GAVE ME A BALLOON DOG.
ENJOYING YOUR COTTON CANDY?
IT'S DELECTABLE.
WHAP!
MY NOSE!
HEY! WHY DIDN'T I GET ANY COTTON CANDY?
LET ME FIX THAT!
RRRIIIPPP!
GEE, TANKS!

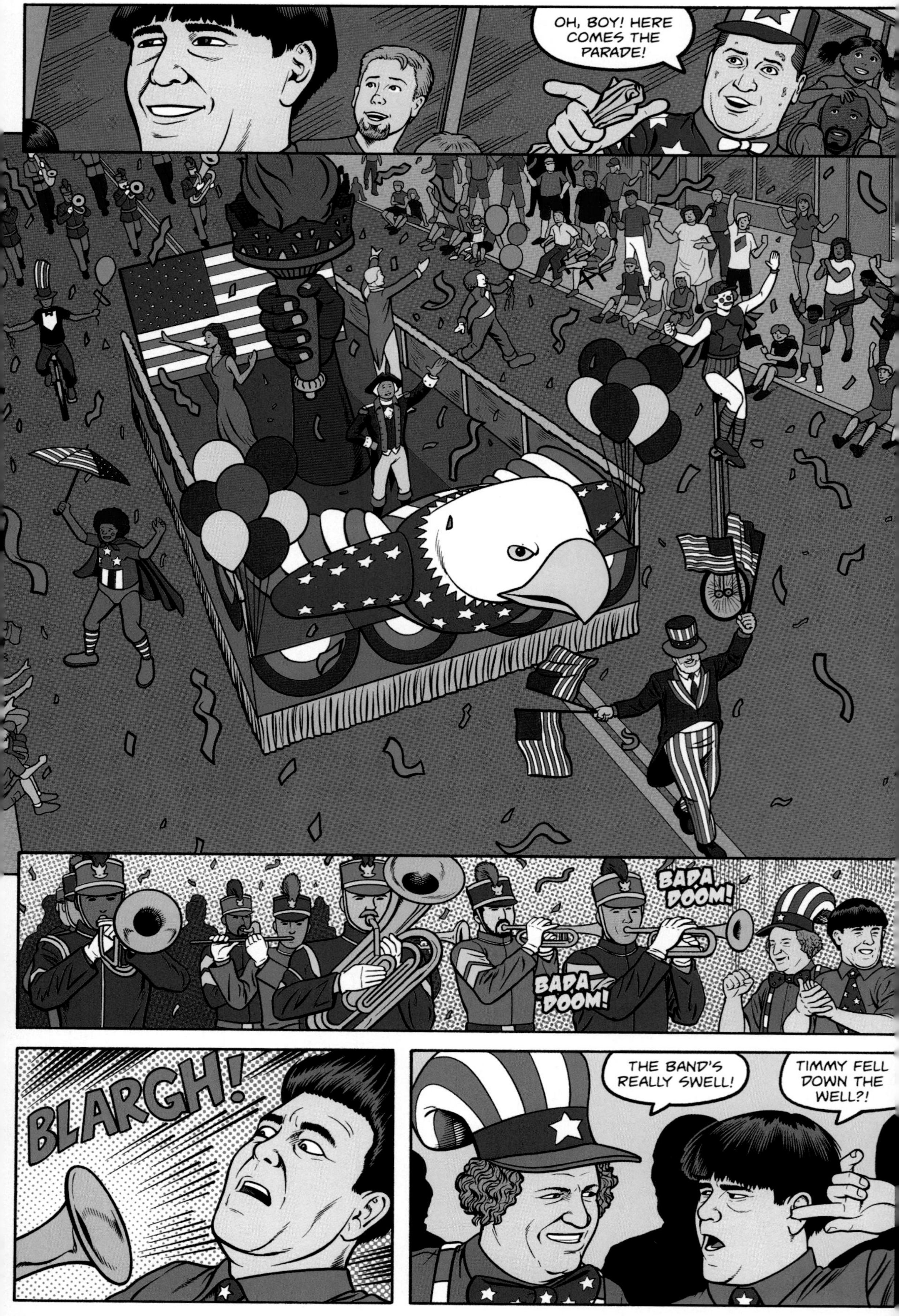
OH, BOY! HERE COMES THE PARADE!
BADA DOOM!
BADA DOOM!
BLARGH!
THE BAND'S REALLY SWELL!
TIMMY FELL DOWN THE WELL?!

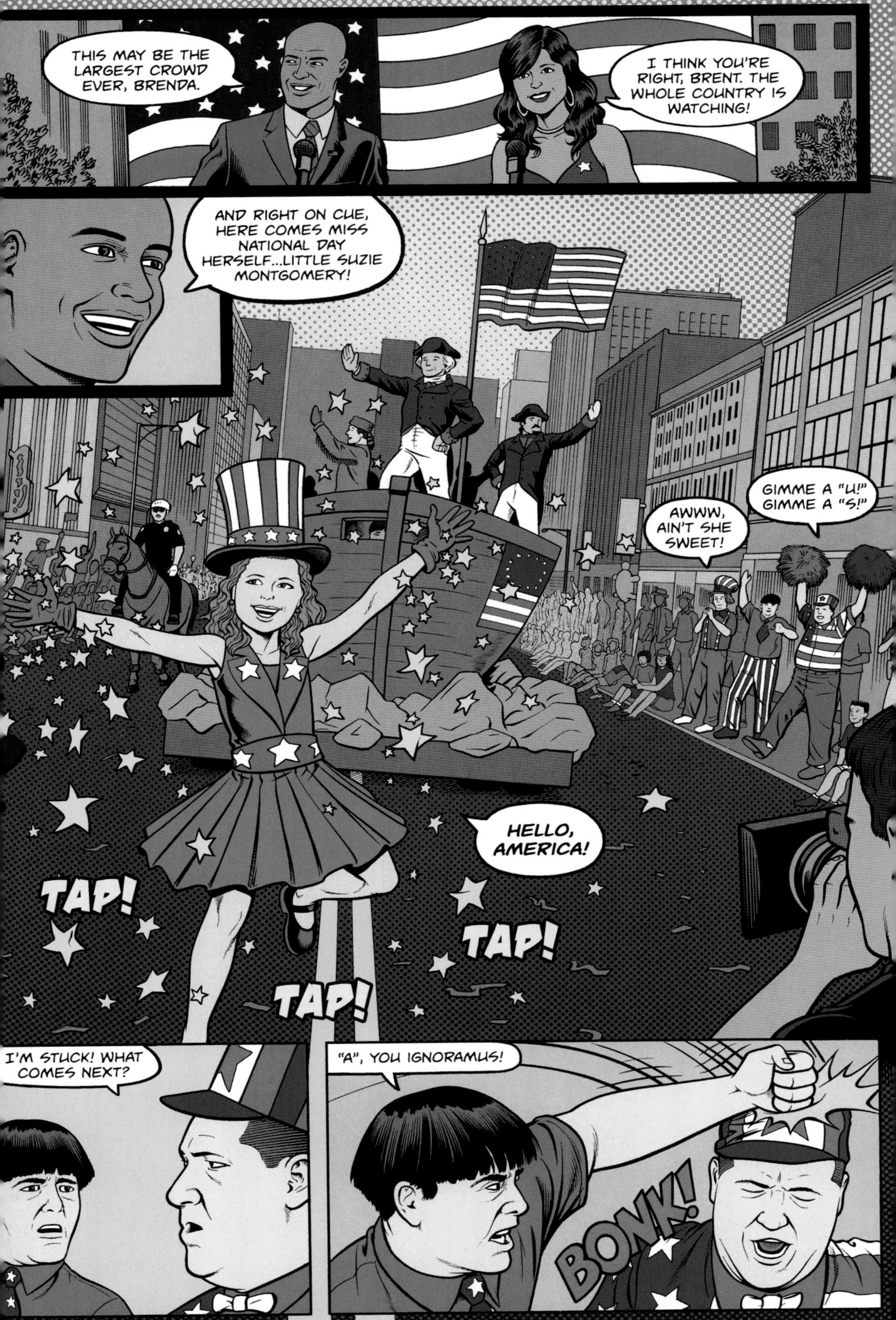
THIS MAY BE THE LARGEST CROWD EVER, BRENDA.
I THINK YOU'RE RIGHT, BRENT. THE WHOLE COUNTRY IS WATCHING!
AND RIGHT ON CUE, HERE COMES MISS NATIONAL DAY HERSELF...LITTLE SUZIE MONTGOMERY!
GIMME A "U!" GIMME A "S!"
AWWW, AIN'T SHE SWEET!
HELLO, AMERICA!
TAP!
TAP!
TAP!
I'M STUCK! WHAT COMES NEXT?
"A", YOU IGNORAMUS!
BONK!

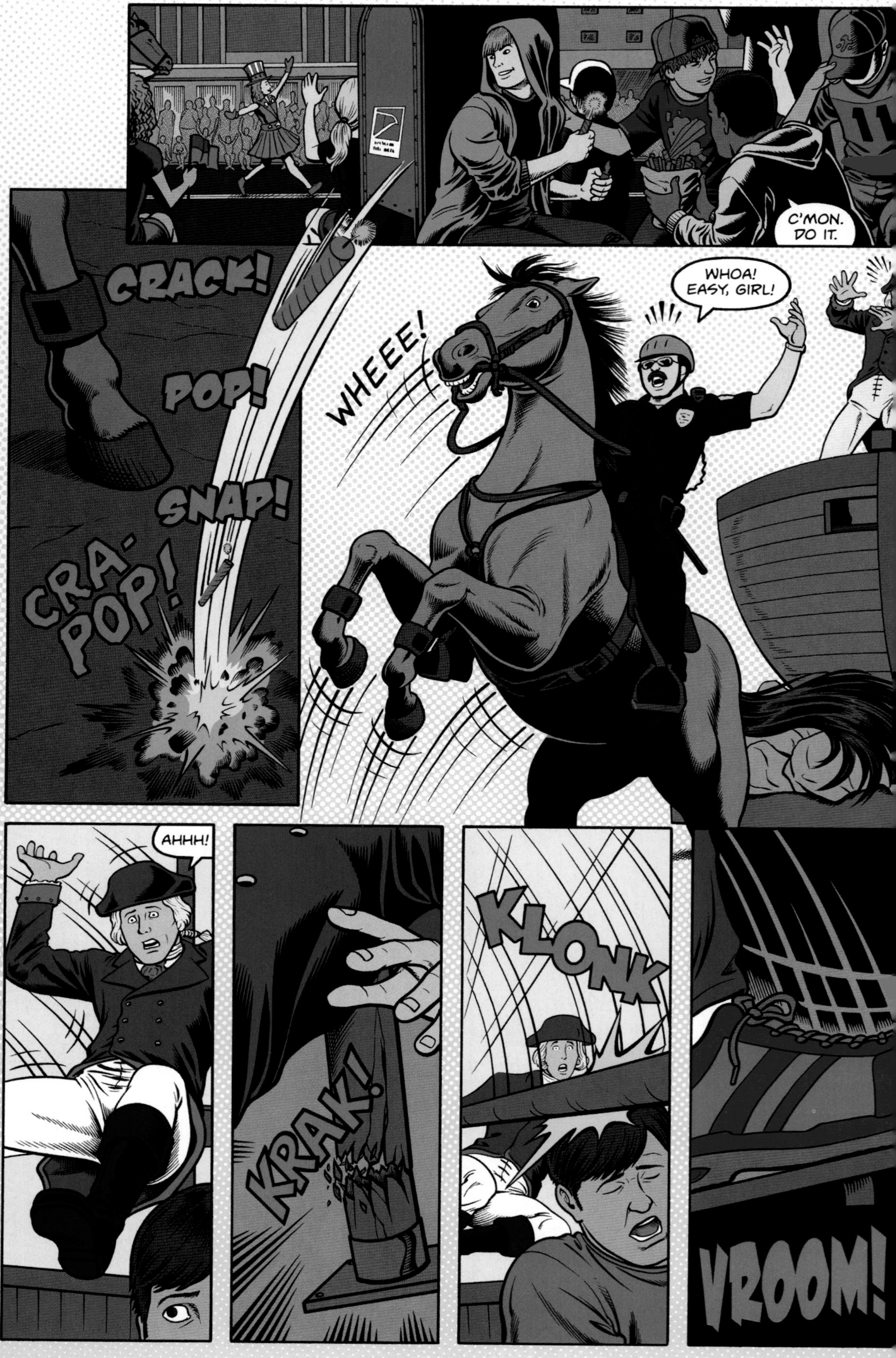
C'MON. DO IT.
CRACK!
POP!
SNAP!
CRA-POP!
WHEEE!
WHOA! EASY, GIRL!
AHHH!
KRAK!
KLONK
VROOM!

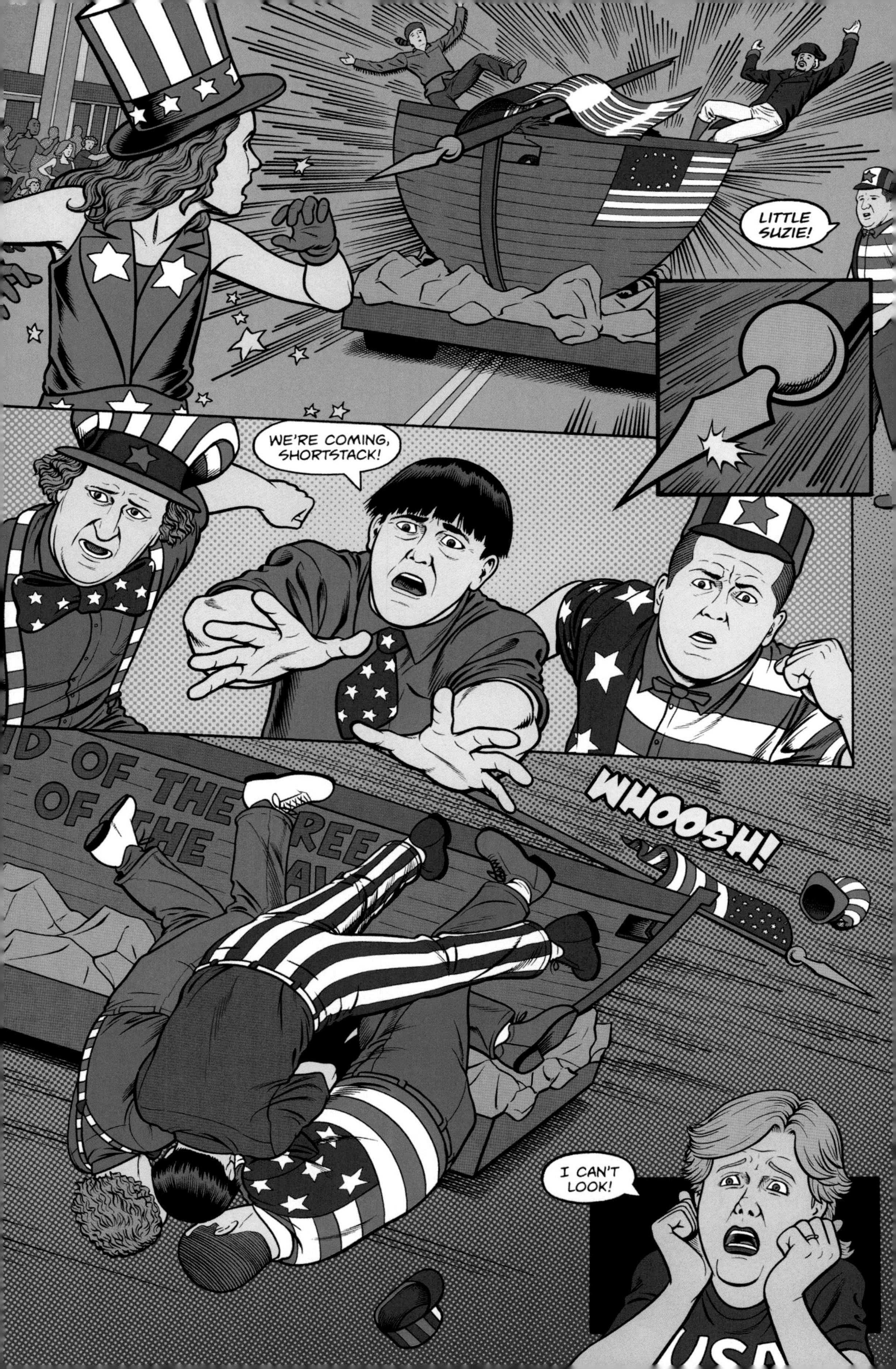

LITTLE SUZIE!
WE'RE COMING, SHORTSTACK!
WHOOSH!
I CAN'T LOOK!

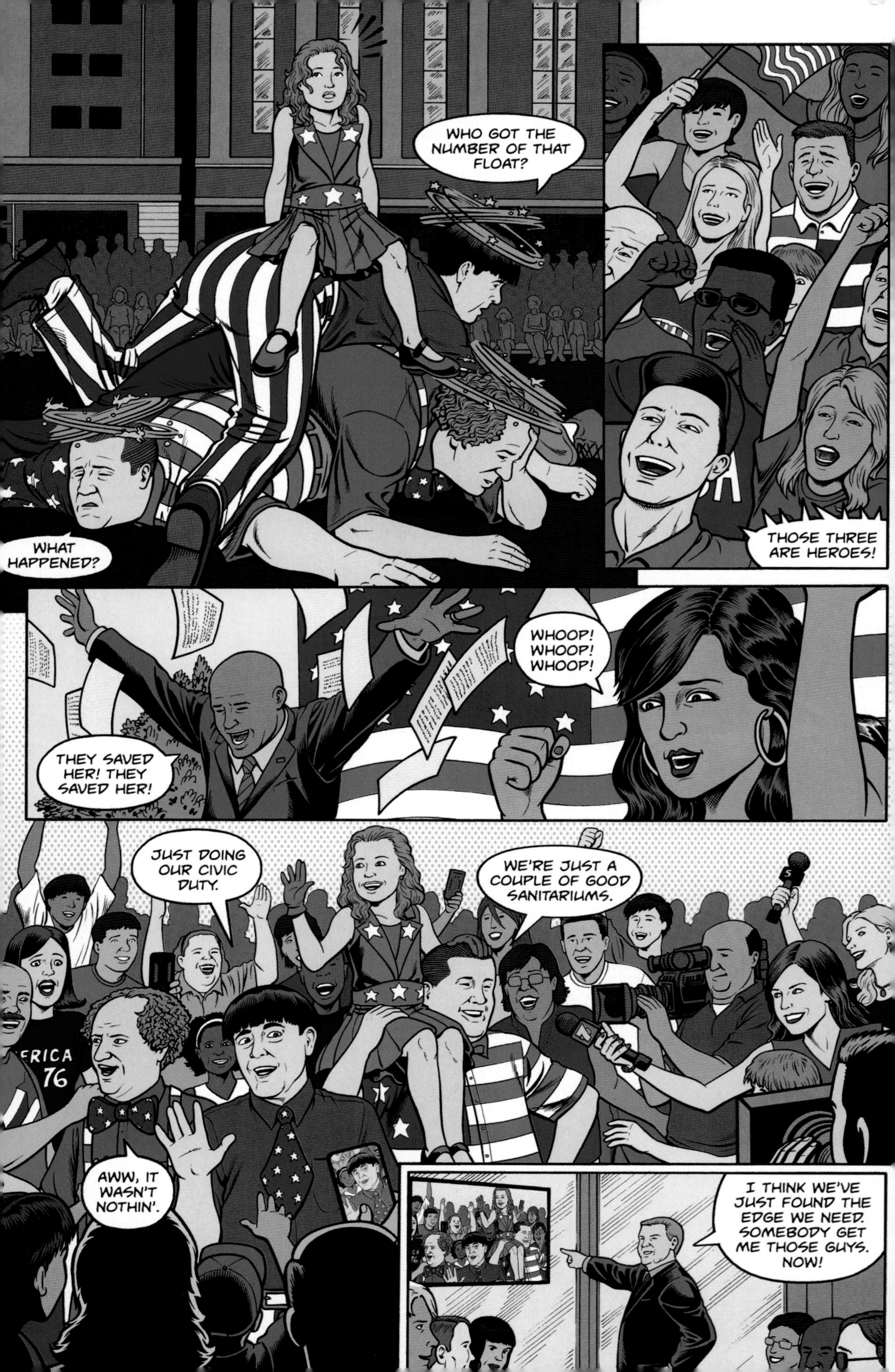
WHO GOT THE NUMBER OF THAT FLOAT?
WHAT HAPPENED?
THOSE THREE ARE HEROES!
THEY SAVED HER! THEY SAVED HER!
WHOOP! WHOOP! WHOOP!
JUST DOING OUR CIVIC DUTY.
WE'RE JUST A COUPLE OF GOOD SANITARIUMS.
ERICA 76
AWW, IT WASN'T NOTHIN'.
I THINK WE'VE JUST FOUND THE EDGE WE NEED. SOMEBODY GET ME THOSE GUYS. NOW!

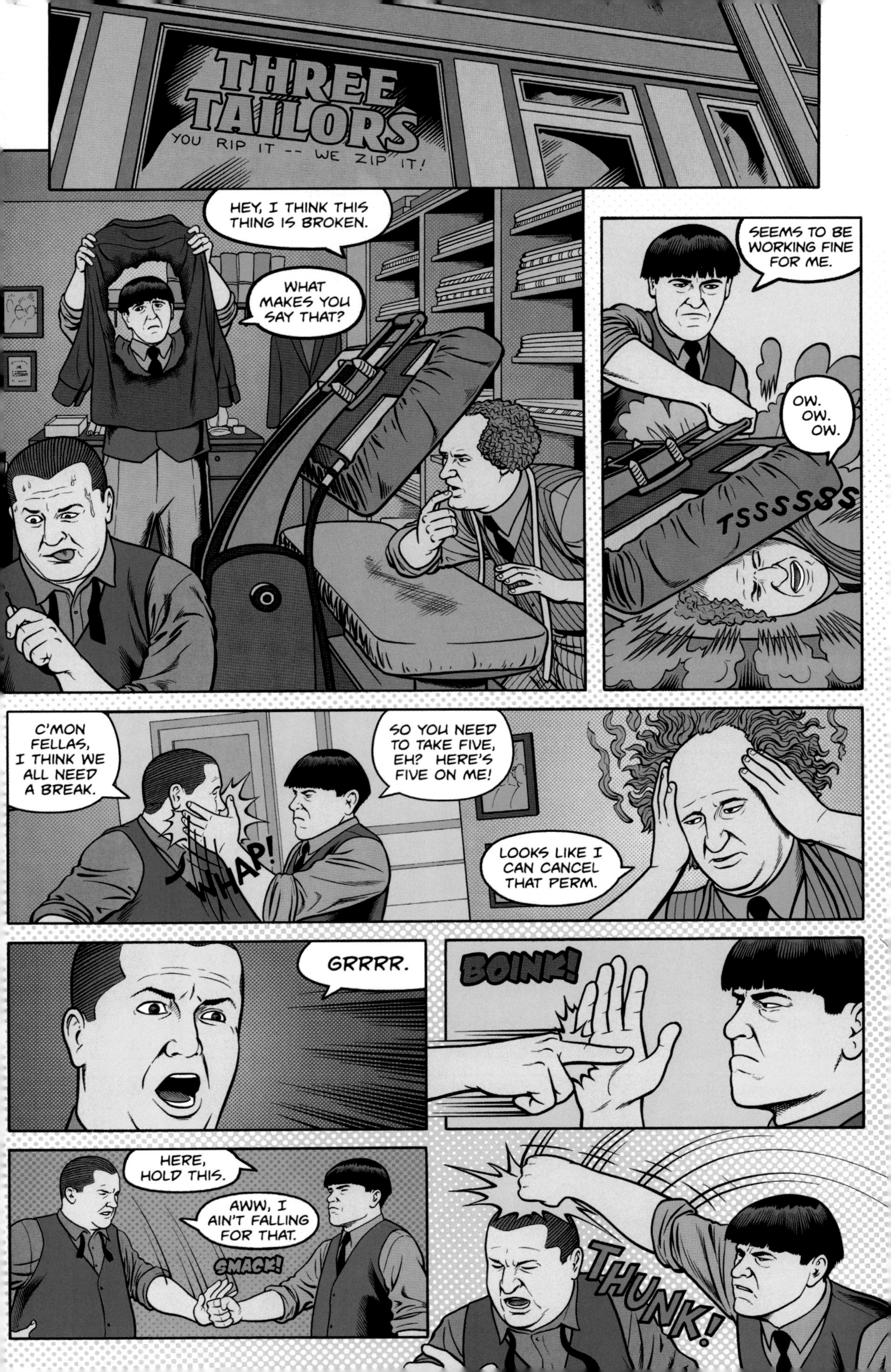
THREE TAILORS
YOU RIP IT -- WE ZIP IT!
HEY, I THINK THIS THING IS BROKEN.
WHAT MAKES YOU SAY THAT?
SEEMS TO BE WORKING FINE FOR ME.
OW. OW. OW.
TSSSSSS
C'MON FELLAS, I THINK WE ALL NEED A BREAK.
SO YOU NEED TO TAKE FIVE, EH? HERE'S FIVE ON ME!
WHAP!
LOOKS LIKE I CAN CANCEL THAT PERM.
GRRRR.
BOINK!
HERE, HOLD THIS.
AWW, I AIN'T FALLING FOR THAT.
SMACK!
THUNK!

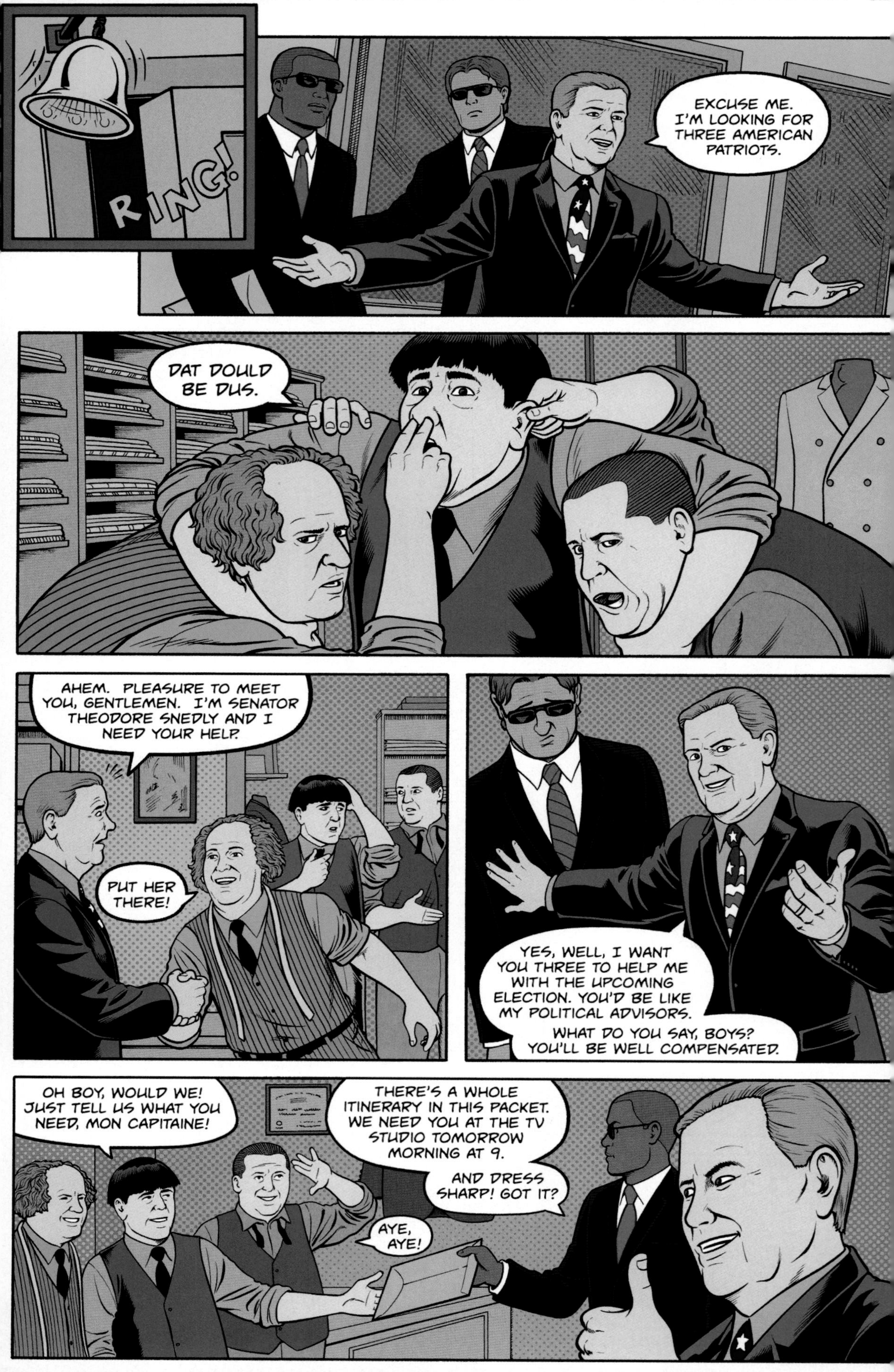
RING!
EXCUSE ME. I'M LOOKING FOR THREE AMERICAN PATRIOTS.
DAT DOULD BE DUS.
AHEM. PLEASURE TO MEET YOU, GENTLEMEN. I'M SENATOR THEODORE SNEDLY AND I NEED YOUR HELP.
PUT HER THERE!
YES, WELL, I WANT YOU THREE TO HELP ME WITH THE UPCOMING ELECTION. YOU'D BE LIKE MY POLITICAL ADVISORS.
WHAT DO YOU SAY, BOYS? YOU'LL BE WELL COMPENSATED.
OH BOY, WOULD WE! JUST TELL US WHAT YOU NEED, MON CAPITAINE!
THERE'S A WHOLE ITINERARY IN THIS PACKET. WE NEED YOU AT THE TV STUDIO TOMORROW MORNING AT 9.
AND DRESS SHARP! GOT IT?
AYE, AYE!

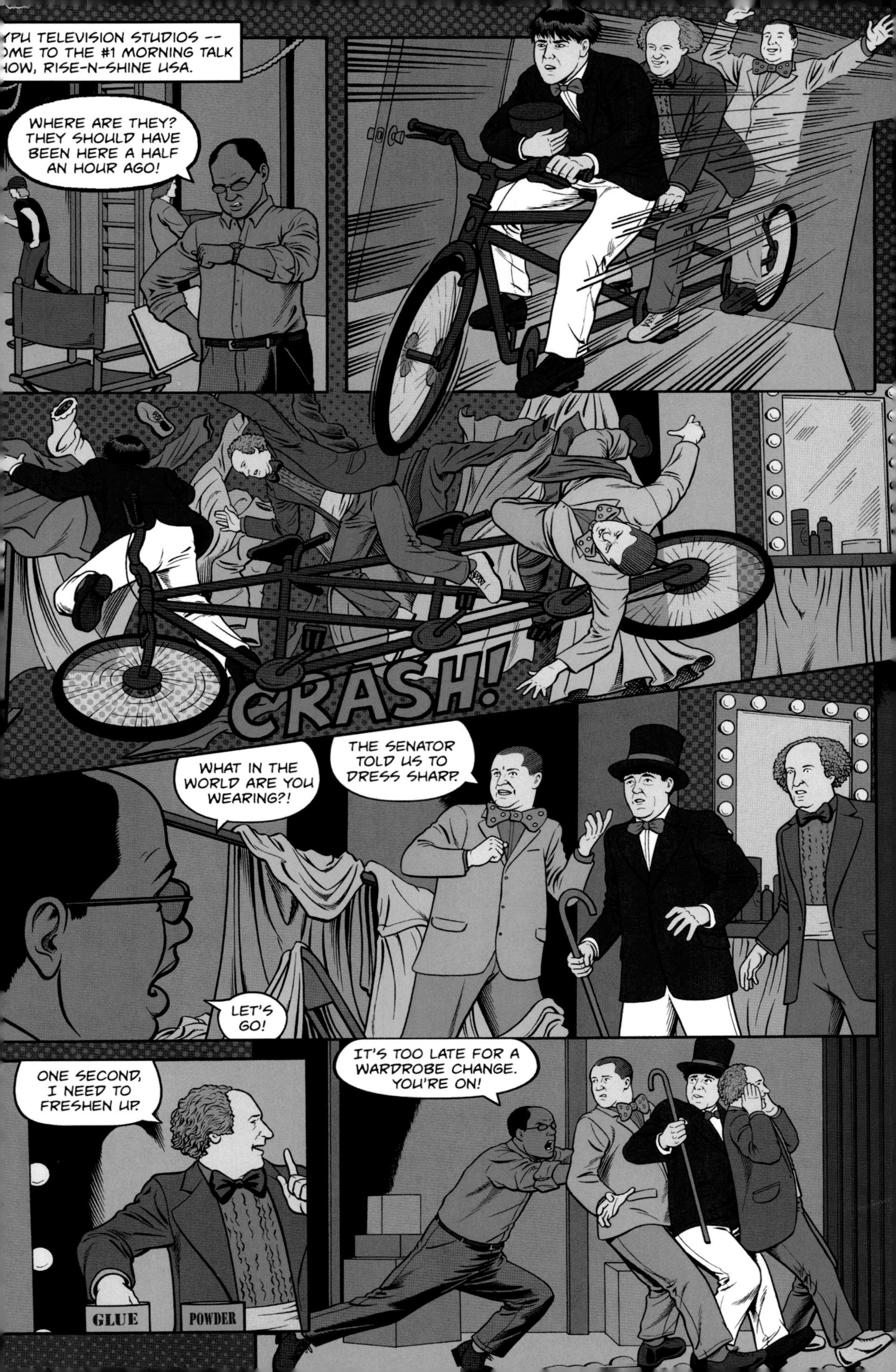
YPU TELEVISION STUDIOS --
OME TO THE #1 MORNING TALK
HOW, RISE-N-SHINE USA.
WHERE ARE THEY? THEY SHOULD HAVE BEEN HERE A HALF AN HOUR AGO!
CRASH!
WHAT IN THE WORLD ARE YOU WEARING?!
THE SENATOR TOLD US TO DRESS SHARP.
LET'S GO!
ONE SECOND, I NEED TO FRESHEN UP.
GLUE
POWDER
IT'S TOO LATE FOR A WARDROBE CHANGE. YOU'RE ON!

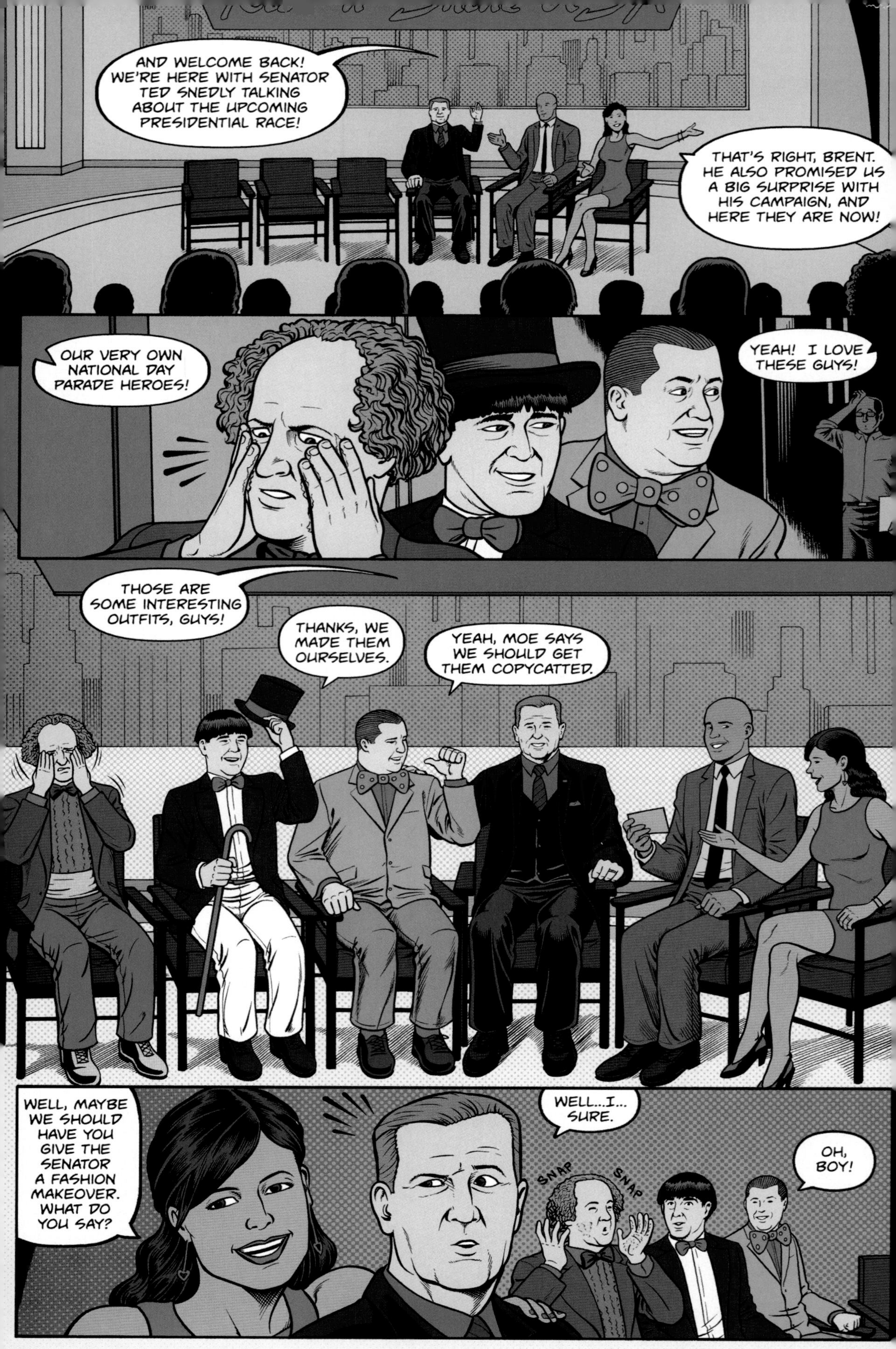
AND WELCOME BACK! WE'RE HERE WITH SENATOR TED SNEDLY TALKING ABOUT THE UPCOMING PRESIDENTIAL RACE!
THAT'S RIGHT, BRENT. HE ALSO PROMISED US A BIG SURPRISE WITH HIS CAMPAIGN, AND HERE THEY ARE NOW!
OUR VERY OWN NATIONAL DAY PARADE HEROES!
YEAH! I LOVE THESE GUYS!
THOSE ARE SOME INTERESTING OUTFITS, GUYS!
THANKS, WE MADE THEM OURSELVES.
YEAH, MOE SAYS WE SHOULD GET THEM COPYCATTED.
WELL, MAYBE WE SHOULD HAVE YOU GIVE THE SENATOR A FASHION MAKEOVER. WHAT DO YOU SAY?
WELL...I... SURE.
SNAP
SNAP
OH, BOY!

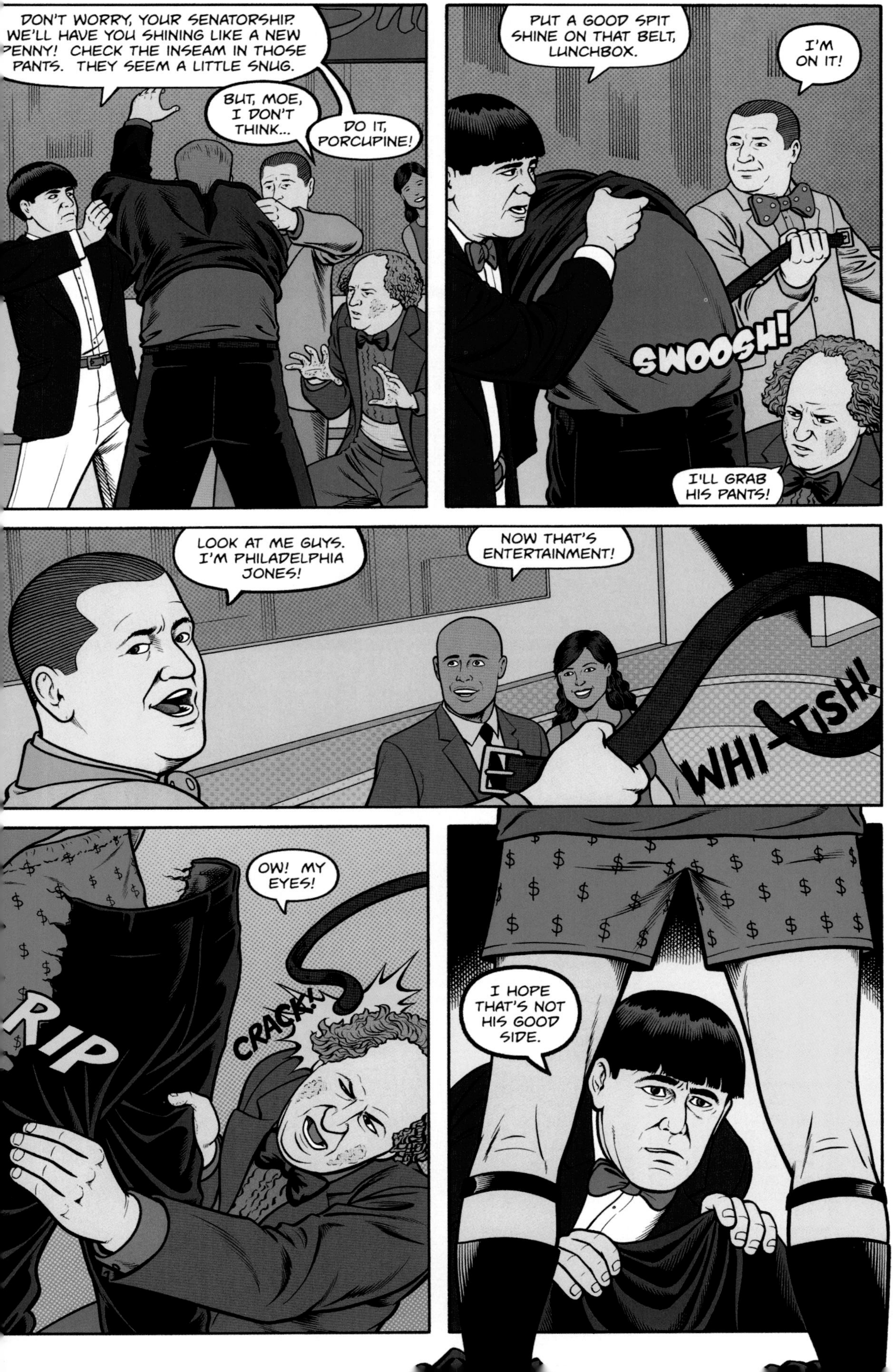
DON'T WORRY, YOUR SENATORSHIP. WE'LL HAVE YOU SHINING LIKE A NEW PENNY! CHECK THE INSEAM IN THOSE PANTS. THEY SEEM A LITTLE SNUG.
BUT, MOE, I DON'T THINK...
DO IT, PORCUPINE!
PUT A GOOD SPIT SHINE ON THAT BELT, LUNCHBOX.
I'M ON IT!
SWOOSH!
I'LL GRAB HIS PANTS!
LOOK AT ME GUYS. I'M PHILADELPHIA JONES!
NOW THAT'S ENTERTAINMENT!
WHI-TISH!
OW! MY EYES!
RIP
CRACK!
I HOPE THAT'S NOT HIS GOOD SIDE.

AFTER THE SHOW.

I WANT THOSE IDIOTS GONE!

BUT SENATOR, WE'VE GOT THEM BOOKED WITH US ALL WEEK UP UNTIL THE BIG BANQUET.

JUST KEEP THEM AWAY FROM ME.

WELL, IT'S BEEN ONE HECKUVA WEEK FOR PRESIDENTIAL HOPEFUL SENATOR SNEDLY.

THAT'S RIGHT, BRENT. HE'S BEEN MAKING NEWS ALL OVER THE COUNTRY!

ENTERTAINMENT HOURLY

SNEDLY MET WITH THE FRENCH AMBASSADOR ON TUESDAY TO DISCUSS FOREIGN POLICY.

I THINK IT'S STUCK IN HIS ASPARAGUS!

STAND BACK! I'LL GIVE HIM THE HEINIELICK MANEUVER!

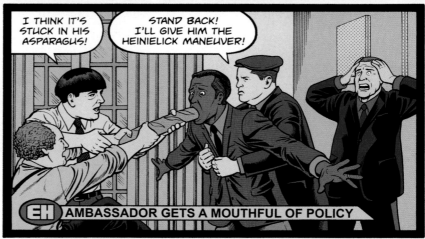

EH AMBASSADOR GETS A MOUTHFUL OF POLICY

WEDNESDAY, HE MADE HIS ROUNDS TO AN AREA SOUP KITCHEN TO HELP FEED THE HOMELESS.

I TOLD YOU THERE WAS TOO MUCH OREGANO.

WHY I OUGHTA...

SMACK!

EH "SOUP'S ON!" SAYS SENATOR SNEDLY

THURSDAY, THE SENATOR PAYED A VISIT TO JFK ELEMENTARY TO PROMOTE HIS NEW AUTOBIOGRAPHY, MY COUNTRY – MY WAY.

GET THESE RUGRATS OFF OF ME!

I THOUGHT WE'D TEACH THEM HOW TO FACE PAINT INSTEAD.

HE ALWAYS WAS THE ARTISTIC ONE.

EH A COLORFUL GREETING AT JFK ELEMENTARY SCHOOL

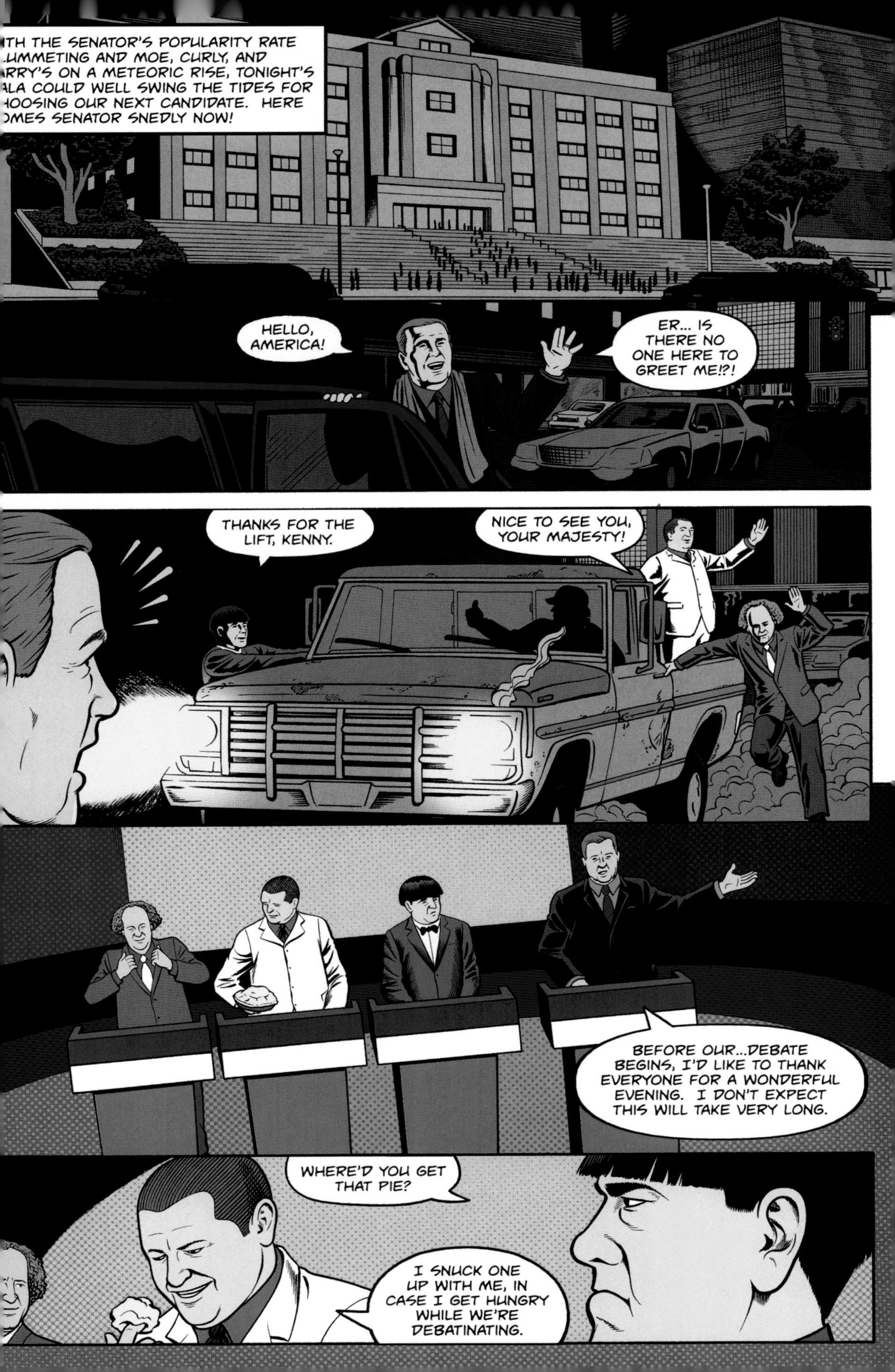

TH THE SENATOR'S POPULARITY RATE
LUMMETING AND MOE, CURLY, AND
RRY'S ON A METEORIC RISE, TONIGHT'S
ALA COULD WELL SWING THE TIDES FOR
HOOSING OUR NEXT CANDIDATE. HERE
OMES SENATOR SNEDLY NOW!
HELLO, AMERICA!
ER... IS THERE NO ONE HERE TO GREET ME!?!
THANKS FOR THE LIFT, KENNY.
NICE TO SEE YOU, YOUR MAJESTY!
BEFORE OUR...DEBATE BEGINS, I'D LIKE TO THANK EVERYONE FOR A WONDERFUL EVENING. I DON'T EXPECT THIS WILL TAKE VERY LONG.
WHERE'D YOU GET THAT PIE?
I SNUCK ONE UP WITH ME, IN CASE I GET HUNGRY WHILE WE'RE DEBATINATING.

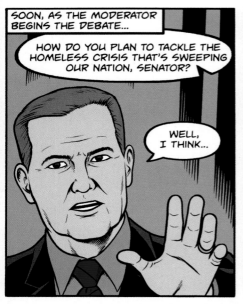

SOON, AS THE MODERATOR BEGINS THE DEBATE...

HOW DO YOU PLAN TO TACKLE THE HOMELESS CRISIS THAT'S SWEEPING OUR NATION, SENATOR?

WELL, I THINK...

I'LL TAKE THE POINT ON THIS ONE IF YOU DON'T MIND!

AMERICA IS OUR HOME. TO SAY THESE FOLKS ARE HOMELESS IS LIKE SAYING THEY AIN'T GOT NO COUNTRY. WE JUST NEED TO SHARE WHAT WE ALREADY HAVE. JUST LIKE WE DO WITH KENNY. HI, KENNY!

YOU TELL 'EM, LARRY!

GET BACK BEHIND YOUR PODIUM! YOU'RE MAKIN' US LOOK BAD.

CURLY, HOW WOULD YOU RESPOND TO THAT?

YEAH... WHAT HE SAID?

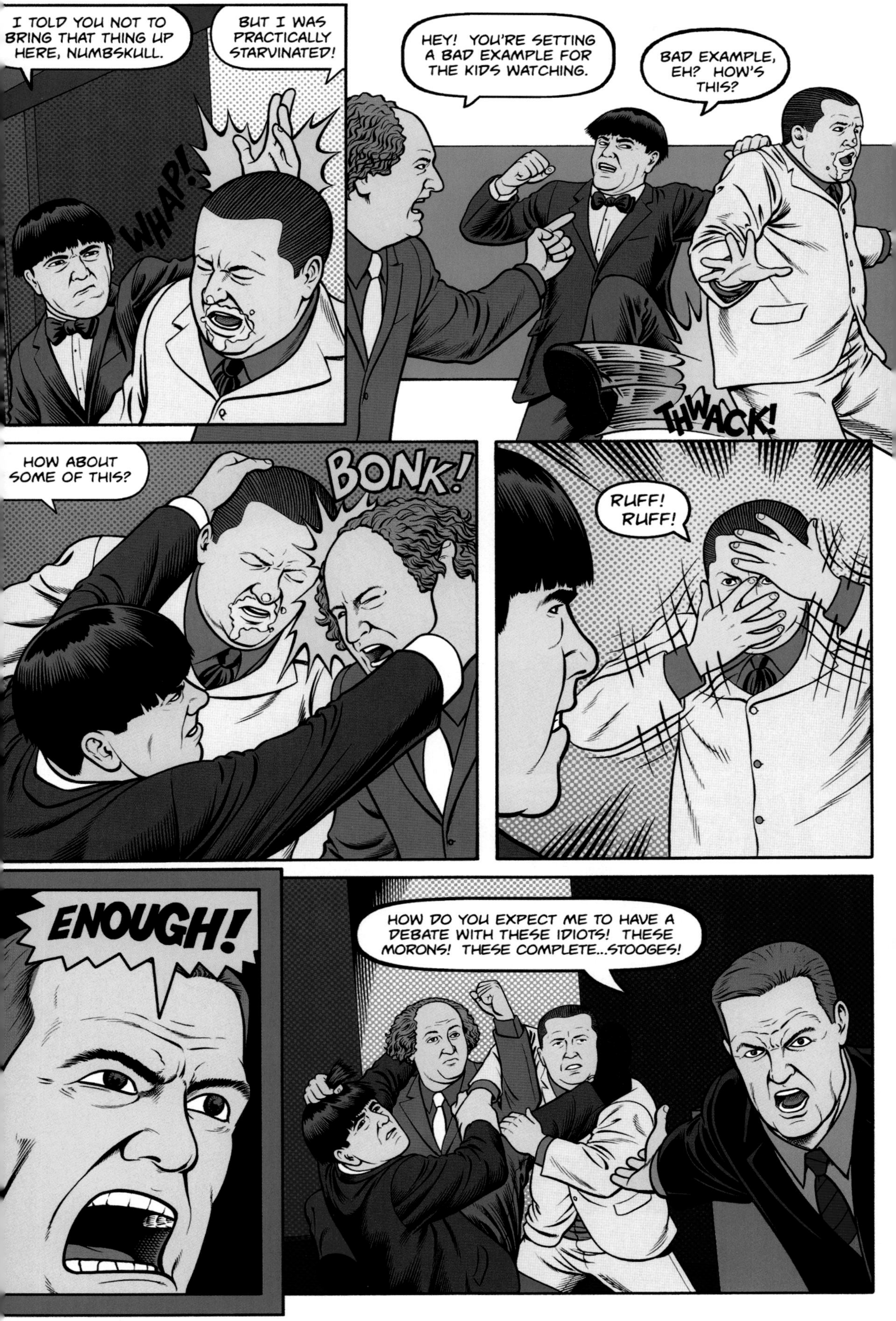
I TOLD YOU NOT TO BRING THAT THING UP HERE, NUMBSKULL.
BUT I WAS PRACTICALLY STARVINATED!
WHAP!
HEY! YOU'RE SETTING A BAD EXAMPLE FOR THE KIDS WATCHING.
BAD EXAMPLE, EH? HOW'S THIS?
THWACK!
HOW ABOUT SOME OF THIS?
BONK!
RUFF! RUFF!
ENOUGH!
HOW DO YOU EXPECT ME TO HAVE A DEBATE WITH THESE IDIOTS! THESE MORONS! THESE COMPLETE...STOOGES!

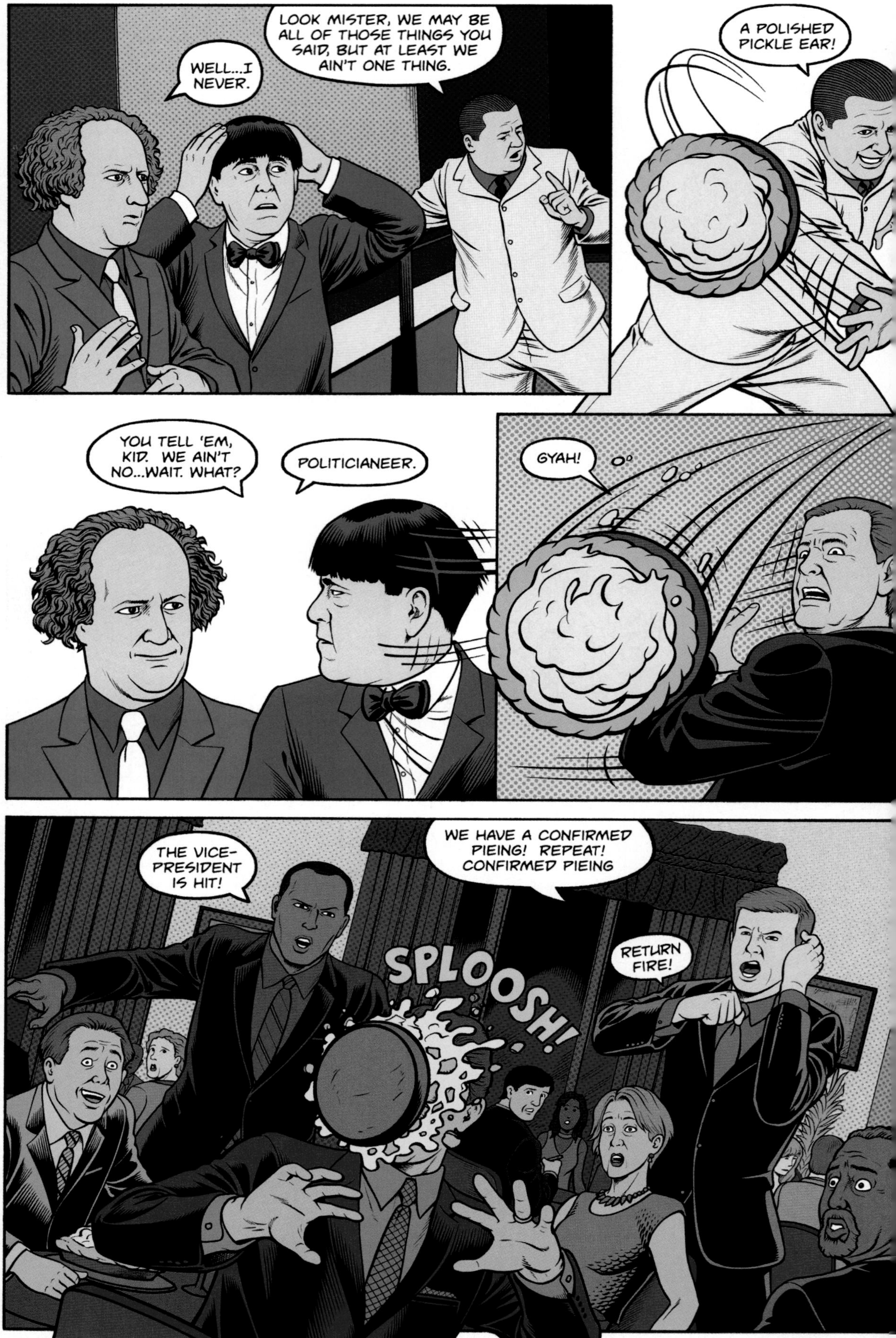

WELL...I NEVER.
LOOK MISTER, WE MAY BE ALL OF THOSE THINGS YOU SAID, BUT AT LEAST WE AIN'T ONE THING.
A POLISHED PICKLE EAR!
YOU TELL 'EM, KID. WE AIN'T NO...WAIT. WHAT?
POLITICIANEER.
GYAH!
THE VICE-PRESIDENT IS HIT!
WE HAVE A CONFIRMED PIEING! REPEAT! CONFIRMED PIEING
SPLOOSH!
RETURN FIRE!

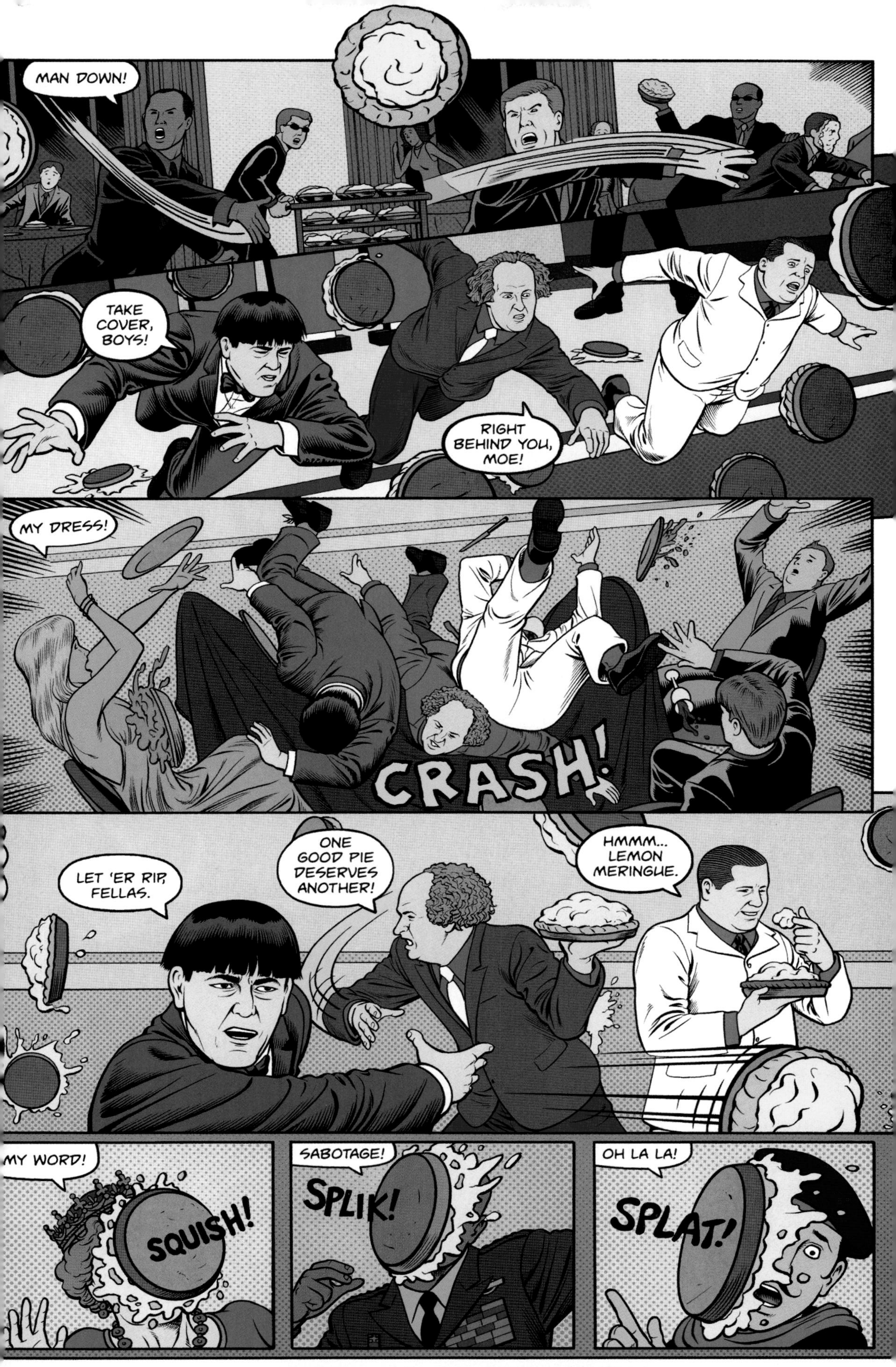
MAN DOWN!
TAKE COVER, BOYS!
RIGHT BEHIND YOU, MOE!
MY DRESS!
CRASH!
LET 'ER RIP, FELLAS.
ONE GOOD PIE DESERVES ANOTHER!
HMMM... LEMON MERINGUE.
MY WORD!
SQUISH!
SABOTAGE!
SPLIK!
OH LA LA!
SPLAT!

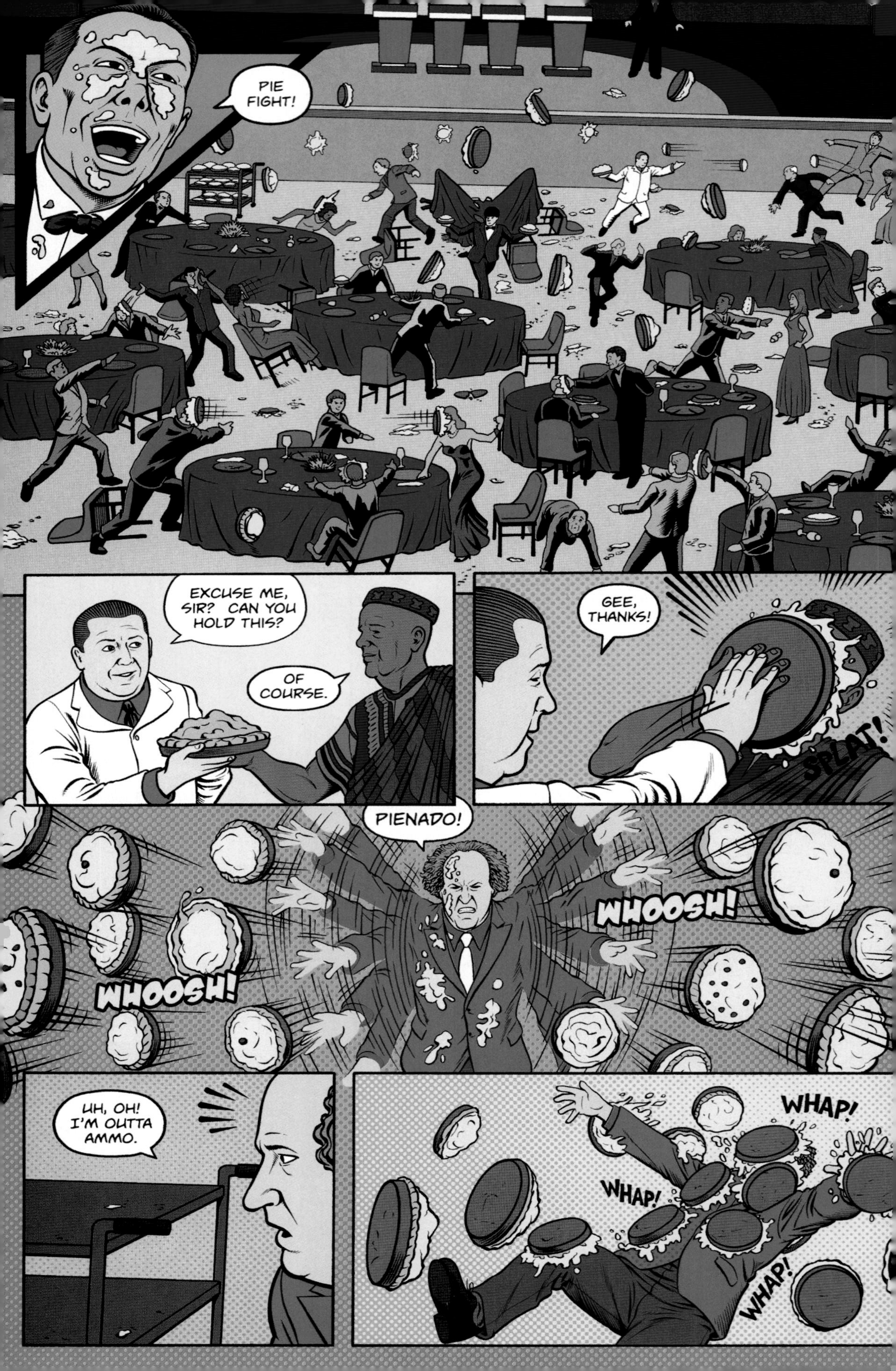
PIE FIGHT!
EXCUSE ME, SIR? CAN YOU HOLD THIS?
OF COURSE.
GEE, THANKS!
SPLAT!
PIENADO!
WHOOSH!
WHOOSH!
UH, OH! I'M OUTTA AMMO.
WHAP!
WHAP!
WHAP!

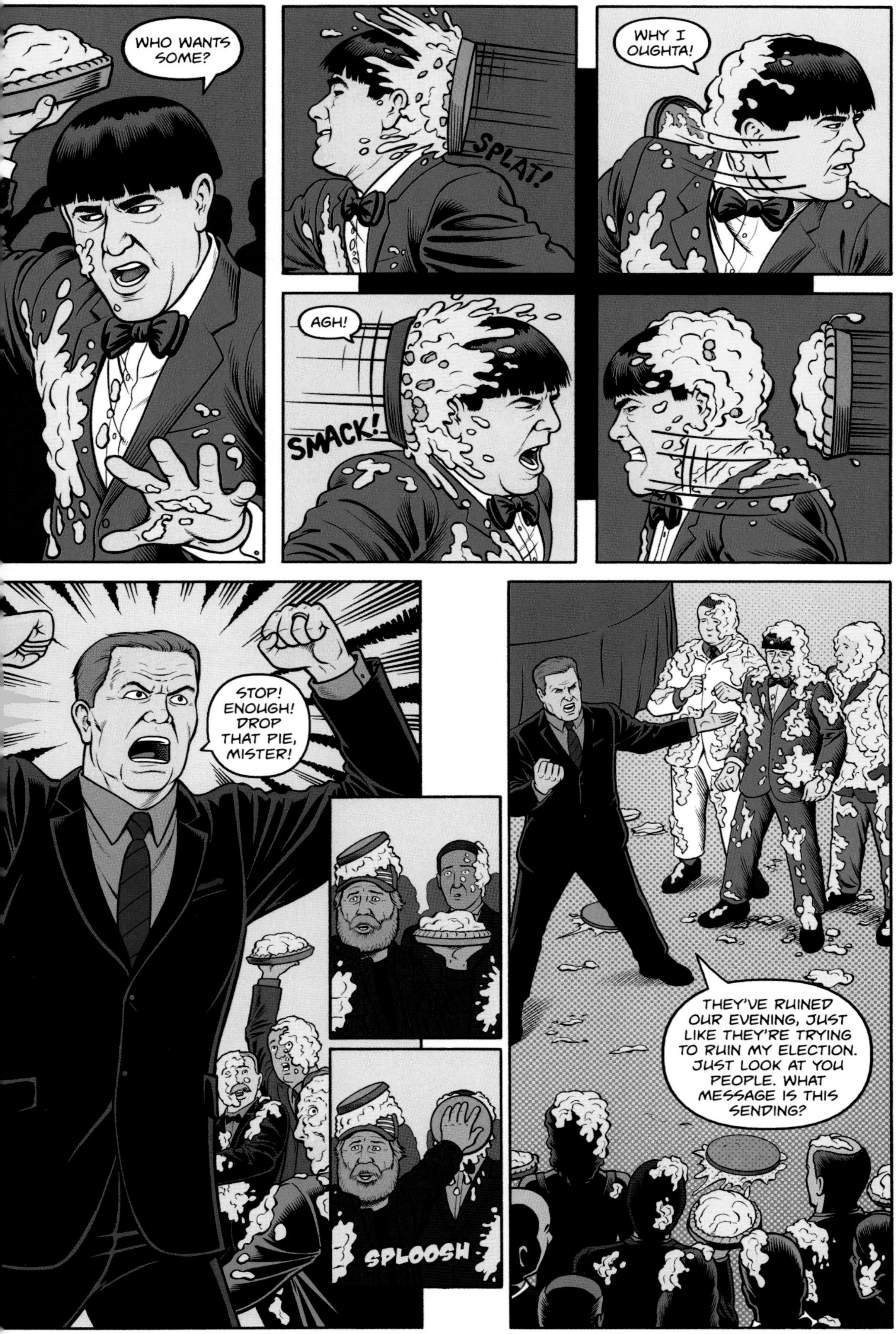
WHO WANTS SOME?
SPLAT!
WHY I OUGHTA!
AGH!
SMACK!
STOP! ENOUGH! DROP THAT PIE, MISTER!
SPLOOSH
THEY'VE RUINED OUR EVENING, JUST LIKE THEY'RE TRYING TO RUIN MY ELECTION. JUST LOOK AT YOU PEOPLE. WHAT MESSAGE IS THIS SENDING?

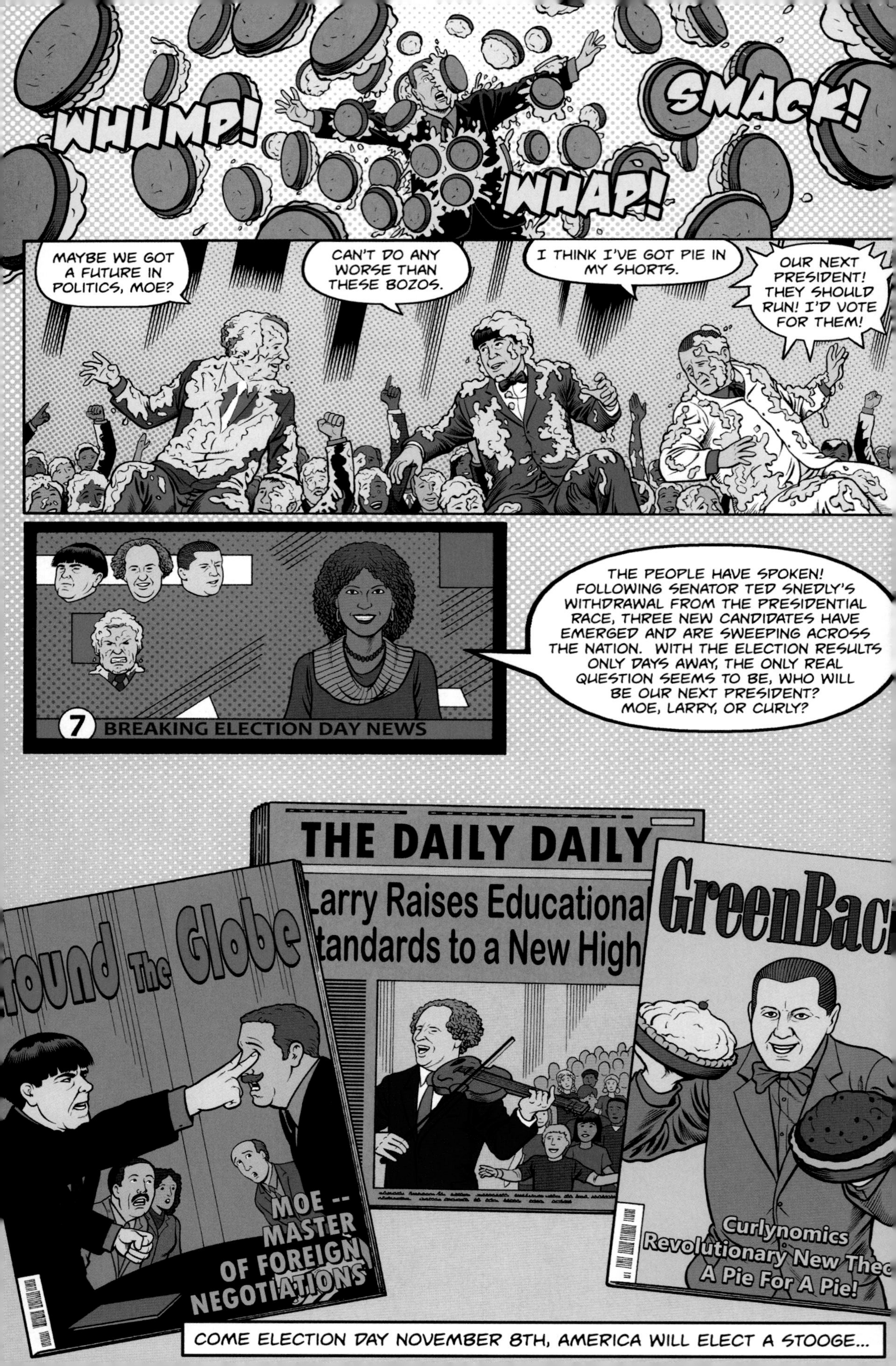
WHUMP!
SMACK!
WHAP!
MAYBE WE GOT A FUTURE IN POLITICS, MOE?
CAN'T DO ANY WORSE THAN THESE BOZOS.
I THINK I'VE GOT PIE IN MY SHORTS.
OUR NEXT PRESIDENT! THEY SHOULD RUN! I'D VOTE FOR THEM!
7 BREAKING ELECTION DAY NEWS
THE PEOPLE HAVE SPOKEN! FOLLOWING SENATOR TED SNEDLY'S WITHDRAWAL FROM THE PRESIDENTIAL RACE, THREE NEW CANDIDATES HAVE EMERGED AND ARE SWEEPING ACROSS THE NATION. WITH THE ELECTION RESULTS ONLY DAYS AWAY, THE ONLY REAL QUESTION SEEMS TO BE, WHO WILL BE OUR NEXT PRESIDENT? MOE, LARRY, OR CURLY?
THE DAILY DAILY
Larry Raises Educational Standards to a New High
round The Globe
MOE -- MASTER OF FOREIGN NEGOTIATIONS
GreenBac
Curlynomics
Revolutionary New Theo
A Pie For A Pie!
COME ELECTION DAY NOVEMBER 8TH, AMERICA WILL ELECT A STOOGE...

THE VOTES ARE IN! YOUR NEW PRESIDENT IS...CURLY!

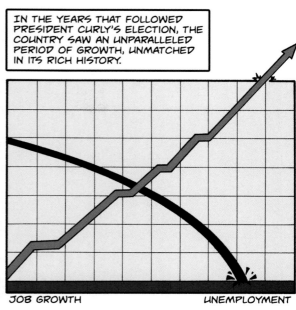

IN THE YEARS THAT FOLLOWED PRESIDENT CURLY'S ELECTION, THE COUNTRY SAW AN UNPARALLELED PERIOD OF GROWTH, UNMATCHED IN ITS RICH HISTORY.

JOB GROWTH

UNEMPLOYMENT

PRESIDENT CURLY DECREED THAT ONCE A YEAR THERE WOULD BE A NEW NATIONAL HOLIDAY, "PIE DAY."

IT'S A TIME WHEN EVERY AMERICAN CAN WORK OUT THEIR PROBLEMS WITH EACH OTHER WITH THIS NEW TRADITION.

SNEDLY'S USED CA

PRESIDENT CURLY, VICE-PRESIDENT LARRY, AND SPEAKER OF THE HOUSE MOE, HAVE PROMISED TO KEEP AMERICA MOVING FORWARD AS THEY LOOK FORWARD TO ANOTHER ELECTION.

SEE YA IN 2020!

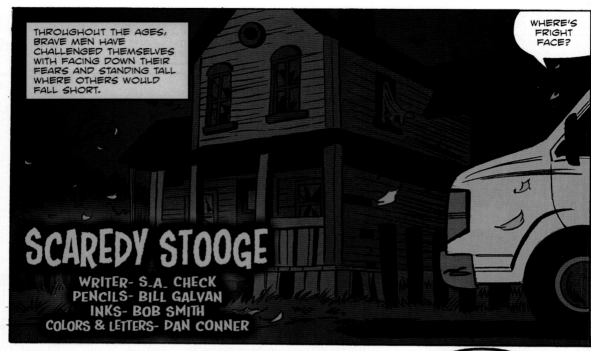

THROUGHOUT THE AGES, BRAVE MEN HAVE CHALLENGED THEMSELVES WITH FACING DOWN THEIR FEARS AND STANDING TALL WHERE OTHERS WOULD FALL SHORT.

WHERE'S FRIGHT FACE?

SCAREDY STOOGE

WRITER- S.A. CHECK
PENCILS- BILL GALVAN
INKS- BOB SMITH
COLORS & LETTERS- DAN CONNER

"THE ONLY THING WITH HAVE TO FEAR IS FEAR ITSELF," FRANKLIN D. ROOSEVELT.

3S VIDEO
WEDDINGS
BIRTHDAYS
GRATULATIONS
GRAND JUBILATIONS
OTHER STUFF

"THE BRAVE MAN IS NOT HE WHO DOES NOT FEEL AFRAID, BUT HE WHO CONQUERS THAT FEAR," NELSON MANDELA.

I DUNNO. HE SAID HE'D MEET US HERE.

THEIR WORDS INSPIRE OTHERS TO STRIVE FOR THAT SAME LEVEL OF GREATNESS.

IS THIS STUPID THING EVEN ON?

MAKE SURE YOU GET MY GOOD SIDE, MUFFIN TOP!

I STILL DON'T KNOW WHY WE HAD TO DO THIS IN THE DARK. THE LIGHTING IS TERRIBLE.

CURLY

WHO CARES! SOME MORON'S PAYING US $1,000 BUCKS JUST TO STAY THE NIGHT AND PROVE THE JOINT AIN'T HAUNTED.

HHHH.. HAUNTED?!

OKAY, MEN, FAN OUT! I'LL TAKE THE STUDY.

I'LL TAKE THE KITCHEN!

I'LL TAKE THE EXIT!

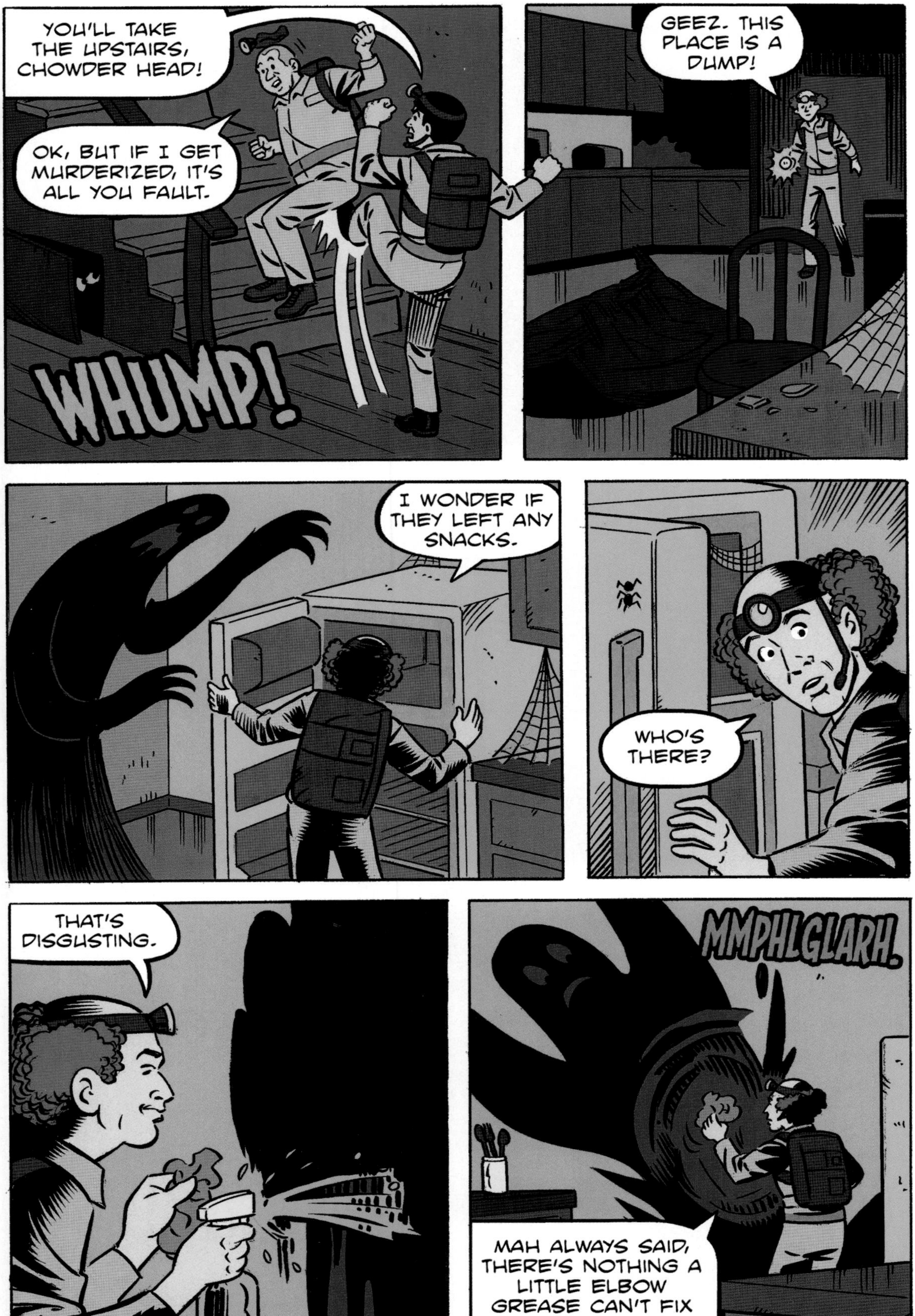
YOU'LL TAKE THE UPSTAIRS, CHOWDER HEAD!
OK, BUT IF I GET MURDERIZED, IT'S ALL YOU FAULT.
WHUMP!
GEEZ. THIS PLACE IS A DUMP!
I WONDER IF THEY LEFT ANY SNACKS.
WHO'S THERE?
THAT'S DISGUSTING.
MMPHLGLARH.
MAH ALWAYS SAID, THERE'S NOTHING A LITTLE ELBOW GREASE CAN'T FIX

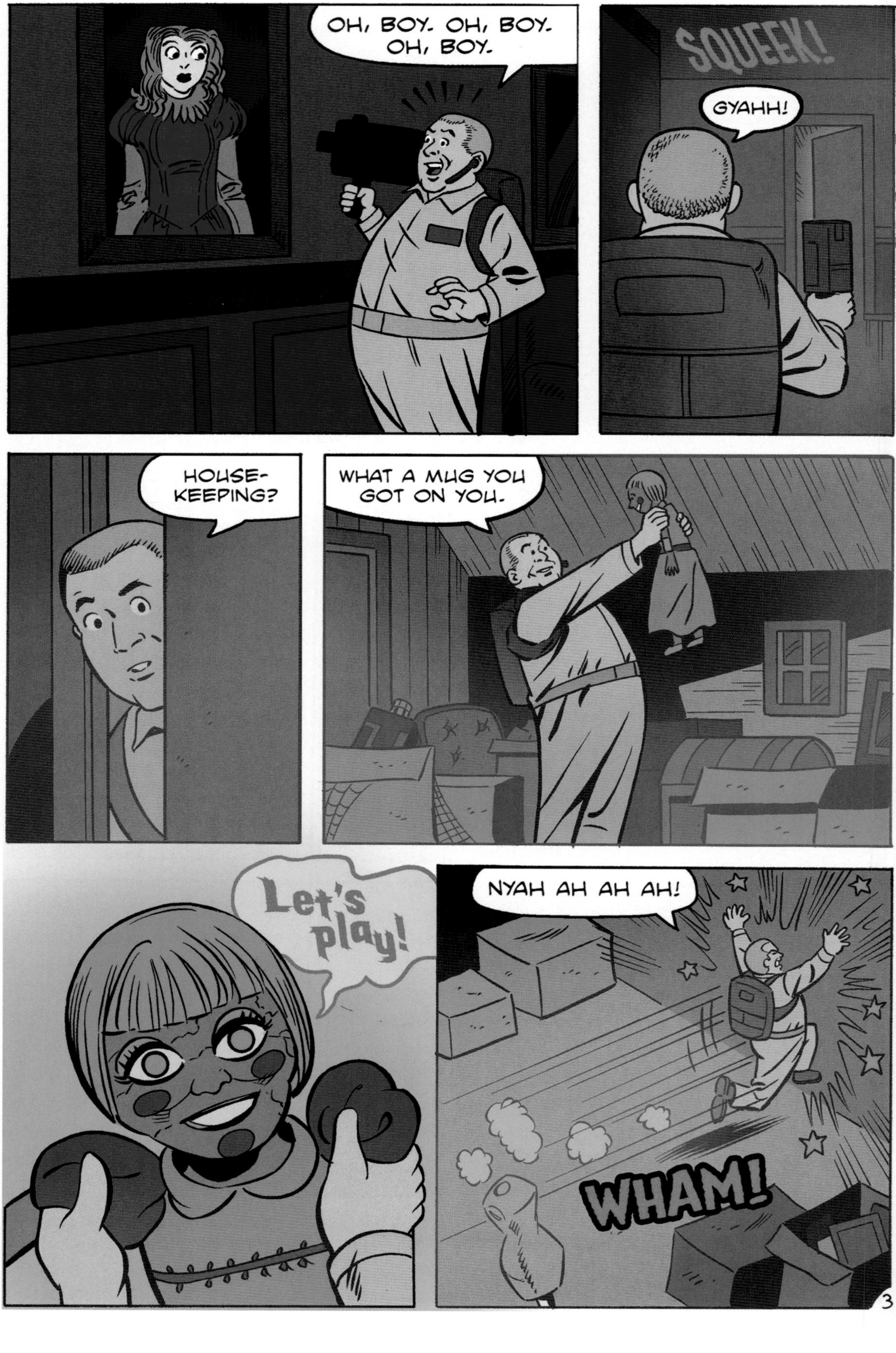
OH, BOY. OH, BOY.
OH, BOY.
SQUEEK!
GYAHH!
HOUSE-
KEEPING?
WHAT A MUG YOU
GOT ON YOU.
Let's
play!
NYAH AH AH AH!
WHAM!

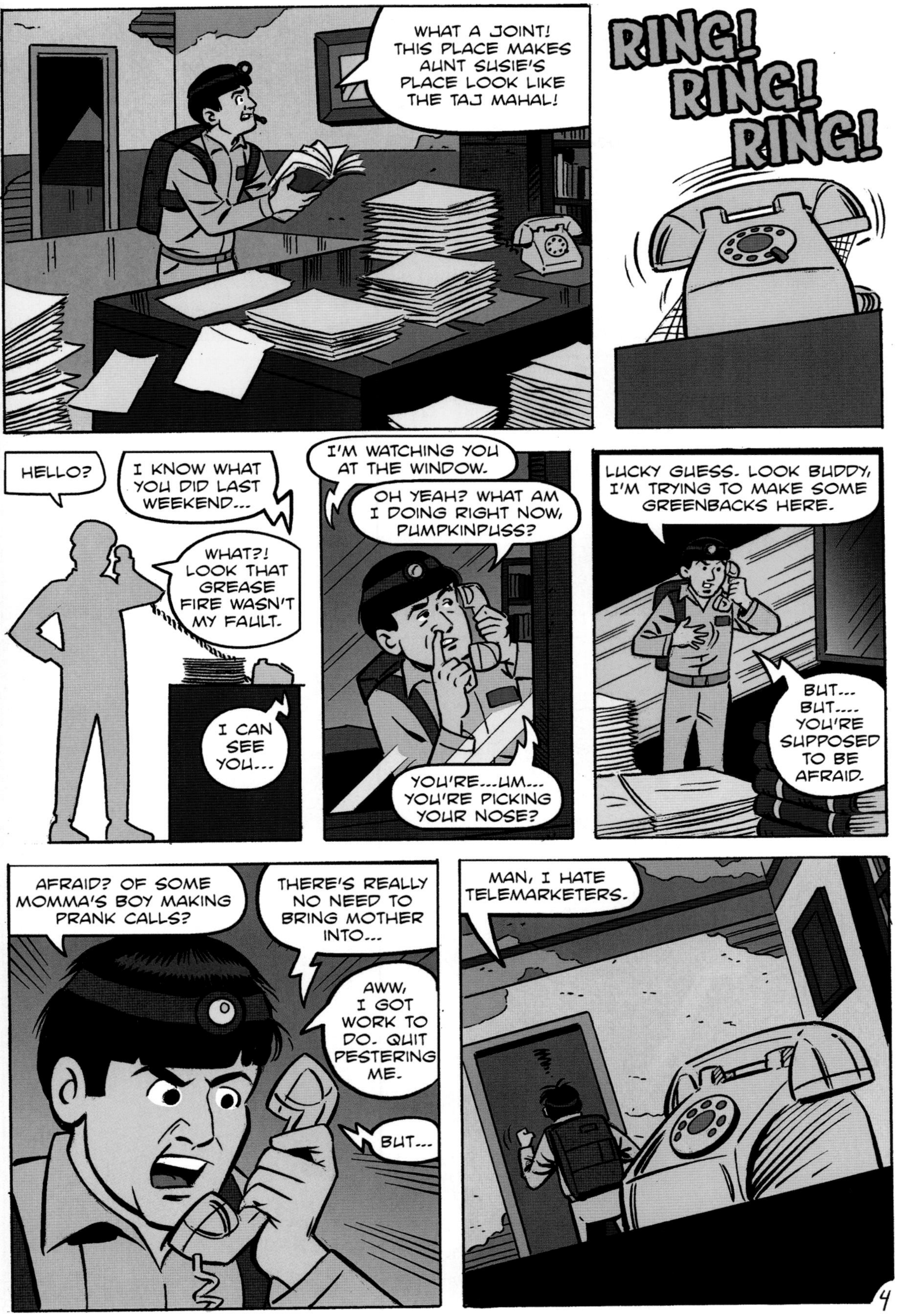
WHAT A JOINT! THIS PLACE MAKES AUNT SUSIE'S PLACE LOOK LIKE THE TAJ MAHAL!
RING! RING! RING!
HELLO?
I KNOW WHAT YOU DID LAST WEEKEND...
WHAT?! LOOK THAT GREASE FIRE WASN'T MY FAULT.
I CAN SEE YOU...
I'M WATCHING YOU AT THE WINDOW.
OH YEAH? WHAT AM I DOING RIGHT NOW, PUMPKINPUSS?
YOU'RE...UM... YOU'RE PICKING YOUR NOSE?
LUCKY GUESS. LOOK BUDDY, I'M TRYING TO MAKE SOME GREENBACKS HERE.
BUT... BUT.... YOU'RE SUPPOSED TO BE AFRAID.
AFRAID? OF SOME MOMMA'S BOY MAKING PRANK CALLS?
THERE'S REALLY NO NEED TO BRING MOTHER INTO...
AWW, I GOT WORK TO DO. QUIT PESTERING ME.
BUT...
MAN, I HATE TELEMARKETERS.

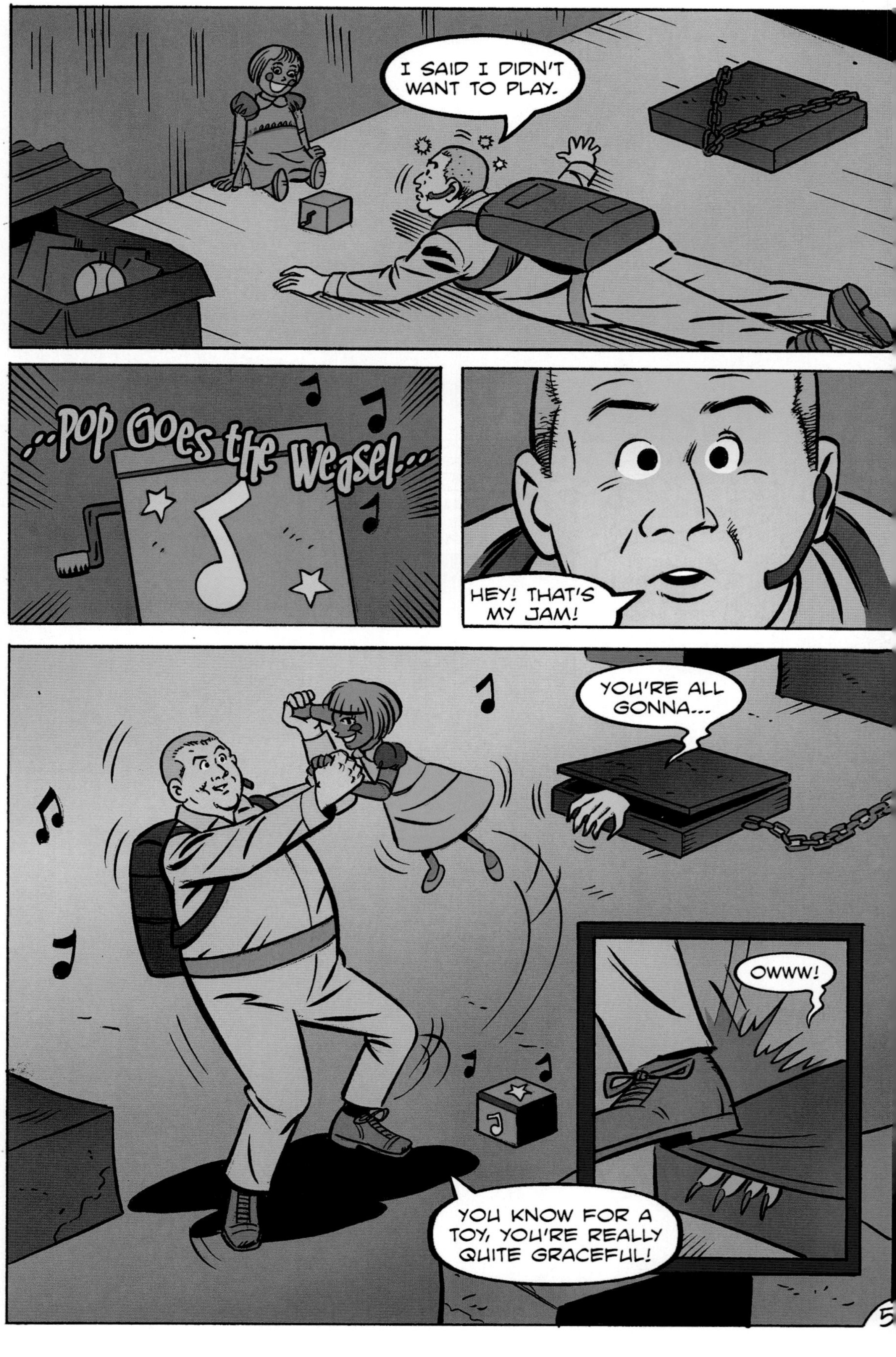
I SAID I DIDN'T WANT TO PLAY.
...Pop Goes the Weasel...
HEY! THAT'S MY JAM!
YOU'RE ALL GONNA...
OWWW!
YOU KNOW FOR A TOY, YOU'RE REALLY QUITE GRACEFUL!

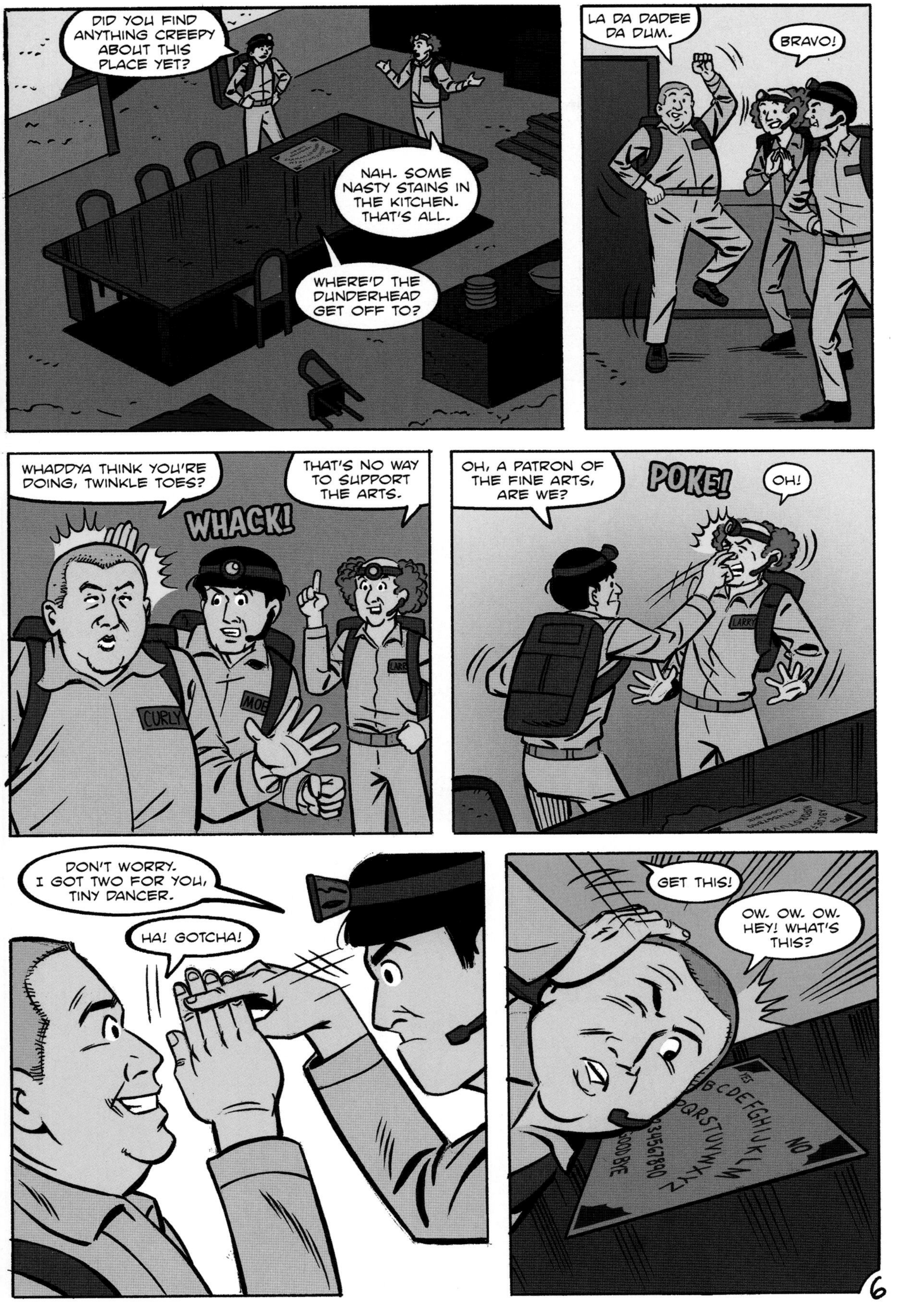
DID YOU FIND ANYTHING CREEPY ABOUT THIS PLACE YET?
NAH. SOME NASTY STAINS IN THE KITCHEN. THAT'S ALL.
WHERE'D THE DUNDERHEAD GET OFF TO?
LA DA DADEE DA DUM.
BRAVO!
WHADDYA THINK YOU'RE DOING, TWINKLE TOES?
WHACK!
THAT'S NO WAY TO SUPPORT THE ARTS.
OH, A PATRON OF THE FINE ARTS, ARE WE?
POKE!
OH!
DON'T WORRY. I GOT TWO FOR YOU, TINY DANCER.
HA! GOTCHA!
GET THIS!
OW. OW. OW. HEY! WHAT'S THIS?

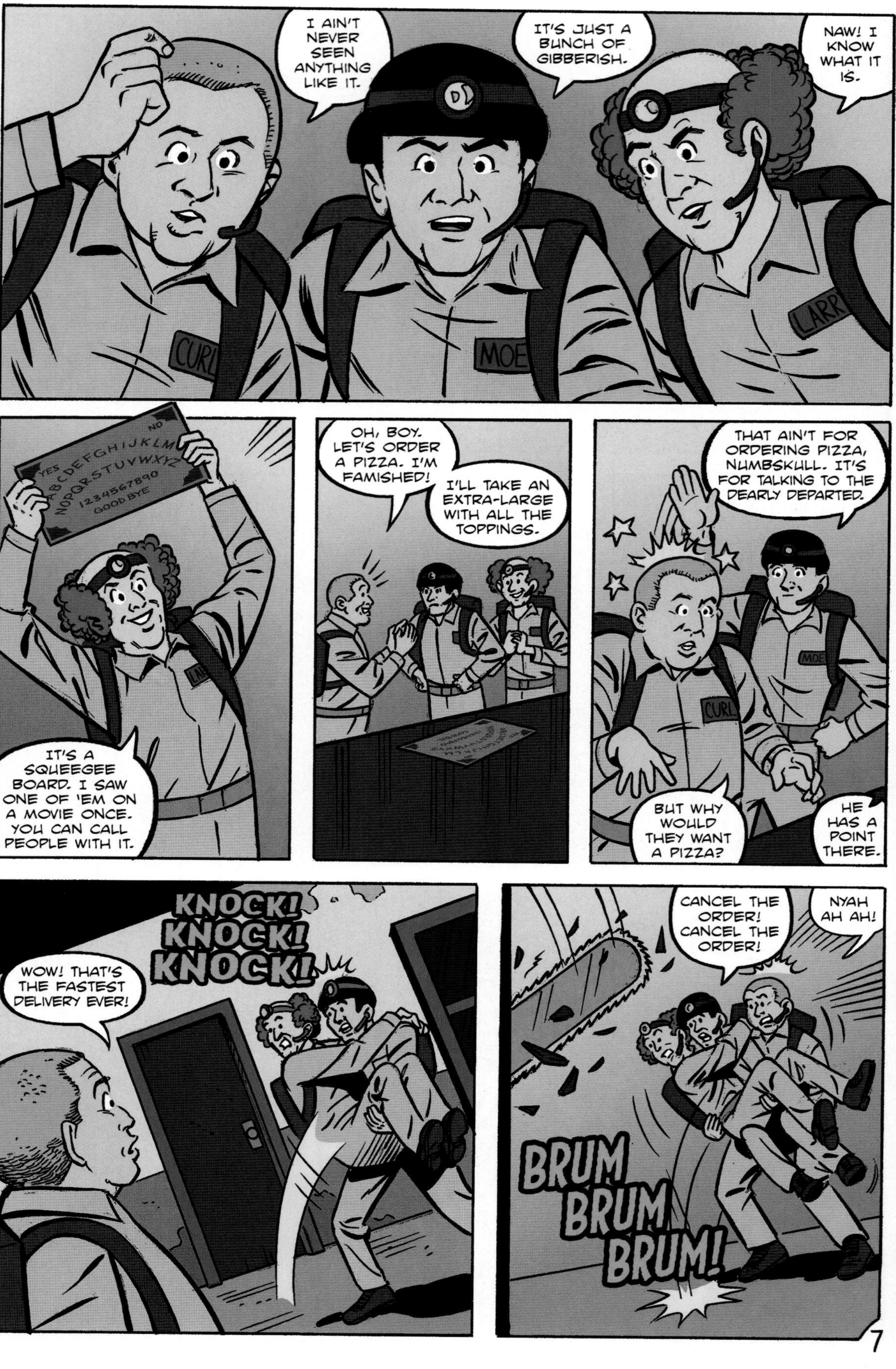
I AIN'T NEVER SEEN ANYTHING LIKE IT.
IT'S JUST A BUNCH OF GIBBERISH.
NAW! I KNOW WHAT IT IS.
CURL
MOE
LARR
YES
NO
ABCDEFGHIJKLM
NOPQRSTUVWXYZ
1234567890
GOOD BYE
IT'S A SQUEEGEE BOARD. I SAW ONE OF 'EM ON A MOVIE ONCE. YOU CAN CALL PEOPLE WITH IT.
OH, BOY. LET'S ORDER A PIZZA. I'M FAMISHED!
I'LL TAKE AN EXTRA-LARGE WITH ALL THE TOPPINGS.
THAT AIN'T FOR ORDERING PIZZA, NUMBSKULL. IT'S FOR TALKING TO THE DEARLY DEPARTED.
BUT WHY WOULD THEY WANT A PIZZA?
HE HAS A POINT THERE.
KNOCK! KNOCK! KNOCK!
WOW! THAT'S THE FASTEST DELIVERY EVER!
CANCEL THE ORDER! CANCEL THE ORDER!
NYAH AH AH!
BRUM BRUM BRUM!

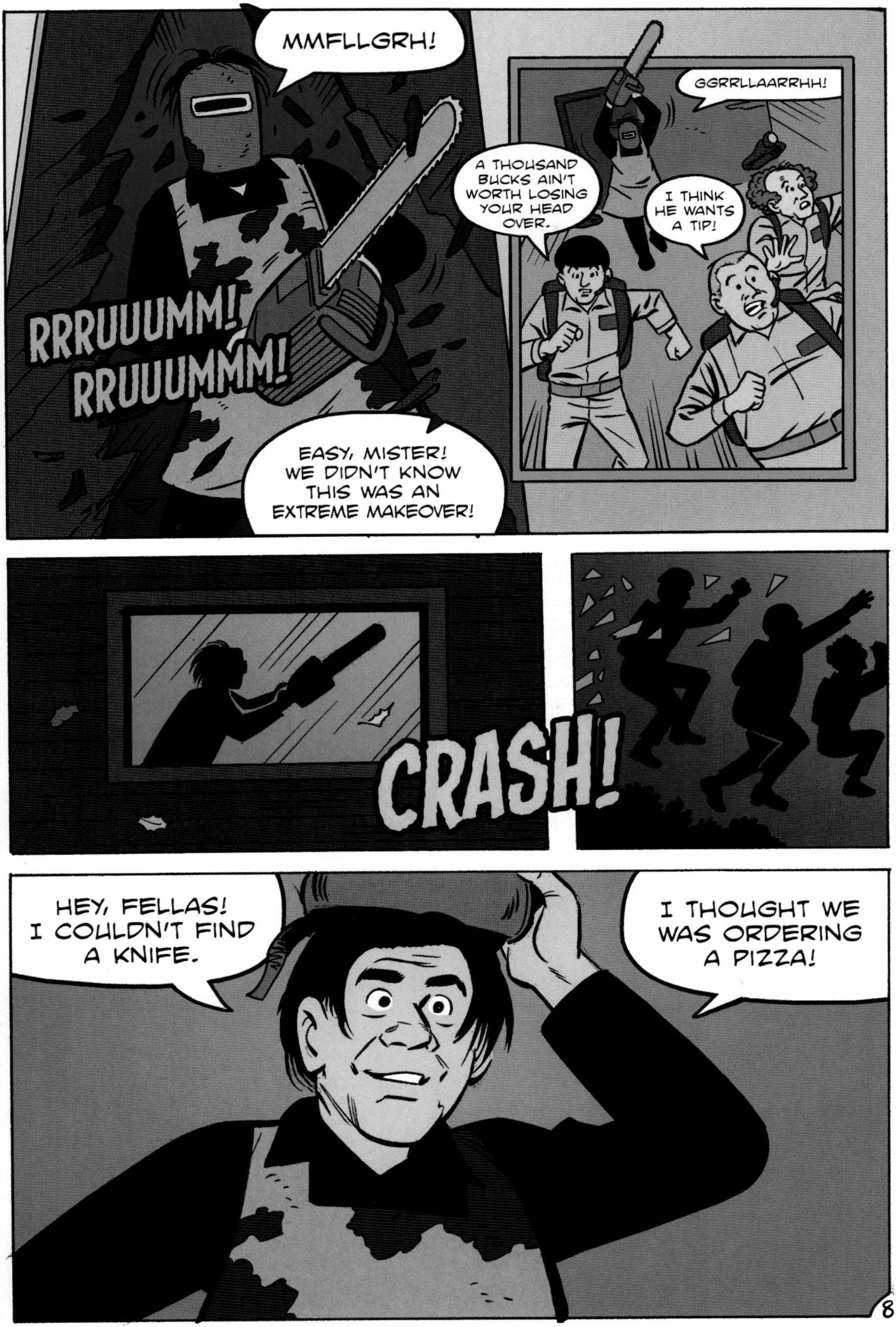
MMFLLGRH!
RRRUUUMM! RRUUUMMM!
EASY, MISTER! WE DIDN'T KNOW THIS WAS AN EXTREME MAKEOVER!
GGRRLLAARRHH!
A THOUSAND BUCKS AIN'T WORTH LOSING YOUR HEAD OVER.
I THINK HE WANTS A TIP!
CRASH!
HEY, FELLAS! I COULDN'T FIND A KNIFE.
I THOUGHT WE WAS ORDERING A PIZZA!

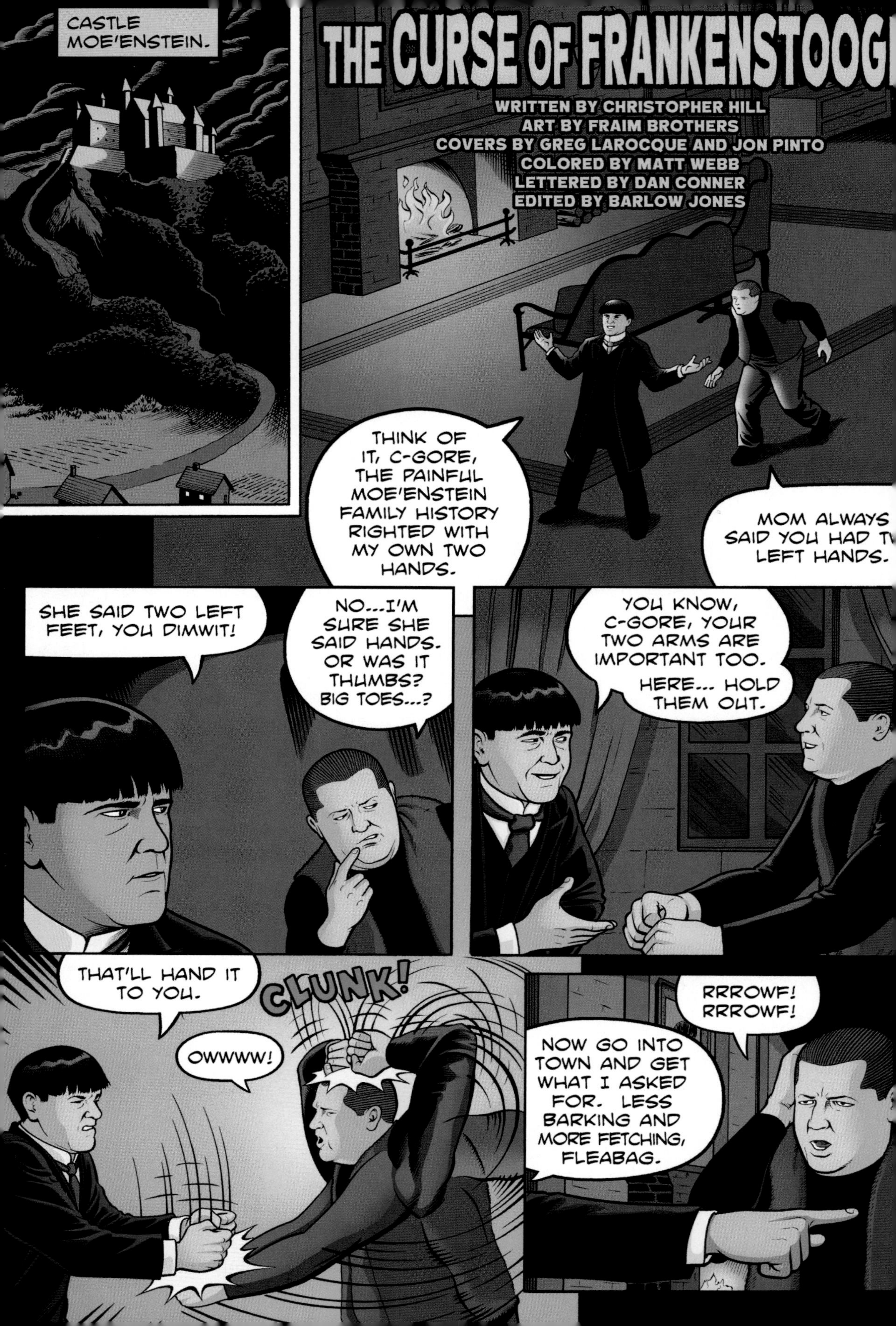
CASTLE MOE'ENSTEIN.
THE CURSE OF FRANKENSTOOG
WRITTEN BY CHRISTOPHER HILL
ART BY FRAIM BROTHERS
COVERS BY GREG LAROCQUE AND JON PINTO
COLORED BY MATT WEBB
LETTERED BY DAN CONNER
EDITED BY BARLOW JONES
THINK OF IT, C-GORE, THE PAINFUL MOE'ENSTEIN FAMILY HISTORY RIGHTED WITH MY OWN TWO HANDS.
MOM ALWAYS SAID YOU HAD T LEFT HANDS.
SHE SAID TWO LEFT FEET, YOU DIMWIT!
NO...I'M SURE SHE SAID HANDS. OR WAS IT THUMBS? BIG TOES...?
YOU KNOW, C-GORE, YOUR TWO ARMS ARE IMPORTANT TOO.
HERE... HOLD THEM OUT.
THAT'LL HAND IT TO YOU.
CLUNK!
OWWWW!
RRROWF! RRROWF!
NOW GO INTO TOWN AND GET WHAT I ASKED FOR. LESS BARKING AND MORE FETCHING, FLEABAG.

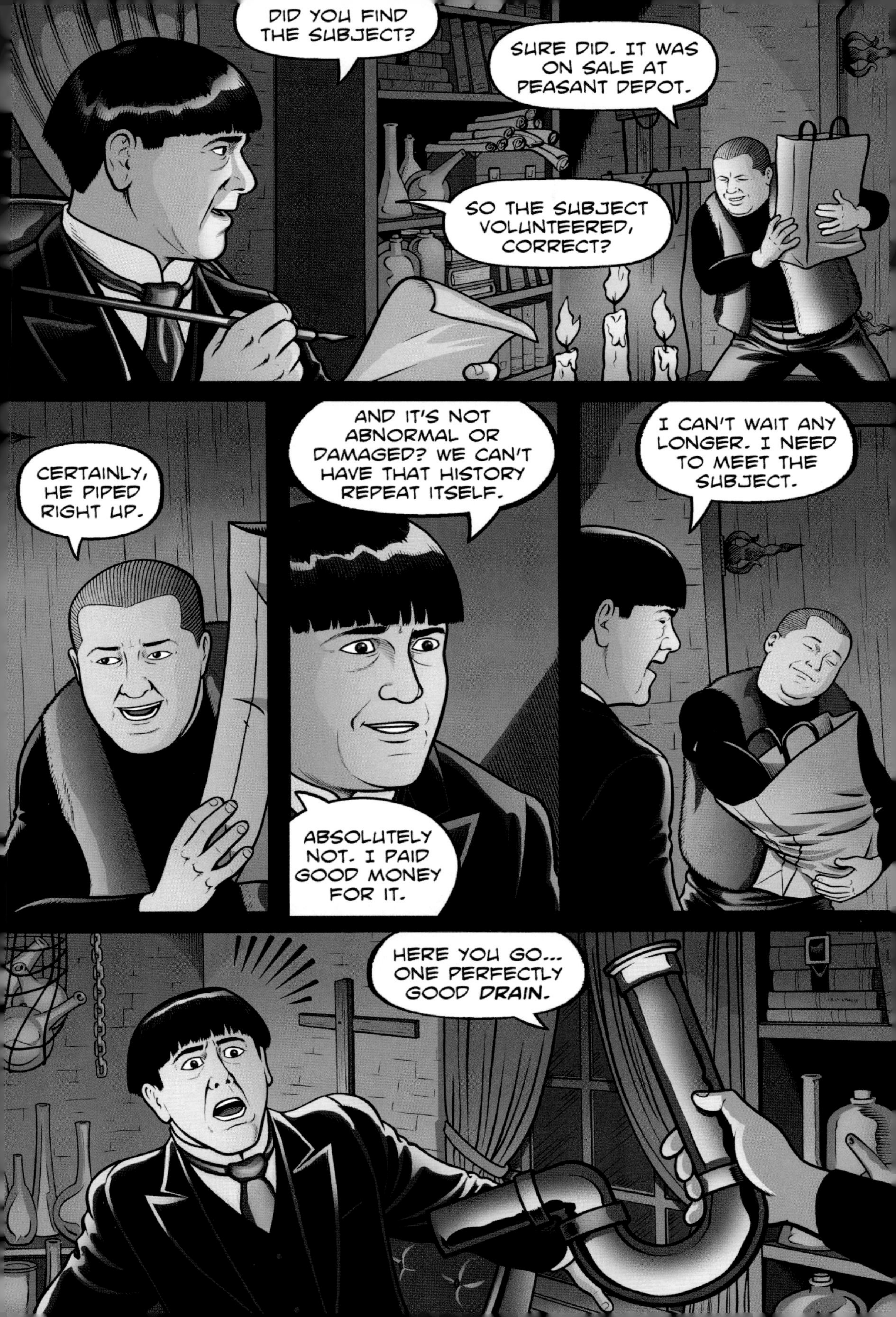
DID YOU FIND THE SUBJECT?
SURE DID. IT WAS ON SALE AT PEASANT DEPOT.
SO THE SUBJECT VOLUNTEERED, CORRECT?
CERTAINLY, HE PIPED RIGHT UP.
AND IT'S NOT ABNORMAL OR DAMAGED? WE CAN'T HAVE THAT HISTORY REPEAT ITSELF.
ABSOLUTELY NOT. I PAID GOOD MONEY FOR IT.
I CAN'T WAIT ANY LONGER. I NEED TO MEET THE SUBJECT.
HERE YOU GO... ONE PERFECTLY GOOD DRAIN.

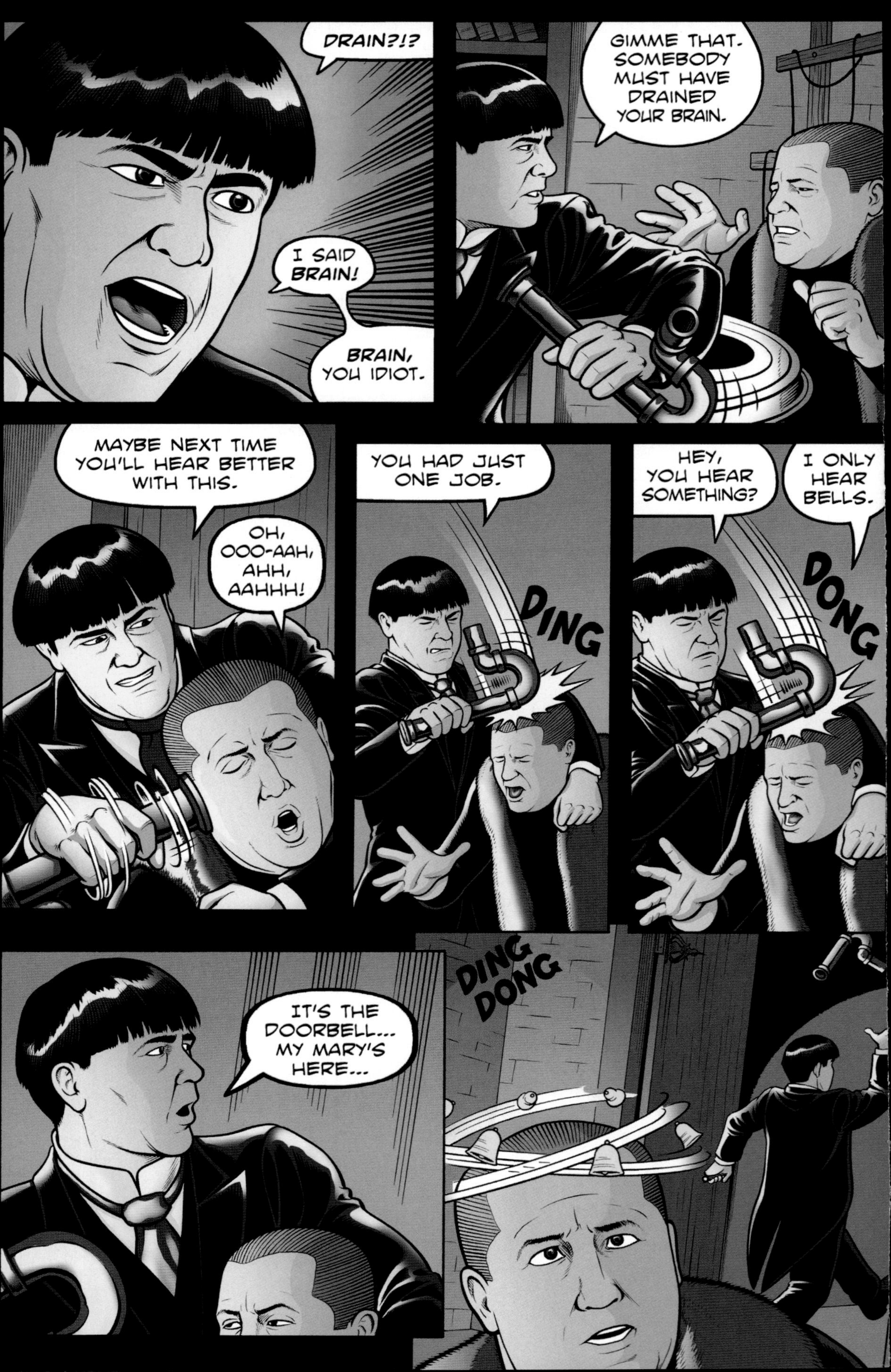
DRAIN?!?
I SAID BRAIN!
BRAIN, YOU IDIOT.
GIMME THAT. SOMEBODY MUST HAVE DRAINED YOUR BRAIN.
MAYBE NEXT TIME YOU'LL HEAR BETTER WITH THIS.
OH, OOO-AAH, AHH, AAHHH!
YOU HAD JUST ONE JOB.
DING
HEY, YOU HEAR SOMETHING?
I ONLY HEAR BELLS.
DONG
IT'S THE DOORBELL... MY MARY'S HERE...
DING DONG

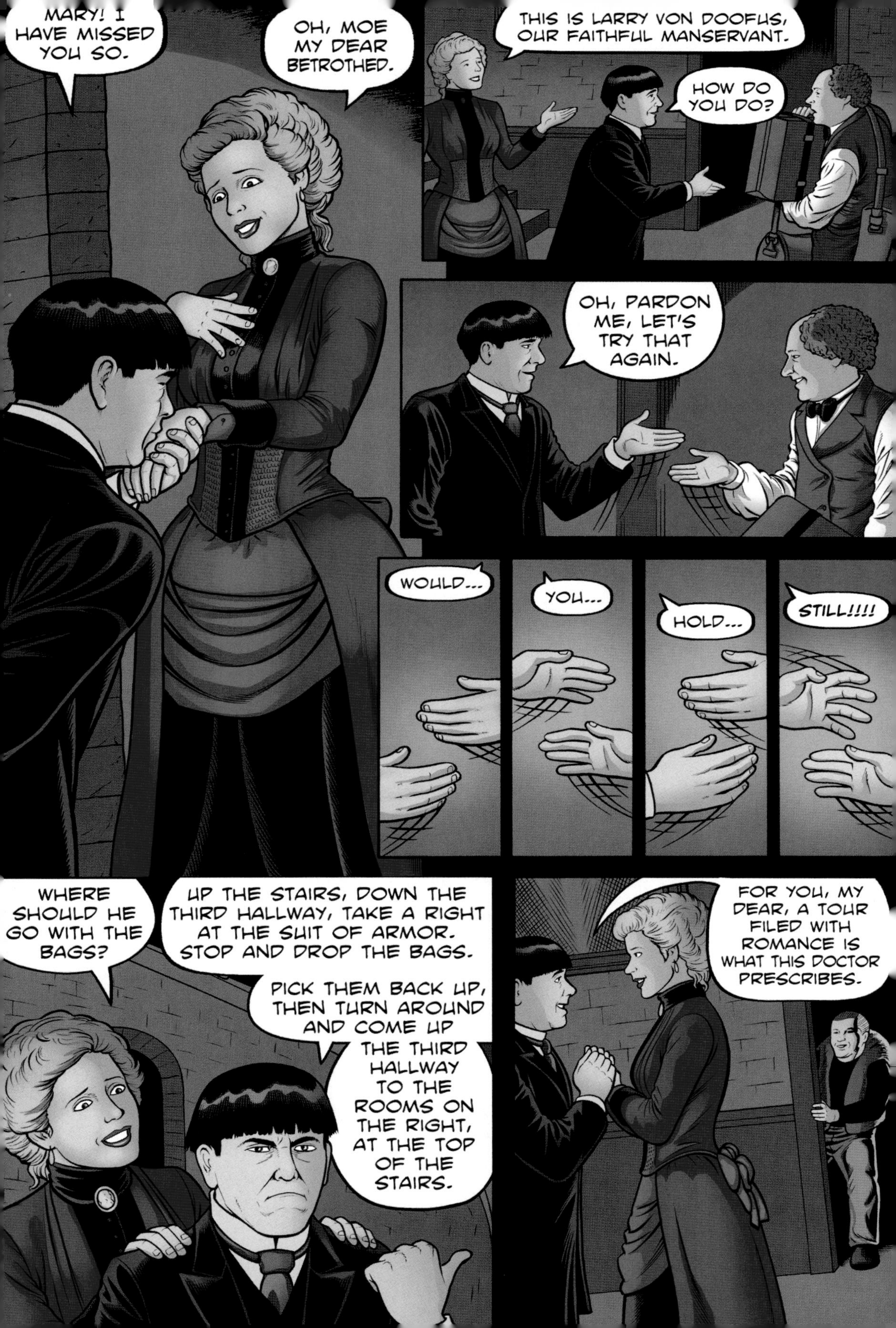
MARY! I HAVE MISSED YOU SO.
OH, MOE MY DEAR BETROTHED.
THIS IS LARRY VON DOOFUS, OUR FAITHFUL MANSERVANT.
HOW DO YOU DO?
OH, PARDON ME, LET'S TRY THAT AGAIN.
WOULD...
YOU...
HOLD...
STILL!!!!
WHERE SHOULD HE GO WITH THE BAGS?
UP THE STAIRS, DOWN THE THIRD HALLWAY, TAKE A RIGHT AT THE SUIT OF ARMOR. STOP AND DROP THE BAGS.
PICK THEM BACK UP, THEN TURN AROUND AND COME UP THE THIRD HALLWAY TO THE ROOMS ON THE RIGHT, AT THE TOP OF THE STAIRS.
FOR YOU, MY DEAR, A TOUR FILED WITH ROMANCE IS WHAT THIS DOCTOR PRESCRIBES.

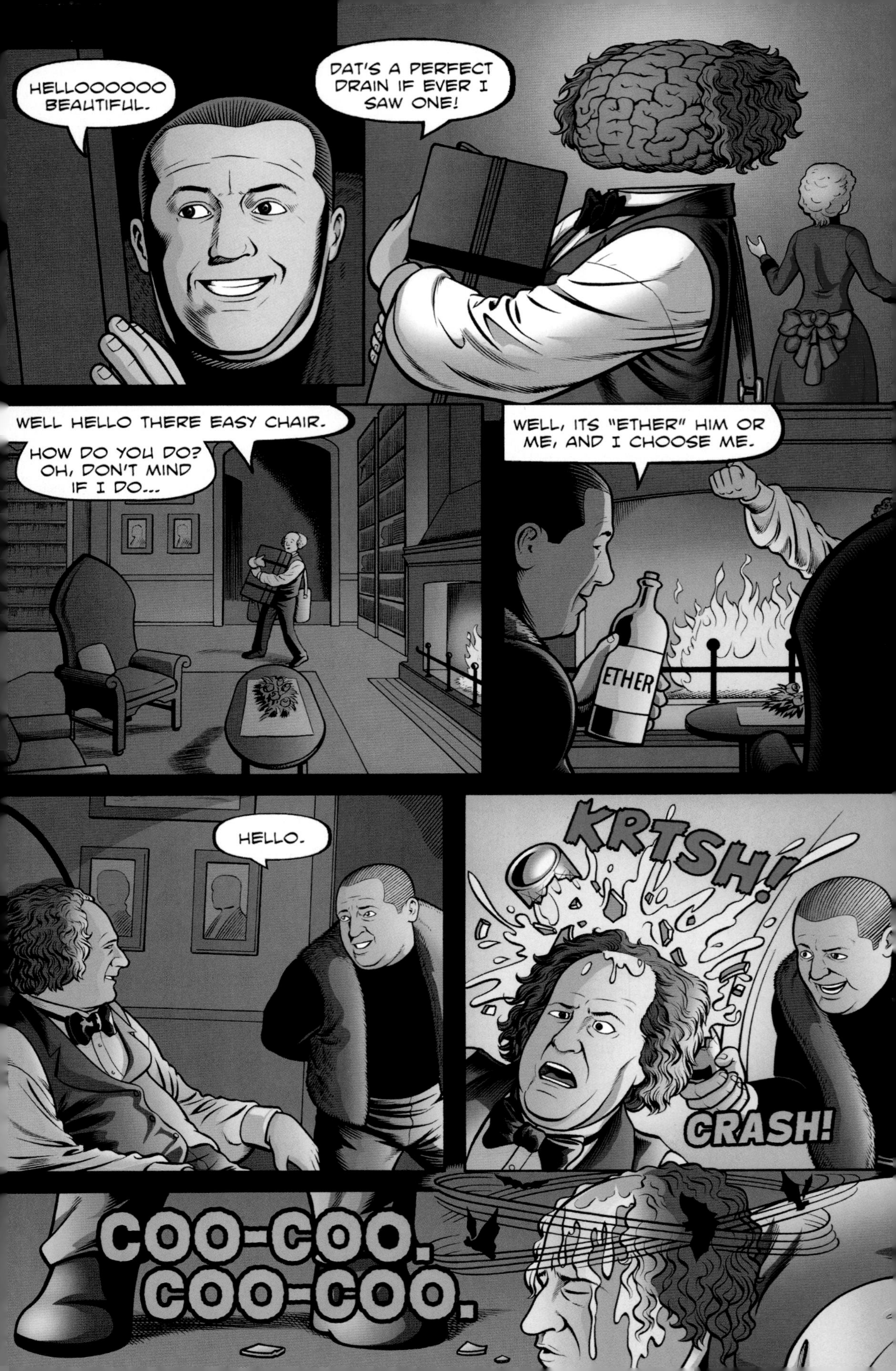
HELLOOOOOO BEAUTIFUL.
DAT'S A PERFECT DRAIN IF EVER I SAW ONE!
WELL HELLO THERE EASY CHAIR.
HOW DO YOU DO? OH, DON'T MIND IF I DO...
WELL, ITS "ETHER" HIM OR ME, AND I CHOOSE ME.
ETHER
HELLO.
KRTSH!
CRASH!
COO-COO. COO-COO.

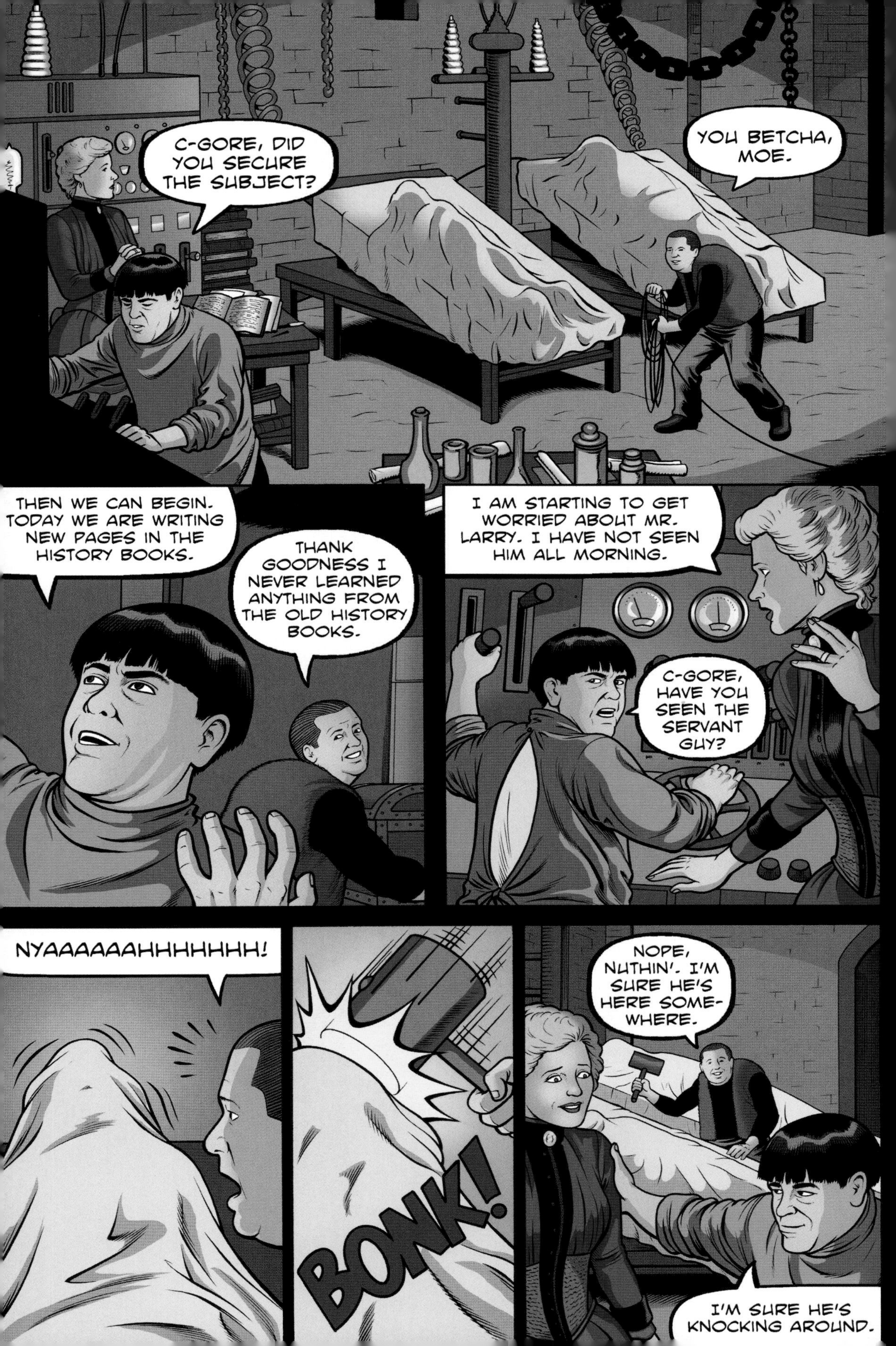
C-GORE, DID YOU SECURE THE SUBJECT?
YOU BETCHA, MOE.
THEN WE CAN BEGIN. TODAY WE ARE WRITING NEW PAGES IN THE HISTORY BOOKS.
THANK GOODNESS I NEVER LEARNED ANYTHING FROM THE OLD HISTORY BOOKS.
I AM STARTING TO GET WORRIED ABOUT MR. LARRY. I HAVE NOT SEEN HIM ALL MORNING.
C-GORE, HAVE YOU SEEN THE SERVANT GUY?
NYAAAAAAHHHHHHH!
BONK!
NOPE, NUTHIN'. I'M SURE HE'S HERE SOME-WHERE.
I'M SURE HE'S KNOCKING AROUND.

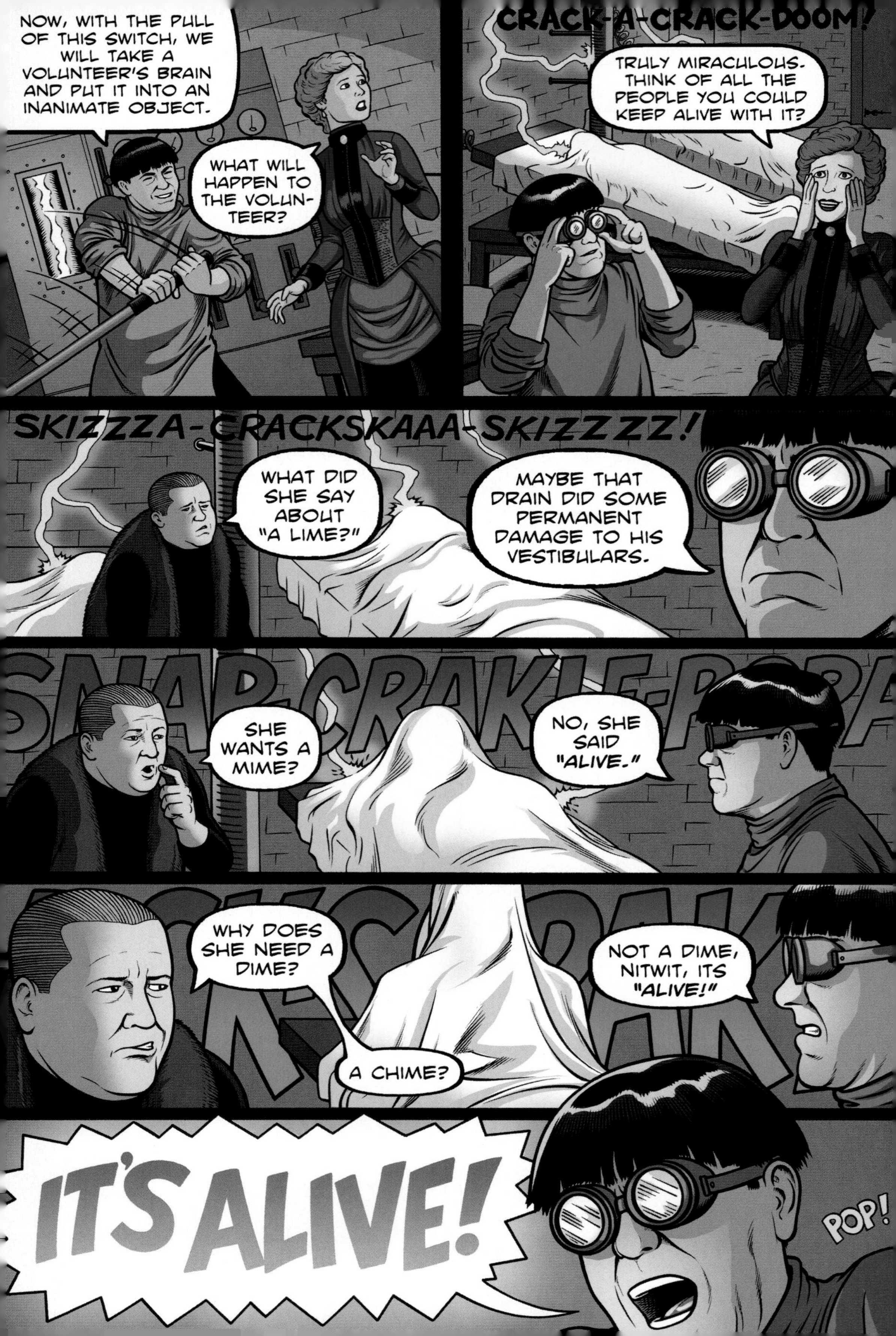
NOW, WITH THE PULL OF THIS SWITCH, WE WILL TAKE A VOLUNTEER'S BRAIN AND PUT IT INTO AN INANIMATE OBJECT.
WHAT WILL HAPPEN TO THE VOLUN-TEER?
CRACK-A-CRACK-DOOM!
TRULY MIRACULOUS. THINK OF ALL THE PEOPLE YOU COULD KEEP ALIVE WITH IT?
SKIZZZA-CRACKSKAAA-SKIZZZZZ!
WHAT DID SHE SAY ABOUT "A LIME?"
MAYBE THAT DRAIN DID SOME PERMANENT DAMAGE TO HIS VESTIBULARS.
SHE WANTS A MIME?
NO, SHE SAID "ALIVE."
WHY DOES SHE NEED A DIME?
A CHIME?
NOT A DIME, NITWIT, ITS "ALIVE!"
IT'S ALIVE!
POP!

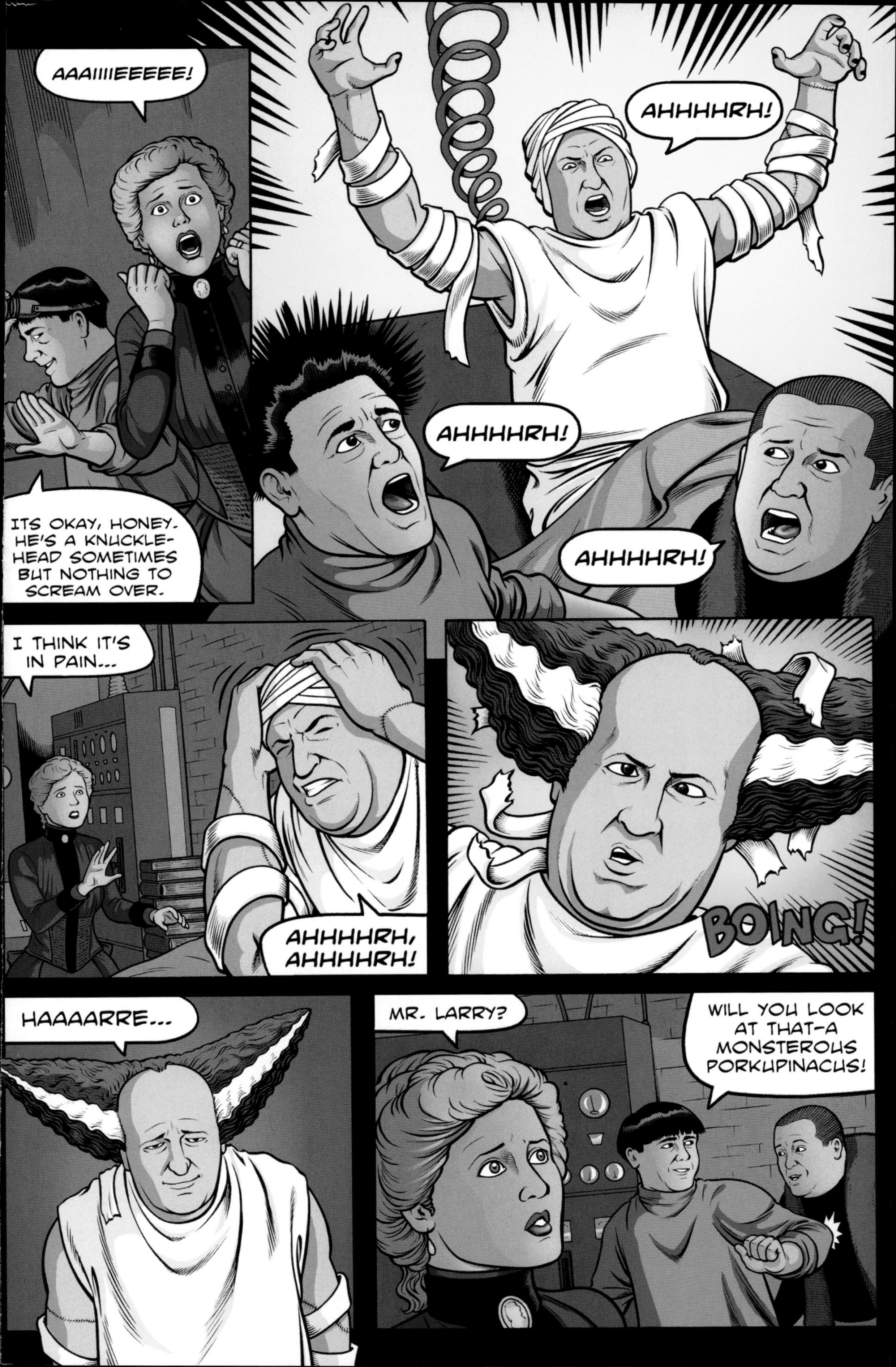
AAAIIIIEEEEE!
AHHHHRH!
AHHHHRH!
AHHHHRH!
ITS OKAY, HONEY. HE'S A KNUCKLE-HEAD SOMETIMES BUT NOTHING TO SCREAM OVER.
I THINK IT'S IN PAIN...
AHHHHRH, AHHHHRH!
BOING!
HAAAARRE...
MR. LARRY?
WILL YOU LOOK AT THAT-A MONSTEROUS PORKUPINACUS!

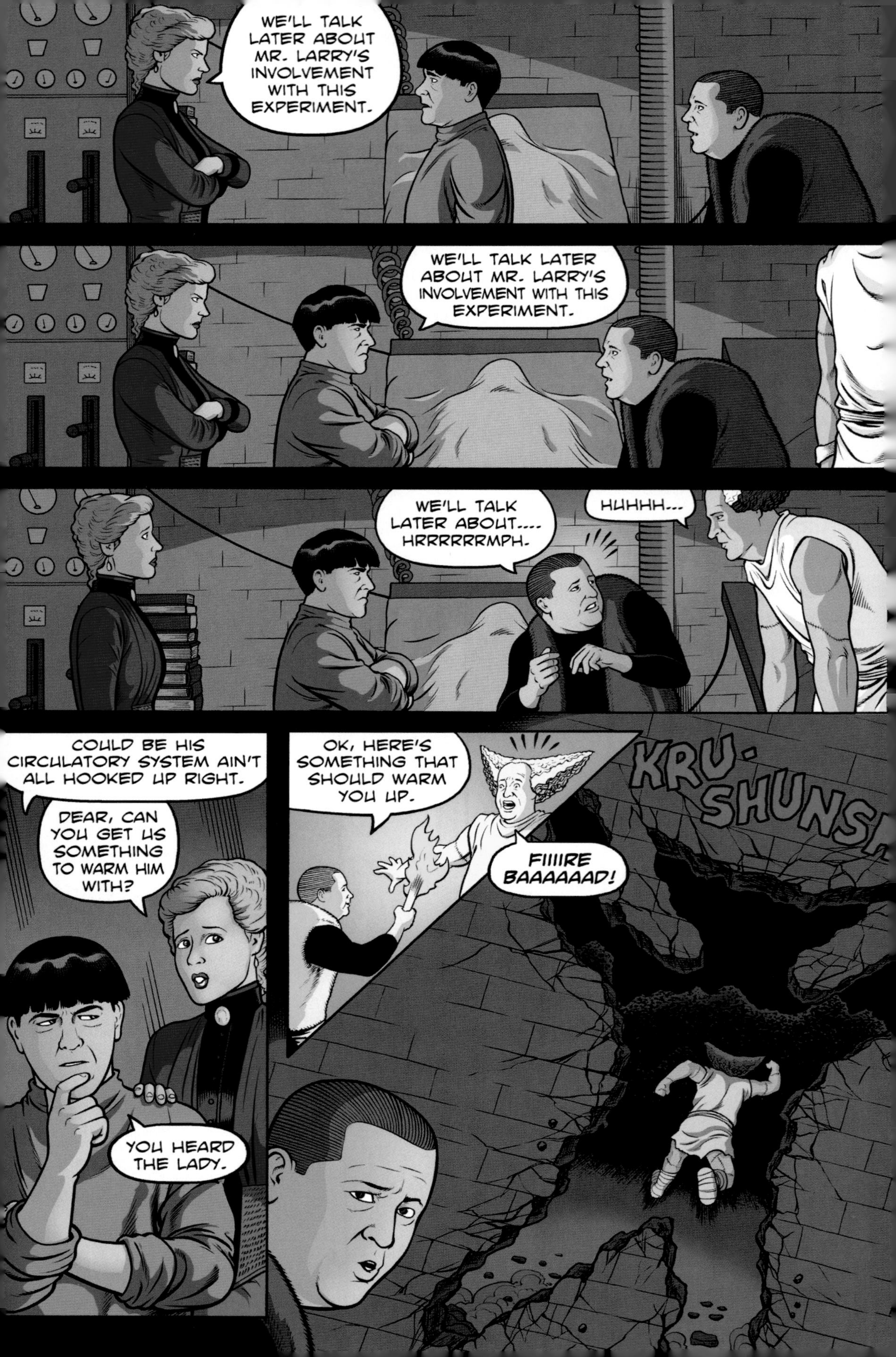

WE'LL TALK LATER ABOUT MR. LARRY'S INVOLVEMENT WITH THIS EXPERIMENT.
WE'LL TALK LATER ABOUT MR. LARRY'S INVOLVEMENT WITH THIS EXPERIMENT.
WE'LL TALK LATER ABOUT.... HRRRRRRMPH.
HUHHH...
COULD BE HIS CIRCULATORY SYSTEM AIN'T ALL HOOKED UP RIGHT.
DEAR, CAN YOU GET US SOMETHING TO WARM HIM WITH?
YOU HEARD THE LADY.
OK, HERE'S SOMETHING THAT SHOULD WARM YOU UP.
FIIIIRE BAAAAAAD!
KRU-SHUNSH

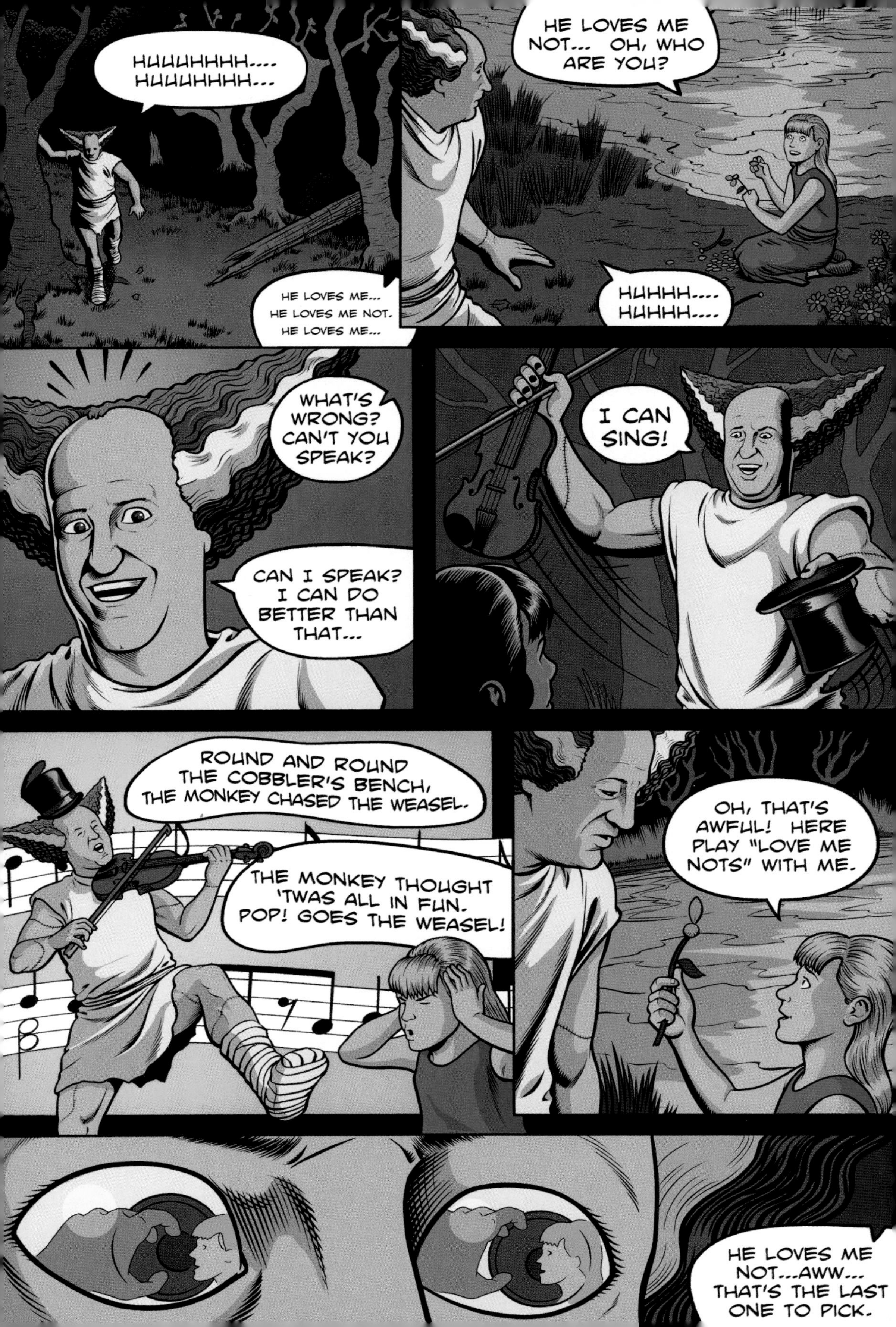
HUUUHHHH....
HUUUHHHH...
HE LOVES ME...
HE LOVES ME NOT.
HE LOVES ME...
HE LOVES ME NOT... OH, WHO ARE YOU?
HUHHH.... HUHHH....
WHAT'S WRONG? CAN'T YOU SPEAK?
CAN I SPEAK? I CAN DO BETTER THAN THAT...
I CAN SING!
ROUND AND ROUND THE COBBLER'S BENCH, THE MONKEY CHASED THE WEASEL.
THE MONKEY THOUGHT 'TWAS ALL IN FUN. POP! GOES THE WEASEL!
OH, THAT'S AWFUL! HERE PLAY "LOVE ME NOTS" WITH ME.
HE LOVES ME NOT...AWW... THAT'S THE LAST ONE TO PICK.

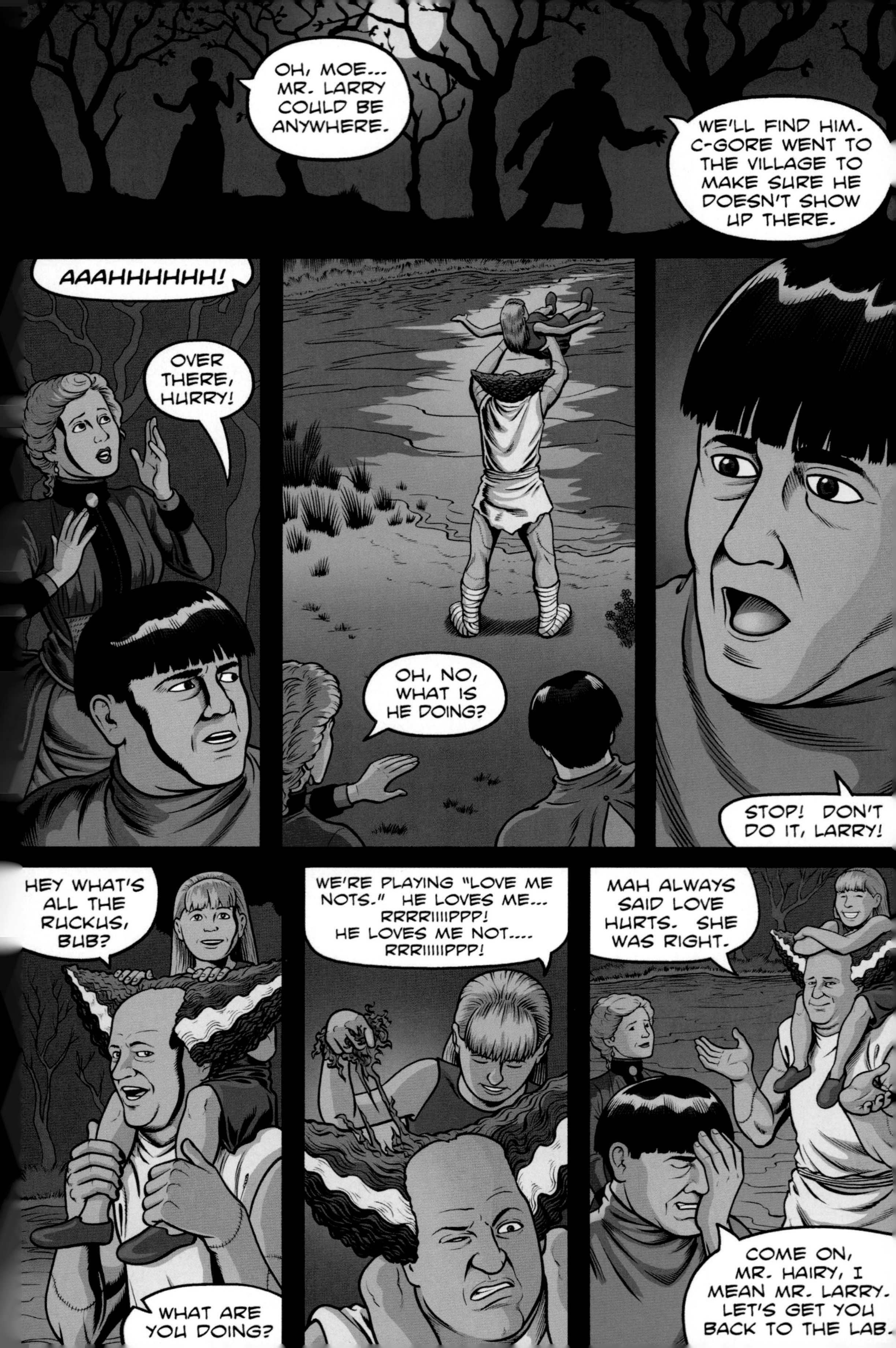
OH, MOE... MR. LARRY COULD BE ANYWHERE.
WE'LL FIND HIM. C-GORE WENT TO THE VILLAGE TO MAKE SURE HE DOESN'T SHOW UP THERE.
AAAHHHHHH!
OVER THERE, HURRY!
OH, NO, WHAT IS HE DOING?
STOP! DON'T DO IT, LARRY!
HEY WHAT'S ALL THE RUCKUS, BUB?
WHAT ARE YOU DOING?
WE'RE PLAYING "LOVE ME NOTS." HE LOVES ME... RRRRIIIIPPP! HE LOVES ME NOT.... RRRIIIIIPPP!
MAH ALWAYS SAID LOVE HURTS. SHE WAS RIGHT.
COME ON, MR. HAIRY, I MEAN MR. LARRY. LET'S GET YOU BACK TO THE LAB.

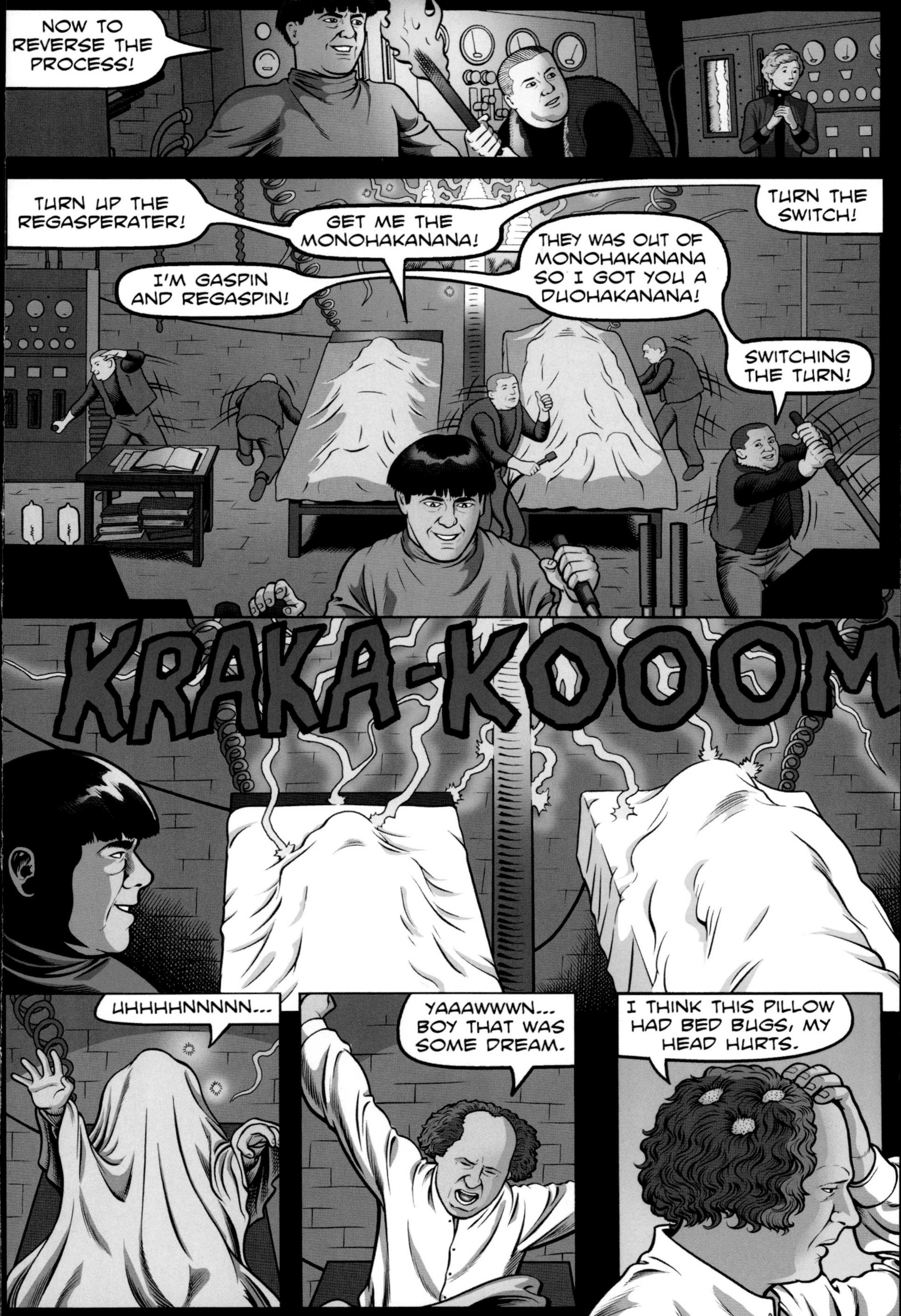
NOW TO REVERSE THE PROCESS!
TURN UP THE REGASPERATER!
GET ME THE MONOHAKANANA!
TURN THE SWITCH!
I'M GASPIN AND REGASPIN!
THEY WAS OUT OF MONOHAKANANA SO I GOT YOU A DUOHAKANANA!
SWITCHING THE TURN!
KRAKA-KOOOM
UHHHHNNNNN...
YAAAWWWN... BOY THAT WAS SOME DREAM.
I THINK THIS PILLOW HAD BED BUGS, MY HEAD HURTS.

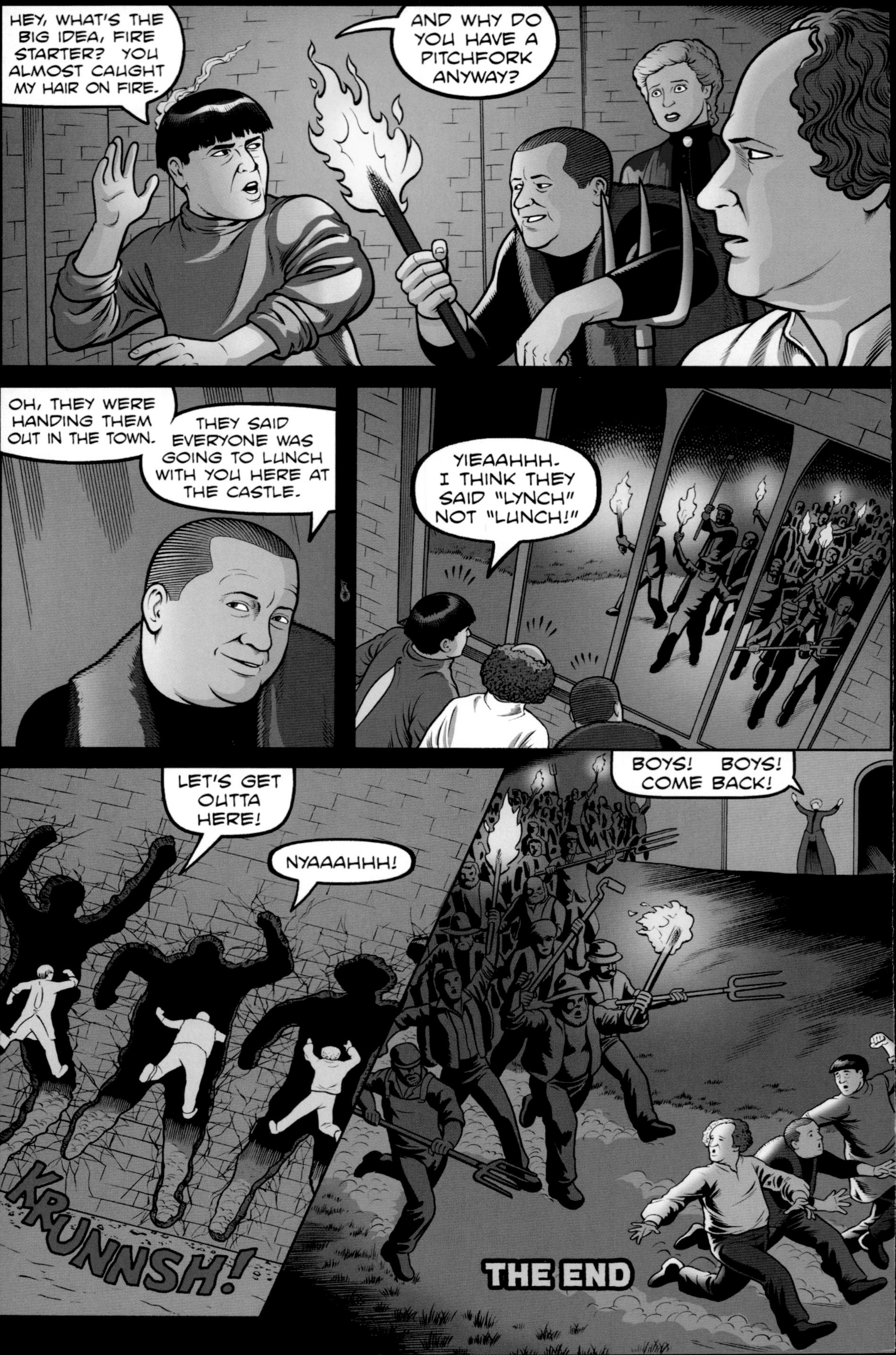
HEY, WHAT'S THE BIG IDEA, FIRE STARTER? YOU ALMOST CAUGHT MY HAIR ON FIRE.
AND WHY DO YOU HAVE A PITCHFORK ANYWAY?
OH, THEY WERE HANDING THEM OUT IN THE TOWN.
THEY SAID EVERYONE WAS GOING TO LUNCH WITH YOU HERE AT THE CASTLE.
YIEAAHHH. I THINK THEY SAID "LYNCH" NOT "LUNCH!"
LET'S GET OUTTA HERE!
NYAAAHHH!
BOYS! BOYS! COME BACK!
KRUNNSH!
THE END

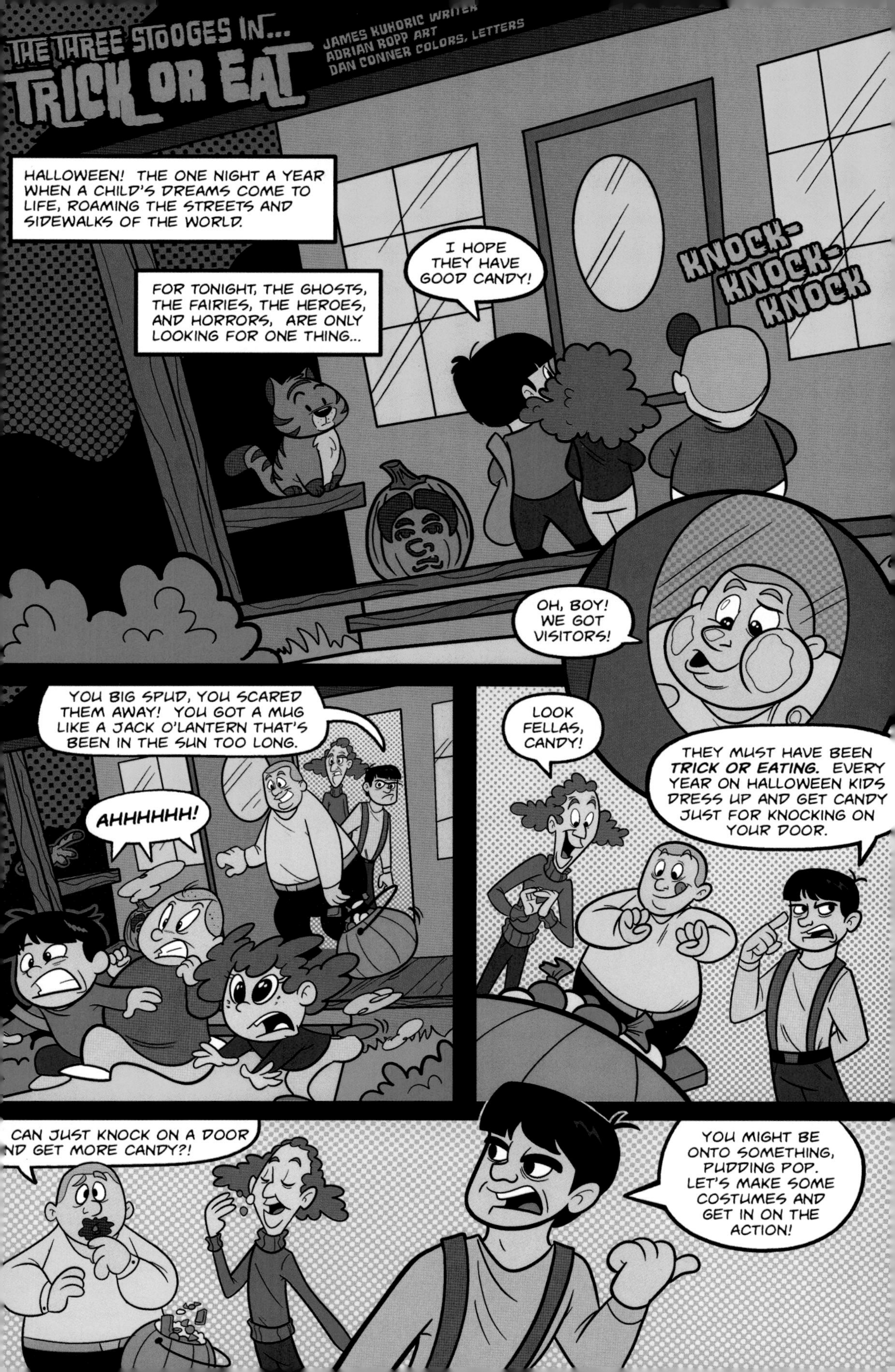
THE THREE STOOGES IN...
TRICK OR EAT
JAMES KUHORIC WRITER
ADRIAN ROPP ART
DAN CONNER COLORS, LETTERS
HALLOWEEN! THE ONE NIGHT A YEAR WHEN A CHILD'S DREAMS COME TO LIFE, ROAMING THE STREETS AND SIDEWALKS OF THE WORLD.
FOR TONIGHT, THE GHOSTS, THE FAIRIES, THE HEROES, AND HORRORS, ARE ONLY LOOKING FOR ONE THING...
I HOPE THEY HAVE GOOD CANDY!
KNOCK-KNOCK-KNOCK
OH, BOY! WE GOT VISITORS!
YOU BIG SPUD, YOU SCARED THEM AWAY! YOU GOT A MUG LIKE A JACK O'LANTERN THAT'S BEEN IN THE SUN TOO LONG.
AHHHHHH!
LOOK FELLAS, CANDY!
THEY MUST HAVE BEEN TRICK OR EATING. EVERY YEAR ON HALLOWEEN KIDS DRESS UP AND GET CANDY JUST FOR KNOCKING ON YOUR DOOR.
CAN JUST KNOCK ON A DOOR
ND GET MORE CANDY?!
YOU MIGHT BE ONTO SOMETHING, PUDDING POP. LET'S MAKE SOME COSTUMES AND GET IN ON THE ACTION!

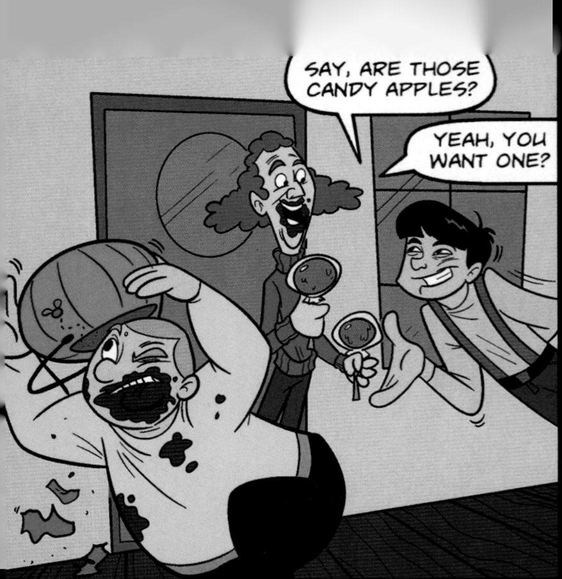
SAY, ARE THOSE CANDY APPLES?
YEAH, YOU WANT ONE?

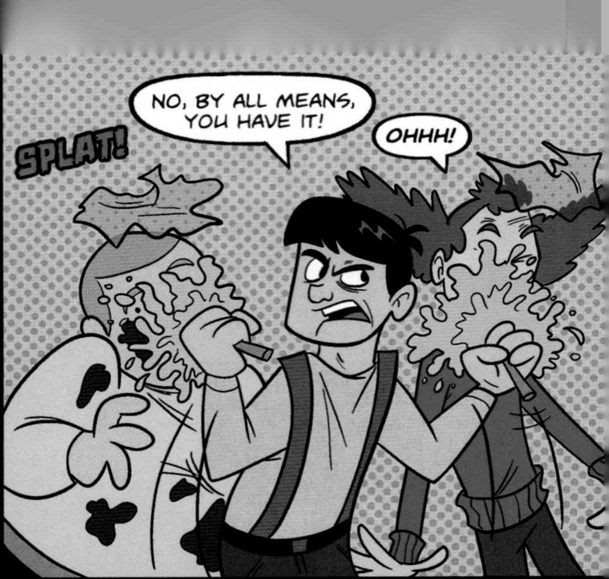
SPLAT!
NO, BY ALL MEANS, YOU HAVE IT!
OHHH!

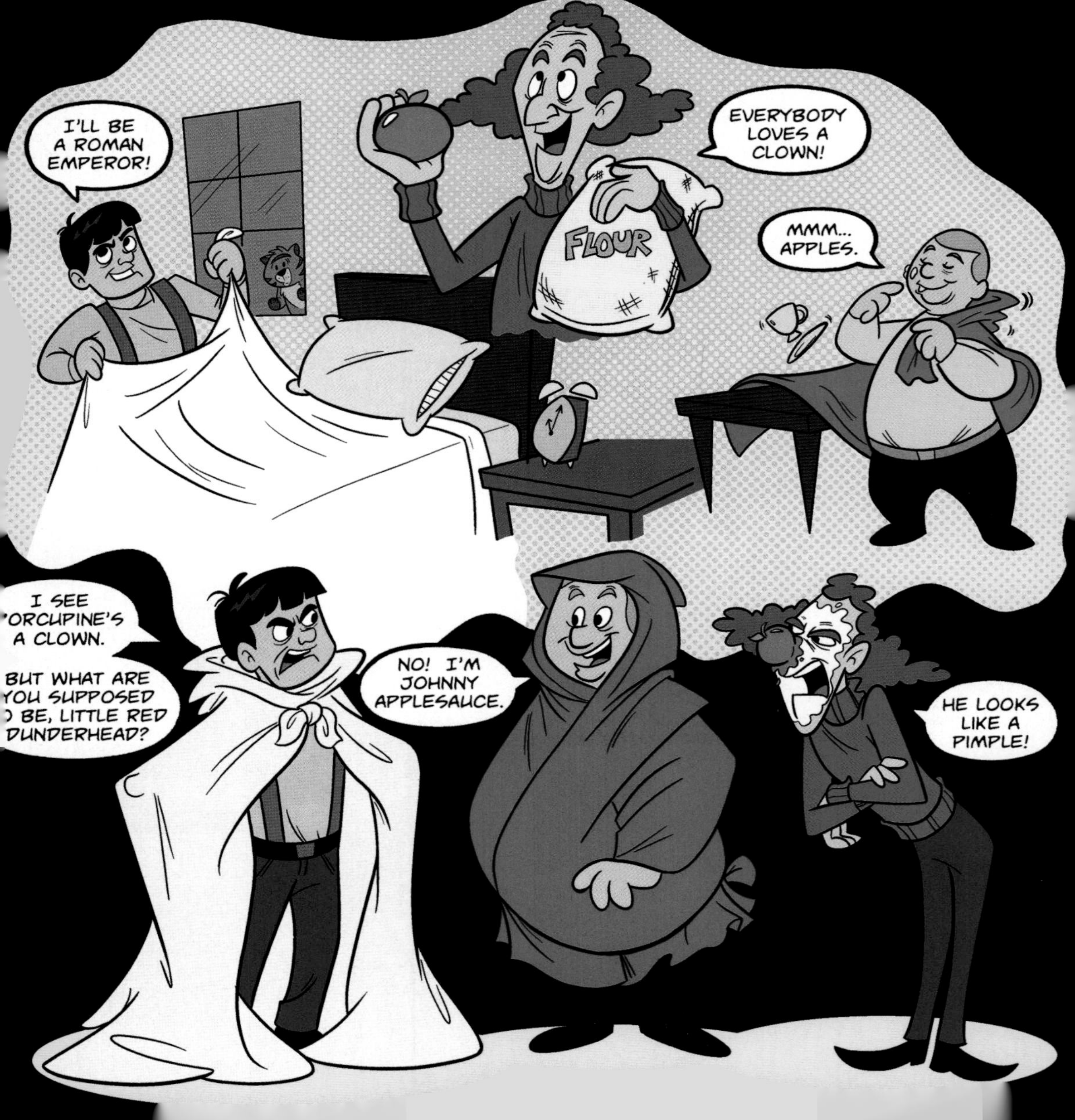
I'LL BE A ROMAN EMPEROR!
EVERYBODY LOVES A CLOWN!
FLOUR
MMM... APPLES.
I SEE PORCUPINE'S A CLOWN.
BUT WHAT ARE YOU SUPPOSED TO BE, LITTLE RED DUNDERHEAD?
NO! I'M JOHNNY APPLESAUCE.
HE LOOKS LIKE A PIMPLE!

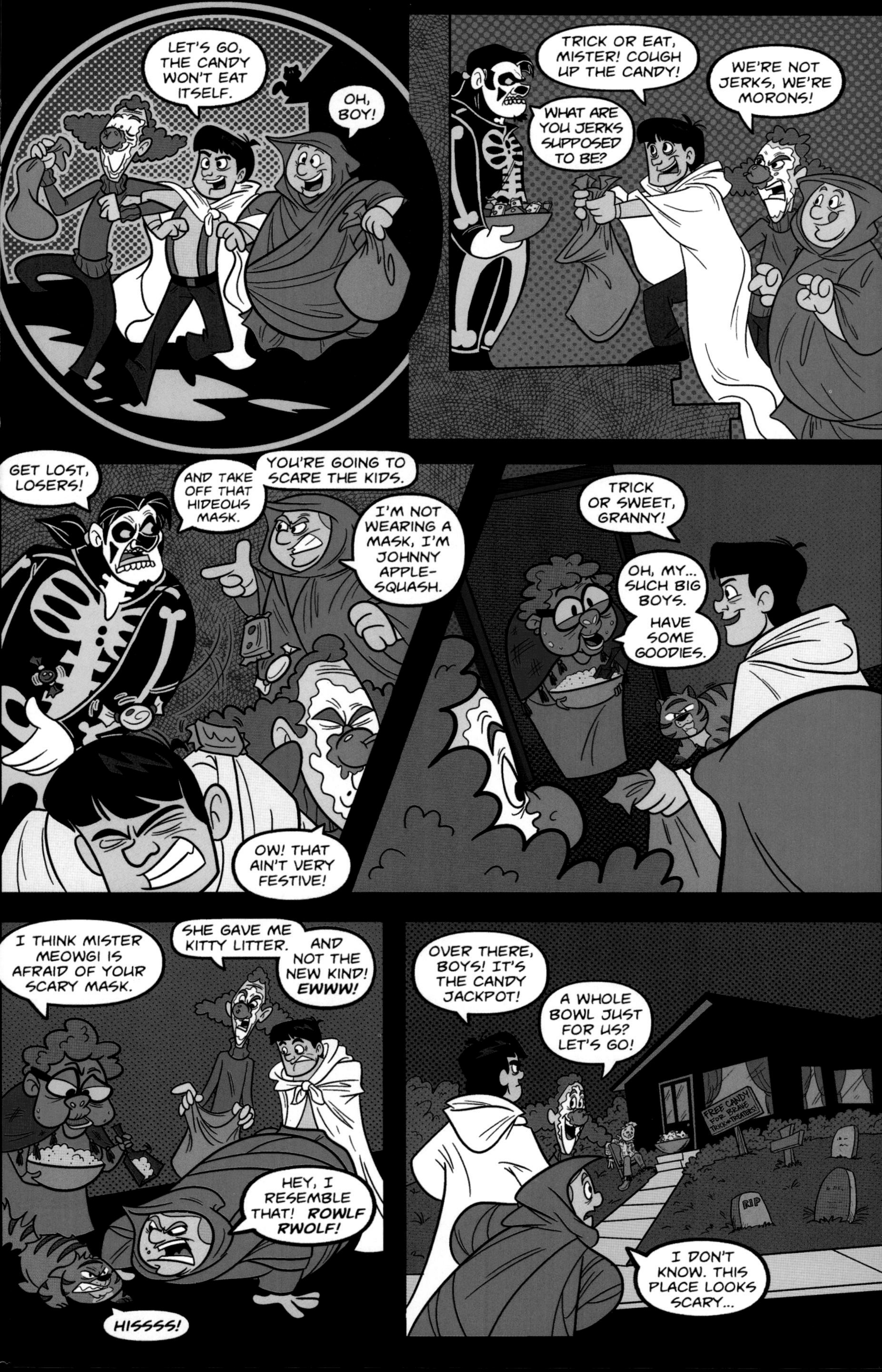

LET'S GO, THE CANDY WON'T EAT ITSELF.
OH, BOY!
TRICK OR EAT, MISTER! COUGH UP THE CANDY!
WHAT ARE YOU JERKS SUPPOSED TO BE?
WE'RE NOT JERKS, WE'RE MORONS!
GET LOST, LOSERS!
AND TAKE OFF THAT HIDEOUS MASK.
YOU'RE GOING TO SCARE THE KIDS.
I'M NOT WEARING A MASK, I'M JOHNNY APPLE-SQUASH.
OW! THAT AIN'T VERY FESTIVE!
TRICK OR SWEET, GRANNY!
OH, MY... SUCH BIG BOYS.
HAVE SOME GOODIES.
I THINK MISTER MEOWGI IS AFRAID OF YOUR SCARY MASK.
SHE GAVE ME KITTY LITTER.
AND NOT THE NEW KIND! **EWWW!**
HEY, I RESEMBLE THAT! ***ROWLF RWOLF!***
HISSSS!
OVER THERE, BOYS! IT'S THE CANDY JACKPOT!
A WHOLE BOWL JUST FOR US? LET'S GO!
FREE CANDY FOR BRAVE TRICK-OR-TREATERS!
RIP
I DON'T KNOW. THIS PLACE LOOKS SCARY...

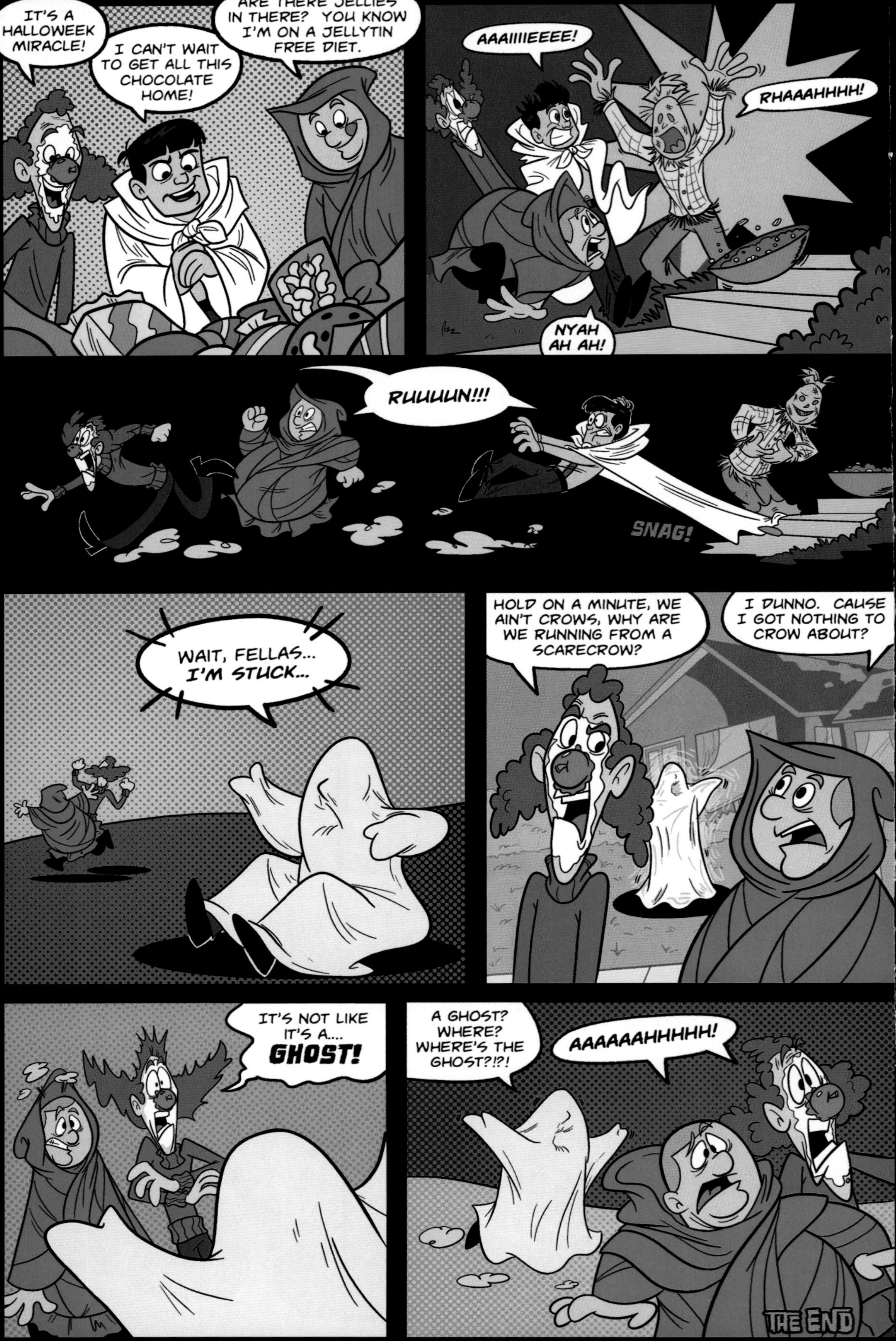
IT'S A HALLOWEEK MIRACLE!
I CAN'T WAIT TO GET ALL THIS CHOCOLATE HOME!
ARE THERE JELLIES IN THERE? YOU KNOW I'M ON A JELLYTIN FREE DIET.
AAAIIIIEEEE!
RHAAAHHHH!
NYAH AH AH!
RUUUUN!!!
SNAG!
WAIT, FELLAS... I'M STUCK...
HOLD ON A MINUTE, WE AIN'T CROWS, WHY ARE WE RUNNING FROM A SCARECROW?
I DUNNO. CAUSE I GOT NOTHING TO CROW ABOUT?
IT'S NOT LIKE IT'S A.... GHOST!
A GHOST? WHERE? WHERE'S THE GHOST?!?!
AAAAAAHHHHH!
THE END

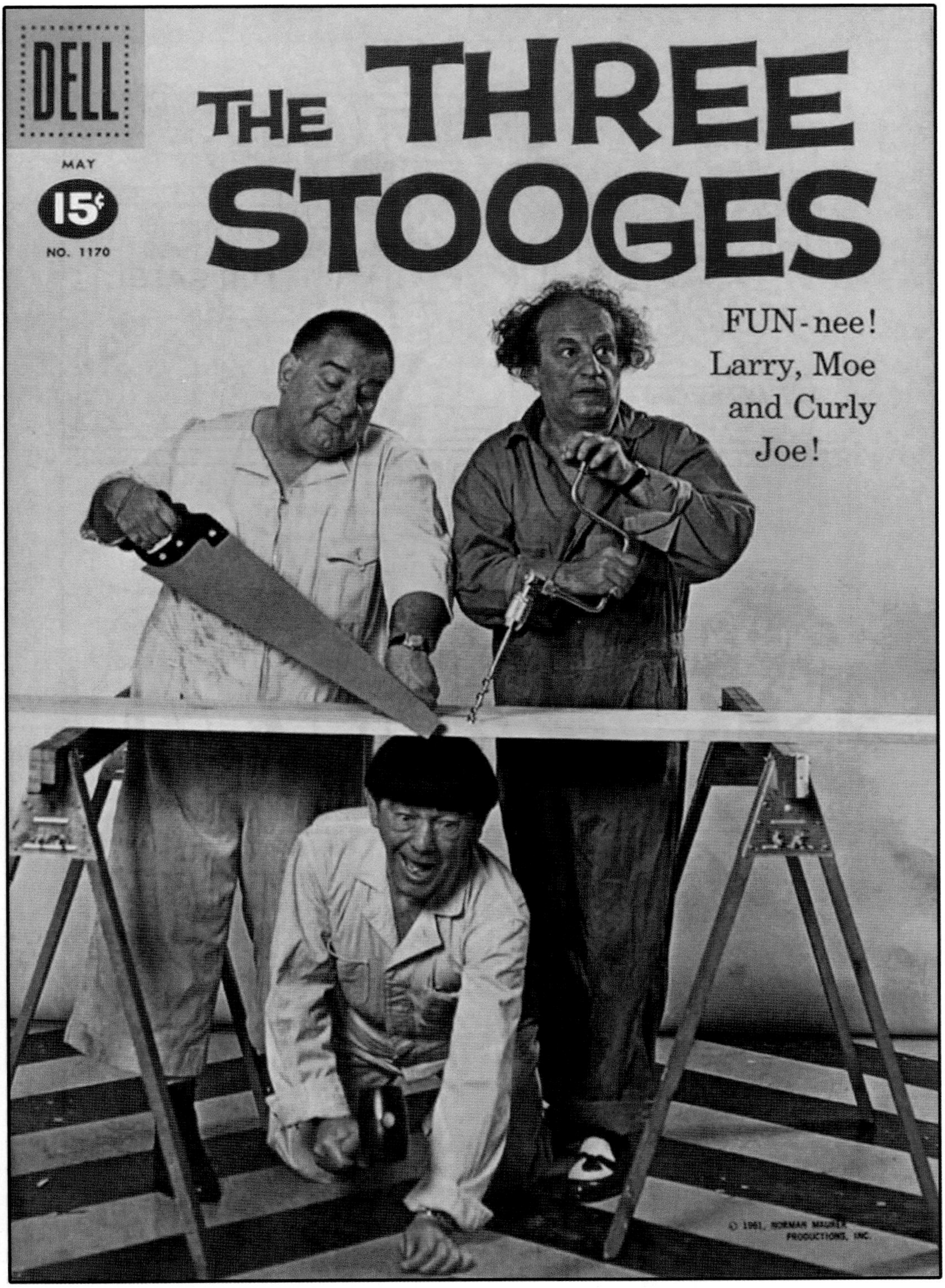
DELL
MAY
15¢
NO. 1170
THE THREE STOOGES
FUN-nee! Larry, Moe and Curly Joe!
© 1961, NORMAN MAURER PRODUCTIONS, INC.

AMERICAN MYTHOLOGY PROUDLY PRESENTS A TALE FROM THE THREE STOOGES PAST FEATURING LARRY, MOE, AND CURLY JOE!

Originally published in *Dell Four Color* #1170 (1961)
Writer: Jerry Belson   Artist: Sparky Moore

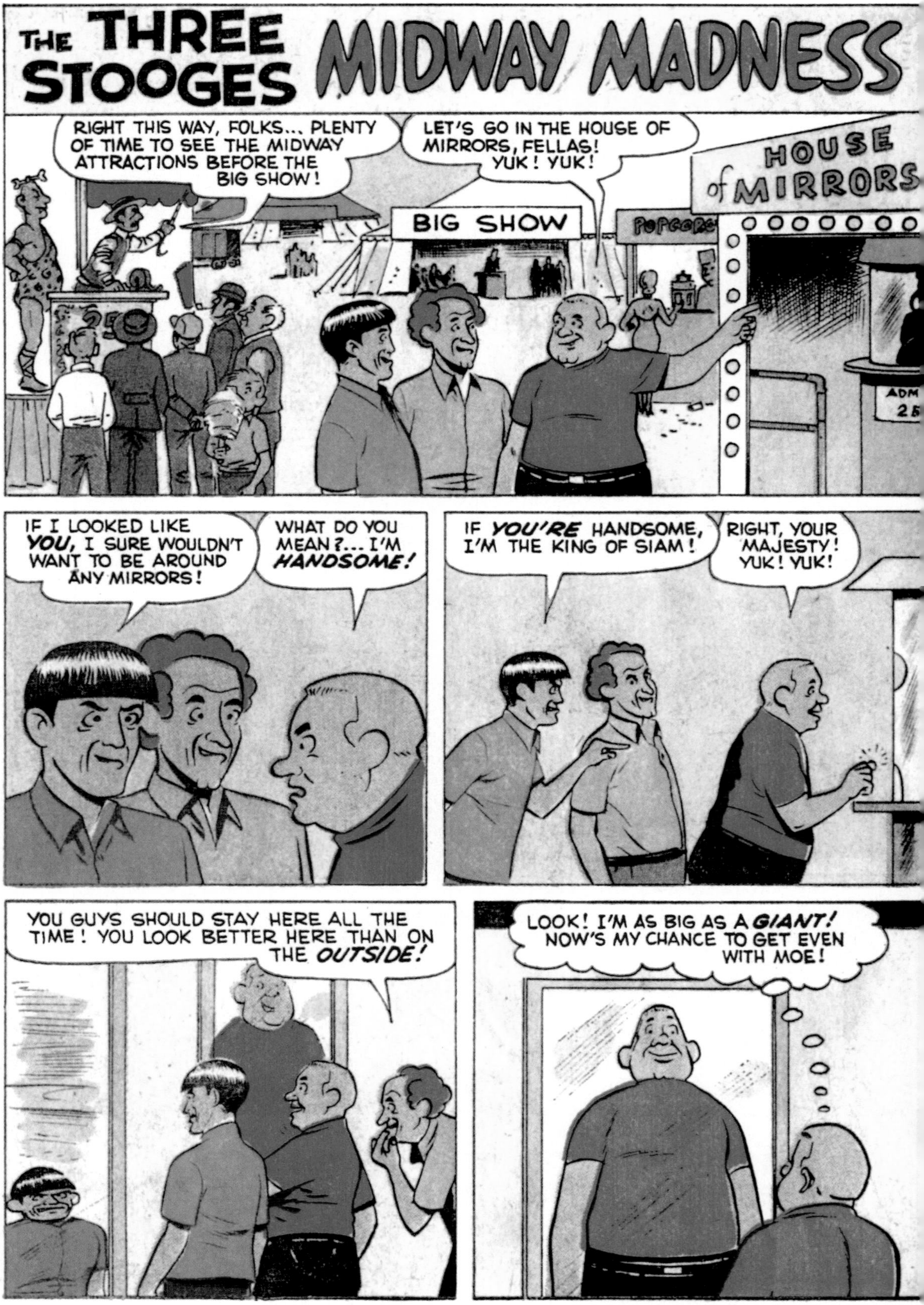

THE THREE STOOGES
MIDWAY MADNESS
RIGHT THIS WAY, FOLKS... PLENTY OF TIME TO SEE THE MIDWAY ATTRACTIONS BEFORE THE BIG SHOW!
LET'S GO IN THE HOUSE OF MIRRORS, FELLAS! YUK! YUK!
HOUSE of MIRRORS
BIG SHOW
IF I LOOKED LIKE YOU, I SURE WOULDN'T WANT TO BE AROUND ANY MIRRORS!
WHAT DO YOU MEAN?... I'M HANDSOME!
IF YOU'RE HANDSOME, I'M THE KING OF SIAM!
RIGHT, YOUR MAJESTY! YUK! YUK!
YOU GUYS SHOULD STAY HERE ALL THE TIME! YOU LOOK BETTER HERE THAN ON THE OUTSIDE!
LOOK! I'M AS BIG AS A GIANT! NOW'S MY CHANCE TO GET EVEN WITH MOE!

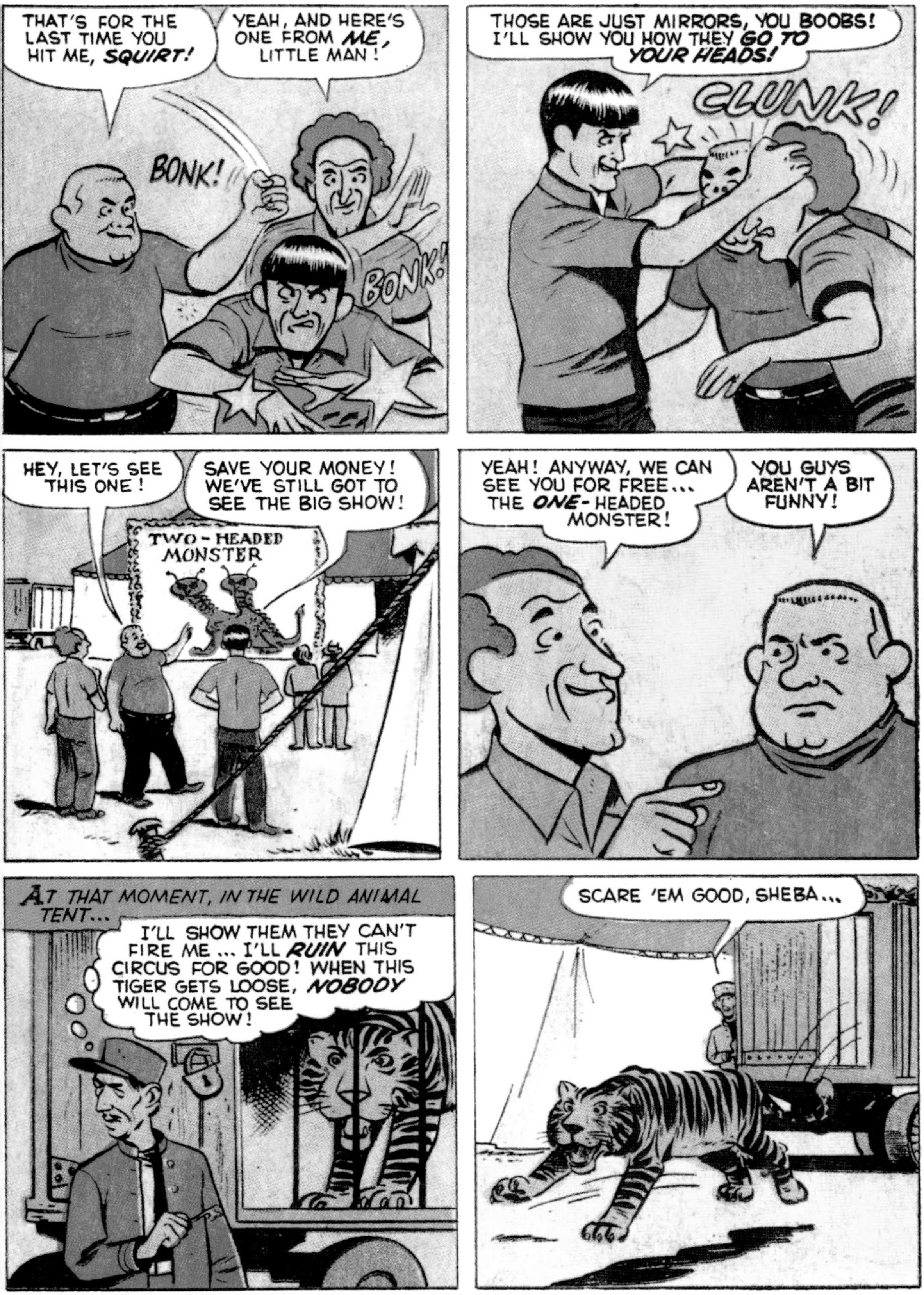
THAT'S FOR THE LAST TIME YOU HIT ME, SQUIRT!
YEAH, AND HERE'S ONE FROM ME, LITTLE MAN!
BONK!
BONK!
THOSE ARE JUST MIRRORS, YOU BOOBS! I'LL SHOW YOU HOW THEY GO TO YOUR HEADS!
CLUNK!
HEY, LET'S SEE THIS ONE!
SAVE YOUR MONEY! WE'VE STILL GOT TO SEE THE BIG SHOW!
TWO-HEADED MONSTER
YEAH! ANYWAY, WE CAN SEE YOU FOR FREE... THE ONE-HEADED MONSTER!
YOU GUYS AREN'T A BIT FUNNY!
AT THAT MOMENT, IN THE WILD ANIMAL TENT...
I'LL SHOW THEM THEY CAN'T FIRE ME ... I'LL RUIN THIS CIRCUS FOR GOOD! WHEN THIS TIGER GETS LOOSE, NOBODY WILL COME TO SEE THE SHOW!
SCARE 'EM GOOD, SHEBA...

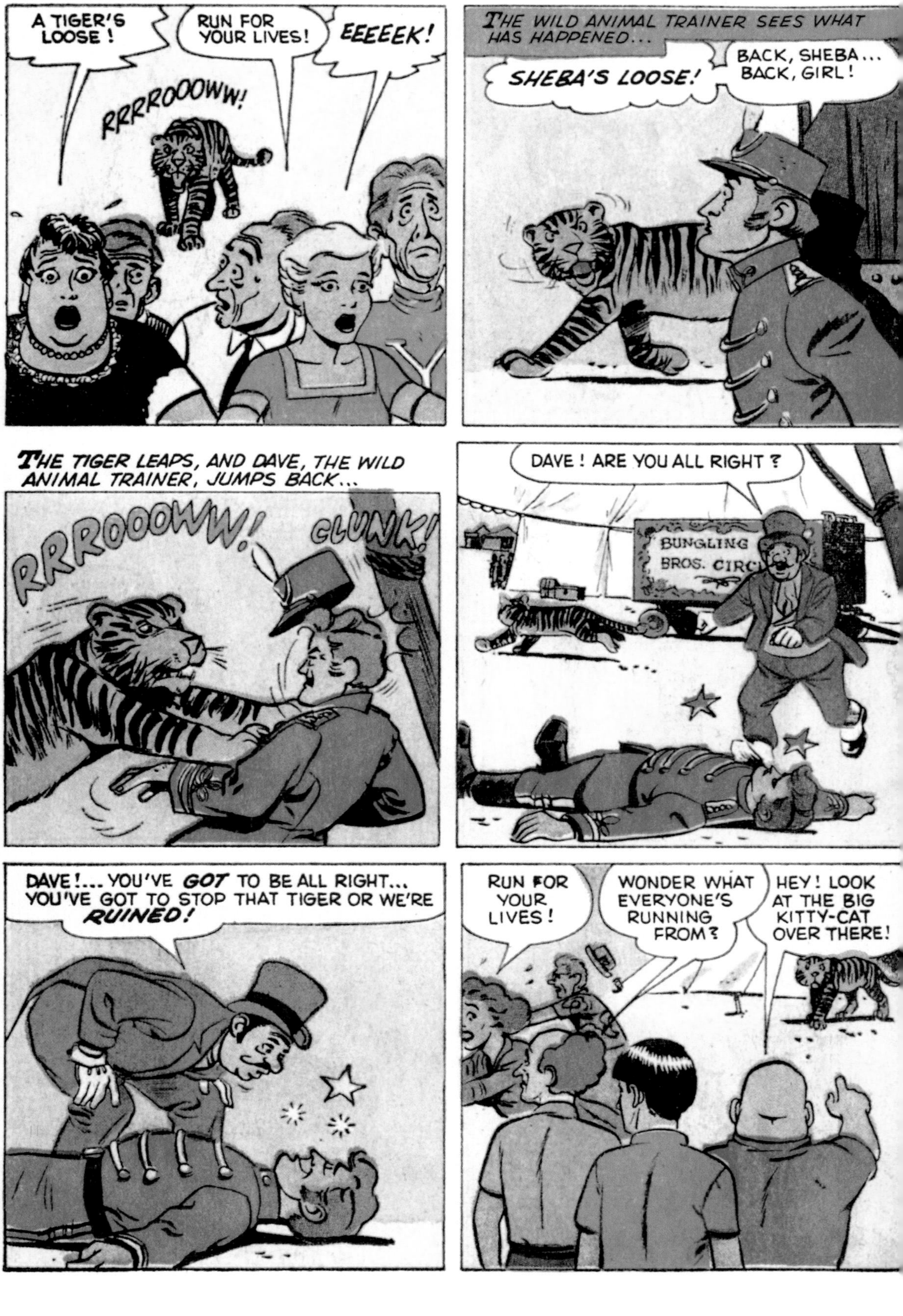
A TIGER'S LOOSE!
RUN FOR YOUR LIVES!
EEEEEK!
RRRROOOWW!
THE WILD ANIMAL TRAINER SEES WHAT HAS HAPPENED...
SHEBA'S LOOSE!
BACK, SHEBA... BACK, GIRL!
THE TIGER LEAPS, AND DAVE, THE WILD ANIMAL TRAINER, JUMPS BACK...
RRROOOWW!
CLUNK!
DAVE! ARE YOU ALL RIGHT?
BUNGLING BROS. CIRC
DAVE!... YOU'VE GOT TO BE ALL RIGHT... YOU'VE GOT TO STOP THAT TIGER OR WE'RE RUINED!
RUN FOR YOUR LIVES!
WONDER WHAT EVERYONE'S RUNNING FROM?
HEY! LOOK AT THE BIG KITTY-CAT OVER THERE!

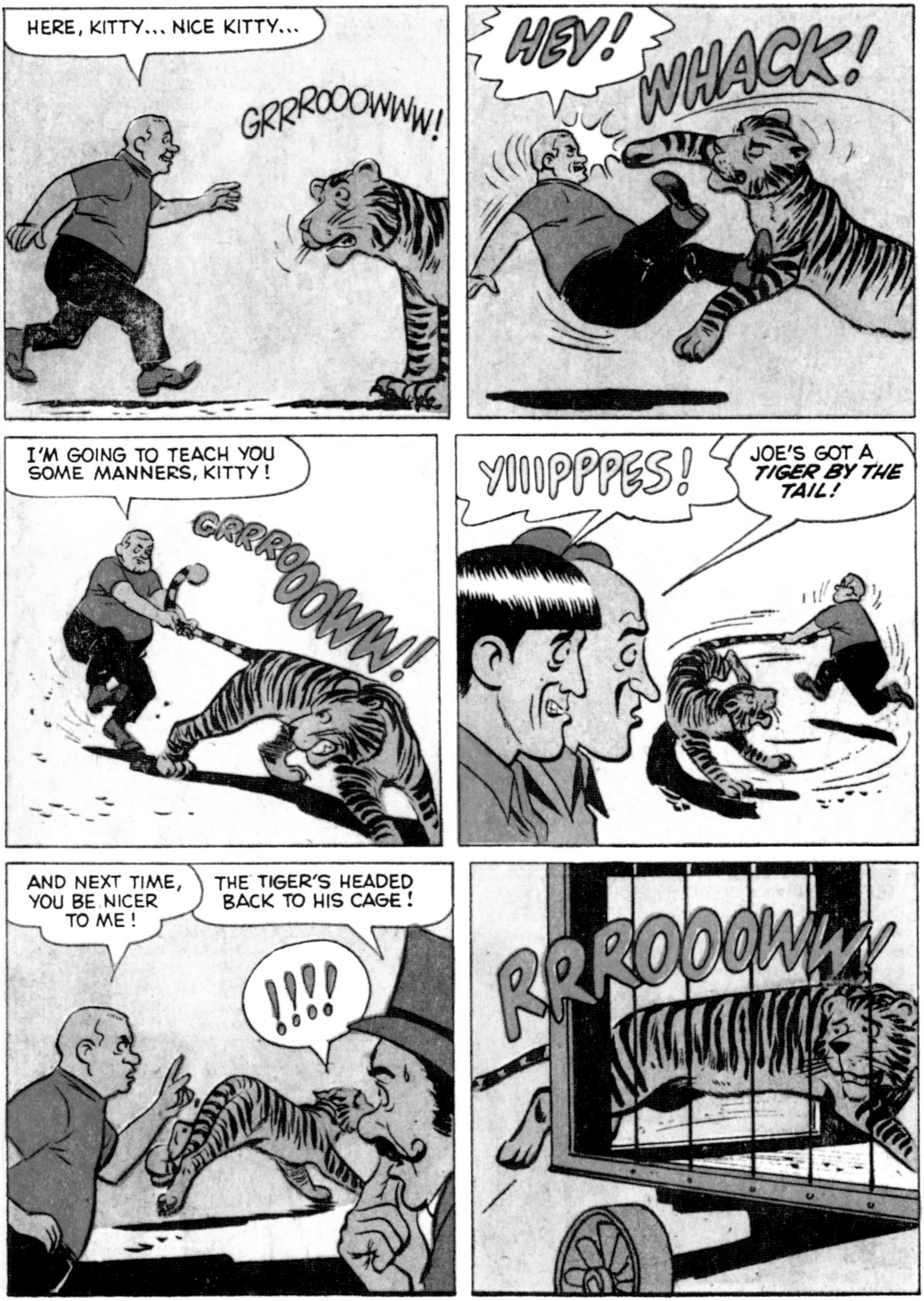
HERE, KITTY... NICE KITTY...
GRRROOOWWW!
HEY!
WHACK!
I'M GOING TO TEACH YOU SOME MANNERS, KITTY!
GRRROOOWW!
YIIIPPPES!
JOE'S GOT A *TIGER BY THE TAIL!*
AND NEXT TIME, YOU BE NICER TO ME!
THE TIGER'S HEADED BACK TO HIS CAGE!
!!!!
RRROOOWW!

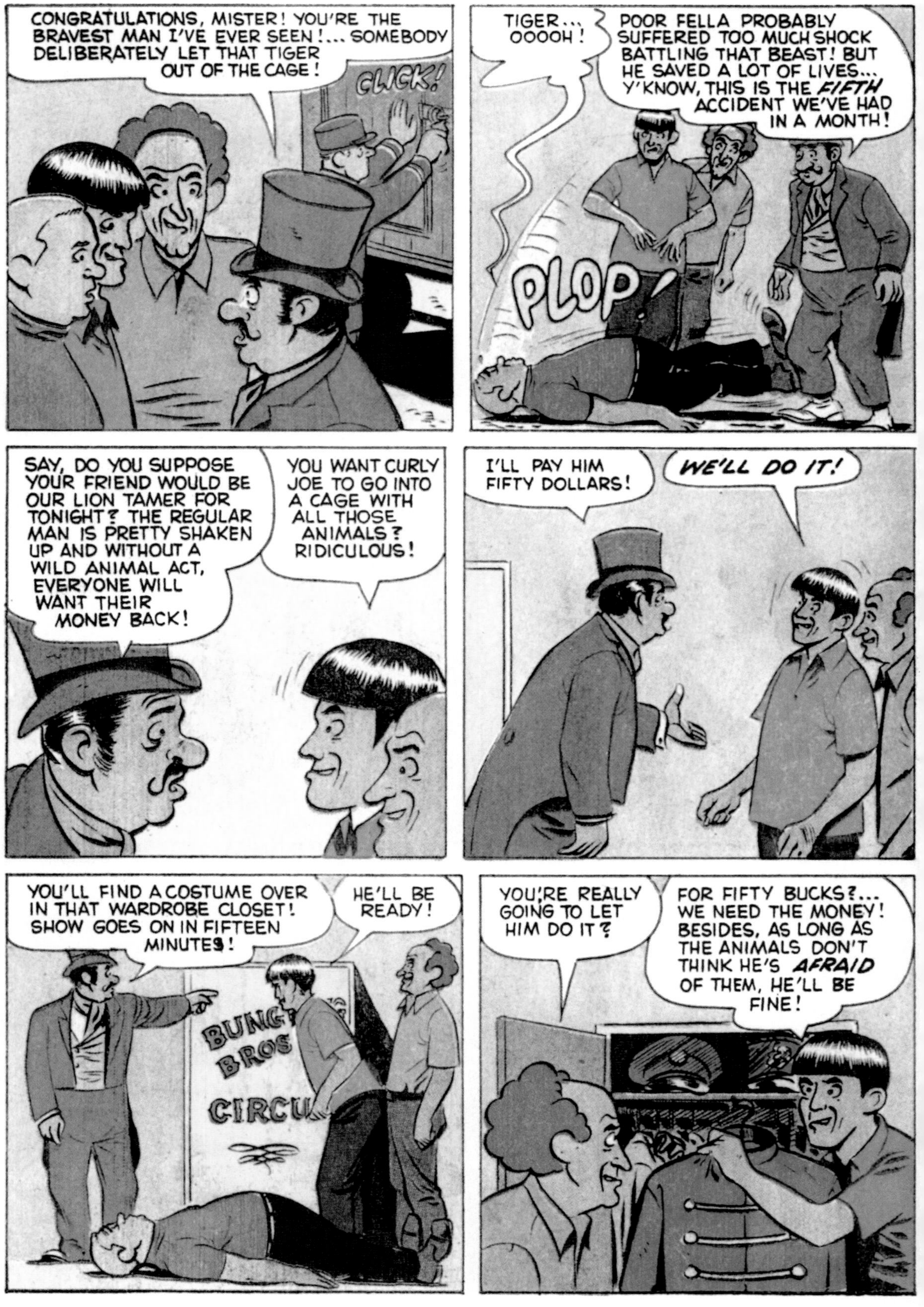
CONGRATULATIONS, MISTER! YOU'RE THE BRAVEST MAN I'VE EVER SEEN!... SOMEBODY DELIBERATELY LET THAT TIGER OUT OF THE CAGE!
CLICK!
TIGER... OOOOH!
POOR FELLA PROBABLY SUFFERED TOO MUCH SHOCK BATTLING THAT BEAST! BUT HE SAVED A LOT OF LIVES... Y'KNOW, THIS IS THE FIFTH ACCIDENT WE'VE HAD IN A MONTH!
PLOP!
SAY, DO YOU SUPPOSE YOUR FRIEND WOULD BE OUR LION TAMER FOR TONIGHT? THE REGULAR MAN IS PRETTY SHAKEN UP AND WITHOUT A WILD ANIMAL ACT, EVERYONE WILL WANT THEIR MONEY BACK!
YOU WANT CURLY JOE TO GO INTO A CAGE WITH ALL THOSE ANIMALS? RIDICULOUS!
I'LL PAY HIM FIFTY DOLLARS!
WE'LL DO IT!
YOU'LL FIND A COSTUME OVER IN THAT WARDROBE CLOSET! SHOW GOES ON IN FIFTEEN MINUTES!
HE'LL BE READY!
BUNG BROS CIRCU
YOU'RE REALLY GOING TO LET HIM DO IT?
FOR FIFTY BUCKS?... WE NEED THE MONEY! BESIDES, AS LONG AS THE ANIMALS DON'T THINK HE'S AFRAID OF THEM, HE'LL BE FINE!

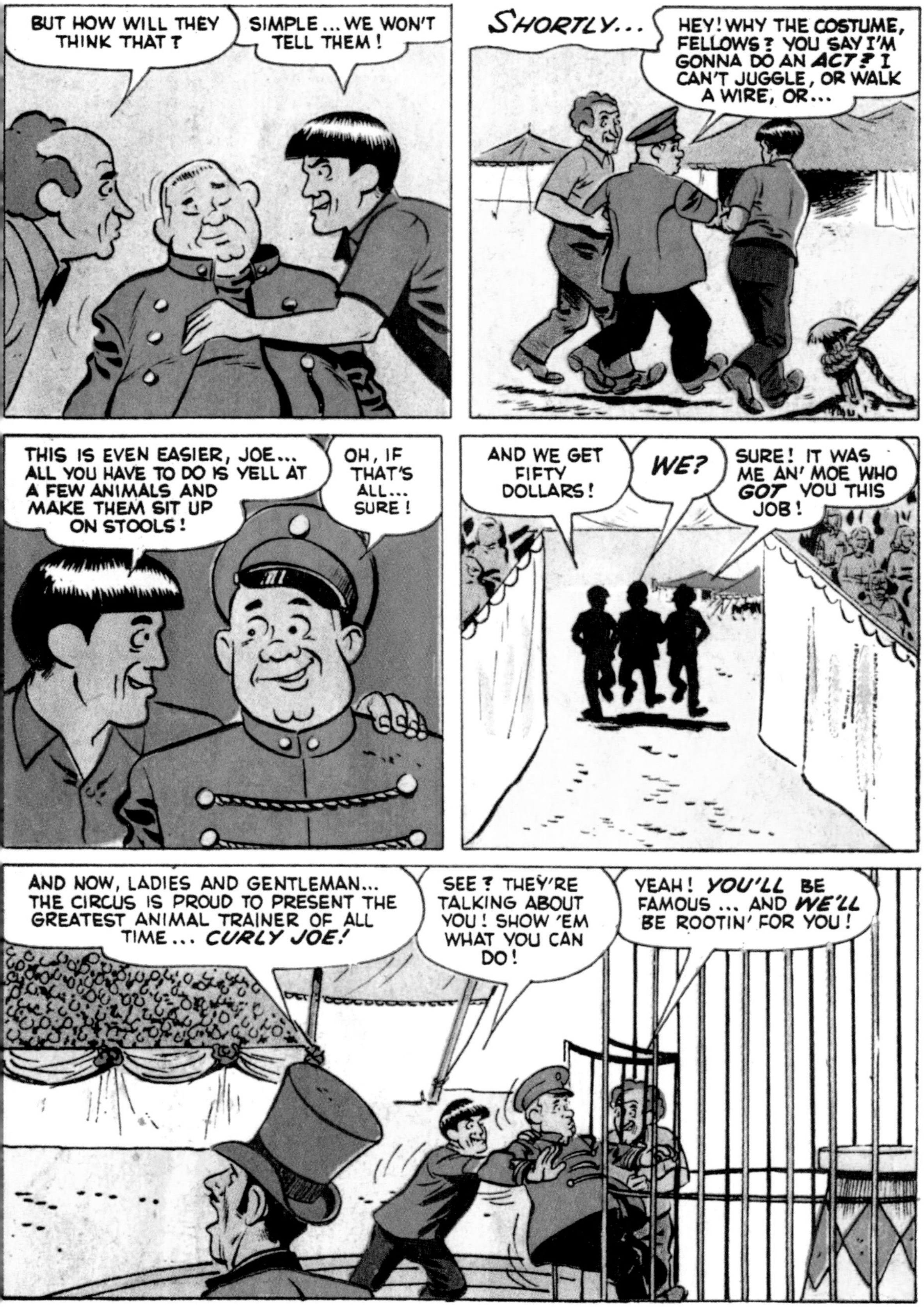
BUT HOW WILL THEY THINK THAT ?
SIMPLE ... WE WON'T TELL THEM !
SHORTLY...
HEY! WHY THE COSTUME, FELLOWS ? YOU SAY I'M GONNA DO AN ACT ? I CAN'T JUGGLE, OR WALK A WIRE, OR...
THIS IS EVEN EASIER, JOE... ALL YOU HAVE TO DO IS YELL AT A FEW ANIMALS AND MAKE THEM SIT UP ON STOOLS !
OH, IF THAT'S ALL... SURE !
AND WE GET FIFTY DOLLARS !
WE?
SURE ! IT WAS ME AN' MOE WHO GOT YOU THIS JOB !
AND NOW, LADIES AND GENTLEMAN... THE CIRCUS IS PROUD TO PRESENT THE GREATEST ANIMAL TRAINER OF ALL TIME... CURLY JOE!
SEE ? THEY'RE TALKING ABOUT YOU ! SHOW 'EM WHAT YOU CAN DO !
YEAH ! YOU'LL BE FAMOUS ... AND WE'LL BE ROOTIN' FOR YOU !

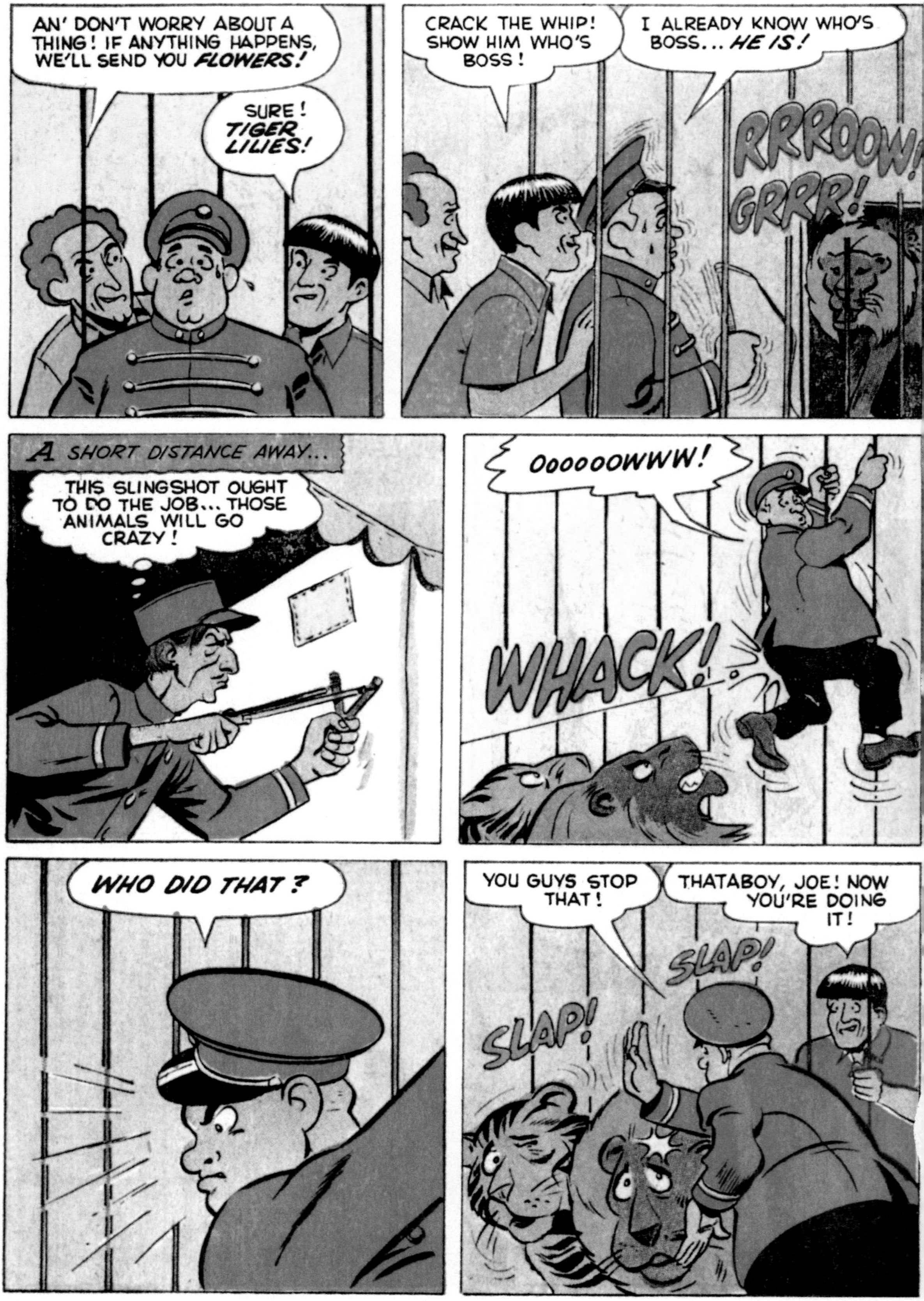
AN' DON'T WORRY ABOUT A THING! IF ANYTHING HAPPENS, WE'LL SEND YOU FLOWERS!
SURE! TIGER LILIES!
CRACK THE WHIP! SHOW HIM WHO'S BOSS!
I ALREADY KNOW WHO'S BOSS... HE IS!
RRROOW! GRRR!
A SHORT DISTANCE AWAY...
THIS SLINGSHOT OUGHT TO DO THE JOB... THOSE ANIMALS WILL GO CRAZY!
OOOOOOWWW!
WHACK!
WHO DID THAT?
YOU GUYS STOP THAT!
THATABOY, JOE! NOW YOU'RE DOING IT!
SLAP!
SLAP!

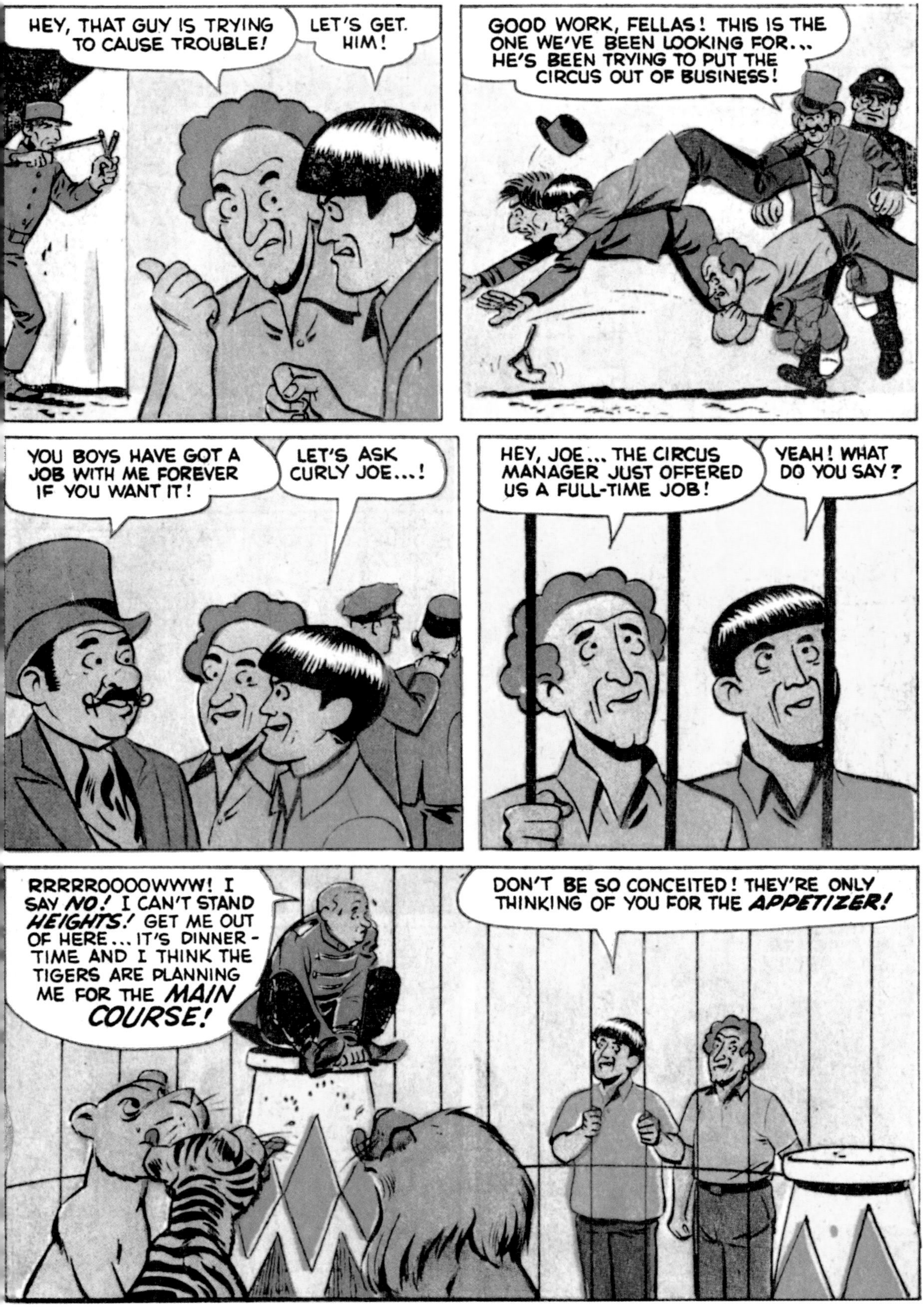
HEY, THAT GUY IS TRYING TO CAUSE TROUBLE!
LET'S GET. HIM!
GOOD WORK, FELLAS! THIS IS THE ONE WE'VE BEEN LOOKING FOR... HE'S BEEN TRYING TO PUT THE CIRCUS OUT OF BUSINESS!
YOU BOYS HAVE GOT A JOB WITH ME FOREVER IF YOU WANT IT!
LET'S ASK CURLY JOE...!
HEY, JOE... THE CIRCUS MANAGER JUST OFFERED US A FULL-TIME JOB!
YEAH! WHAT DO YOU SAY?
RRRRROOOOWWW! I SAY NO! I CAN'T STAND HEIGHTS! GET ME OUT OF HERE... IT'S DINNER-TIME AND I THINK THE TIGERS ARE PLANNING ME FOR THE MAIN COURSE!
DON'T BE SO CONCEITED! THEY'RE ONLY THINKING OF YOU FOR THE APPETIZER!

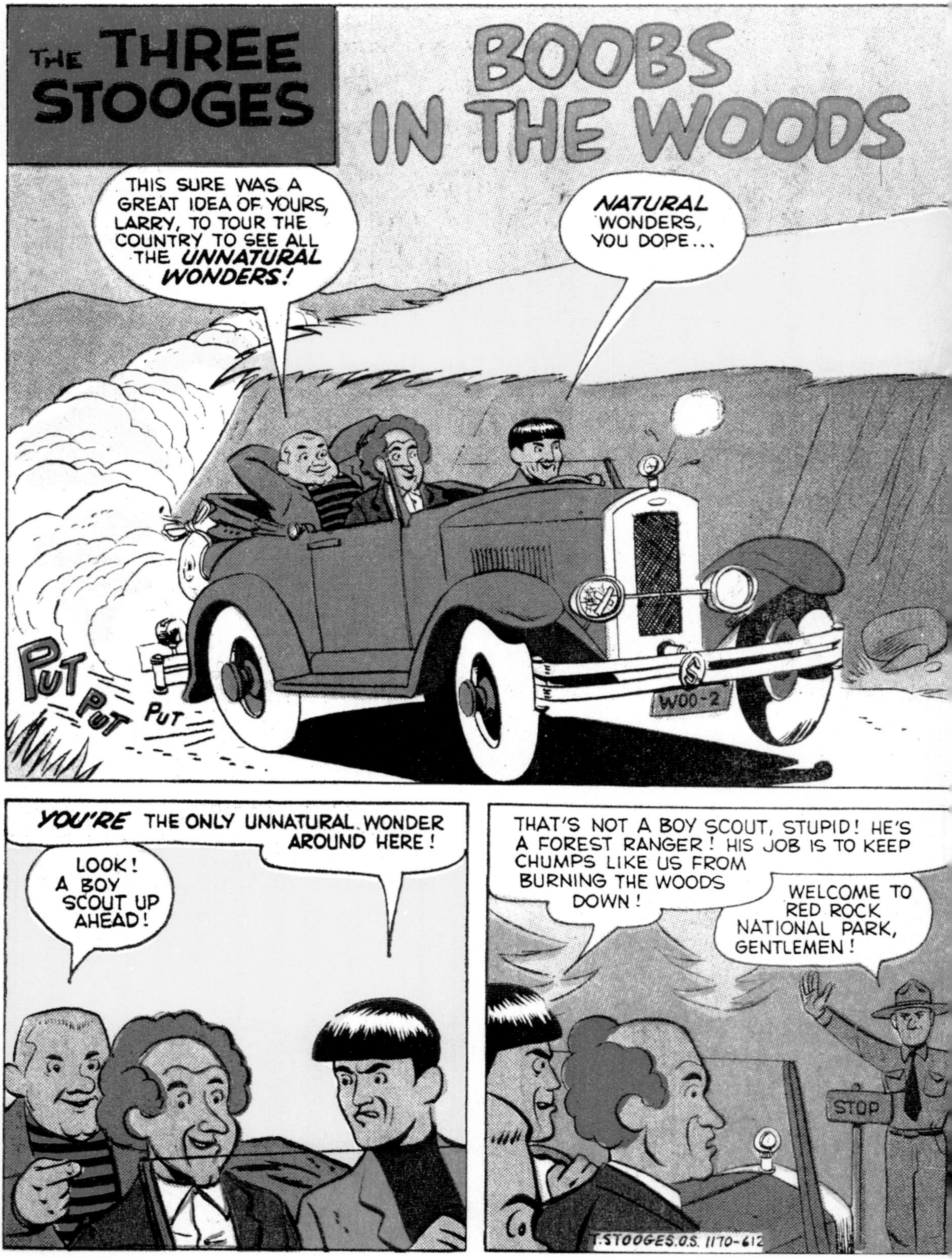
THE THREE STOOGES
BOOBS IN THE WOODS
THIS SURE WAS A GREAT IDEA OF YOURS, LARRY, TO TOUR THE COUNTRY TO SEE ALL THE UNNATURAL WONDERS!
NATURAL WONDERS, YOU DOPE...
PUT PUT PUT
WOO-2
YOU'RE THE ONLY UNNATURAL WONDER AROUND HERE!
LOOK! A BOY SCOUT UP AHEAD!
THAT'S NOT A BOY SCOUT, STUPID! HE'S A FOREST RANGER! HIS JOB IS TO KEEP CHUMPS LIKE US FROM BURNING THE WOODS DOWN!
WELCOME TO RED ROCK NATIONAL PARK, GENTLEMEN!
STOP
T.STOOGES.O.S. 1170-612

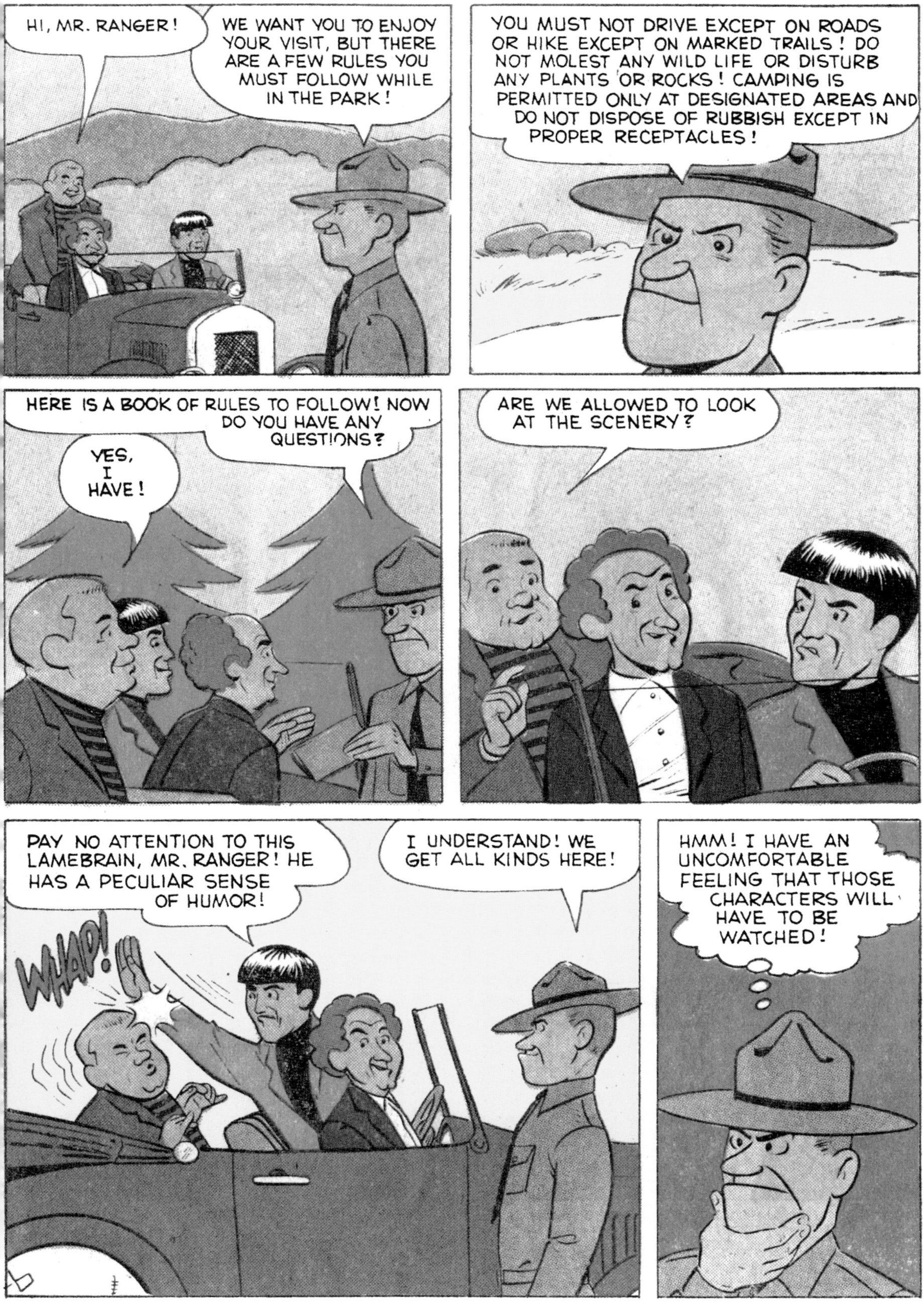

HI, MR. RANGER!
WE WANT YOU TO ENJOY YOUR VISIT, BUT THERE ARE A FEW RULES YOU MUST FOLLOW WHILE IN THE PARK!
YOU MUST NOT DRIVE EXCEPT ON ROADS OR HIKE EXCEPT ON MARKED TRAILS! DO NOT MOLEST ANY WILD LIFE OR DISTURB ANY PLANTS OR ROCKS! CAMPING IS PERMITTED ONLY AT DESIGNATED AREAS AND DO NOT DISPOSE OF RUBBISH EXCEPT IN PROPER RECEPTACLES!
HERE IS A BOOK OF RULES TO FOLLOW! NOW DO YOU HAVE ANY QUESTIONS?
YES, I HAVE!
ARE WE ALLOWED TO LOOK AT THE SCENERY?
PAY NO ATTENTION TO THIS LAMEBRAIN, MR. RANGER! HE HAS A PECULIAR SENSE OF HUMOR!
WHAP!
I UNDERSTAND! WE GET ALL KINDS HERE!
HMM! I HAVE AN UNCOMFORTABLE FEELING THAT THOSE CHARACTERS WILL HAVE TO BE WATCHED!

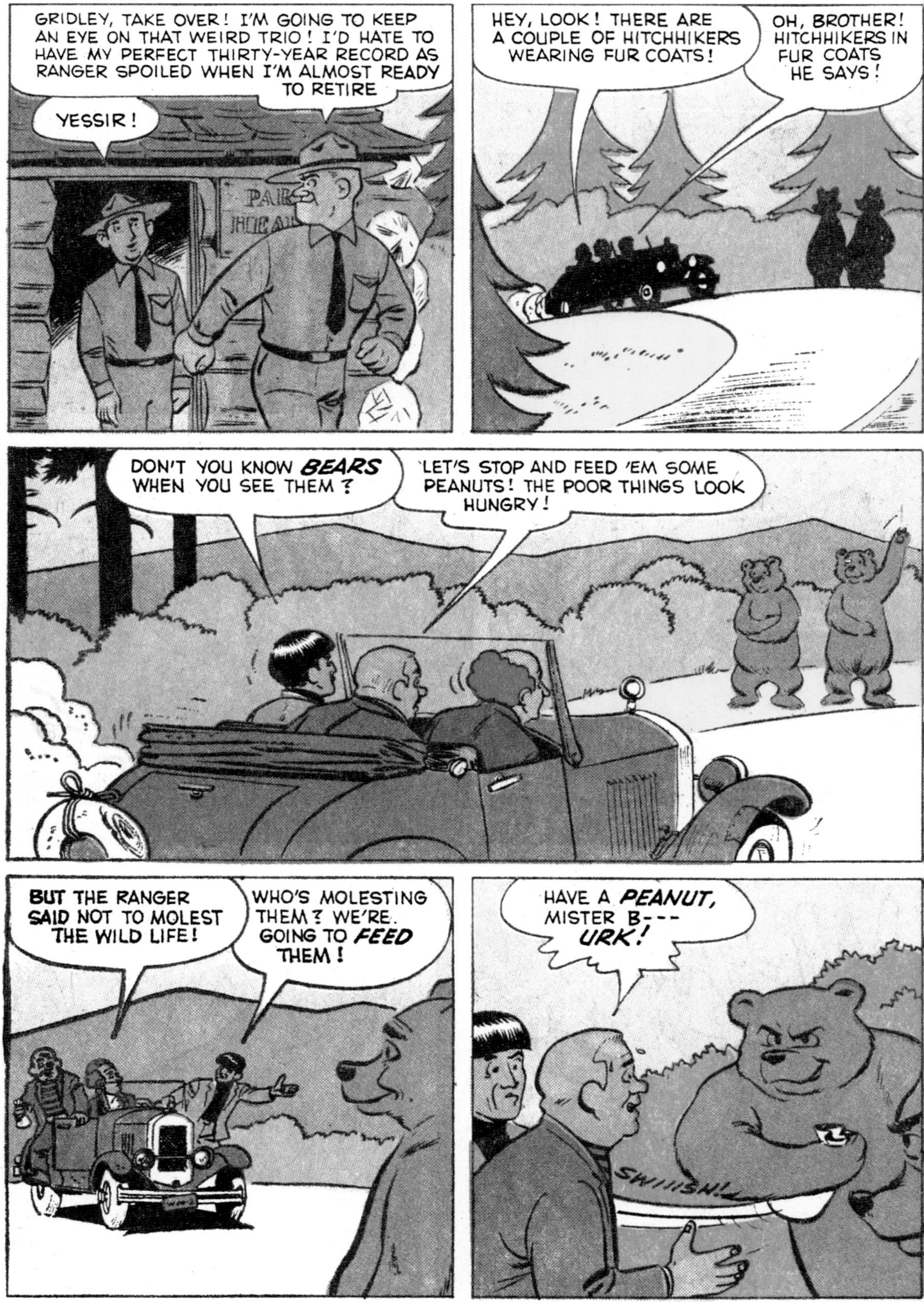
GRIDLEY, TAKE OVER! I'M GOING TO KEEP AN EYE ON THAT WEIRD TRIO! I'D HATE TO HAVE MY PERFECT THIRTY-YEAR RECORD AS RANGER SPOILED WHEN I'M ALMOST READY TO RETIRE
YESSIR!
HEY, LOOK! THERE ARE A COUPLE OF HITCHHIKERS WEARING FUR COATS!
OH, BROTHER! HITCHHIKERS IN FUR COATS HE SAYS!
DON'T YOU KNOW BEARS WHEN YOU SEE THEM?
LET'S STOP AND FEED 'EM SOME PEANUTS! THE POOR THINGS LOOK HUNGRY!
BUT THE RANGER SAID NOT TO MOLEST THE WILD LIFE!
WHO'S MOLESTING THEM? WE'RE GOING TO FEED THEM!
HAVE A PEANUT, MISTER B---
URK!
SWIIISH!

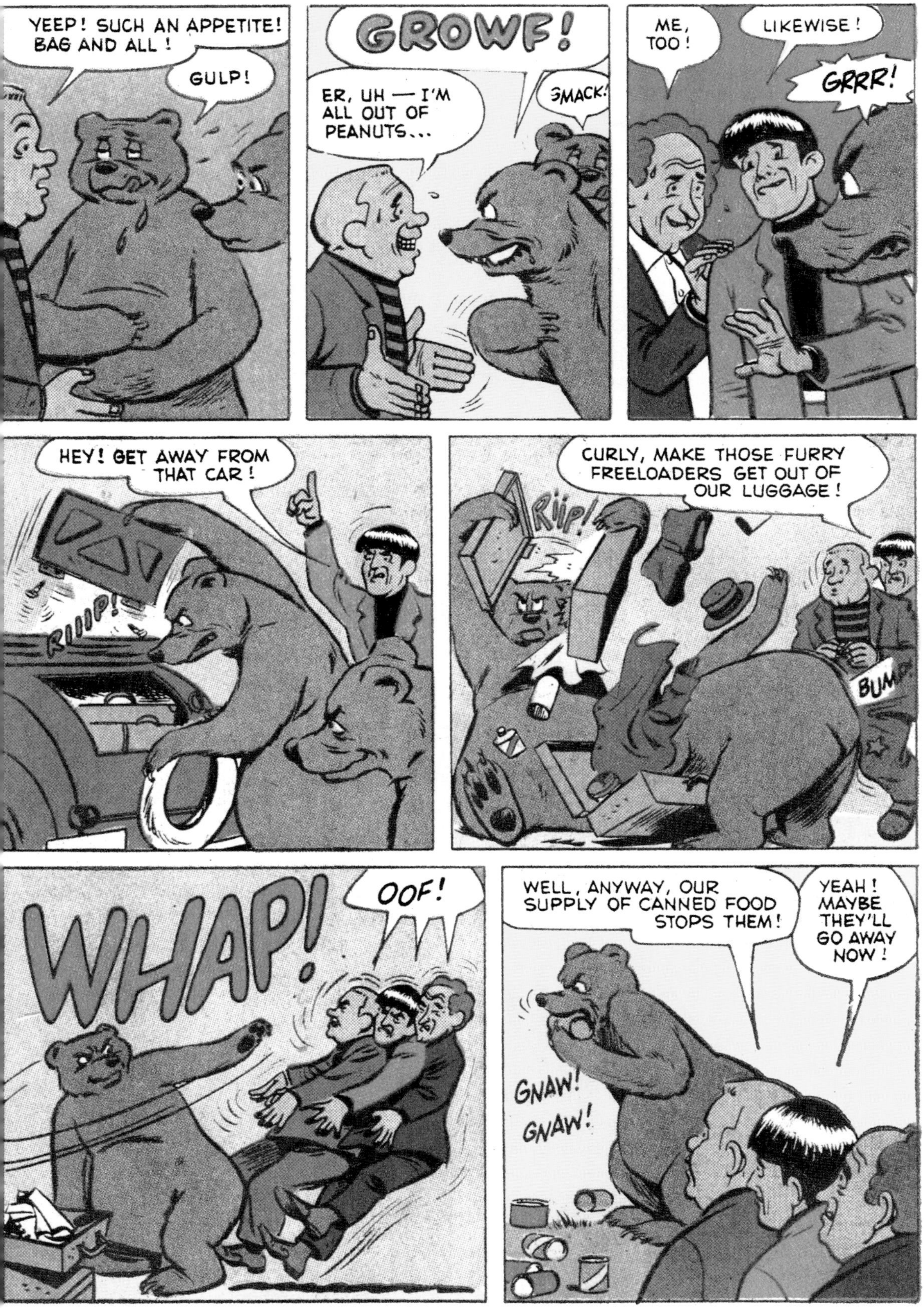

YEEP! SUCH AN APPETITE! BAG AND ALL!
GULP!
GROWF!
ER, UH — I'M ALL OUT OF PEANUTS...
SMACK!
ME, TOO!
LIKEWISE!
GRRR!
HEY! GET AWAY FROM THAT CAR!
RIIIP!
CURLY, MAKE THOSE FURRY FREELOADERS GET OUT OF OUR LUGGAGE!
RIIIP!
WHAP!
OOF!
WELL, ANYWAY, OUR SUPPLY OF CANNED FOOD STOPS THEM!
YEAH! MAYBE THEY'LL GO AWAY NOW!
GNAW! GNAW!

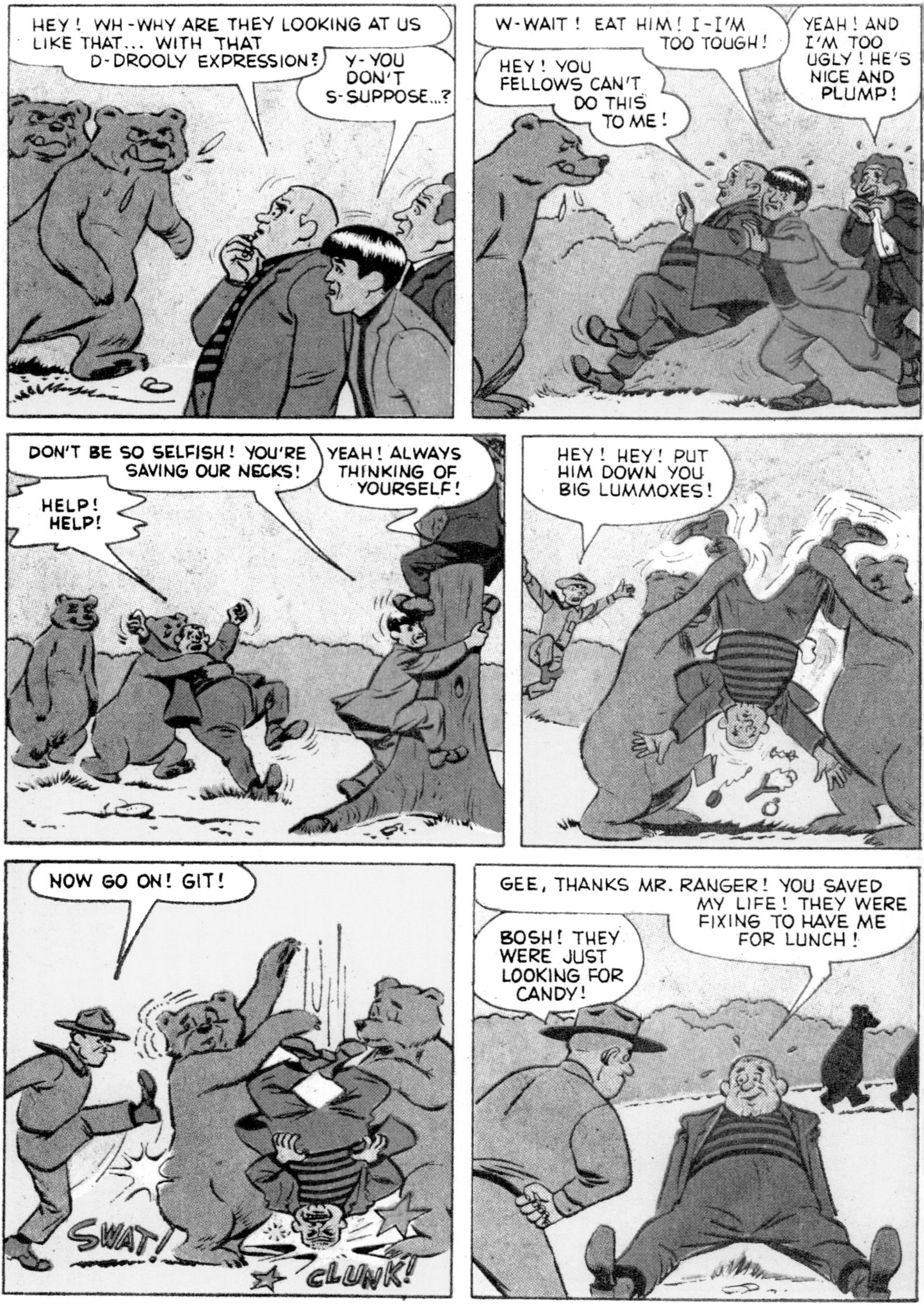
HEY! WH-WHY ARE THEY LOOKING AT US LIKE THAT... WITH THAT D-DROOLY EXPRESSION?
Y-YOU DON'T S-SUPPOSE...?
W-WAIT! EAT HIM! I-I'M TOO TOUGH!
HEY! YOU FELLOWS CAN'T DO THIS TO ME!
YEAH! AND I'M TOO UGLY! HE'S NICE AND PLUMP!
DON'T BE SO SELFISH! YOU'RE SAVING OUR NECKS!
YEAH! ALWAYS THINKING OF YOURSELF!
HELP! HELP!
HEY! HEY! PUT HIM DOWN YOU BIG LUMMOXES!
NOW GO ON! GIT!
SWAT!
CLUNK!
GEE, THANKS MR. RANGER! YOU SAVED MY LIFE! THEY WERE FIXING TO HAVE ME FOR LUNCH!
BOSH! THEY WERE JUST LOOKING FOR CANDY!

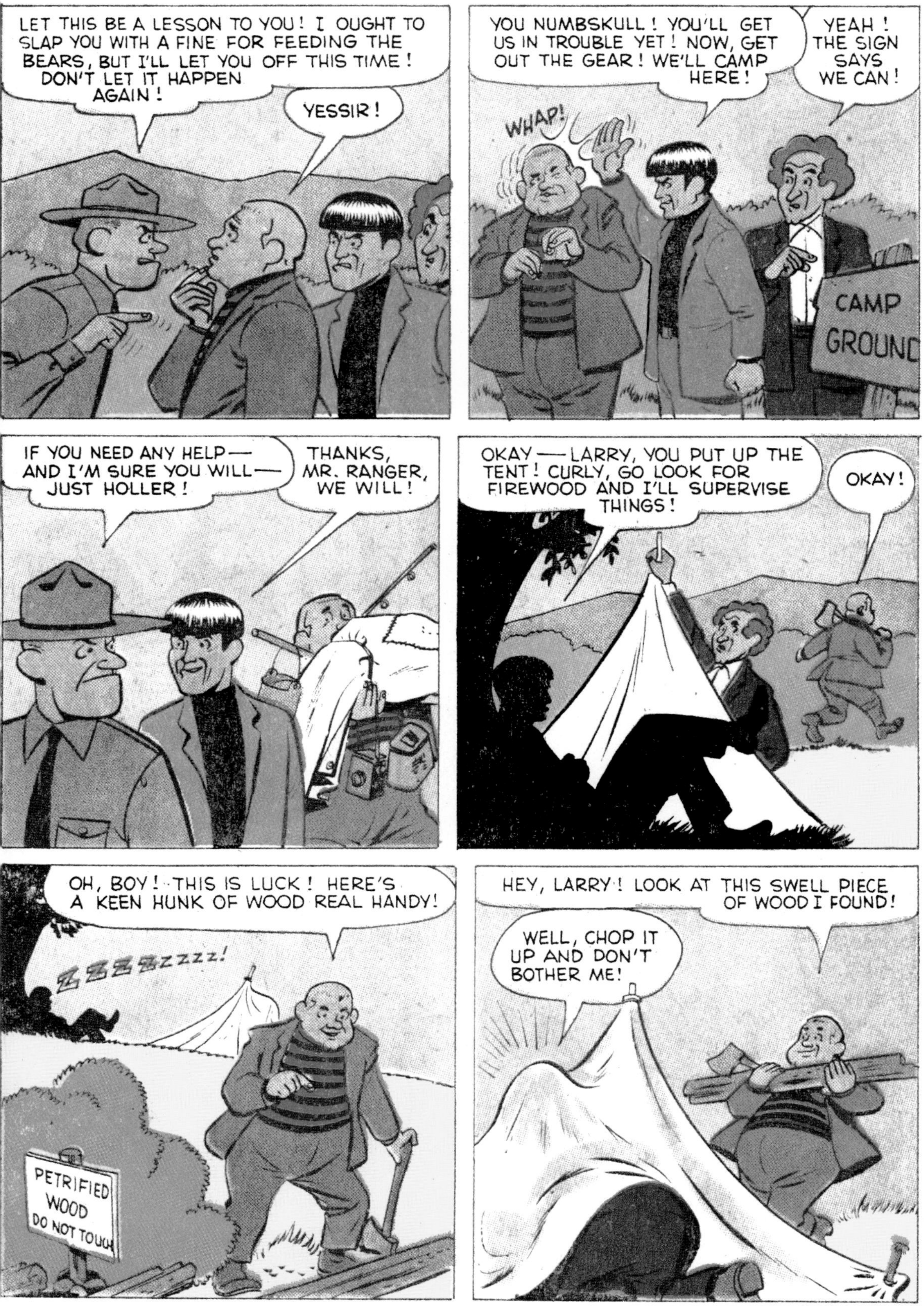
LET THIS BE A LESSON TO YOU! I OUGHT TO SLAP YOU WITH A FINE FOR FEEDING THE BEARS, BUT I'LL LET YOU OFF THIS TIME! DON'T LET IT HAPPEN AGAIN!
YESSIR!
YOU NUMBSKULL! YOU'LL GET US IN TROUBLE YET! NOW, GET OUT THE GEAR! WE'LL CAMP HERE!
YEAH! THE SIGN SAYS WE CAN!
WHAP!
CAMP GROUND
IF YOU NEED ANY HELP— AND I'M SURE YOU WILL— JUST HOLLER!
THANKS, MR. RANGER, WE WILL!
OKAY — LARRY, YOU PUT UP THE TENT! CURLY, GO LOOK FOR FIREWOOD AND I'LL SUPERVISE THINGS!
OKAY!
OH, BOY! THIS IS LUCK! HERE'S A KEEN HUNK OF WOOD REAL HANDY!
ZZZZzzzz!
PETRIFIED WOOD DO NOT TOUCH
HEY, LARRY! LOOK AT THIS SWELL PIECE OF WOOD I FOUND!
WELL, CHOP IT UP AND DON'T BOTHER ME!

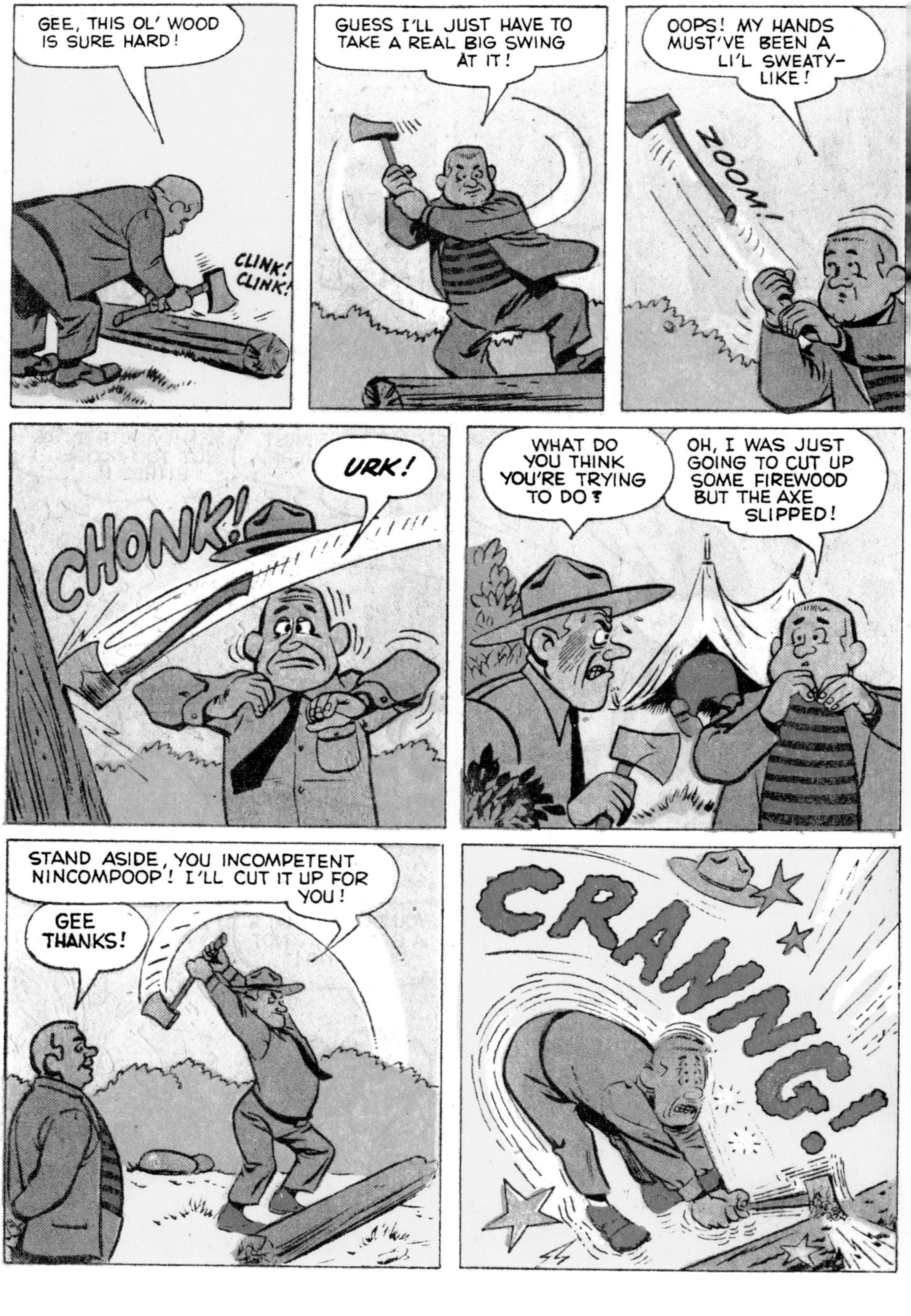

GEE, THIS OL' WOOD IS SURE HARD!
CLINK! CLINK!
GUESS I'LL JUST HAVE TO TAKE A REAL BIG SWING AT IT!
OOPS! MY HANDS MUST'VE BEEN A LI'L SWEATY-LIKE!
ZOOM!
CHONK!
URK!
WHAT DO YOU THINK YOU'RE TRYING TO DO?
OH, I WAS JUST GOING TO CUT UP SOME FIREWOOD BUT THE AXE SLIPPED!
STAND ASIDE, YOU INCOMPETENT NINCOMPOOP! I'LL CUT IT UP FOR YOU!
GEE THANKS!
CRANNG!

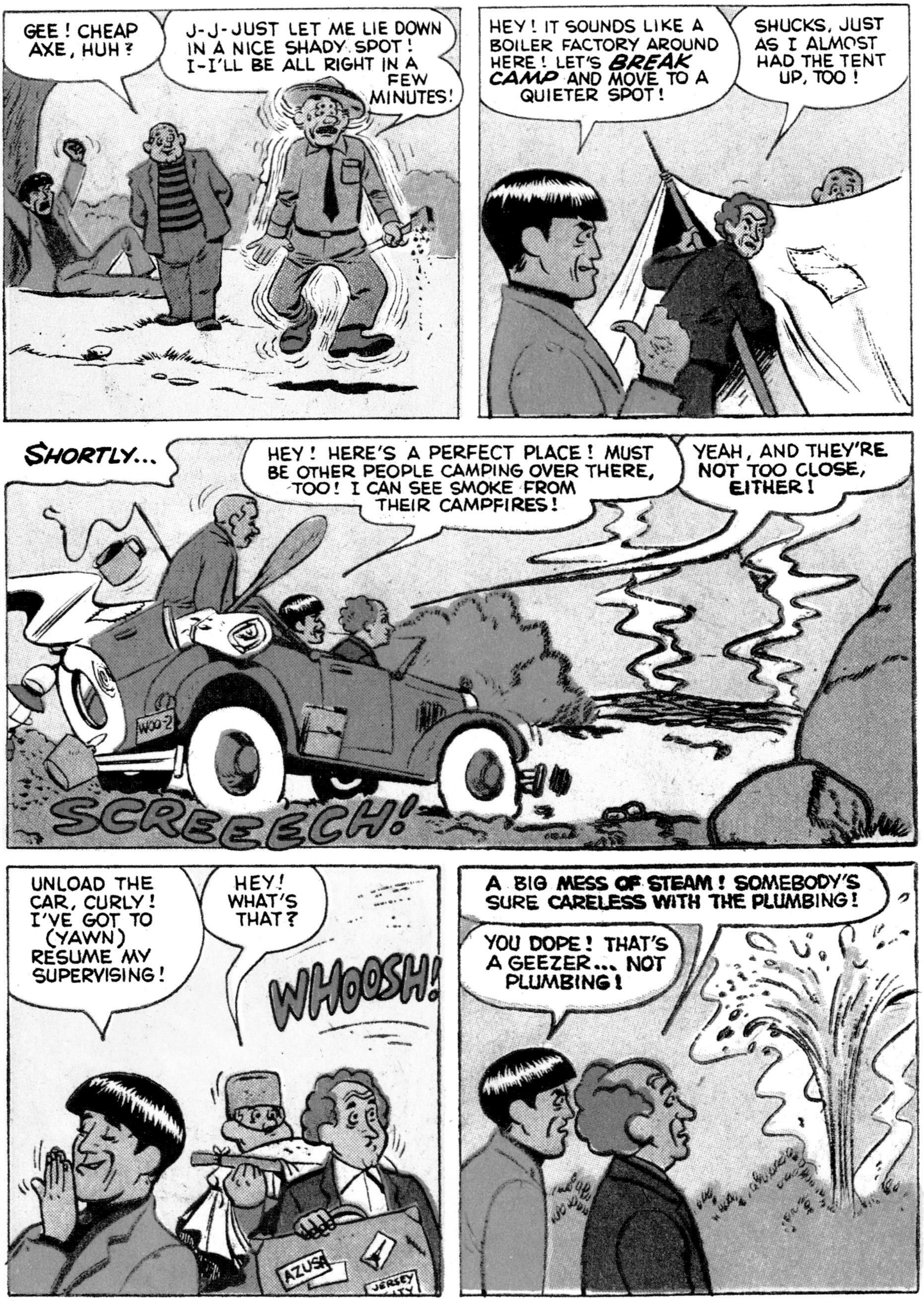

GEE! CHEAP AXE, HUH?
J-J-JUST LET ME LIE DOWN IN A NICE SHADY SPOT! I-I'LL BE ALL RIGHT IN A FEW MINUTES!
HEY! IT SOUNDS LIKE A BOILER FACTORY AROUND HERE! LET'S BREAK CAMP AND MOVE TO A QUIETER SPOT!
SHUCKS, JUST AS I ALMOST HAD THE TENT UP, TOO!
SHORTLY...
HEY! HERE'S A PERFECT PLACE! MUST BE OTHER PEOPLE CAMPING OVER THERE, TOO! I CAN SEE SMOKE FROM THEIR CAMPFIRES!
YEAH, AND THEY'RE NOT TOO CLOSE, EITHER!
WOO-2
SCREEECH!
UNLOAD THE CAR, CURLY! I'VE GOT TO (YAWN) RESUME MY SUPERVISING!
HEY! WHAT'S THAT?
WHOOSH!
AZUSA
JERSEY
A BIG MESS OF STEAM! SOMEBODY'S SURE CARELESS WITH THE PLUMBING!
YOU DOPE! THAT'S A GEEZER... NOT PLUMBING!

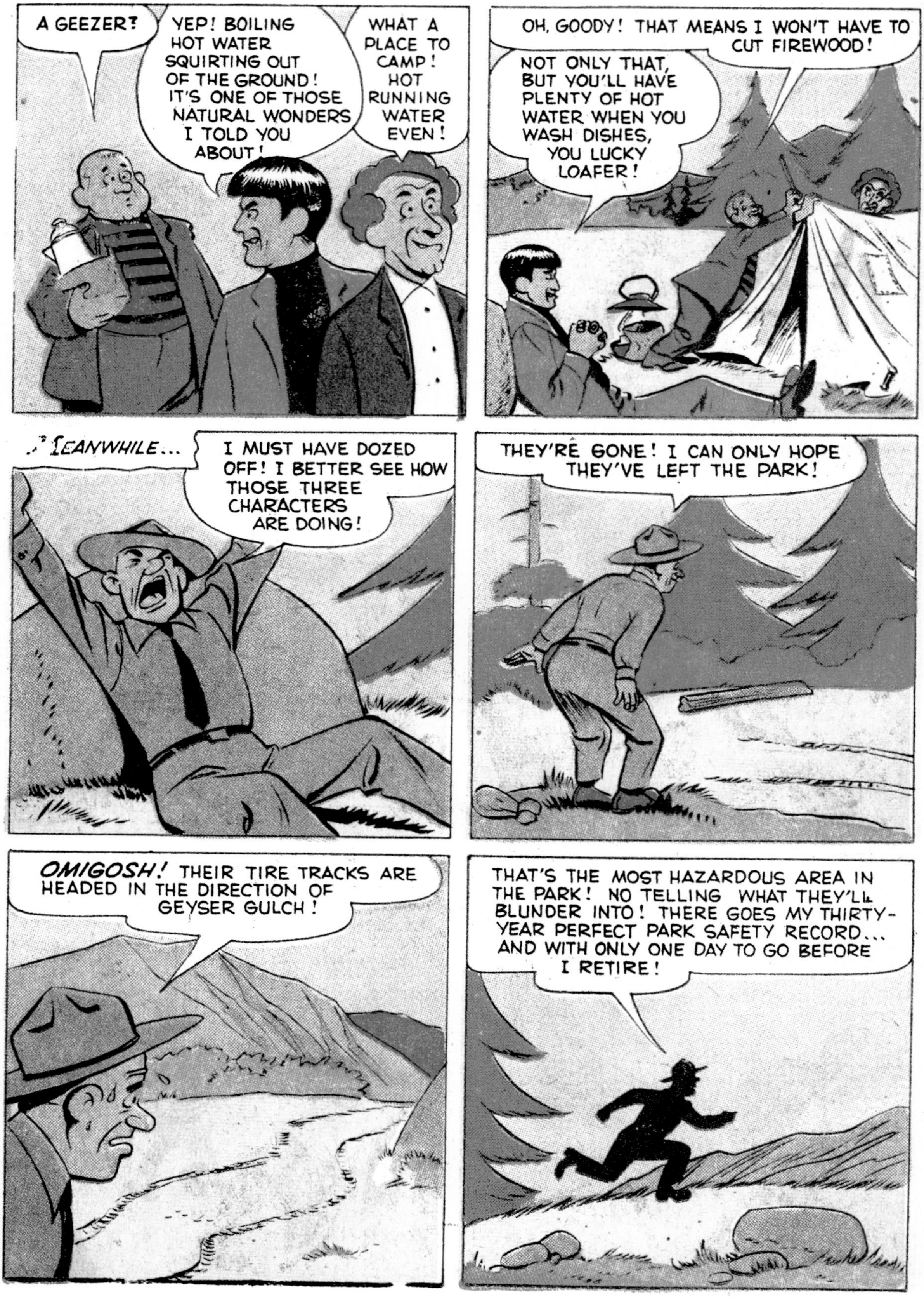
A GEEZER?
YEP! BOILING HOT WATER SQUIRTING OUT OF THE GROUND! IT'S ONE OF THOSE NATURAL WONDERS I TOLD YOU ABOUT!
WHAT A PLACE TO CAMP! HOT RUNNING WATER EVEN!
OH, GOODY! THAT MEANS I WON'T HAVE TO CUT FIREWOOD!
NOT ONLY THAT, BUT YOU'LL HAVE PLENTY OF HOT WATER WHEN YOU WASH DISHES, YOU LUCKY LOAFER!
MEANWHILE...
I MUST HAVE DOZED OFF! I BETTER SEE HOW THOSE THREE CHARACTERS ARE DOING!
THEY'RE GONE! I CAN ONLY HOPE THEY'VE LEFT THE PARK!
OMIGOSH! THEIR TIRE TRACKS ARE HEADED IN THE DIRECTION OF GEYSER GULCH!
THAT'S THE MOST HAZARDOUS AREA IN THE PARK! NO TELLING WHAT THEY'LL BLUNDER INTO! THERE GOES MY THIRTY-YEAR PERFECT PARK SAFETY RECORD... AND WITH ONLY ONE DAY TO GO BEFORE I RETIRE!

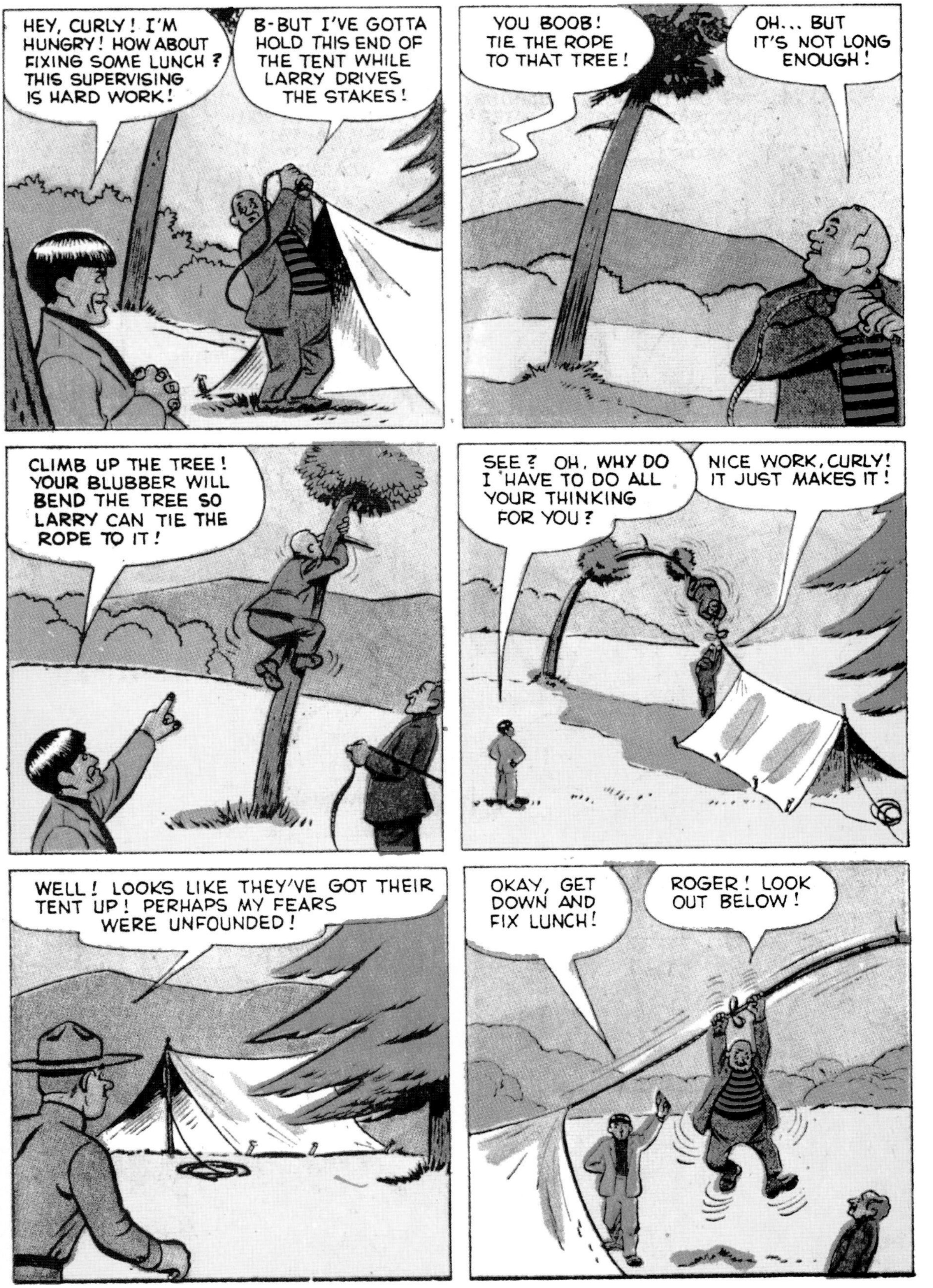
HEY, CURLY! I'M HUNGRY! HOW ABOUT FIXING SOME LUNCH? THIS SUPERVISING IS HARD WORK!
B-BUT I'VE GOTTA HOLD THIS END OF THE TENT WHILE LARRY DRIVES THE STAKES!
YOU BOOB! TIE THE ROPE TO THAT TREE!
OH... BUT IT'S NOT LONG ENOUGH!
CLIMB UP THE TREE! YOUR BLUBBER WILL BEND THE TREE SO LARRY CAN TIE THE ROPE TO IT!
SEE? OH, WHY DO I HAVE TO DO ALL YOUR THINKING FOR YOU?
NICE WORK, CURLY! IT JUST MAKES IT!
WELL! LOOKS LIKE THEY'VE GOT THEIR TENT UP! PERHAPS MY FEARS WERE UNFOUNDED!
OKAY, GET DOWN AND FIX LUNCH!
ROGER! LOOK OUT BELOW!

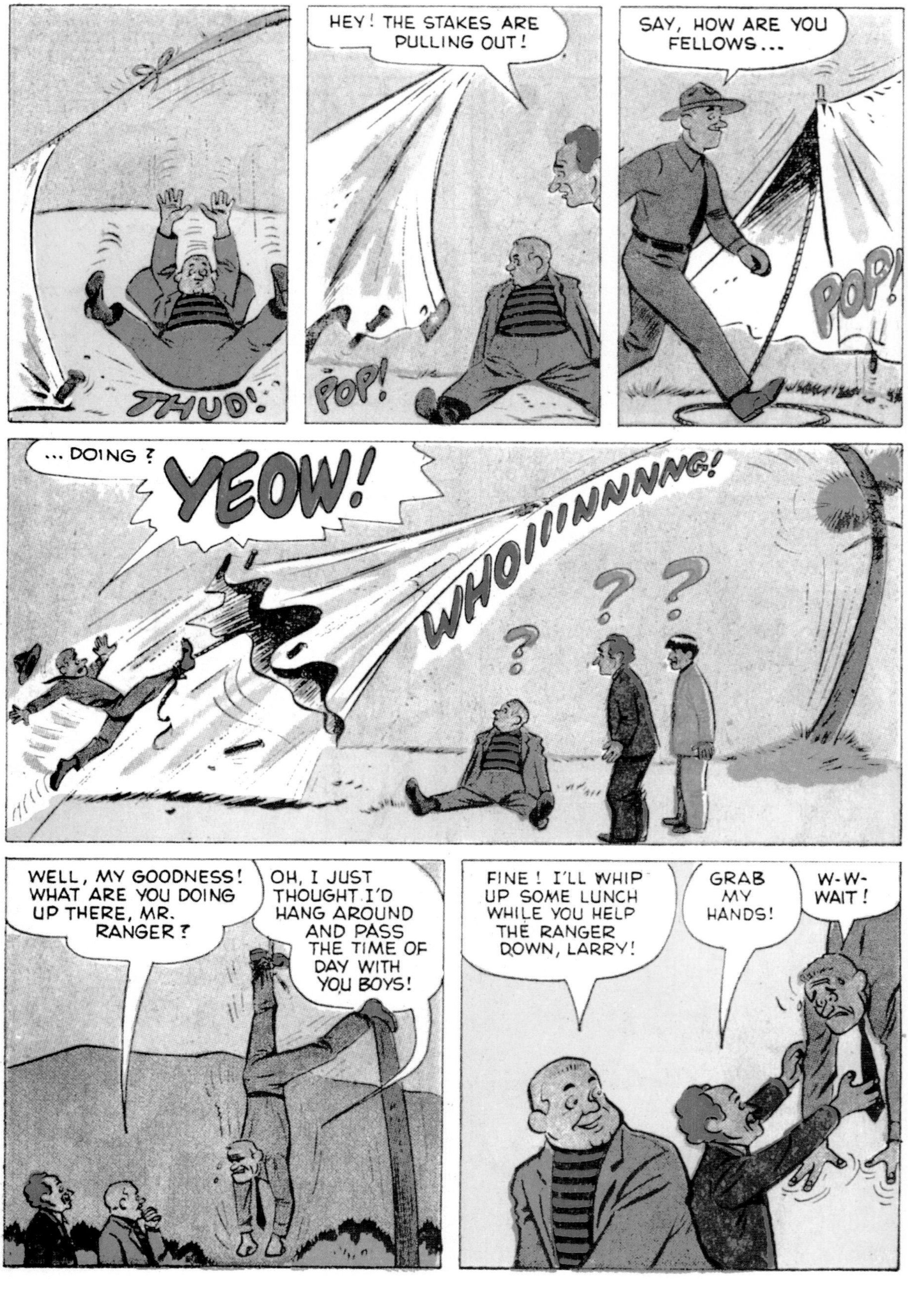
THUD!
HEY! THE STAKES ARE PULLING OUT!
POP!
SAY, HOW ARE YOU FELLOWS...
POP!
...DOING?
YEOW!
WHOIIINNNNG!
?
??
WELL, MY GOODNESS! WHAT ARE YOU DOING UP THERE, MR. RANGER?
OH, I JUST THOUGHT I'D HANG AROUND AND PASS THE TIME OF DAY WITH YOU BOYS!
FINE! I'LL WHIP UP SOME LUNCH WHILE YOU HELP THE RANGER DOWN, LARRY!
GRAB MY HANDS!
W-W-WAIT!

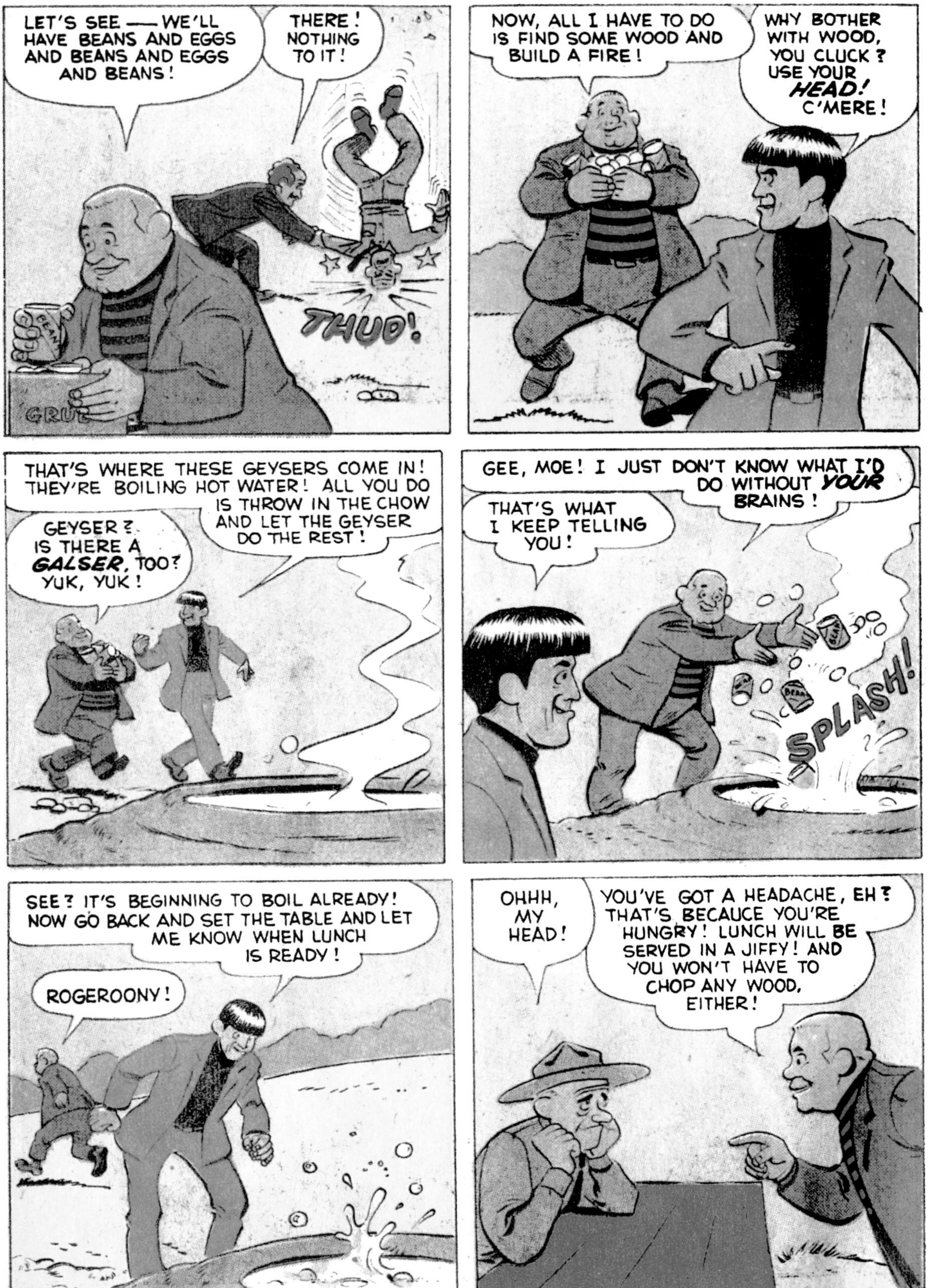
LET'S SEE — WE'LL HAVE BEANS AND EGGS AND BEANS AND EGGS AND BEANS!
THERE! NOTHING TO IT!
THUD!
NOW, ALL I HAVE TO DO IS FIND SOME WOOD AND BUILD A FIRE!
WHY BOTHER WITH WOOD, YOU CLUCK? USE YOUR HEAD! C'MERE!
THAT'S WHERE THESE GEYSERS COME IN! THEY'RE BOILING HOT WATER! ALL YOU DO IS THROW IN THE CHOW AND LET THE GEYSER DO THE REST!
GEYSER? IS THERE A GALSER, TOO? YUK, YUK!
GEE, MOE! I JUST DON'T KNOW WHAT I'D DO WITHOUT YOUR BRAINS!
THAT'S WHAT I KEEP TELLING YOU!
SPLASH!
SEE? IT'S BEGINNING TO BOIL ALREADY! NOW GO BACK AND SET THE TABLE AND LET ME KNOW WHEN LUNCH IS READY!
ROGEROONY!
OHHH, MY HEAD!
YOU'VE GOT A HEADACHE, EH? THAT'S BECAUCE YOU'RE HUNGRY! LUNCH WILL BE SERVED IN A JIFFY! AND YOU WON'T HAVE TO CHOP ANY WOOD, EITHER!

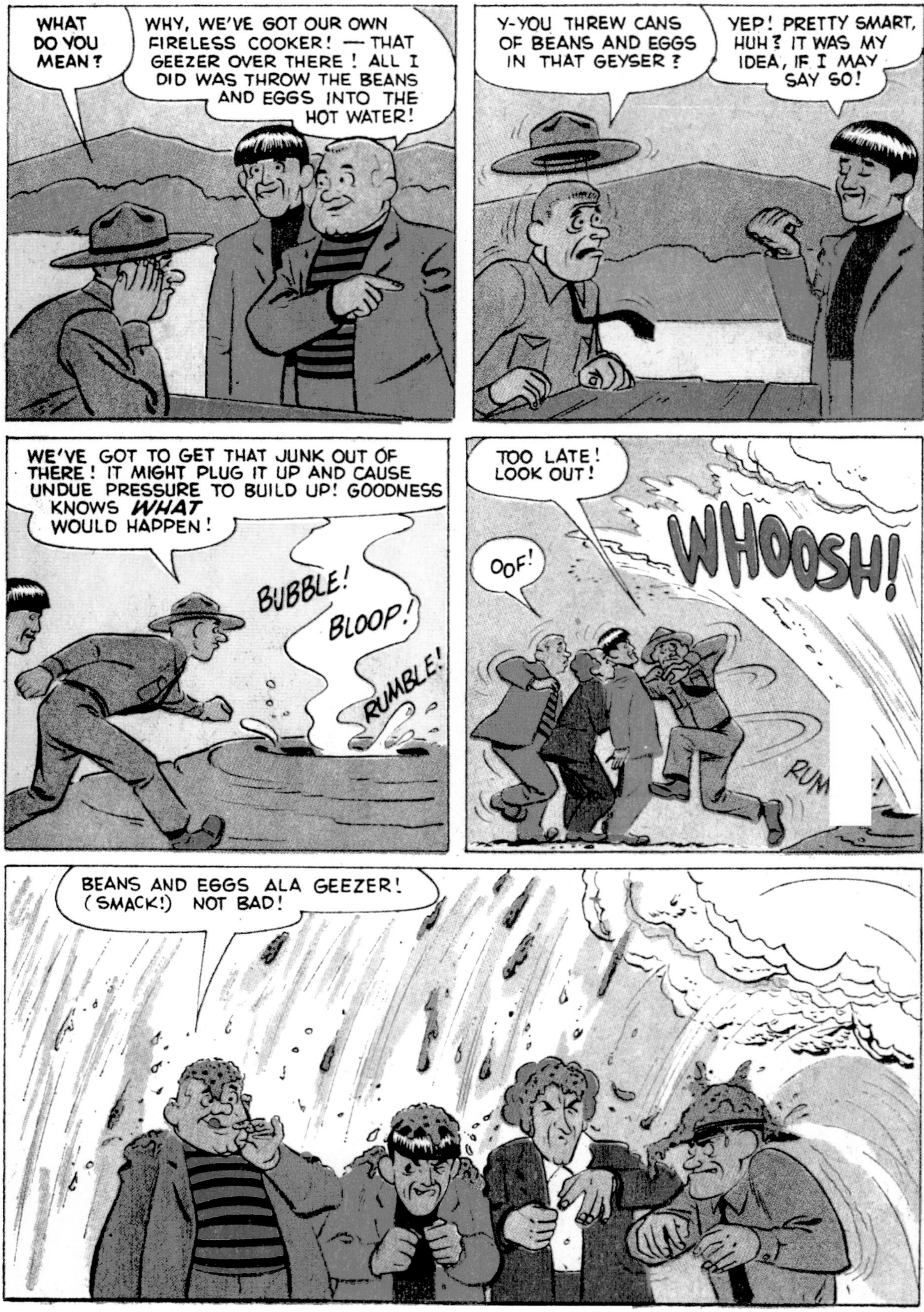
WHAT DO YOU MEAN?
WHY, WE'VE GOT OUR OWN FIRELESS COOKER! — THAT GEEZER OVER THERE! ALL I DID WAS THROW THE BEANS AND EGGS INTO THE HOT WATER!
Y-YOU THREW CANS OF BEANS AND EGGS IN THAT GEYSER?
YEP! PRETTY SMART, HUH? IT WAS MY IDEA, IF I MAY SAY SO!
WE'VE GOT TO GET THAT JUNK OUT OF THERE! IT MIGHT PLUG IT UP AND CAUSE UNDUE PRESSURE TO BUILD UP! GOODNESS KNOWS WHAT WOULD HAPPEN!
BUBBLE!
BLOOP!
RUMBLE!
TOO LATE! LOOK OUT!
OOF!
WHOOSH!
BEANS AND EGGS ALA GEEZER! (SMACK!) NOT BAD!

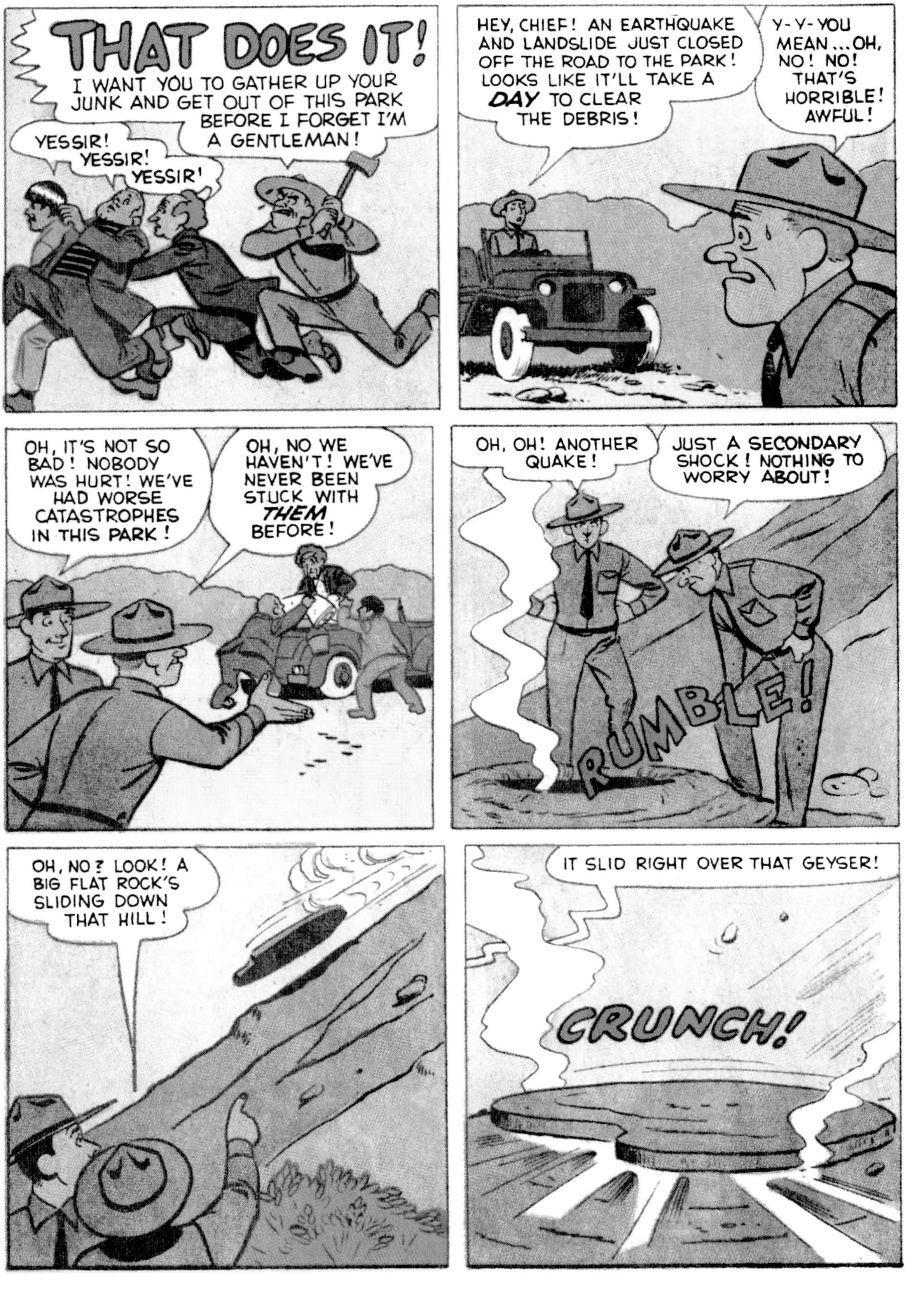
THAT DOES IT!
I WANT YOU TO GATHER UP YOUR JUNK AND GET OUT OF THIS PARK BEFORE I FORGET I'M A GENTLEMAN!
YESSIR! YESSIR! YESSIR!
HEY, CHIEF! AN EARTHQUAKE AND LANDSLIDE JUST CLOSED OFF THE ROAD TO THE PARK! LOOKS LIKE IT'LL TAKE A DAY TO CLEAR THE DEBRIS!
Y-Y-YOU MEAN...OH, NO! NO! THAT'S HORRIBLE! AWFUL!
OH, IT'S NOT SO BAD! NOBODY WAS HURT! WE'VE HAD WORSE CATASTROPHES IN THIS PARK!
OH, NO WE HAVEN'T! WE'VE NEVER BEEN STUCK WITH THEM BEFORE!
OH, OH! ANOTHER QUAKE!
JUST A SECONDARY SHOCK! NOTHING TO WORRY ABOUT!
RUMBLE!
OH, NO? LOOK! A BIG FLAT ROCK'S SLIDING DOWN THAT HILL!
IT SLID RIGHT OVER THAT GEYSER!
CRUNCH!

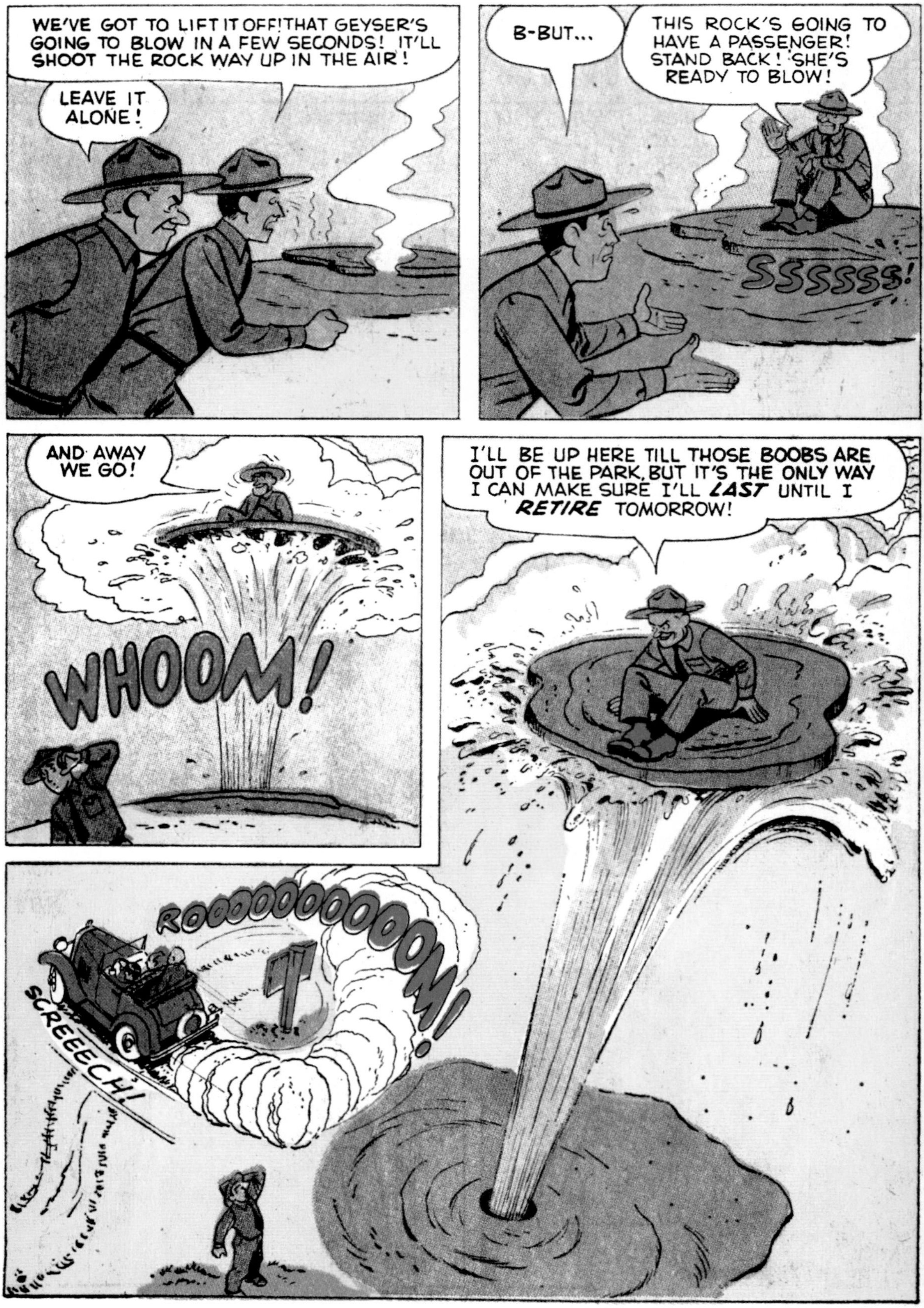
WE'VE GOT TO LIFT IT OFF! THAT GEYSER'S GOING TO BLOW IN A FEW SECONDS! IT'LL SHOOT THE ROCK WAY UP IN THE AIR!
LEAVE IT ALONE!
B-BUT...
THIS ROCK'S GOING TO HAVE A PASSENGER! STAND BACK! SHE'S READY TO BLOW!
SSSSSS!
AND AWAY WE GO!
WHOOM!
I'LL BE UP HERE TILL THOSE BOOBS ARE OUT OF THE PARK, BUT IT'S THE ONLY WAY I CAN MAKE SURE I'LL LAST UNTIL I RETIRE TOMORROW!
ROOOOOOOOOOOM!
SCREEECH!

AMERICAN MYTHOLOGY PRODUCTIONS

10005-909
SEPTEMBER

THE THREE STOOGES

15c

the **Three Stooges**

Fun in the sun with the
BEACH BOO-BOOBS

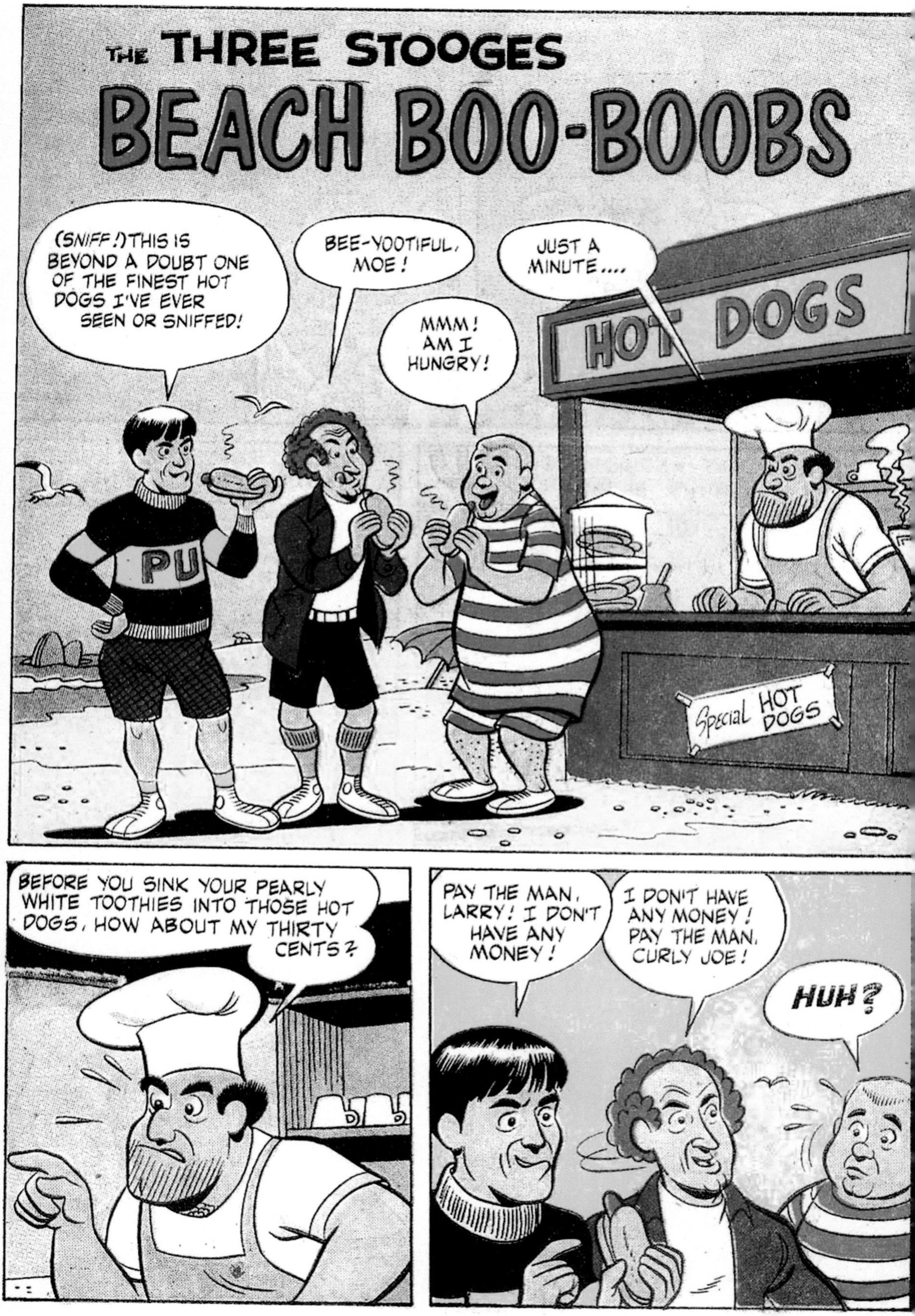
THE THREE STOOGES
BEACH BOO-BOOBS
(SNIFF!) THIS IS BEYOND A DOUBT ONE OF THE FINEST HOT DOGS I'VE EVER SEEN OR SNIFFED!
BEE-YOOTIFUL, MOE!
MMM! AM I HUNGRY!
JUST A MINUTE....
HOT DOGS
Special HOT DOGS
PU
BEFORE YOU SINK YOUR PEARLY WHITE TOOTHIES INTO THOSE HOT DOGS, HOW ABOUT MY THIRTY CENTS?
PAY THE MAN, LARRY! I DON'T HAVE ANY MONEY!
I DON'T HAVE ANY MONEY! PAY THE MAN, CURLY JOE!
HUH?

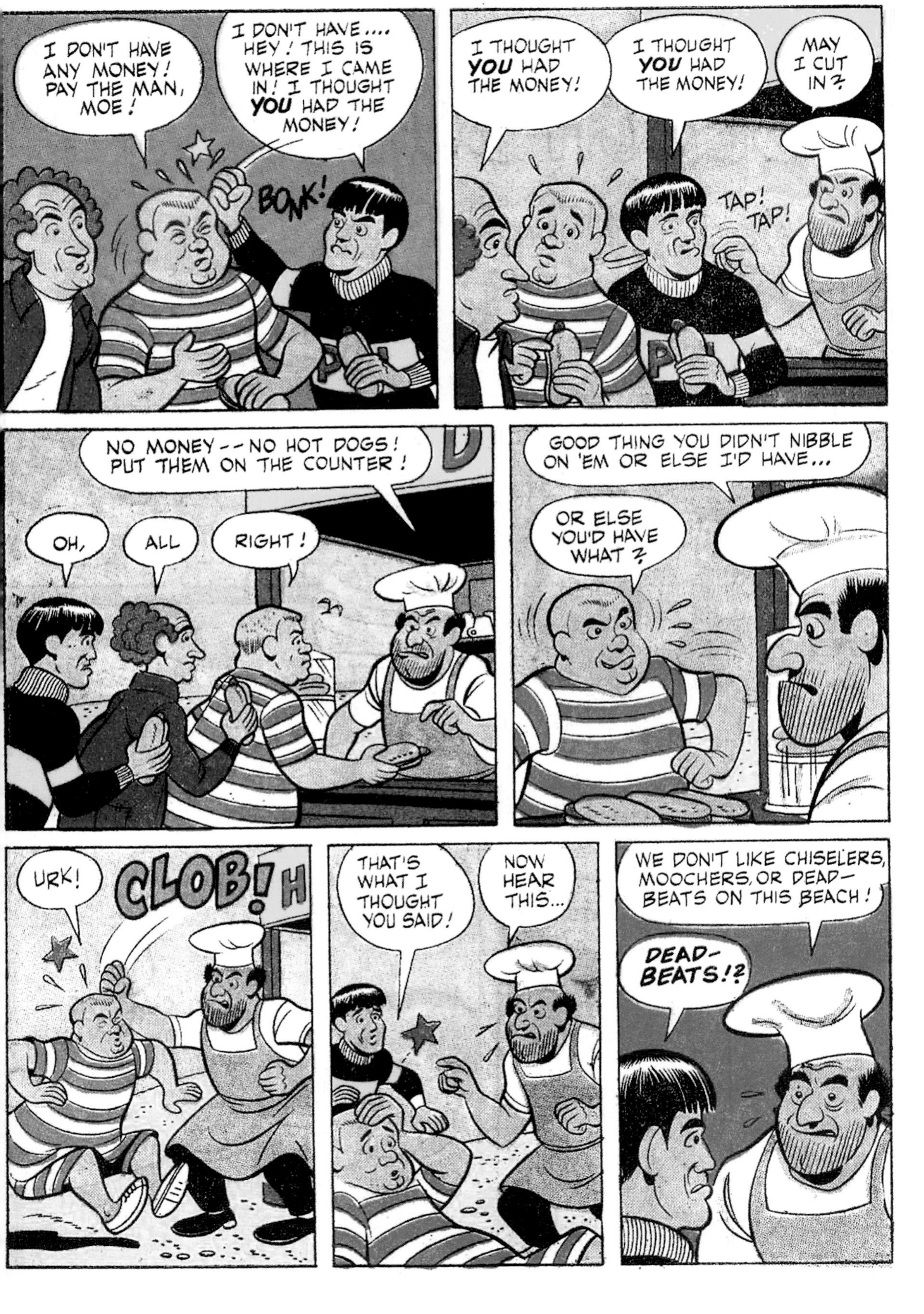
I DON'T HAVE ANY MONEY! PAY THE MAN, MOE!
I DON'T HAVE.... HEY! THIS IS WHERE I CAME IN! I THOUGHT YOU HAD THE MONEY!
BONK!
I THOUGHT YOU HAD THE MONEY!
I THOUGHT YOU HAD THE MONEY!
MAY I CUT IN?
TAP! TAP!
NO MONEY--NO HOT DOGS! PUT THEM ON THE COUNTER!
OH,
ALL
RIGHT!
GOOD THING YOU DIDN'T NIBBLE ON 'EM OR ELSE I'D HAVE...
OR ELSE YOU'D HAVE WHAT?
URK!
CLOB!
THAT'S WHAT I THOUGHT YOU SAID!
NOW HEAR THIS...
WE DON'T LIKE CHISELERS, MOOCHERS, OR DEAD-BEATS ON THIS BEACH!
DEAD-BEATS!?

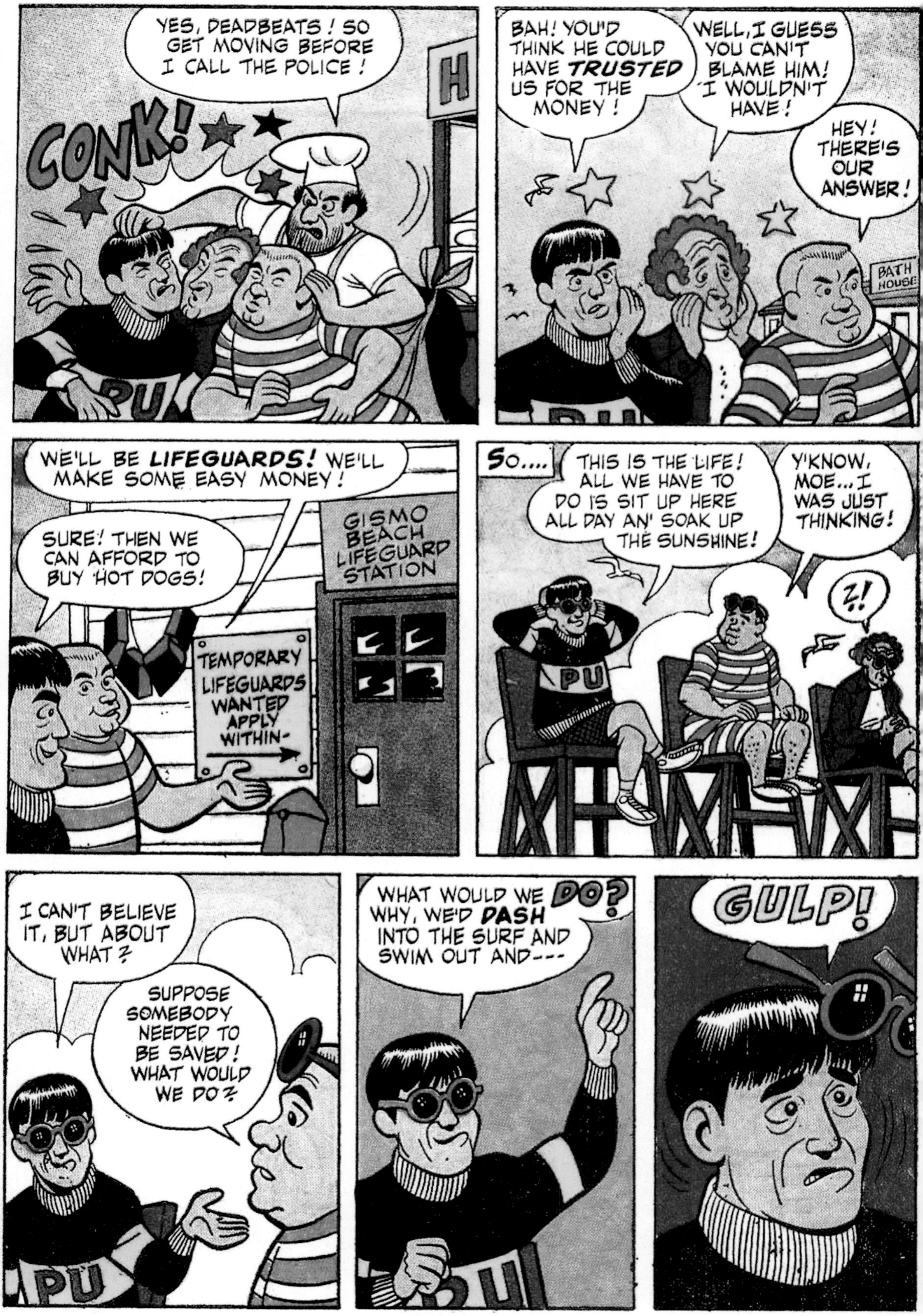
YES, DEADBEATS! SO GET MOVING BEFORE I CALL THE POLICE!
CONK!
H
BAH! YOU'D THINK HE COULD HAVE TRUSTED US FOR THE MONEY!
WELL, I GUESS YOU CAN'T BLAME HIM! I WOULDN'T HAVE!
HEY! THERE'S OUR ANSWER!
BATH HOUSE
WE'LL BE LIFEGUARDS! WE'LL MAKE SOME EASY MONEY!
SURE! THEN WE CAN AFFORD TO BUY HOT DOGS!
GISMO BEACH LIFEGUARD STATION
TEMPORARY LIFEGUARDS WANTED APPLY WITHIN-
SO....
THIS IS THE LIFE! ALL WE HAVE TO DO IS SIT UP HERE ALL DAY AN' SOAK UP THE SUNSHINE!
Y'KNOW, MOE... I WAS JUST THINKING!
Z!
I CAN'T BELIEVE IT, BUT ABOUT WHAT?
SUPPOSE SOMEBODY NEEDED TO BE SAVED! WHAT WOULD WE DO?
WHAT WOULD WE DO? WHY, WE'D DASH INTO THE SURF AND SWIM OUT AND---
GULP!

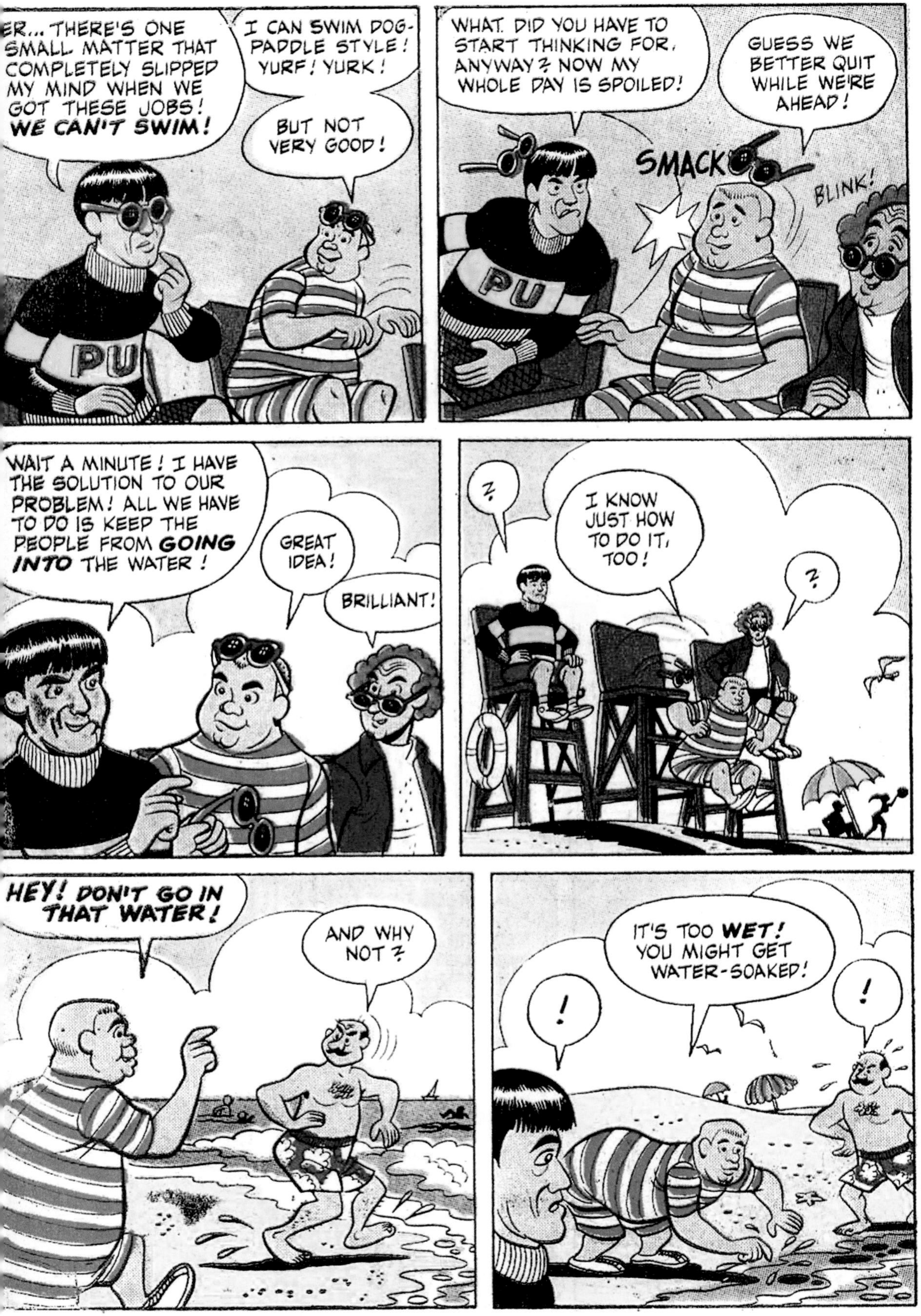
ER... THERE'S ONE SMALL MATTER THAT COMPLETELY SLIPPED MY MIND WHEN WE GOT THESE JOBS! WE CAN'T SWIM!
I CAN SWIM DOG-PADDLE STYLE! YURF! YURK!
BUT NOT VERY GOOD!
PU
WHAT DID YOU HAVE TO START THINKING FOR, ANYWAY? NOW MY WHOLE DAY IS SPOILED!
GUESS WE BETTER QUIT WHILE WE'RE AHEAD!
SMACK
BLINK!
PU
WAIT A MINUTE! I HAVE THE SOLUTION TO OUR PROBLEM! ALL WE HAVE TO DO IS KEEP THE PEOPLE FROM GOING INTO THE WATER!
GREAT IDEA!
BRILLIANT!
?
I KNOW JUST HOW TO DO IT, TOO!
?
HEY! DON'T GO IN THAT WATER!
AND WHY NOT?
!
IT'S TOO WET! YOU MIGHT GET WATER-SOAKED!
!

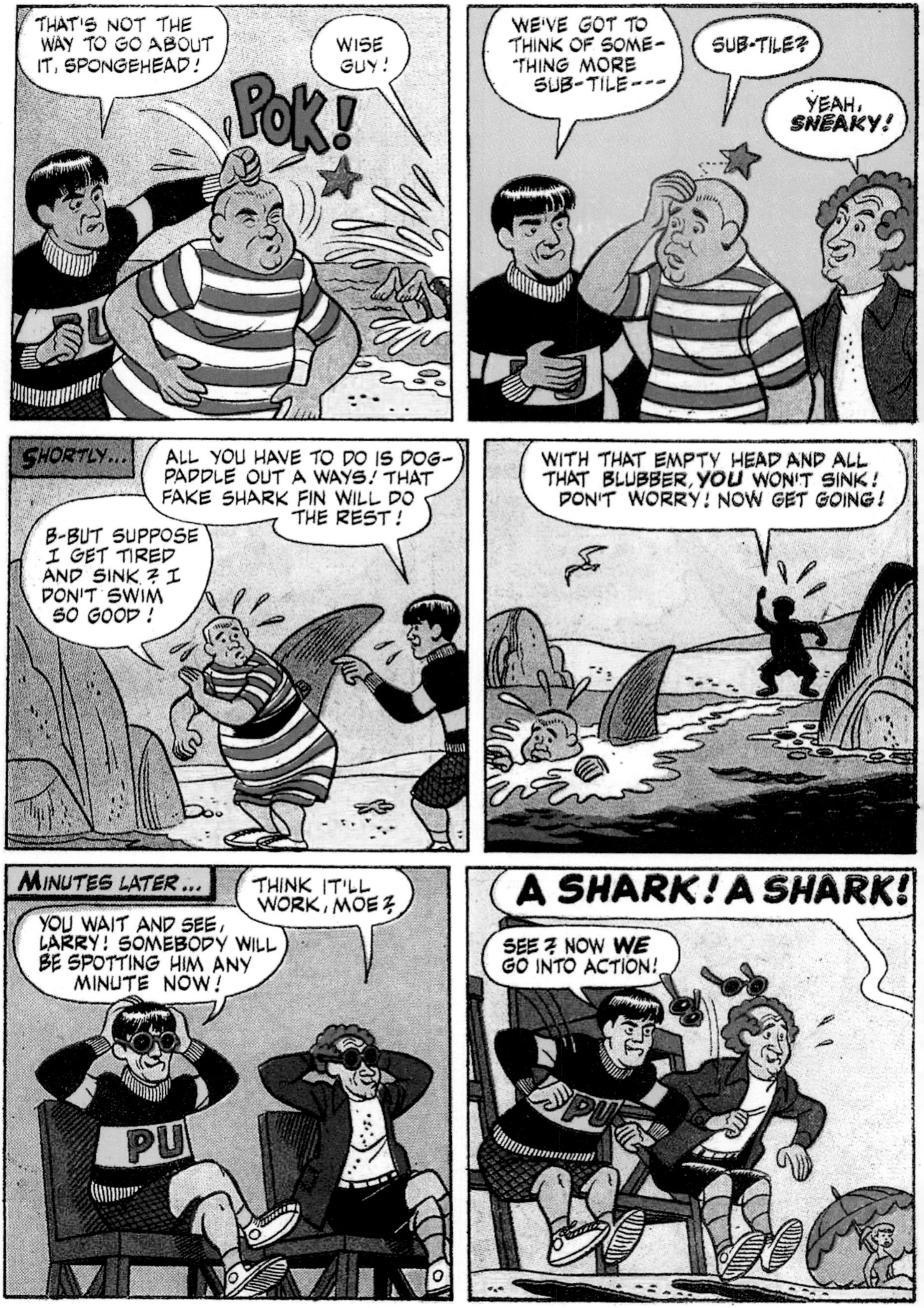
THAT'S NOT THE WAY TO GO ABOUT IT, SPONGEHEAD!
WISE GUY!
POK!
WE'VE GOT TO THINK OF SOME-THING MORE SUB-TILE---
SUB-TILE?
YEAH, SNEAKY!
SHORTLY...
ALL YOU HAVE TO DO IS DOG-PADDLE OUT A WAYS! THAT FAKE SHARK FIN WILL DO THE REST!
B-BUT SUPPOSE I GET TIRED AND SINK? I DON'T SWIM SO GOOD!
WITH THAT EMPTY HEAD AND ALL THAT BLUBBER, YOU WON'T SINK! DON'T WORRY! NOW GET GOING!
MINUTES LATER...
THINK IT'LL WORK, MOE?
YOU WAIT AND SEE, LARRY! SOMEBODY WILL BE SPOTTING HIM ANY MINUTE NOW!
A SHARK! A SHARK!
SEE? NOW WE GO INTO ACTION!

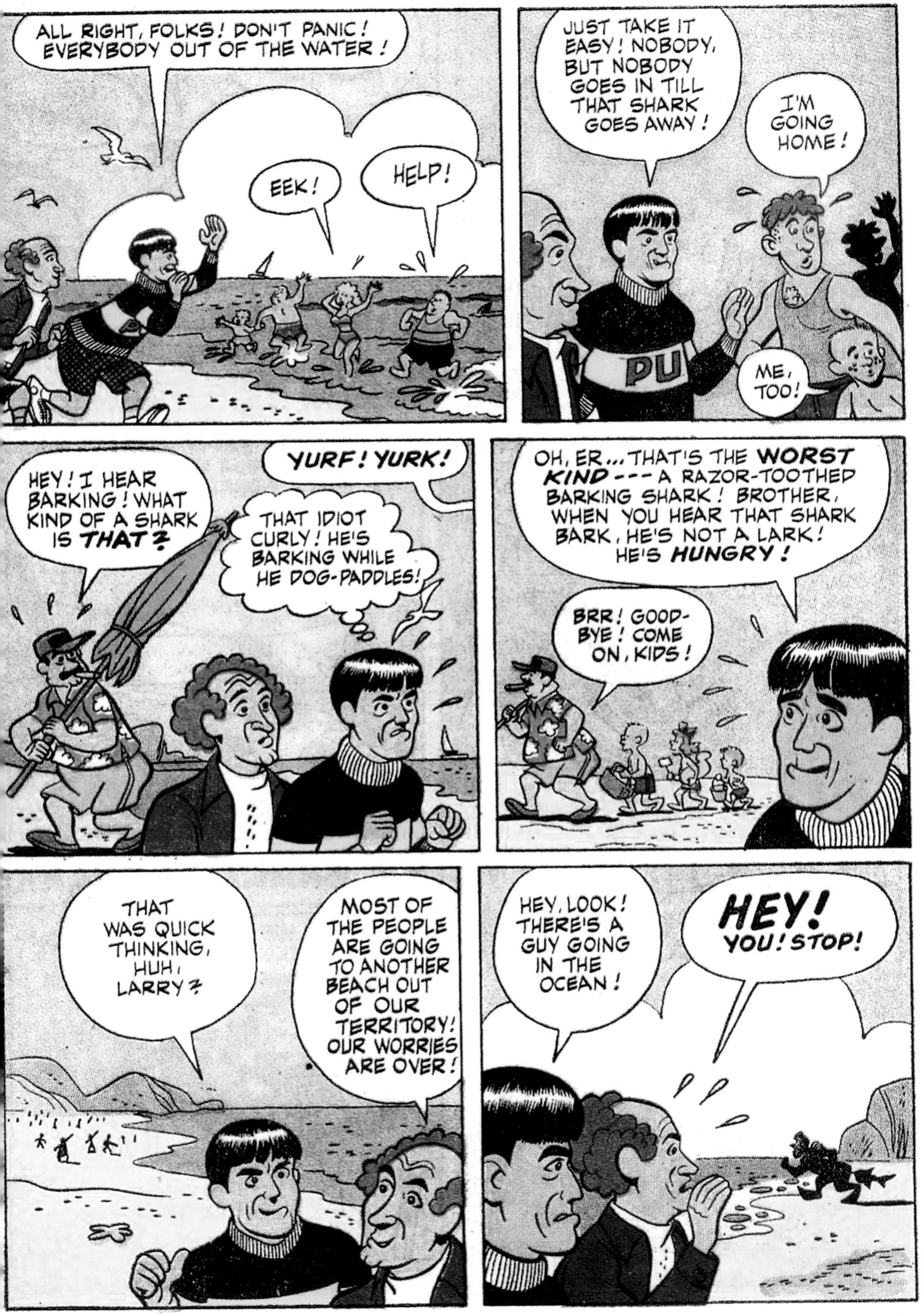
ALL RIGHT, FOLKS! DON'T PANIC! EVERYBODY OUT OF THE WATER!
EEK!
HELP!
JUST TAKE IT EASY! NOBODY, BUT NOBODY GOES IN TILL THAT SHARK GOES AWAY!
I'M GOING HOME!
ME, TOO!
HEY! I HEAR BARKING! WHAT KIND OF A SHARK IS *THAT*?
YURF! YURK!
THAT IDIOT CURLY! HE'S BARKING WHILE HE DOG-PADDLES!
OH, ER... THAT'S THE **WORST KIND**--- A RAZOR-TOOTHED BARKING SHARK! BROTHER, WHEN YOU HEAR THAT SHARK BARK, HE'S NOT A LARK! HE'S **HUNGRY**!
BRR! GOOD-BYE! COME ON, KIDS!
THAT WAS QUICK THINKING, HUH, LARRY?
MOST OF THE PEOPLE ARE GOING TO ANOTHER BEACH OUT OF OUR TERRITORY! OUR WORRIES ARE OVER!
HEY, LOOK! THERE'S A GUY GOING IN THE OCEAN!
HEY! YOU! STOP!

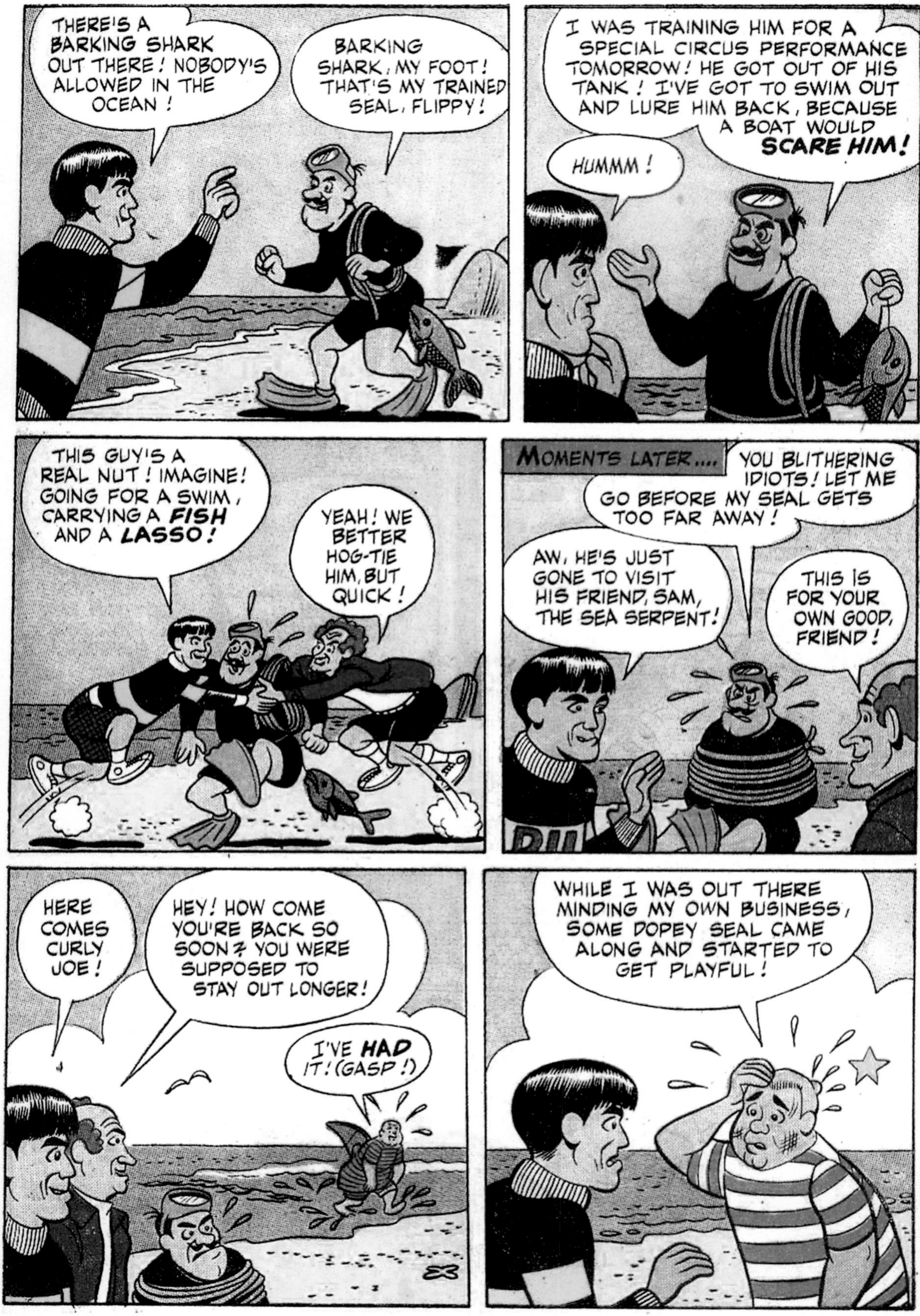
THERE'S A BARKING SHARK OUT THERE! NOBODY'S ALLOWED IN THE OCEAN!
BARKING SHARK, MY FOOT! THAT'S MY TRAINED SEAL, FLIPPY!
I WAS TRAINING HIM FOR A SPECIAL CIRCUS PERFORMANCE TOMORROW! HE GOT OUT OF HIS TANK! I'VE GOT TO SWIM OUT AND LURE HIM BACK, BECAUSE A BOAT WOULD SCARE HIM!
HUMMM!
THIS GUY'S A REAL NUT! IMAGINE! GOING FOR A SWIM, CARRYING A FISH AND A LASSO!
YEAH! WE BETTER HOG-TIE HIM, BUT QUICK!
MOMENTS LATER....
YOU BLITHERING IDIOTS! LET ME GO BEFORE MY SEAL GETS TOO FAR AWAY!
AW, HE'S JUST GONE TO VISIT HIS FRIEND, SAM, THE SEA SERPENT!
THIS IS FOR YOUR OWN GOOD, FRIEND!
HERE COMES CURLY JOE!
HEY! HOW COME YOU'RE BACK SO SOON? YOU WERE SUPPOSED TO STAY OUT LONGER!
I'VE HAD IT! (GASP!)
WHILE I WAS OUT THERE MINDING MY OWN BUSINESS, SOME DOPEY SEAL CAME ALONG AND STARTED TO GET PLAYFUL!

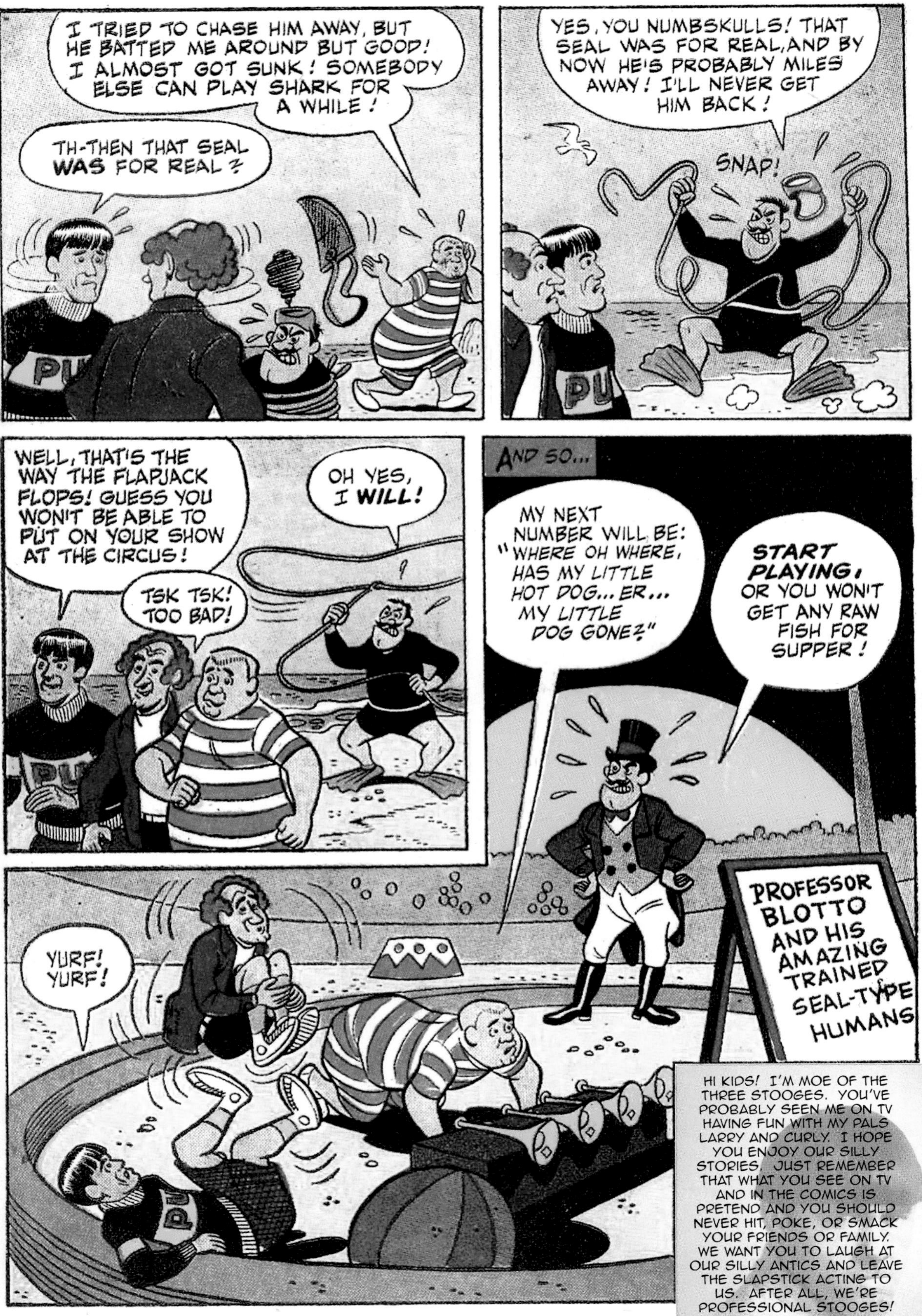
I TRIED TO CHASE HIM AWAY, BUT HE BATTED ME AROUND BUT GOOD! I ALMOST GOT SUNK! SOMEBODY ELSE CAN PLAY SHARK FOR A WHILE!
TH-THEN THAT SEAL **WAS** FOR REAL?
YES, YOU NUMBSKULLS! THAT SEAL WAS FOR REAL, AND BY NOW HE'S PROBABLY MILES AWAY! I'LL NEVER GET HIM BACK!
SNAP!
WELL, THAT'S THE WAY THE FLAPJACK FLOPS! GUESS YOU WON'T BE ABLE TO PUT ON YOUR SHOW AT THE CIRCUS!
TSK TSK! TOO BAD!
OH YES, I **WILL**!
AND SO...
MY NEXT NUMBER WILL BE: "WHERE OH WHERE, HAS MY LITTLE HOT DOG... ER... MY LITTLE DOG GONE?"
START PLAYING, OR YOU WON'T GET ANY RAW FISH FOR SUPPER!
YURF! YURF!
PROFESSOR BLOTTO AND HIS AMAZING TRAINED SEAL-TYPE HUMANS

HI KIDS! I'M MOE OF THE THREE STOOGES. YOU'VE PROBABLY SEEN ME ON TV HAVING FUN WITH MY PALS LARRY AND CURLY. I HOPE YOU ENJOY OUR SILLY STORIES. JUST REMEMBER THAT WHAT YOU SEE ON TV AND IN THE COMICS IS PRETEND AND YOU SHOULD NEVER HIT, POKE, OR SMACK YOUR FRIENDS OR FAMILY. WE WANT YOU TO LAUGH AT OUR SILLY ANTICS AND LEAVE THE SLAPSTICK ACTING TO US. AFTER ALL, WE'RE PROFESSIONAL STOOGES!

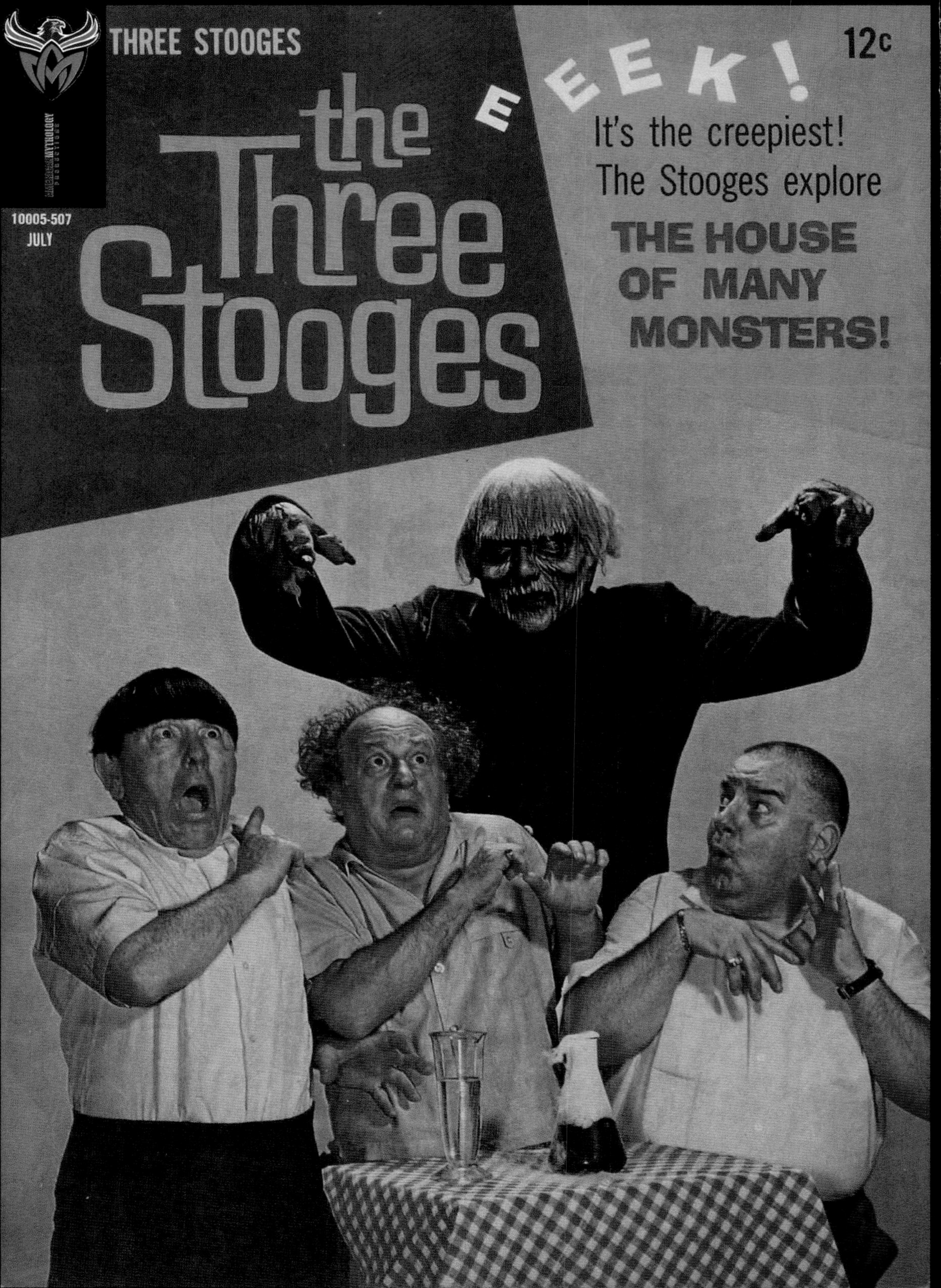
THREE STOOGES
12¢
10005-507
JULY
the Three Stooges
EEEK!
It's the creepiest!
The Stooges explore
THE HOUSE
OF MANY
MONSTERS!

THE THREE STOOGES

THE HOUSE OF MANY MONSTERS

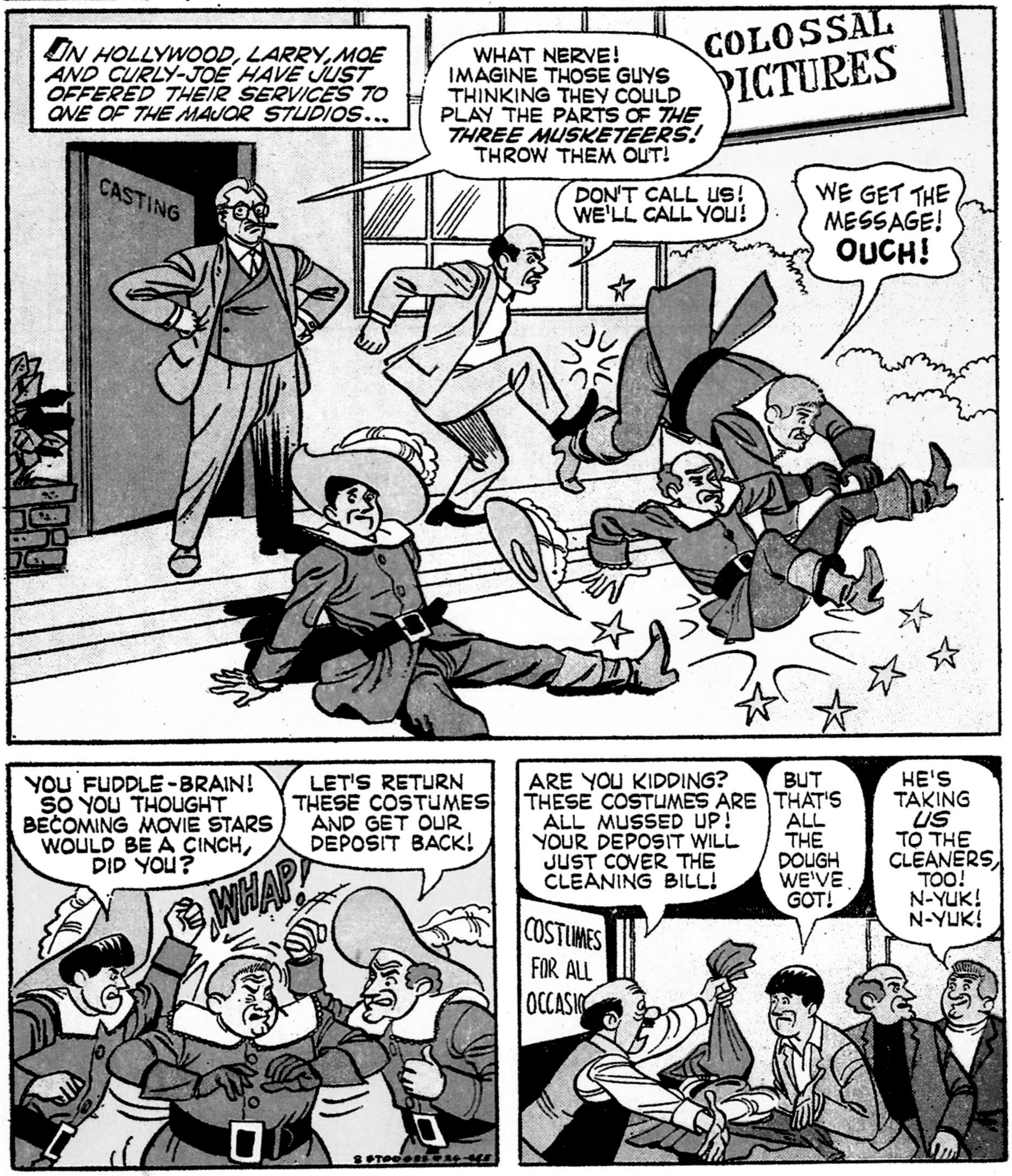
IN HOLLYWOOD, LARRY, MOE AND CURLY-JOE HAVE JUST OFFERED THEIR SERVICES TO ONE OF THE MAJOR STUDIOS...
COLOSSAL PICTURES
WHAT NERVE! IMAGINE THOSE GUYS THINKING THEY COULD PLAY THE PARTS OF THE THREE MUSKETEERS! THROW THEM OUT!
CASTING
DON'T CALL US! WE'LL CALL YOU!
WE GET THE MESSAGE! OUCH!
YOU FUDDLE-BRAIN! SO YOU THOUGHT BECOMING MOVIE STARS WOULD BE A CINCH, DID YOU?
LET'S RETURN THESE COSTUMES AND GET OUR DEPOSIT BACK!
WHAP!
ARE YOU KIDDING? THESE COSTUMES ARE ALL MUSSED UP! YOUR DEPOSIT WILL JUST COVER THE CLEANING BILL!
BUT THAT'S ALL THE DOUGH WE'VE GOT!
HE'S TAKING US TO THE CLEANERS, TOO! N-YUK! N-YUK!
COSTUMES FOR ALL OCCASIO

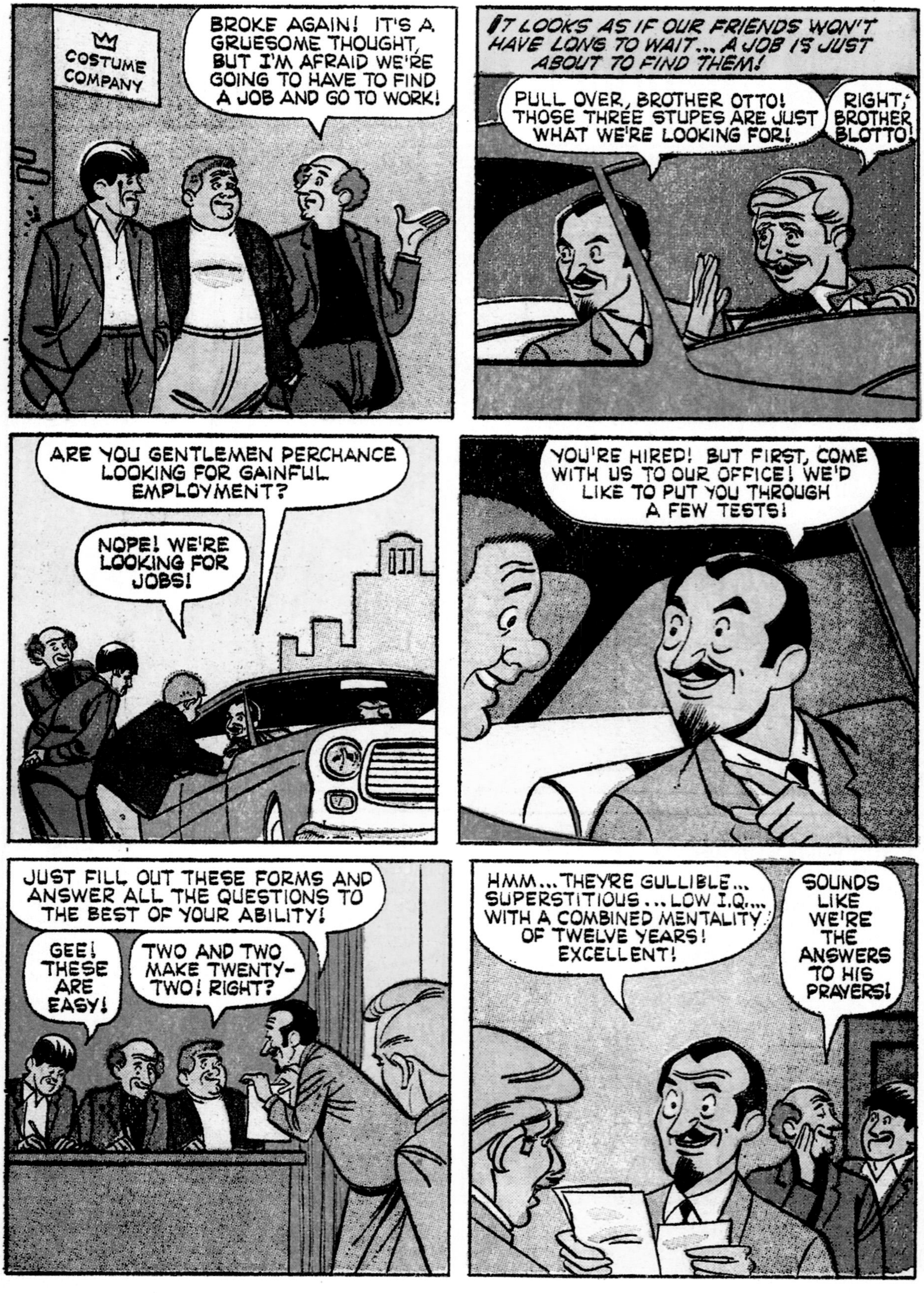
COSTUME COMPANY
BROKE AGAIN! IT'S A GRUESOME THOUGHT, BUT I'M AFRAID WE'RE GOING TO HAVE TO FIND A JOB AND GO TO WORK!
IT LOOKS AS IF OUR FRIENDS WON'T HAVE LONG TO WAIT... A JOB IS JUST ABOUT TO FIND THEM!
PULL OVER, BROTHER OTTO! THOSE THREE STUPES ARE JUST WHAT WE'RE LOOKING FOR!
RIGHT, BROTHER BLOTTO!
ARE YOU GENTLEMEN PERCHANCE LOOKING FOR GAINFUL EMPLOYMENT?
NOPE! WE'RE LOOKING FOR JOBS!
YOU'RE HIRED! BUT FIRST, COME WITH US TO OUR OFFICE! WE'D LIKE TO PUT YOU THROUGH A FEW TESTS!
JUST FILL OUT THESE FORMS AND ANSWER ALL THE QUESTIONS TO THE BEST OF YOUR ABILITY!
GEE! THESE ARE EASY!
TWO AND TWO MAKE TWENTY-TWO! RIGHT?
HMM... THEY'RE GULLIBLE... SUPERSTITIOUS... LOW I.Q.... WITH A COMBINED MENTALITY OF TWELVE YEARS! EXCELLENT!
SOUNDS LIKE WE'RE THE ANSWERS TO HIS PRAYERS!

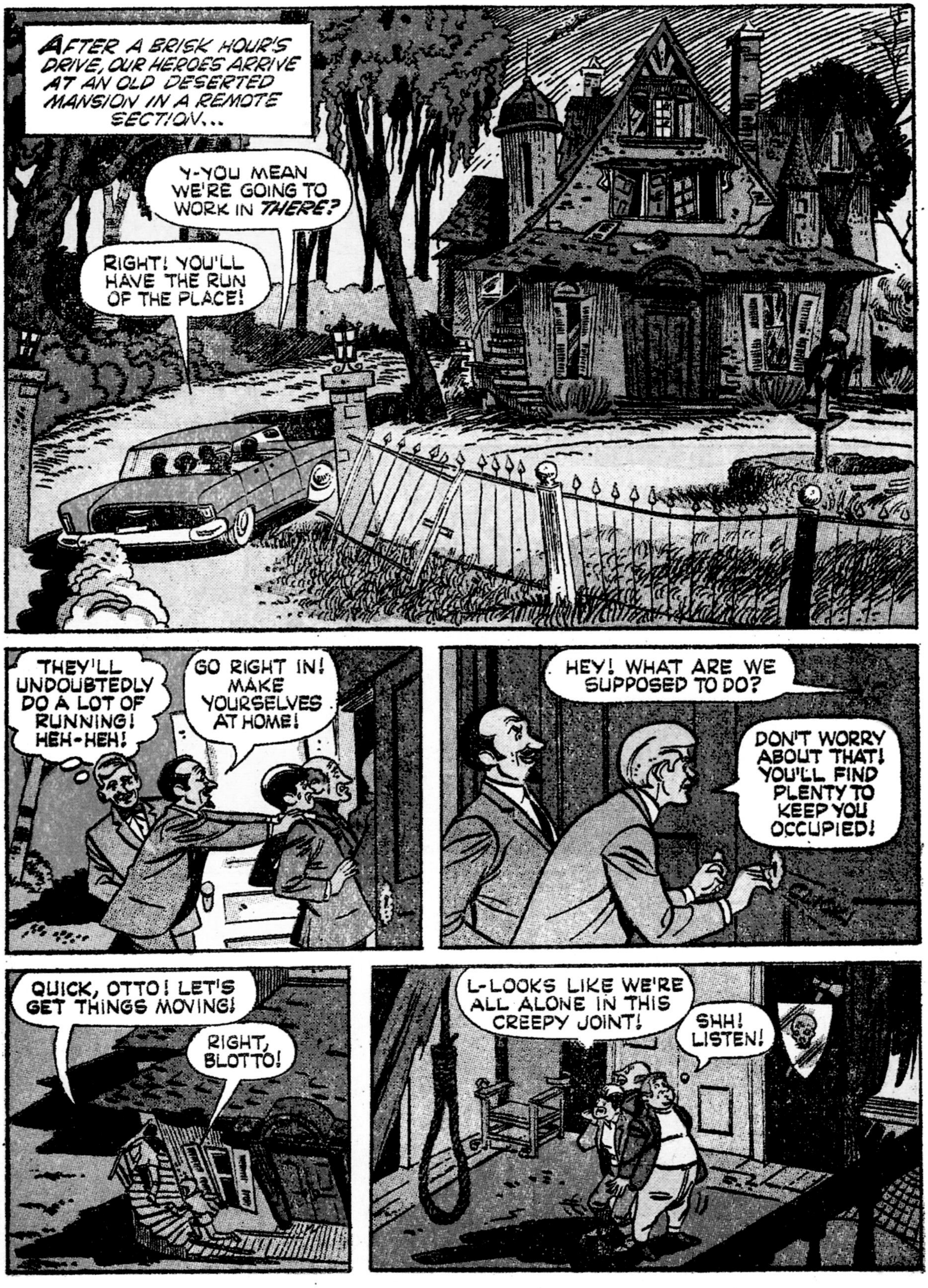
AFTER A BRISK HOUR'S DRIVE, OUR HEROES ARRIVE AT AN OLD DESERTED MANSION IN A REMOTE SECTION...
Y-YOU MEAN WE'RE GOING TO WORK IN THERE?
RIGHT! YOU'LL HAVE THE RUN OF THE PLACE!
THEY'LL UNDOUBTEDLY DO A LOT OF RUNNING! HEH-HEH!
GO RIGHT IN! MAKE YOURSELVES AT HOME!
HEY! WHAT ARE WE SUPPOSED TO DO?
DON'T WORRY ABOUT THAT! YOU'LL FIND PLENTY TO KEEP YOU OCCUPIED!
QUICK, OTTO! LET'S GET THINGS MOVING!
RIGHT, BLOTTO!
L-LOOKS LIKE WE'RE ALL ALONE IN THIS CREEPY JOINT!
SHH! LISTEN!

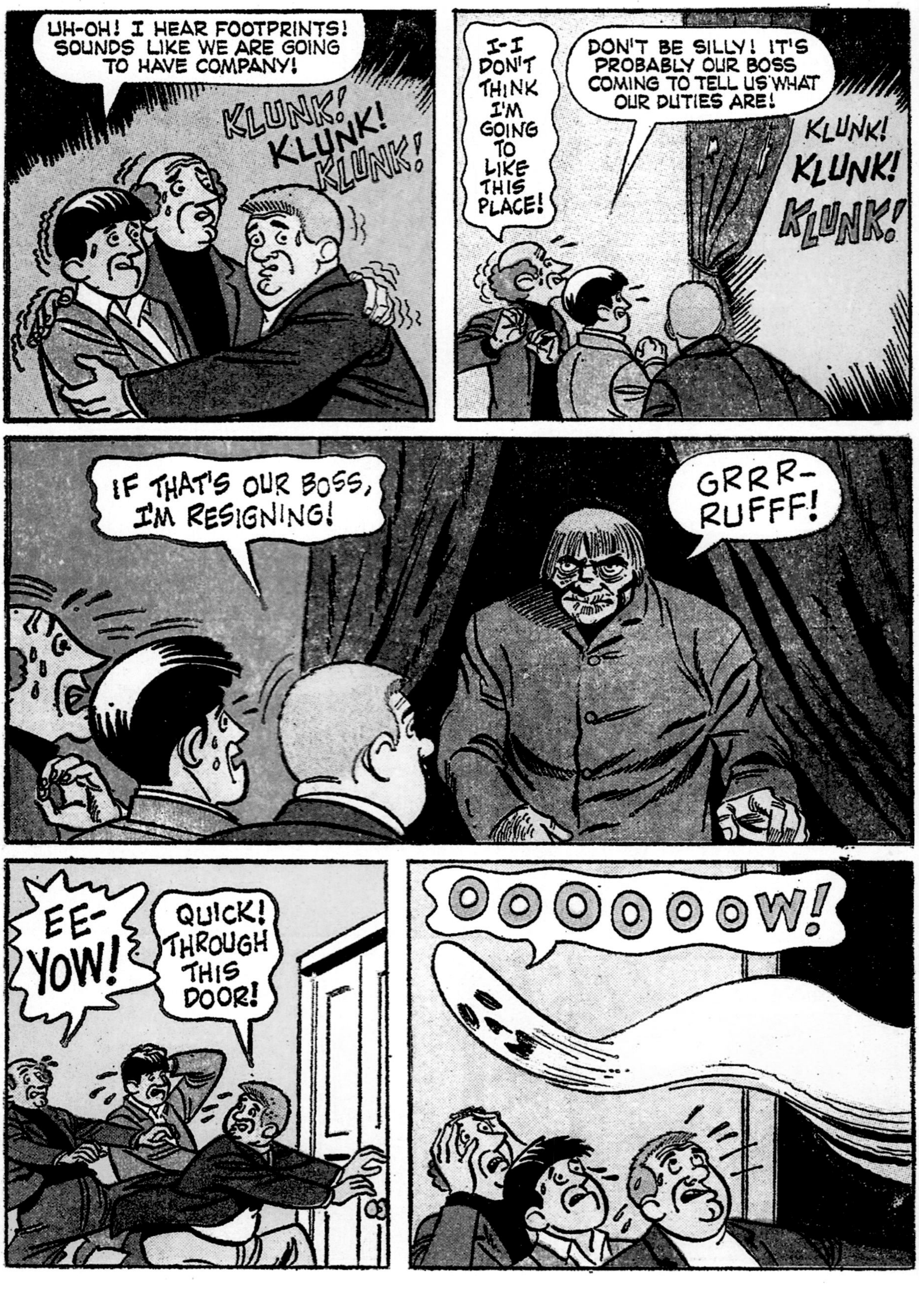
UH-OH! I HEAR FOOTPRINTS! SOUNDS LIKE WE ARE GOING TO HAVE COMPANY!
KLUNK! KLUNK! KLUNK!
I-I DON'T THINK I'M GOING TO LIKE THIS PLACE!
DON'T BE SILLY! IT'S PROBABLY OUR BOSS COMING TO TELL US WHAT OUR DUTIES ARE!
KLUNK! KLUNK! KLUNK!
IF THAT'S OUR BOSS, I'M RESIGNING!
GRRR-RUFFF!
EE-YOW!
QUICK! THROUGH THIS DOOR!
OOOOOOOW!

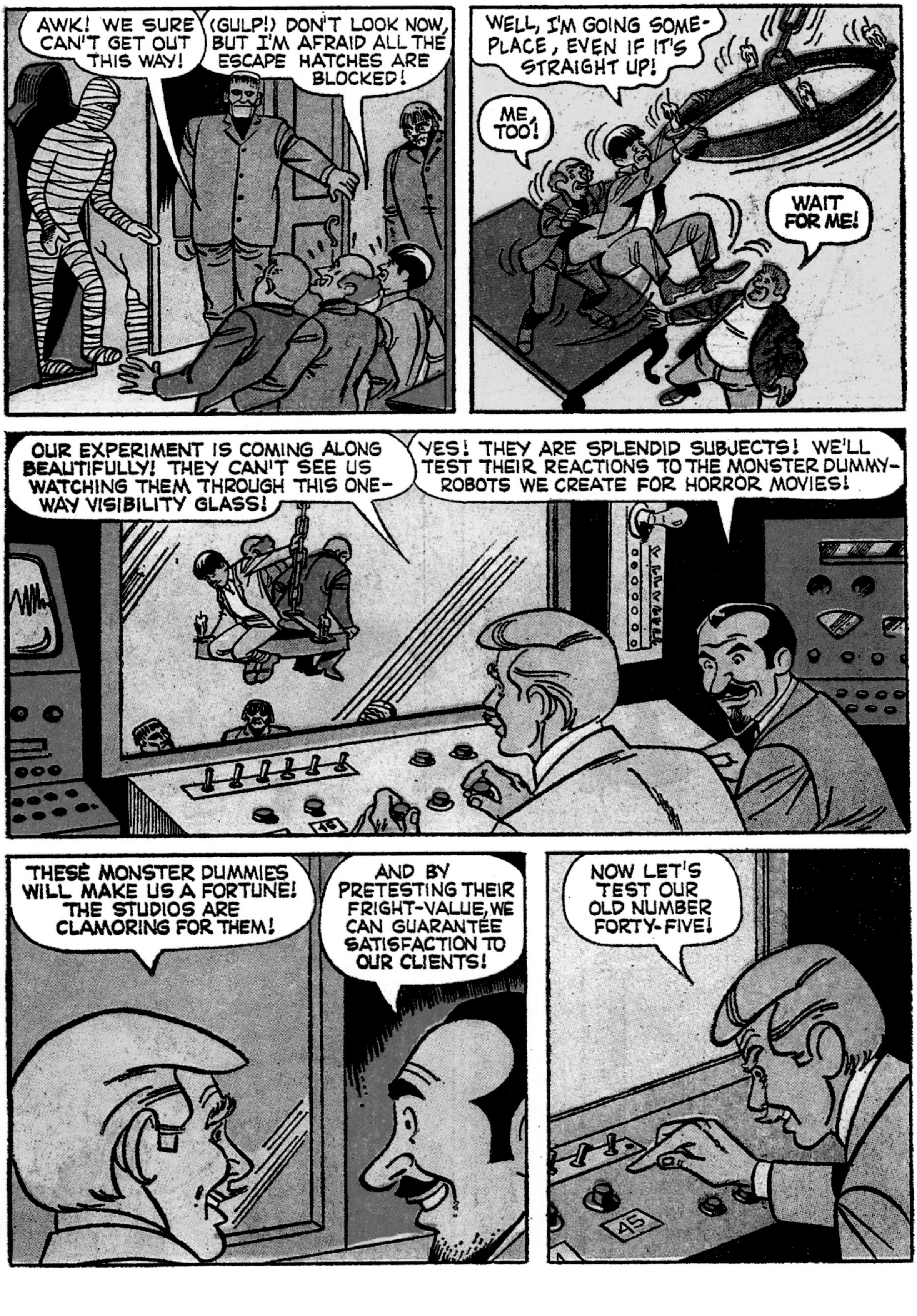
AWK! WE SURE CAN'T GET OUT THIS WAY!
(GULP!) DON'T LOOK NOW, BUT I'M AFRAID ALL THE ESCAPE HATCHES ARE BLOCKED!
WELL, I'M GOING SOME-PLACE, EVEN IF IT'S STRAIGHT UP!
ME, TOO!
WAIT FOR ME!
OUR EXPERIMENT IS COMING ALONG BEAUTIFULLY! THEY CAN'T SEE US WATCHING THEM THROUGH THIS ONE-WAY VISIBILITY GLASS!
YES! THEY ARE SPLENDID SUBJECTS! WE'LL TEST THEIR REACTIONS TO THE MONSTER DUMMY-ROBOTS WE CREATE FOR HORROR MOVIES!
45
THESE MONSTER DUMMIES WILL MAKE US A FORTUNE! THE STUDIOS ARE CLAMORING FOR THEM!
AND BY PRETESTING THEIR FRIGHT-VALUE, WE CAN GUARANTEE SATISFACTION TO OUR CLIENTS!
NOW LET'S TEST OUR OLD NUMBER FORTY-FIVE!
45

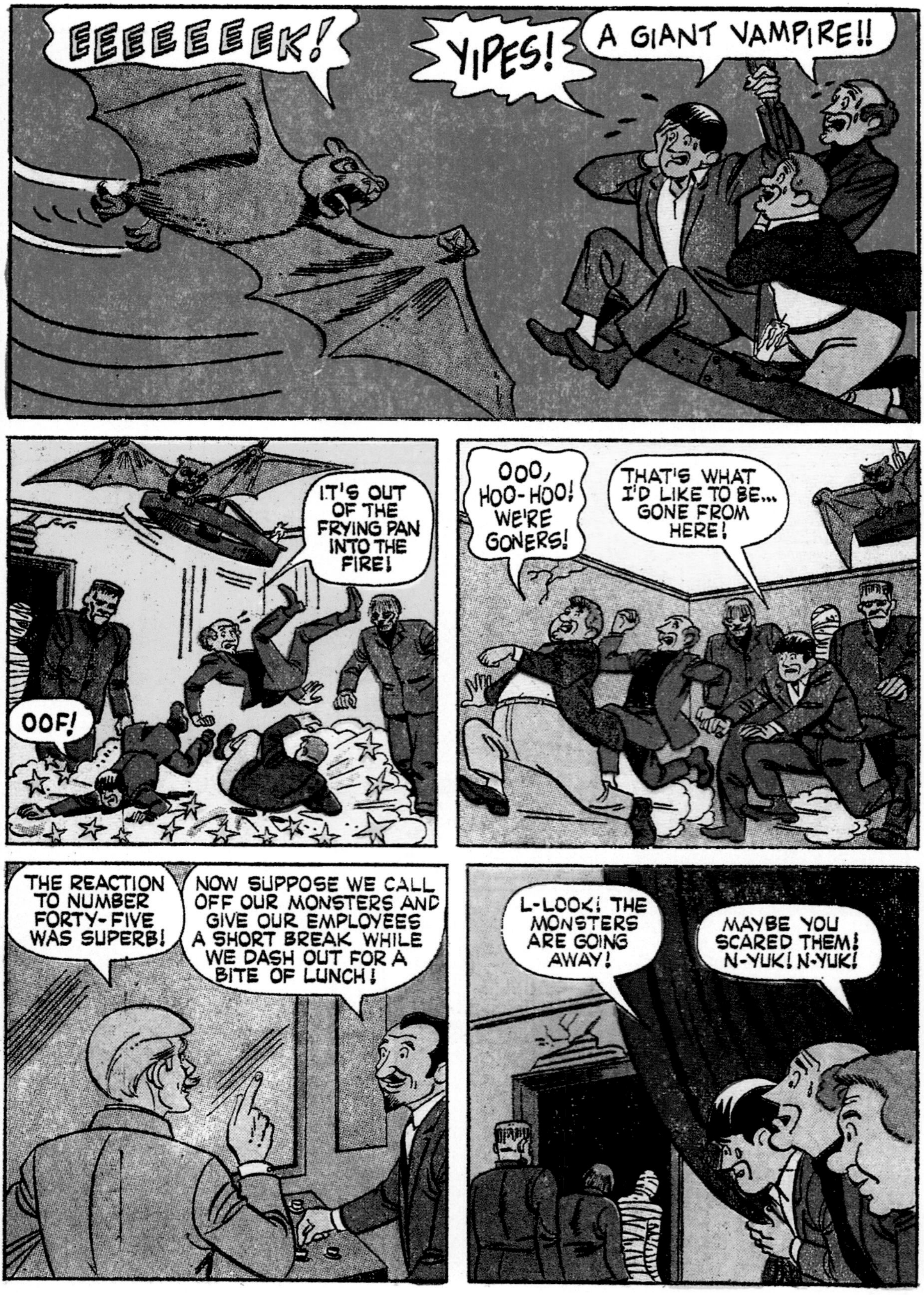
EEEEEEEEK!
YIPES!
A GIANT VAMPIRE!!
IT'S OUT OF THE FRYING PAN INTO THE FIRE!
OOF!
OOO, HOO-HOO! WE'RE GONERS!
THAT'S WHAT I'D LIKE TO BE... GONE FROM HERE!
THE REACTION TO NUMBER FORTY-FIVE WAS SUPERB!
NOW SUPPOSE WE CALL OFF OUR MONSTERS AND GIVE OUR EMPLOYEES A SHORT BREAK WHILE WE DASH OUT FOR A BITE OF LUNCH!
L-LOOK! THE MONSTERS ARE GOING AWAY!
MAYBE YOU SCARED THEM! N-YUK! N-YUK!

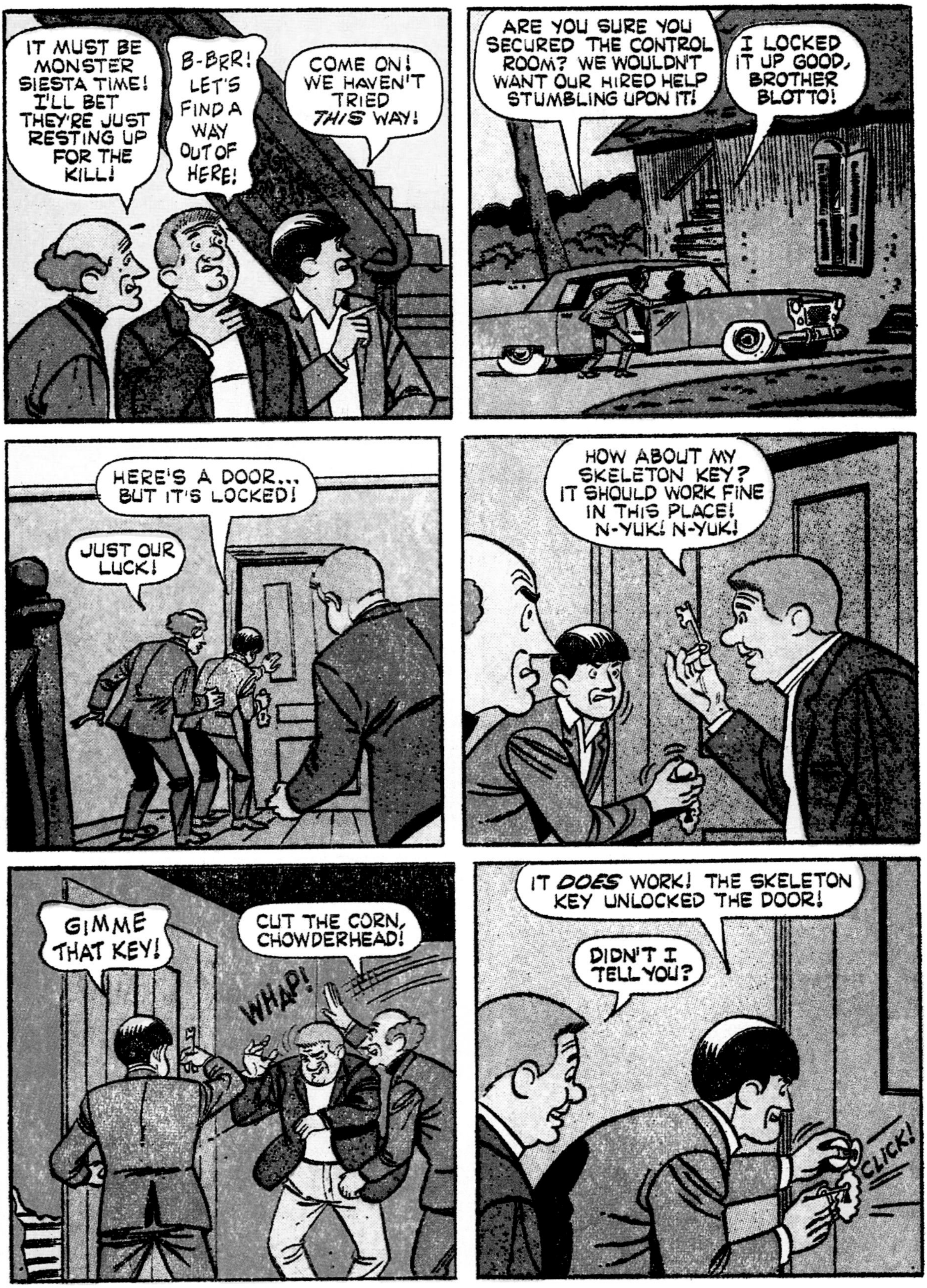
IT MUST BE MONSTER SIESTA TIME! I'LL BET THEY'RE JUST RESTING UP FOR THE KILL!
B-BRR! LET'S FIND A WAY OUT OF HERE!
COME ON! WE HAVEN'T TRIED *THIS* WAY!
ARE YOU SURE YOU SECURED THE CONTROL ROOM? WE WOULDN'T WANT OUR HIRED HELP STUMBLING UPON IT!
I LOCKED IT UP GOOD, BROTHER BLOTTO!
HERE'S A DOOR... BUT IT'S LOCKED!
JUST OUR LUCK!
HOW ABOUT MY SKELETON KEY? IT SHOULD WORK FINE IN THIS PLACE! N-YUK! N-YUK!
GIMME THAT KEY!
CUT THE CORN, CHOWDERHEAD!
WHAP!
IT *DOES* WORK! THE SKELETON KEY UNLOCKED THE DOOR!
DIDN'T I TELL YOU?
CLICK!

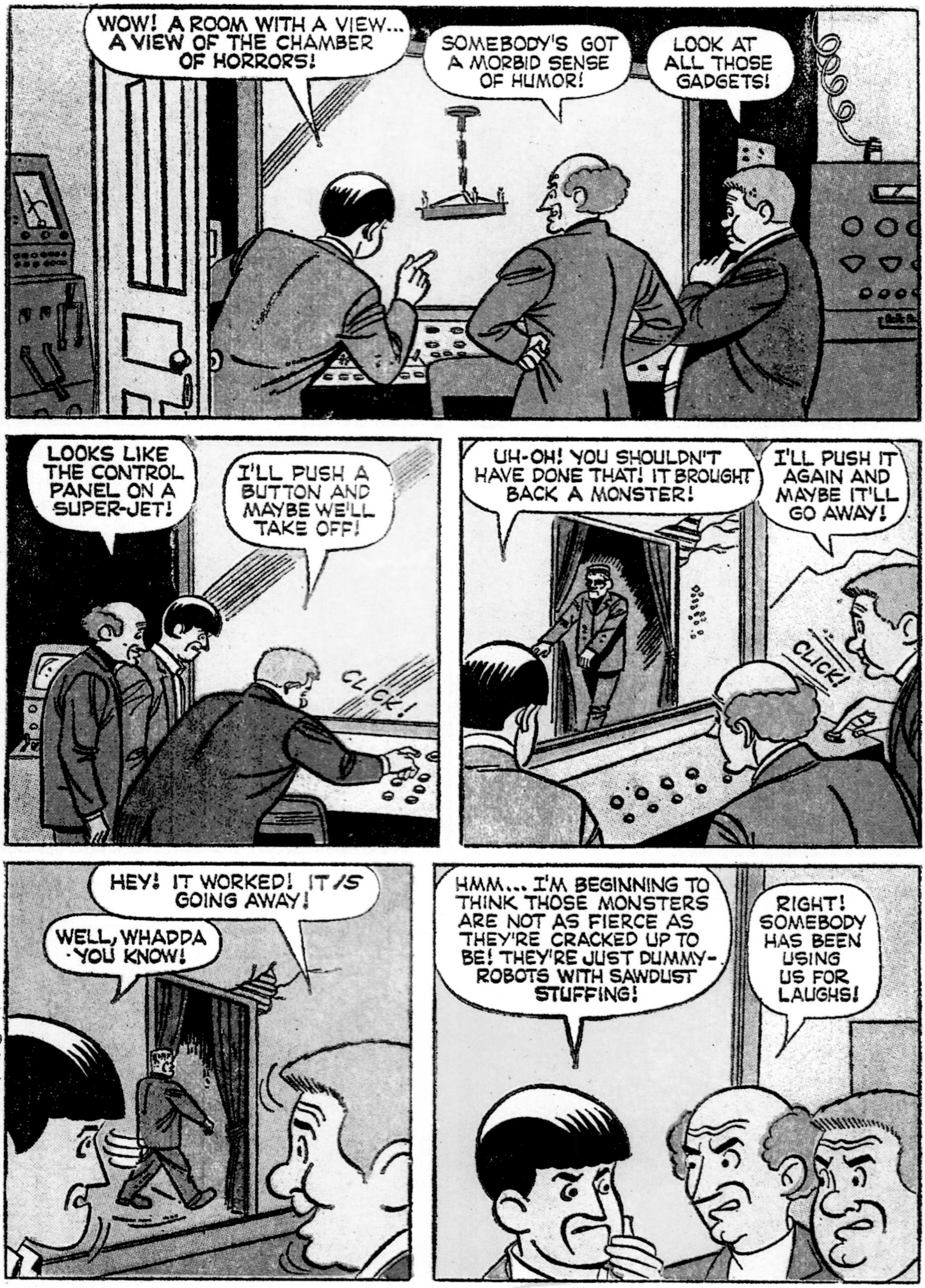
WOW! A ROOM WITH A VIEW... A VIEW OF THE CHAMBER OF HORRORS!
SOMEBODY'S GOT A MORBID SENSE OF HUMOR!
LOOK AT ALL THOSE GADGETS!
LOOKS LIKE THE CONTROL PANEL ON A SUPER-JET!
I'LL PUSH A BUTTON AND MAYBE WE'LL TAKE OFF!
CLICK!
UH-OH! YOU SHOULDN'T HAVE DONE THAT! IT BROUGHT BACK A MONSTER!
I'LL PUSH IT AGAIN AND MAYBE IT'LL GO AWAY!
CLICK!
HEY! IT WORKED! IT IS GOING AWAY!
WELL, WHADDA YOU KNOW!
HMM... I'M BEGINNING TO THINK THOSE MONSTERS ARE NOT AS FIERCE AS THEY'RE CRACKED UP TO BE! THEY'RE JUST DUMMY-ROBOTS WITH SAWDUST STUFFING!
RIGHT! SOMEBODY HAS BEEN USING US FOR LAUGHS!

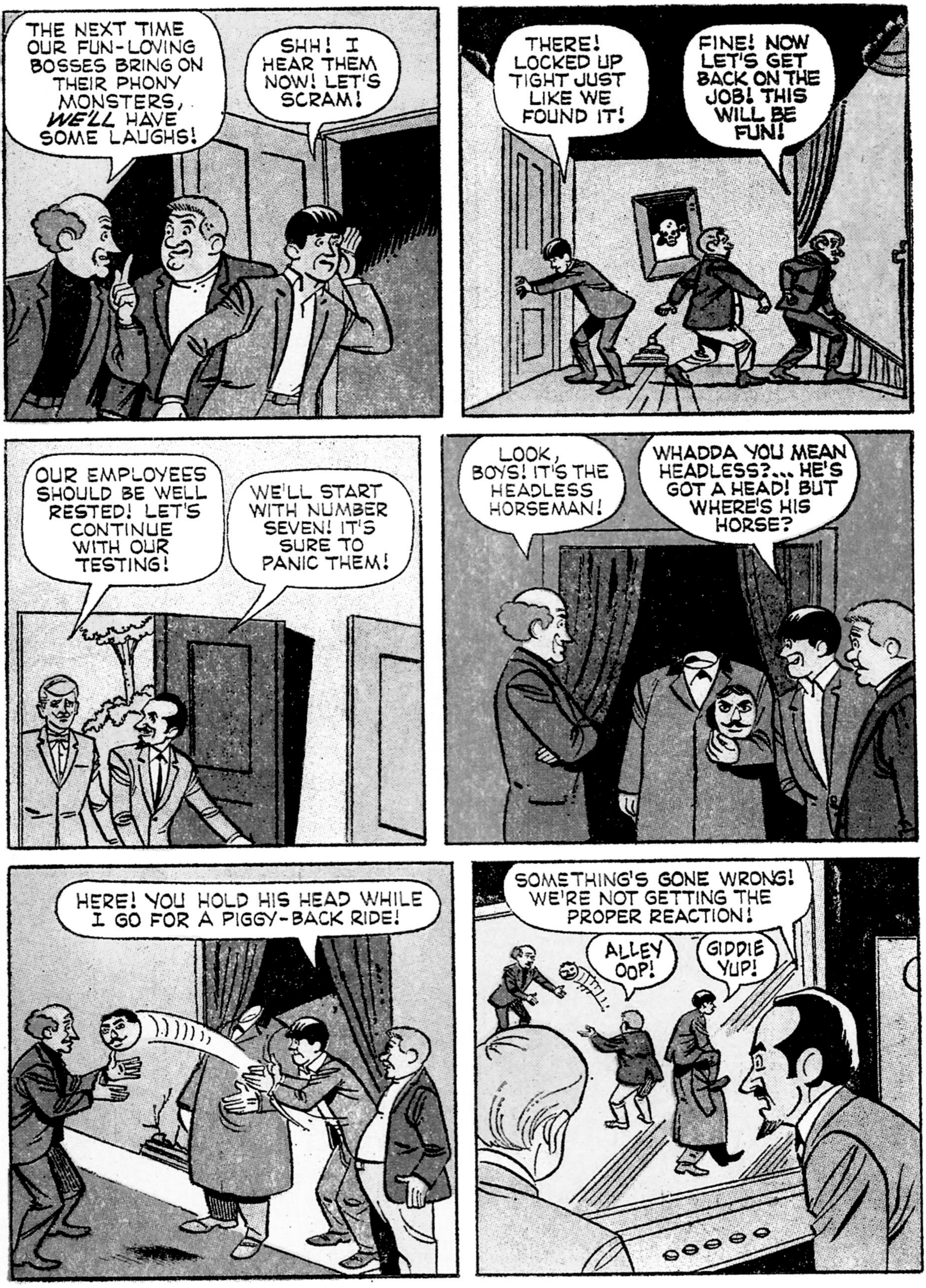
THE NEXT TIME OUR FUN-LOVING BOSSES BRING ON THEIR PHONY MONSTERS, WE'LL HAVE SOME LAUGHS!
SHH! I HEAR THEM NOW! LET'S SCRAM!
THERE! LOCKED UP TIGHT JUST LIKE WE FOUND IT!
FINE! NOW LET'S GET BACK ON THE JOB! THIS WILL BE FUN!
OUR EMPLOYEES SHOULD BE WELL RESTED! LET'S CONTINUE WITH OUR TESTING!
WE'LL START WITH NUMBER SEVEN! IT'S SURE TO PANIC THEM!
LOOK, BOYS! IT'S THE HEADLESS HORSEMAN!
WHADDA YOU MEAN HEADLESS?... HE'S GOT A HEAD! BUT WHERE'S HIS HORSE?
HERE! YOU HOLD HIS HEAD WHILE I GO FOR A PIGGY-BACK RIDE!
SOMETHING'S GONE WRONG! WE'RE NOT GETTING THE PROPER REACTION!
ALLEY OOP!
GIDDIE YUP!

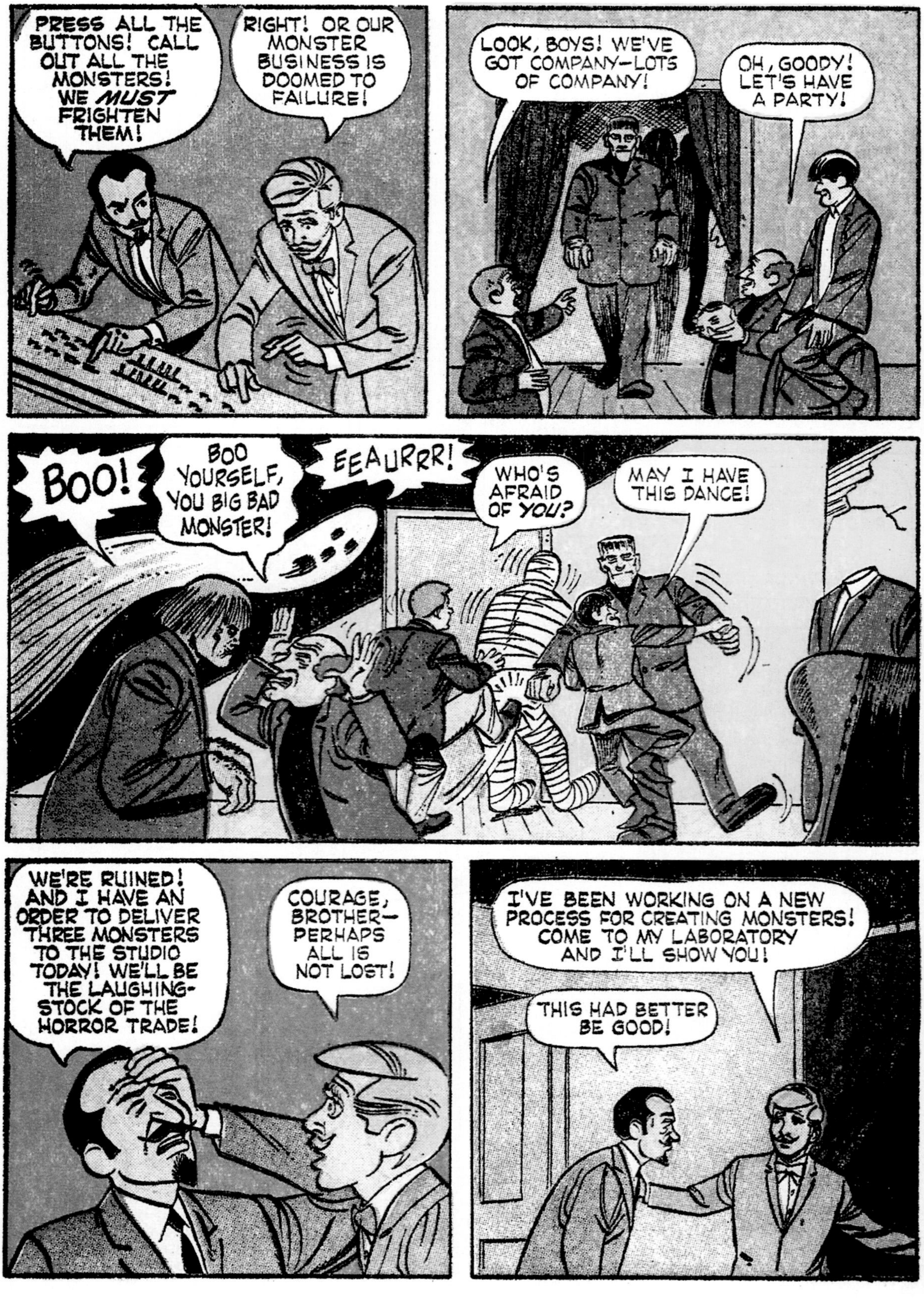
PRESS ALL THE BUTTONS! CALL OUT ALL THE MONSTERS! WE MUST FRIGHTEN THEM!
RIGHT! OR OUR MONSTER BUSINESS IS DOOMED TO FAILURE!
LOOK, BOYS! WE'VE GOT COMPANY—LOTS OF COMPANY!
OH, GOODY! LET'S HAVE A PARTY!
BOO!
BOO YOURSELF, YOU BIG BAD MONSTER!
EEAURRR!
WHO'S AFRAID OF YOU?
MAY I HAVE THIS DANCE!
WE'RE RUINED! AND I HAVE AN ORDER TO DELIVER THREE MONSTERS TO THE STUDIO TODAY! WE'LL BE THE LAUGHING-STOCK OF THE HORROR TRADE!
COURAGE, BROTHER—PERHAPS ALL IS NOT LOST!
I'VE BEEN WORKING ON A NEW PROCESS FOR CREATING MONSTERS! COME TO MY LABORATORY AND I'LL SHOW YOU!
THIS HAD BETTER BE GOOD!

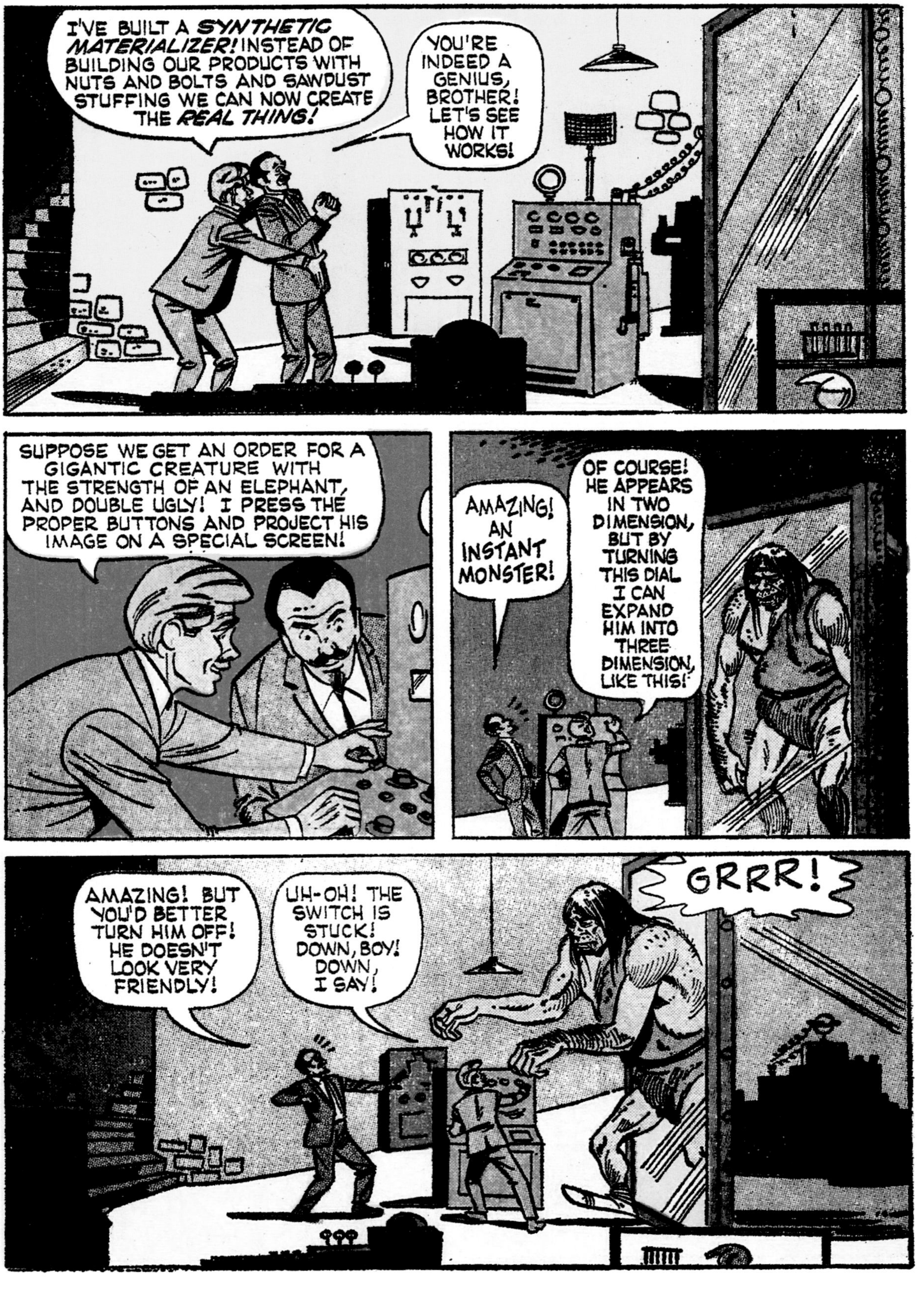

I'VE BUILT A SYNTHETIC MATERIALIZER! INSTEAD OF BUILDING OUR PRODUCTS WITH NUTS AND BOLTS AND SAWDUST STUFFING WE CAN NOW CREATE THE REAL THING!
YOU'RE INDEED A GENIUS, BROTHER! LET'S SEE HOW IT WORKS!
SUPPOSE WE GET AN ORDER FOR A GIGANTIC CREATURE WITH THE STRENGTH OF AN ELEPHANT, AND DOUBLE UGLY! I PRESS THE PROPER BUTTONS AND PROJECT HIS IMAGE ON A SPECIAL SCREEN!
AMAZING! AN INSTANT MONSTER!
OF COURSE! HE APPEARS IN TWO DIMENSION, BUT BY TURNING THIS DIAL I CAN EXPAND HIM INTO THREE DIMENSION, LIKE THIS!
AMAZING! BUT YOU'D BETTER TURN HIM OFF! HE DOESN'T LOOK VERY FRIENDLY!
UH-OH! THE SWITCH IS STUCK! DOWN, BOY! DOWN, I SAY!
GRRR!

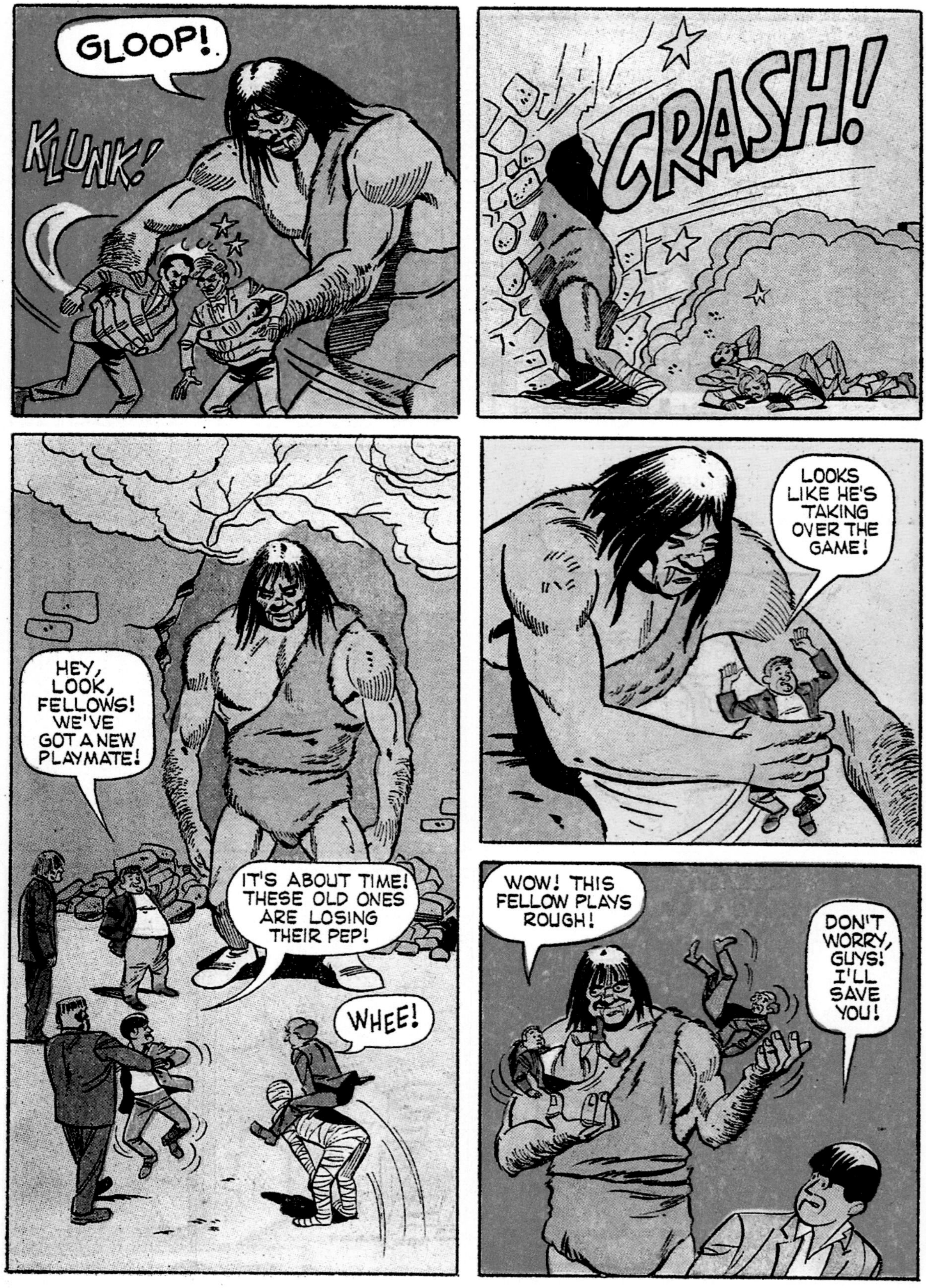
GLOOP!
KLUNK!
CRASH!
HEY, LOOK, FELLOWS! WE'VE GOT A NEW PLAYMATE!
IT'S ABOUT TIME! THESE OLD ONES ARE LOSING THEIR PEP!
WHEE!
LOOKS LIKE HE'S TAKING OVER THE GAME!
WOW! THIS FELLOW PLAYS ROUGH!
DON'T WORRY, GUYS! I'LL SAVE YOU!

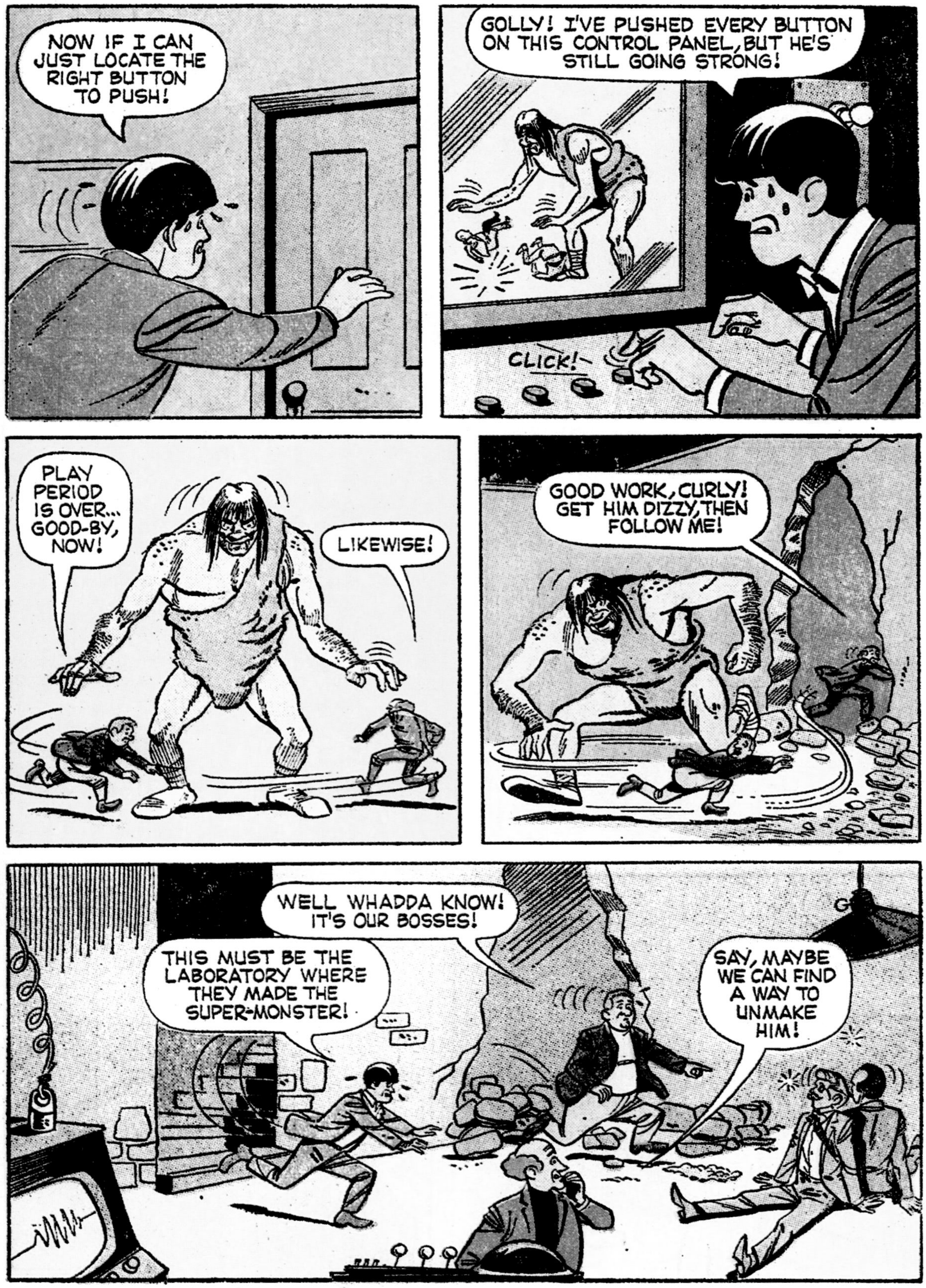
NOW IF I CAN JUST LOCATE THE RIGHT BUTTON TO PUSH!
GOLLY! I'VE PUSHED EVERY BUTTON ON THIS CONTROL PANEL, BUT HE'S STILL GOING STRONG!
CLICK!
PLAY PERIOD IS OVER... GOOD-BY, NOW!
LIKEWISE!
GOOD WORK, CURLY! GET HIM DIZZY, THEN FOLLOW ME!
WELL WHADDA KNOW! IT'S OUR BOSSES!
THIS MUST BE THE LABORATORY WHERE THEY MADE THE SUPER-MONSTER!
SAY, MAYBE WE CAN FIND A WAY TO UNMAKE HIM!

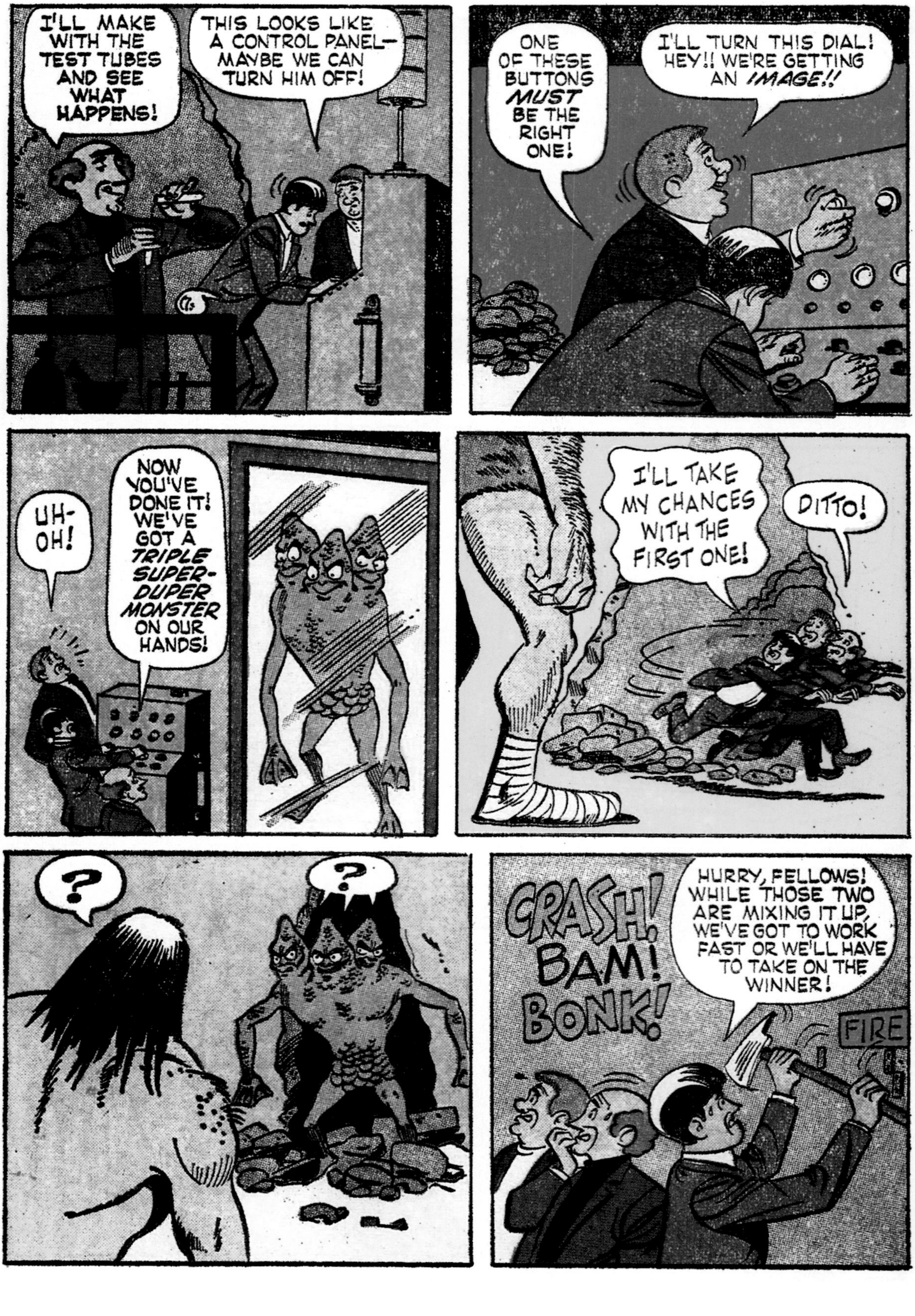
I'LL MAKE WITH THE TEST TUBES AND SEE WHAT HAPPENS!
THIS LOOKS LIKE A CONTROL PANEL— MAYBE WE CAN TURN HIM OFF!
ONE OF THESE BUTTONS MUST BE THE RIGHT ONE!
I'LL TURN THIS DIAL! HEY!! WE'RE GETTING AN IMAGE!!
UH-OH!
NOW YOU'VE DONE IT! WE'VE GOT A TRIPLE SUPER-DUPER MONSTER ON OUR HANDS!
I'LL TAKE MY CHANCES WITH THE FIRST ONE!
DITTO!
?
?
CRASH! BAM! BONK!
HURRY, FELLOWS! WHILE THOSE TWO ARE MIXING IT UP, WE'VE GOT TO WORK FAST OR WE'LL HAVE TO TAKE ON THE WINNER!
FIRE

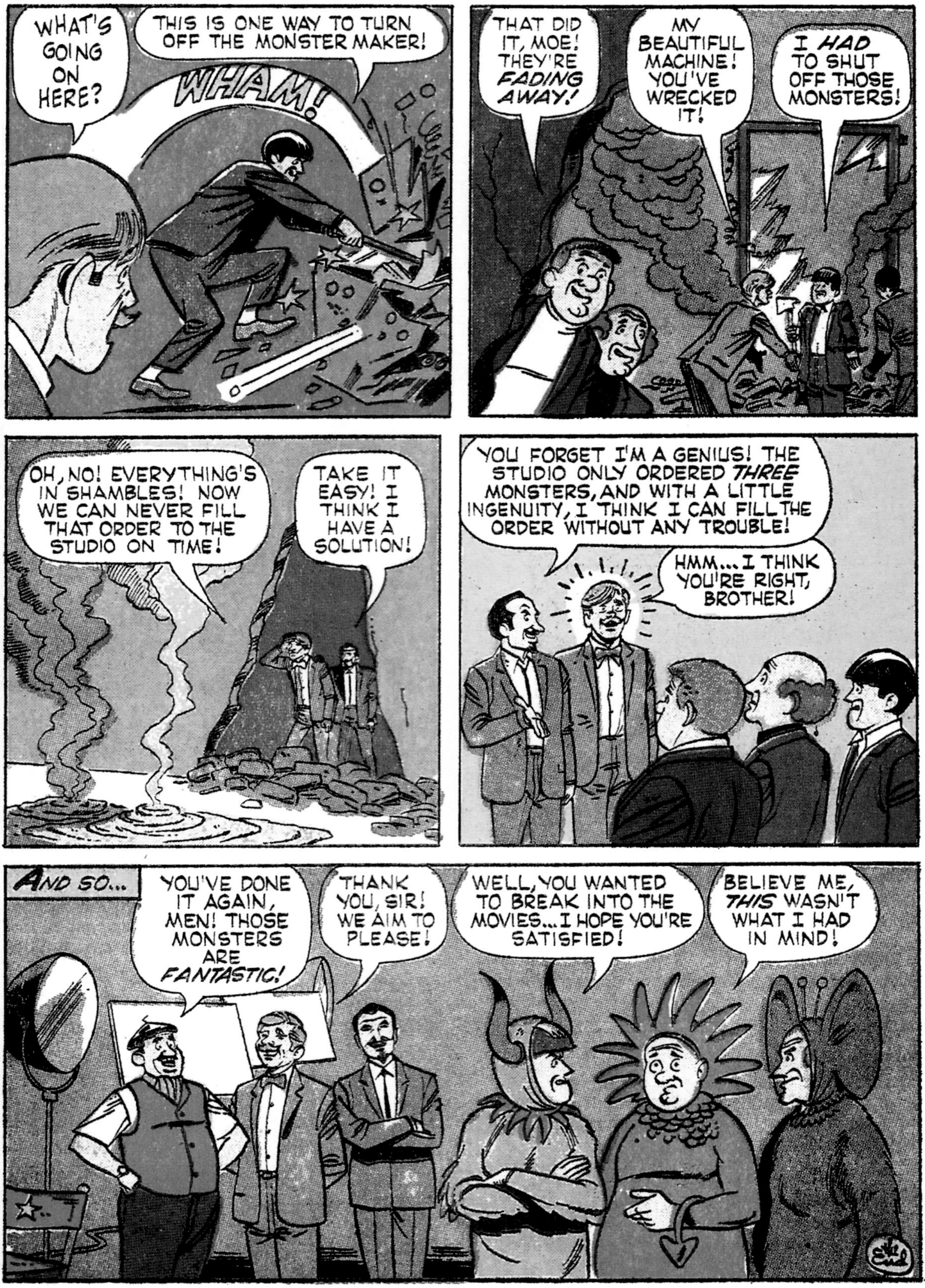

WHAT'S GOING ON HERE?
THIS IS ONE WAY TO TURN OFF THE MONSTER MAKER!
WHAM!
THAT DID IT, MOE! THEY'RE FADING AWAY!
MY BEAUTIFUL MACHINE! YOU'VE WRECKED IT!
I HAD TO SHUT OFF THOSE MONSTERS!
OH, NO! EVERYTHING'S IN SHAMBLES! NOW WE CAN NEVER FILL THAT ORDER TO THE STUDIO ON TIME!
TAKE IT EASY! I THINK I HAVE A SOLUTION!
YOU FORGET I'M A GENIUS! THE STUDIO ONLY ORDERED THREE MONSTERS, AND WITH A LITTLE INGENUITY, I THINK I CAN FILL THE ORDER WITHOUT ANY TROUBLE!
HMM... I THINK YOU'RE RIGHT, BROTHER!
AND SO...
YOU'VE DONE IT AGAIN, MEN! THOSE MONSTERS ARE FANTASTIC!
THANK YOU, SIR! WE AIM TO PLEASE!
WELL, YOU WANTED TO BREAK INTO THE MOVIES... I HOPE YOU'RE SATISFIED!
BELIEVE ME, THIS WASN'T WHAT I HAD IN MIND!
The End

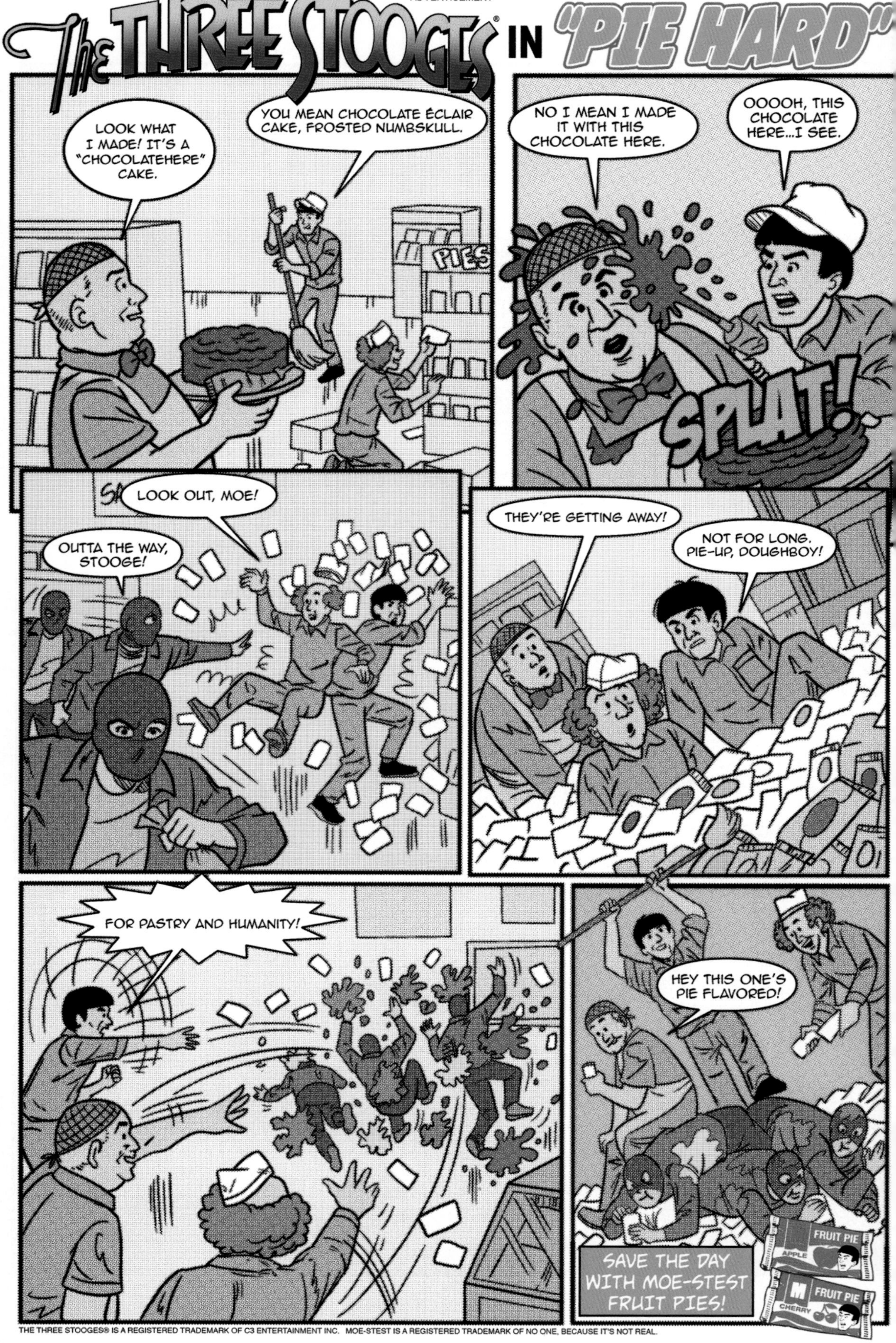
The THREE STOOGES® IN "PIE HARD"
LOOK WHAT I MADE! IT'S A "CHOCOLATEHERE" CAKE.
YOU MEAN CHOCOLATE ÉCLAIR CAKE, FROSTED NUMBSKULL.
PIES
NO I MEAN I MADE IT WITH THIS CHOCOLATE HERE.
OOOOH, THIS CHOCOLATE HERE...I SEE.
SPLAT!
LOOK OUT, MOE!
OUTTA THE WAY, STOOGE!
THEY'RE GETTING AWAY!
NOT FOR LONG. PIE-UP, DOUGHBOY!
FOR PASTRY AND HUMANITY!
HEY THIS ONE'S PIE FLAVORED!
SAVE THE DAY WITH MOE-STEST FRUIT PIES!
FRUIT PIE
APPLE
M FRUIT PIE
CHERRY

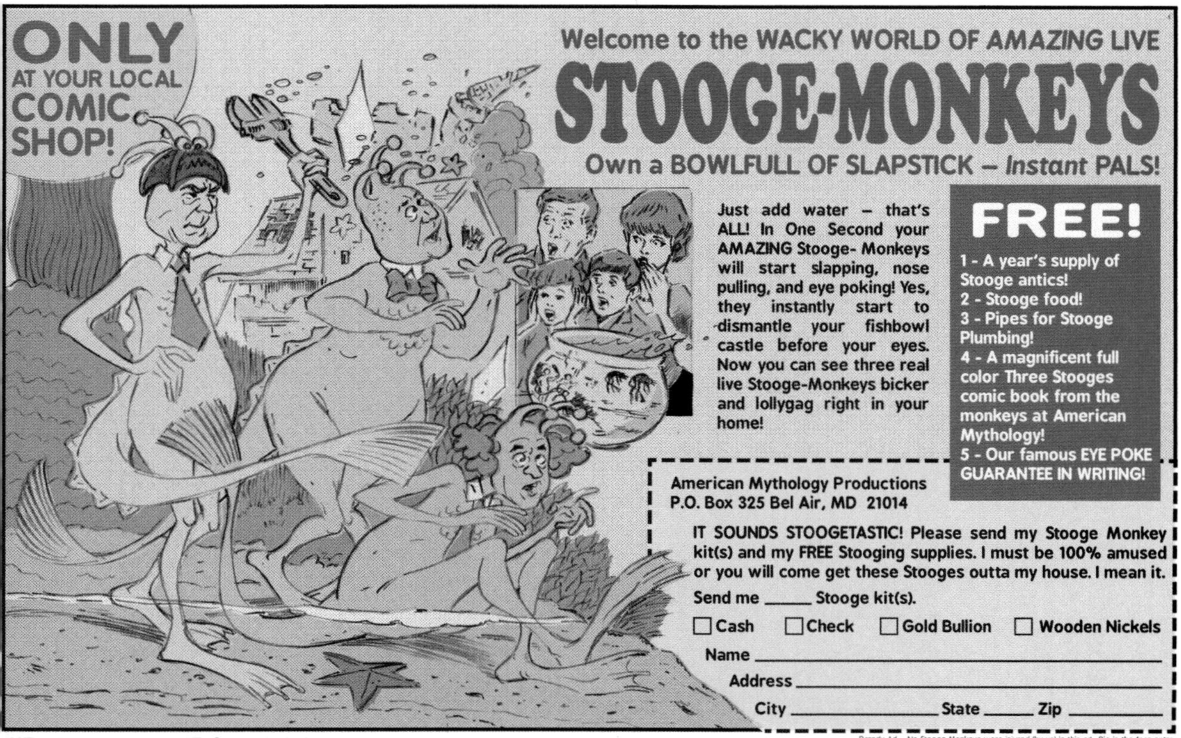

ONLY AT YOUR LOCAL COMIC SHOP!
Welcome to the WACKY WORLD OF AMAZING LIVE
STOOGE-MONKEYS
Own a BOWLFULL OF SLAPSTICK – Instant PALS!
Just add water – that's ALL! In One Second your AMAZING Stooge- Monkeys will start slapping, nose pulling, and eye poking! Yes, they instantly start to dismantle your fishbowl castle before your eyes. Now you can see three real live Stooge-Monkeys bicker and lollygag right in your home!
FREE!
1 - A year's supply of Stooge antics!
2 - Stooge food!
3 - Pipes for Stooge Plumbing!
4 - A magnificent full color Three Stooges comic book from the monkeys at American Mythology!
5 - Our famous EYE POKE GUARANTEE IN WRITING!
American Mythology Productions
P.O. Box 325 Bel Air, MD 21014
IT SOUNDS STOOGETASTIC! Please send my Stooge Monkey kit(s) and my FREE Stooging supplies. I must be 100% amused or you will come get these Stooges outta my house. I mean it.
Send me _____ Stooge kit(s).
☐ Cash ☐ Check ☐ Gold Bullion ☐ Wooden Nickels
Name ____________
Address ____________
City ____________ State _____ Zip ______
Parody Ad – No Stooge Monkeys were injured (by us) in this ad. Pie in the face extra.

TEXT BY JAMES KUHORIC
ART BY S.L. GALLANT

ART BY CHRIS SCALF
LAYOUT BY ADRIAN ROPP

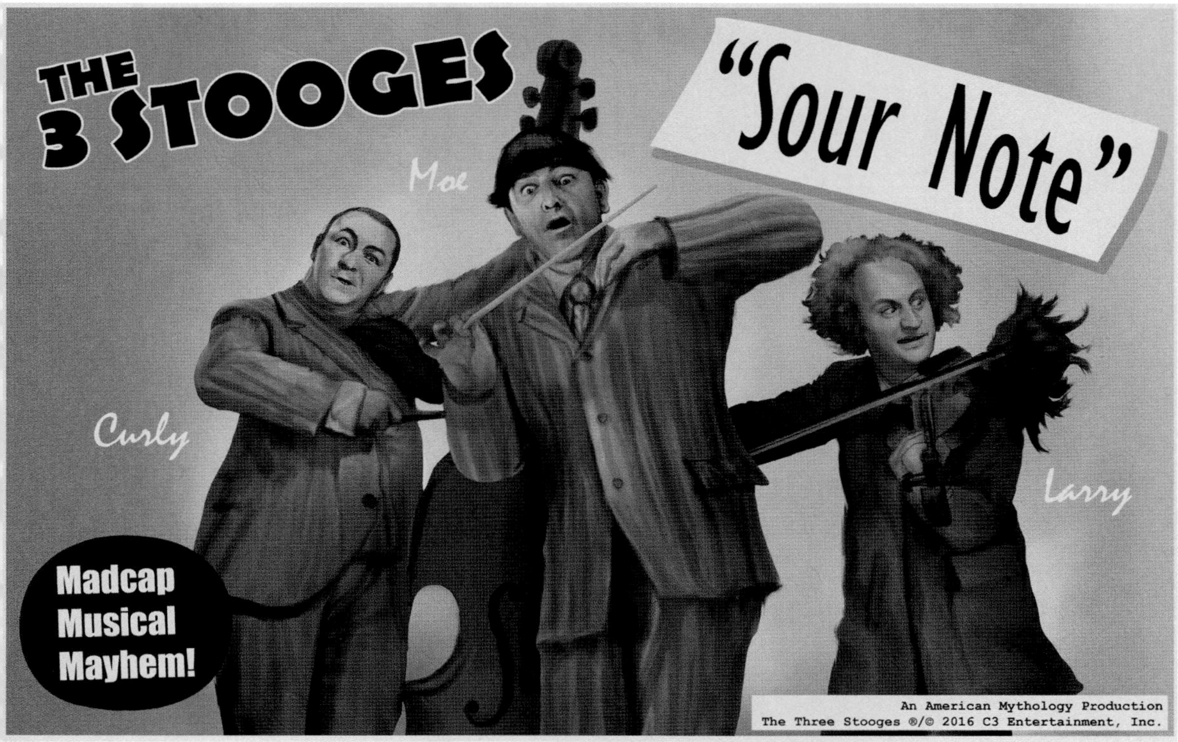

THE 3 STOOGES
"Sour Note"
Moe
Curly
Larry
Madcap Musical Mayhem!
An American Mythology Production
The Three Stooges ®/© 2016 C3 Entertainment, Inc.

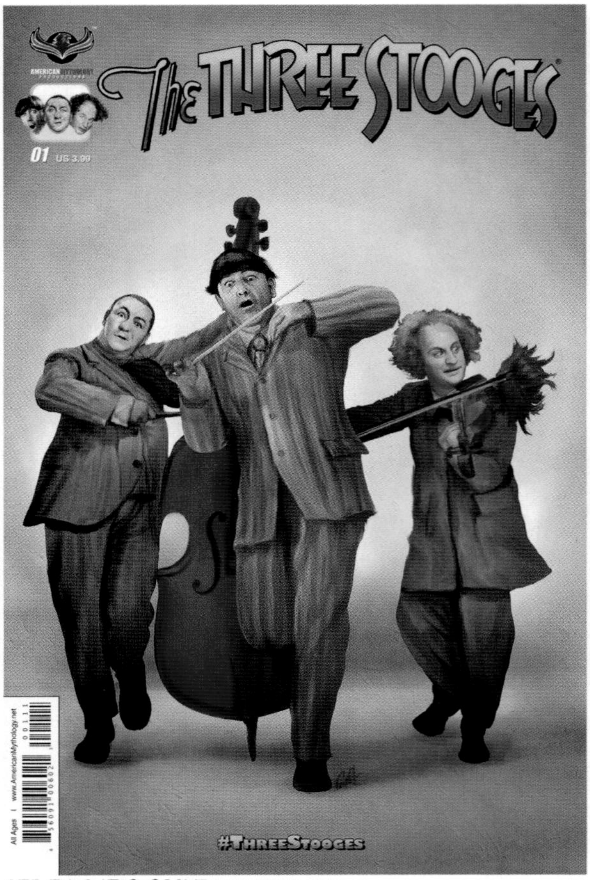
The Three Stooges
01 US 3.99
All Ages | www.AmericanMythology.net
#ThreeStooges

ART BY CHRIS SCALF

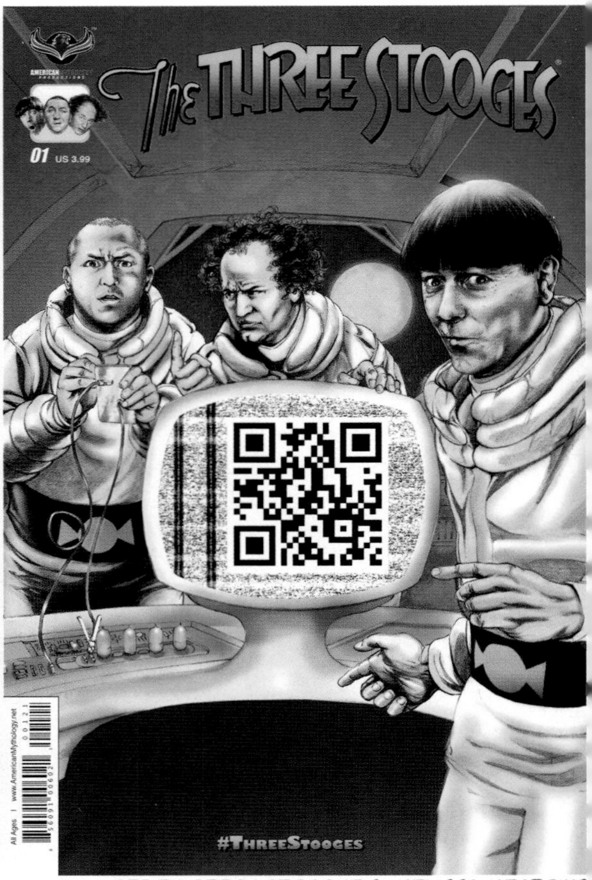
The Three Stooges
01 US 3.99
All Ages | www.AmericanMythology.net
#ThreeStooges

ART BY GREG LAROCQUE & MELISSA MEADOWS

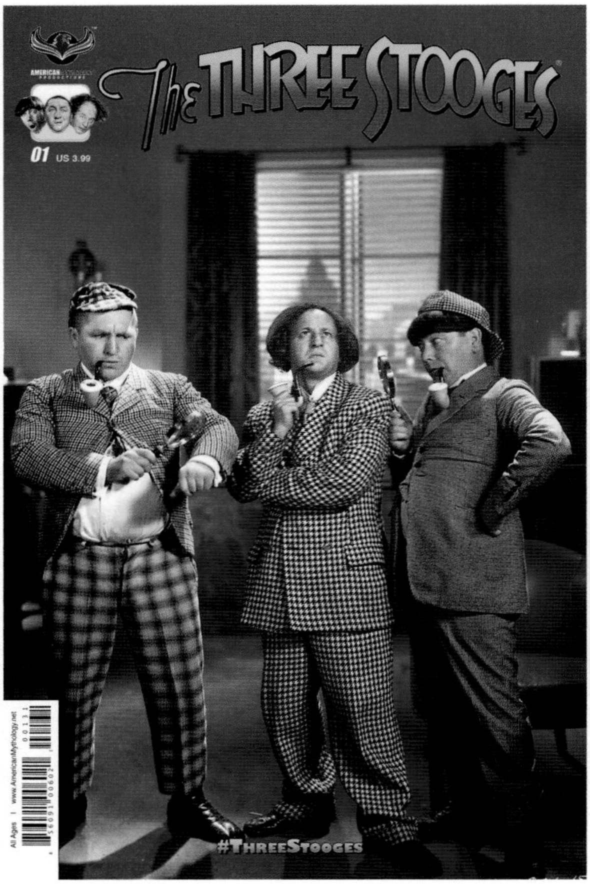
The Three Stooges
01 US 3.99
All Ages | www.AmericanMythology.net
#ThreeStooges

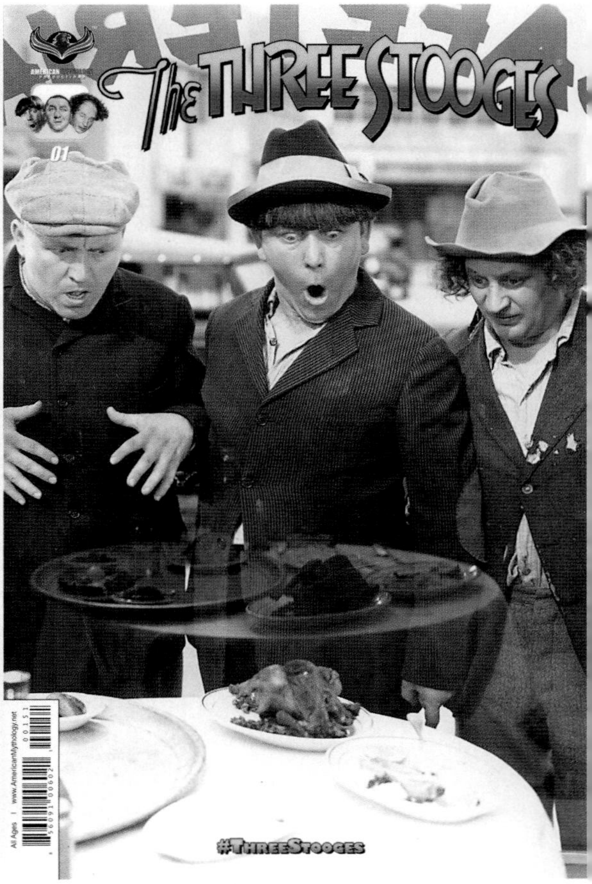
The Three Stooges
01
All Ages | www.AmericanMythology.net
#ThreeStooges

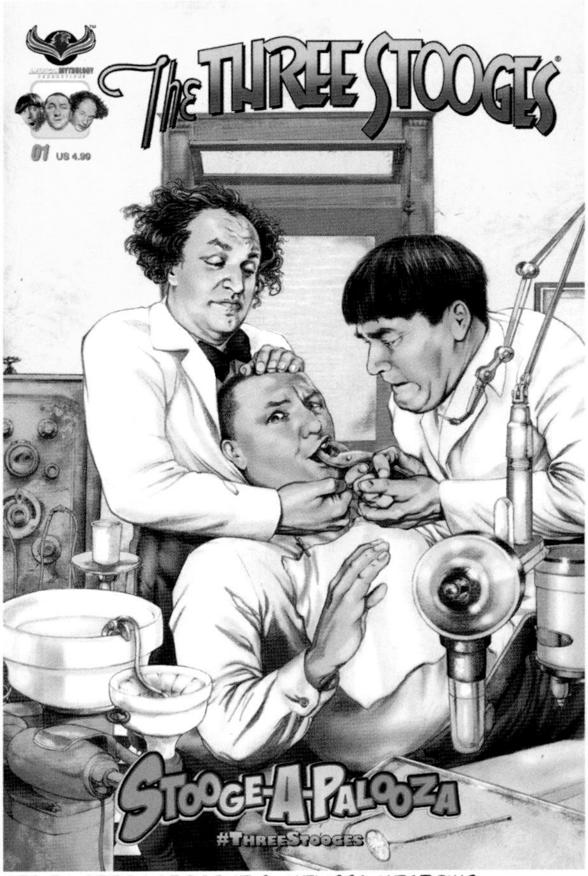
The THREE STOOGES
01 US 4.99
STOOGE-A-PALOOZA
#ThreeStooges
ART BY GREG LAROCQUE & MELISSA MEADOWS

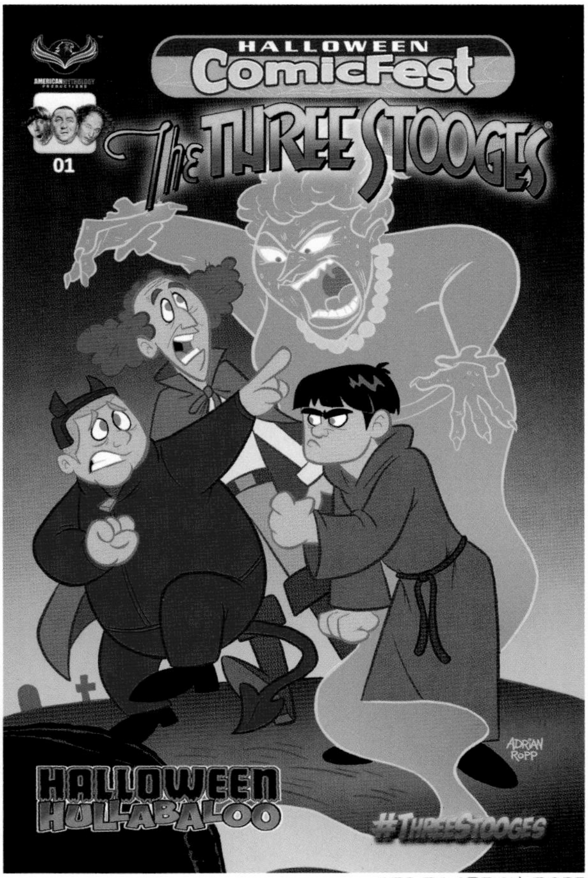
HALLOWEEN
ComicFest
The THREE STOOGES
01
ADRIAN ROPP
HALLOWEEN
HULLABALOO
#ThreeStooges
ART BY ADRIAN ROPP

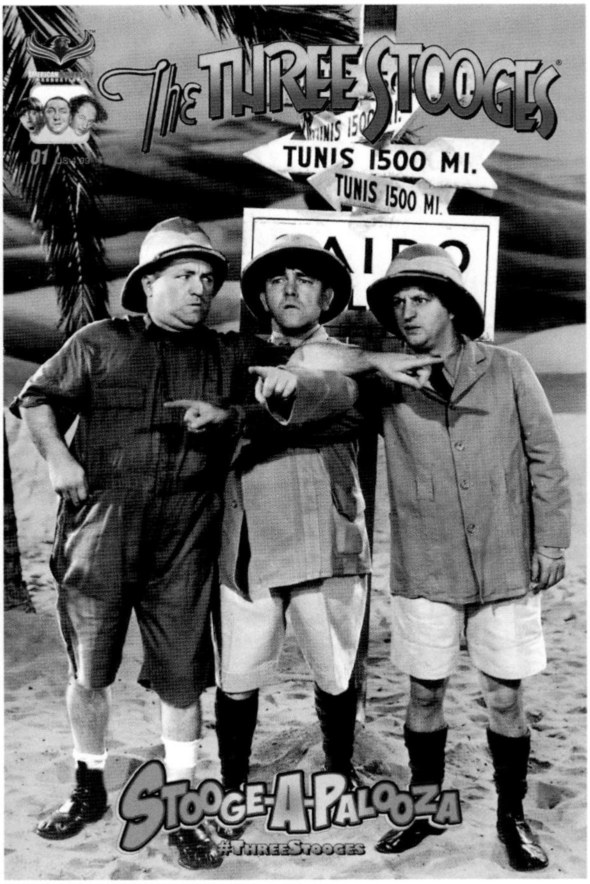
The THREE STOOGES
01
TUNIS 1500 MI.
TUNIS 1500 MI.
STOOGE-A-PALOOZA
#ThreeStooges

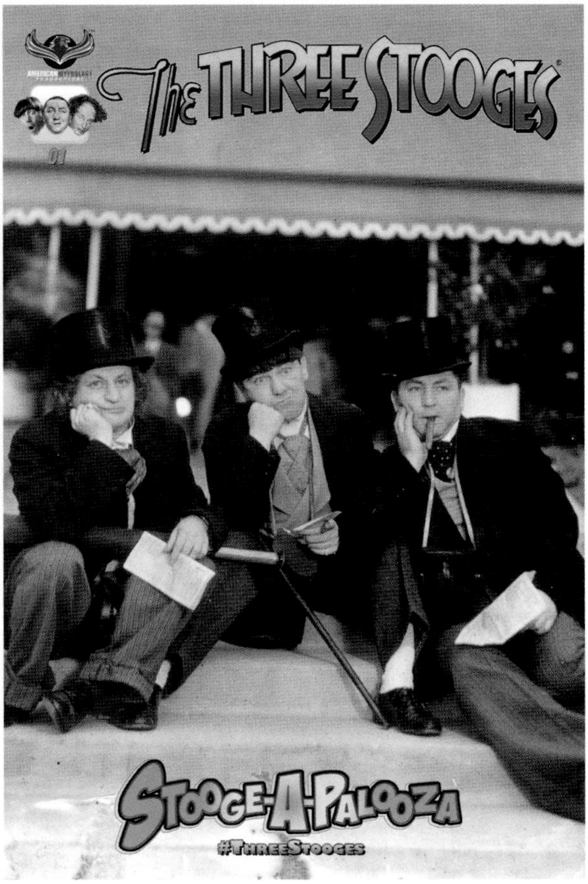
The THREE STOOGES
01
STOOGE-A-PALOOZA
#ThreeStooges

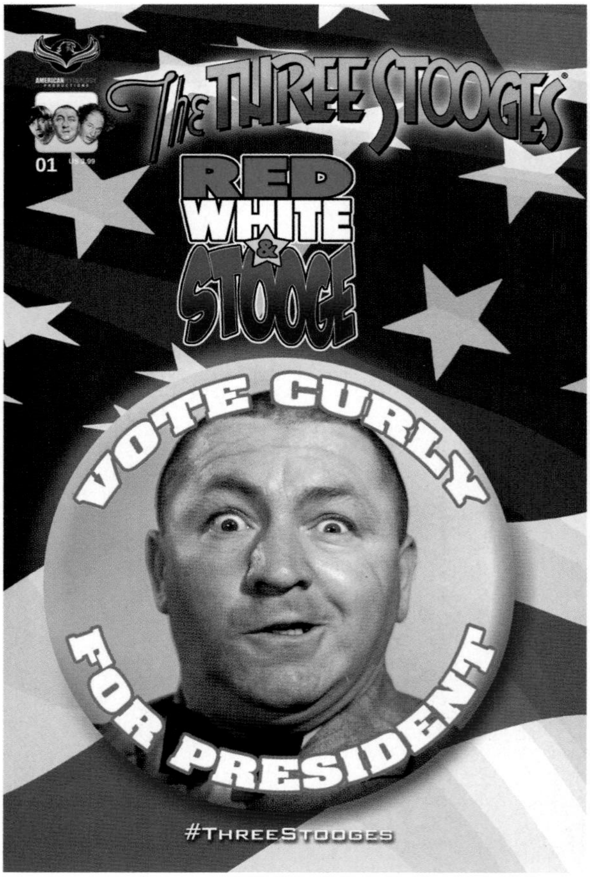

The Three Stooges
01
RED
WHITE
&
STOOGE
VOTE CURLY
FOR PRESIDENT
#ThreeStooges

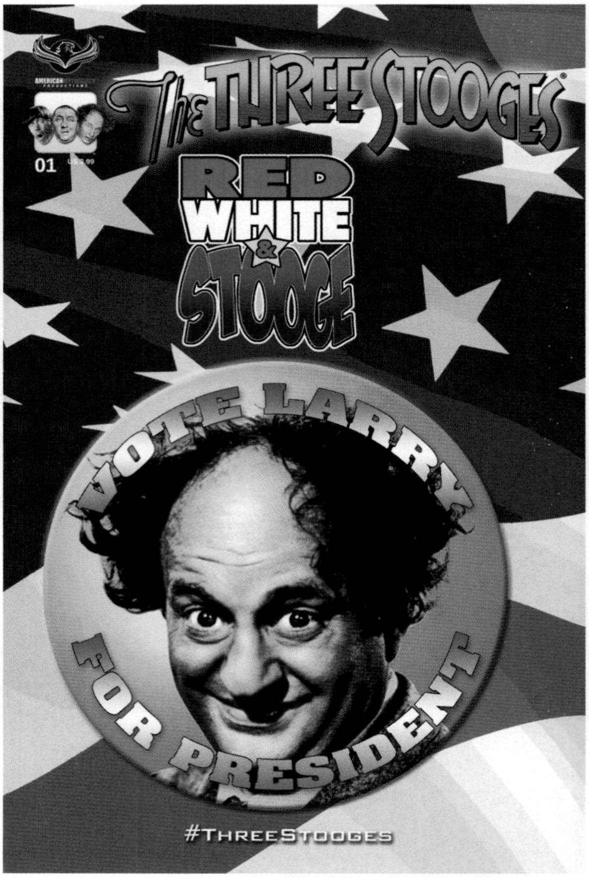

The Three Stooges
01
RED
WHITE
&
STOOGE
VOTE LARRY
FOR PRESIDENT
#ThreeStooges

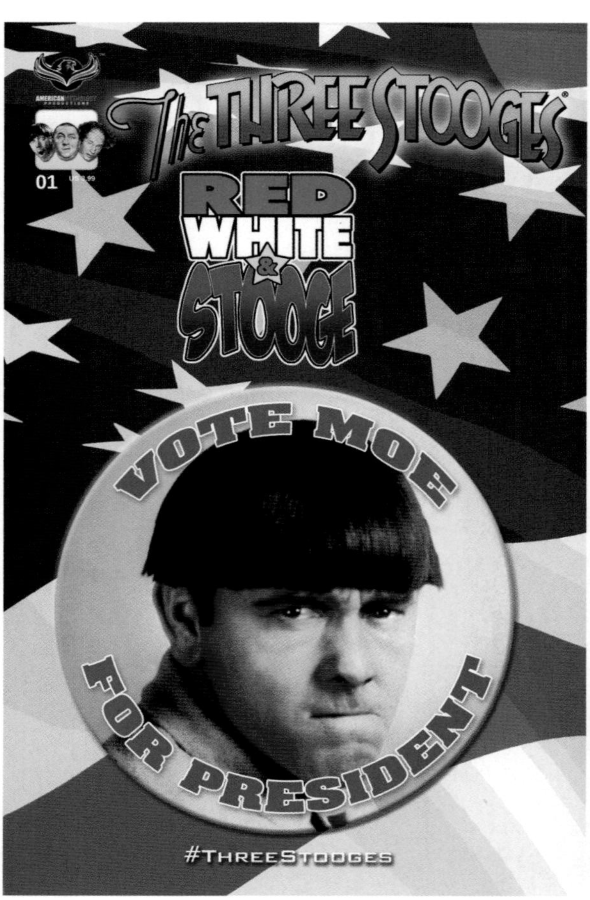

The Three Stooges
01
RED
WHITE
&
STOOGE
VOTE MOE
FOR PRESIDENT
#ThreeStooges

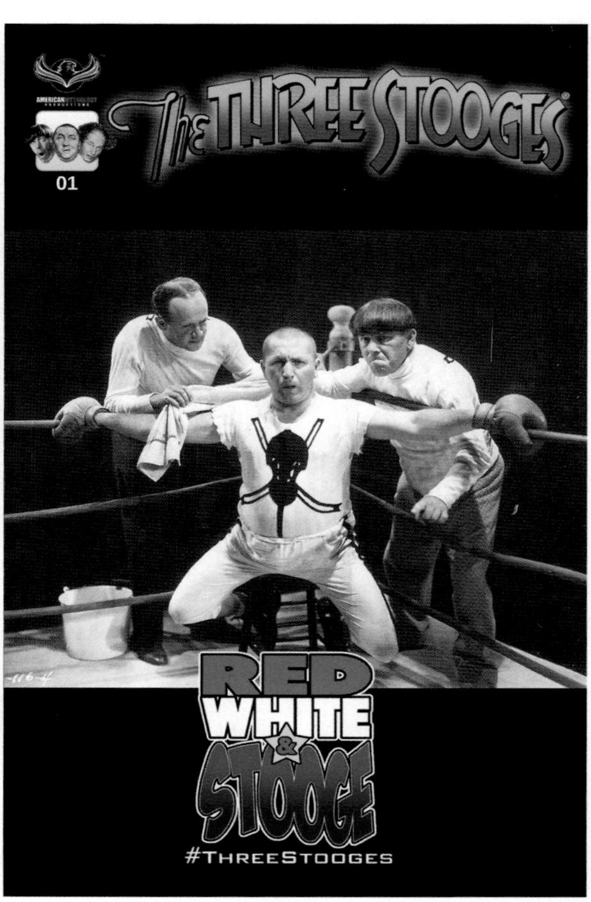

The Three Stooges
01
RED
WHITE
&
STOOGE
#ThreeStooges